That Moaning Saxophone

BRUCE VERMAZEN

THAT MOANING
SAXOPHONE

The Six

Brown

Brothers

and the

Dawning

of a

Musical

Craze

UNIVERSITY PRESS

2004

OXFORD
UNIVERSITY PRESS

Oxford   New York
Auckland   Bangkok   Buenos Aires   Cape Town   Chennai
Dar es Salaam   Delhi   Hong Kong   Istanbul   Karachi   Kolkata
Kuala Lumpur   Madrid   Melbourne   Mexico City   Mumbai   Nairobi
São Paulo   Shanghai   Taipei   Tokyo   Toronto

Published by Oxford University Press, Inc.
198 Madison Avenue, New York, New York 10016

www.oup.com

Oxford is a registered trademark of Oxford University Press

Library of Congress Cataloging-in-Publication Data
Vermazen, Bruce.
That moaning saxophone : the Six Brown Brothers and the dawning of a musical craze /
Bruce Vermazen.
    p. cm.
Includes discography, bibliographic references, and index.
ISBN 0-19-516592-6
1. Six Brown Brothers. 2. Saxophonists—United States—Biography. I. Title.
ML421.S54V47 2004
788.7'092'273—dc21   2003049884
[B]

9 8 7 6 5 4 3 2 1

Printed in the United States of America
on acid-free paper

To Tom Brown Jr.

Acknowledgments

The present book started as a series of articles integrating a decade of casual research on the Six Brown Brothers. It would never have become a serious treatment of the subject without a fortuitous meeting, in 1996, with Tom Brown's son, Tom Brown Jr., and, a few years later, with three of the four children of Alec Brown, Tom's brother and the Brown Brothers' longtime baritone saxophonist. The members of this generation of the family were astonishingly generous in providing the author with the scrapbooks, photographs, letters, contracts, itineraries, and reminiscences that revealed their parents' past and gave a basic shape to the narrative. So I thank them first: Tom Brown Jr. and his wife, Saymie; Myrtle Hendrickson; Helene Bleibdrey; and Allan Brown and his wife, Hazel. Allan and Hazel's son, Thomas E. Brown, furnished a recollection of Alec's old age that forms a part of chapter 16. I also thank Fred Kiemle, another of Alec's grandsons, who put me in touch with that branch of the family. I very much regret that I was unable to speak to his late mother, Alec's daughter, Dorothy Kiemle.

My lucky meeting with Tom Brown Jr. was made possible by Robert Young and Gino Micheletti, when Gino invited Robert to see an original Sax instrument from c. 1863 that was under repair in Gino's shop. A chat about its owner—Tom Jr.—led to Robert getting contact information, which he then relayed to me. My gratitude to both of them is immeasurable.

I thank Larry Larkins, a grandson of Tom Brown's friend, admirer, and emulator Clayton Leroy Brown (not one of the Brown Brothers). Besides sharing with me stories about his grandfather, Larry first alerted me to the existence of the pioneer concert saxophonist Cecil Leeson's collection of research material on the saxophone. Now housed at the National Music Museum in Vermillion, South Dakota, the Leeson Archive is indispensable for anyone studying the history of the saxophone in the United States. Everyone on the museum's staff was helpful, but two stood out from the rest: Dr. Margaret Downie Banks, who graciously shared her own research with me, and Dr. André Larson.

Besides Cecil Leeson, two other researchers I never met collected and synthesized information without which this book would not have been possible: the late Ulysses "Jim" Walsh, longtime columnist for *Hobbies* magazine, and the late Sverre O. Braathen, a midwestern lawyer whose hobby was the history of circus music.

Other scholars who shared their discoveries with me are Doug Caldwell, who is writing a biography of Rudy Wiedoeft; Lawrence Gushee, an authority on early jazz; Mark Miller, who writes about jazz in Canada; Dave Robinson, a fan of early saxophone ensembles; and Chuck Sengstock, who has studied Chicago's night life in the early twentieth century. I thank them all.

I also extend my gratitude to those who helped with advice, contacts, leads, research materials, reminiscences, and recordings, including Eric Bernhoft, Edward A. Berlin, Grey Brechin, Paul Coats, Paul Cohen, Al Dodge, Jack Eagleson, Bob Erdos, Patrick Feaster, Hersha Sue Fisher, Father Vincent Fitzpatrick, Jack Fleming, Judy Gedney, Vince Giordano, Tim Gracyk, Bob Grimes, Richard Hadlock, Alan Hall, Patricia Hall, Ted Hegvik, Meagan Hennessy, Ron Hutchinson, Bob LaBelle, Steven Lederman, the late Irv Levin, Dan Levinson, Stewart Lloyd, David Lovrien, Richard Martin, Peter Mintun, Charlie Moller, George Morrow, Michael Panico, Doug Pomeroy, Jack Raymond, Richard Reutlinger, Brian Rust, the late Wally Rose, Gary Scott, Dr. Thomas Smialek, Janis and Sonny Strunk, Allan Sutton, Alan Timberlake, Susan Walter, Scott Wenzel, and Richard Zimmerman. Special members of this category are my fellow members of the Arts Club at the University of California, Berkeley, who were the first audience for the story of the Six Brown Brothers. Technical work on the photographs used in the book was done by Paul Van Vleck, Naik, Andrew Taylor, and Jennifer Gwirtz.

The warm hospitality of friends and family enabled me to conduct research coast to coast on a low budget: Lillian Farber and Bern Friedelson, Ardis and John Harnagel, Ed Pierce and Rob Saltzmann, Mal and Sandra Sharpe, and Susan Vermazen. My work was made easier by several Faculty Research Grants and Research Enabling Grants awarded by the University of California, Berkeley, Committee on Research, and by a Humanities Research Grant and sabbatical leave during 1998–99. Special thanks are owed to Tony Newcomb for his role in bringing about the 1998–99 grant and leave.

The tough, friendly, and detailed advice of Kimberly Robinson, the music editor at Oxford University Press in New York, helped transform a less than disciplined manuscript into a volume someone might enjoy reading. The comments of two anonymous reviewers were just as important in that respect, but in addition their shared expertise sent me off in new research directions that, I hope, strengthened the historical conclusions of the book. Christi Stanforth, the volume's production editor, and Barbara Norton, its copyeditor, have deployed their considerable skills to produce a "clean" and handsome product.

Besides the National Music Museum, I want to express gratitude to the institutions whose collections, services, and hard-working, resourceful staff personnel helped me gather scraps of the past: the New York Public Library for the Performing Arts; the New York Public Library Manuscripts and Archives Division; the Berkeley (California) Public Library; the Lindsay (Ontario) Public Library; the San Francisco Public Library; the Richard L. Parkinson Library of the Circus World Museum in Baraboo, Wisconsin; the Oakland, California, Temple of the Church of Jesus Christ of Latter-Day Saints; and the libraries at Ball State University, the University of Iowa, the University of California, Berkeley, the University of California, Los Angeles, the University of California, San Diego, the University of Southern California, and San Diego State University.

The many recordings of the Six (and Five) Brown Brothers are difficult to locate. A few may be heard on the Canadian National Library Web site, at www2.nlc-bnc.ca/gramophone/. A few more, with sound excellently restored by Doug Pomeroy and Richard Martin, are available on *Those Moaning Saxophones*, Archeophone Records 6002. And a program of selections including a few original Six Brown Brothers arrangements forms the playlist of *Smiles and Chuckles: Celebrating the Music of the Six Brown Brothers* (CBC Records MVCD 1160), performed by the Royal City Saxophone Quartet.

I acknowledge, with thanks, the permission of *Bandwagon* magazine to quote from Sverre O. Braathen, "Circus Windjammers," *Bandwagon*, May–June 1971, and of *Daily Variety* to quote from "Tom Brown's Minstrels," *Variety*, June 3, 1925.

Finally, I want to express my deepest gratitude and love to my spouse, Juan Miguel Godoy, whose help and encouragement brought me through some very bad stretches during the years of writing, and whose love provides a center for my life.

Contents

That Moaning Saxophone

I

Once a Legend

The Six Brown Brothers were saxophonists, famous throughout the United States, Canada, and Australia during their quarter-century on the vaudeville and musical comedy stages. Playing the hit tunes of the day, they marched, even danced, across the boards, and Tom Brown, the leader, raised waves of laughter with his blackface mime and the repertoire of extra-musical sounds he coaxed from his alto and soprano saxophones. Tom's min-strel-show motley and the other Brothers' extravagant clown costumes and glistening instruments promised what they consistently delivered: the latest music expertly played and a hilarious time listening to it. In 1920, when they opened as a featured act in their third hugely successful Broadway musical, the stage critic for *Life*, one of America's most widely read magazines, began his review with this:

> There are a great many disturbing features about "Tip-Top," the new Fred Stone show at the Globe Theatre. It makes one so dissatisfied with one's own life.
>
> For instance, no one in whose veins flows the stuff which has made this country what it is to-day can listen to the Six Brown Brothers and not feel consumed with a desire to throw over what-ever work he may be doing in the world and take up the saxophone. To be able to play the bass instrument in that aggregation of tuba-dors should be the ambition of every one-hundred-percent Ameri-can. . . . The next best thing would be to work very hard all your life and accumulate enough money to hire the Six Brown Brothers to come and play for you from nine to five every day during your declin-ing years.[1]

In 1924, Gilbert Seldes, a critic for the bohemian intellectual review *Dial* and the leisure-class magazine *Vanity Fair*, writing about "the high levity of the minor arts" in general and the value of vaudeville in particular, named the Six Brown Brothers among the acts that persuaded him that vaudeville was then

3

at as high a point as it had ever reached. A few pages farther on, he compared the Brown Brothers with the jazz bands that were popular stage attractions and the Brothers' degree of perfection with that of several other star acts, ranking them above the Marx Brothers: "the Six Brown Brothers are at the very top with their saxophones. It is an independent act, wholly self-contained, not nearly so appropriate in any other framework, except possibly a one-ring circus; it is a real variety turn where a jazz band is only half and half; and in the case of these performers everything they do is exquisite."[2]

Seldes's opinion was not eccentric. From its debut (as the Five Brown Brothers) in 1908, the act delighted critics and theatregoers across North America in minstrelsy, vaudeville, musical comedy, and even a short film, as well as touring to high acclaim in England, Scotland, and Australia. In 1913, the *Citizen* of Ottawa, Ontario (birthplace of three of the Brothers), asserted that "they possess a perfect mastery of their special instrument, the saxophone, and can draw from it grace, tenderness, and humor in abundance," and continued with strong praise for their comedy, concluding that Tom Brown "showed himself a genius in evoking comical effects."[3] In 1920, when the Brothers were allegedly "the highest paid musical act" on the American stage,[4] Alexander Woollcott, the most powerful of newspaper drama critics, described Tom, "the melancholy one who stands apart and sobs with a saxophone," as "funny beyond words."[5]

Yet by the end of 1933, the Brown Brothers, like so many other stage performers in the ruined show business of the Great Depression, were has-beens, to be remembered after their disbanding as a standard act of the 1910s, as a subject for "Remember When?" and "Whatever Happened To?" items in the newspapers—but also as a legend. For the Six Brown Brothers, according to a story repeated often enough to take on the weight and solidity of truth, had started the craze for saxophones in America, when, beginning around 1914, saxophones "increased and multiplied so that the instrument became, of all instruments, the best known to that general public that frequents dance halls and likes to dine or sup to music."[6]

Their legendary status distinguishes their story from the thousands that might be told about the abundantly talented performers whose turns made up the marvelous spectacle of big-time vaudeville. The legend lingers around their name even today. A 1996 coffee-table book proclaims that "it was Rudy Wiedoeft [a C-melody saxophone virtuoso] and the Six Brown Brothers who gave the saxophone a foothold in popular music in the teens of this century. And it was they who paved the way for its astonishing explosion in popularity in the next decade: the sax-crazy 1920s."[7] A 1989 doctor of arts dissertation calls the Six Brown Brothers "probably responsible in a great part for the initiation of the American saxophone craze."[8] And in their heyday, the legend was pervasive. In 1920, a reviewer in *Variety*, the leading show-business weekly, called Tom Brown "the discoverer of the gold mine concealed in a saxophone" and "the first explorer to learn that you can take nothing but saxos and make music out of them instead of using but one incidentally."[9] In

1921, a piece in *Billboard*, *Variety*'s only serious rival, said, "To this sextet goes the credit for making the saxophone popular."[10] Two years later, the *San Francisco Call and Post* printed a large caricature of Tom Brown under the headline "He's the Bird That Gave the Saxophone Its Start; Now He Can't Stop It."[11] Even after the act had retired and the real-life brothers were struggling to put food on the table, a 1938 general-interest book called *The Story of Musical Instruments: From Shepherd's Pipe to Symphony* reported that "selling the saxophone to the American public has often been credited to Tom Brown and his famous saxophone sextet. He it was who taught America that the saxophone can moan, laugh, cackle, titter, squeal and grunt. . . . Tom Brown was a great showman, and he made the saxophone the most-talked-of instrument in America."[12]

We call a story a legend rather than a myth because we think it has a basis in history. But we think the story as told must have more or less falsehood blended with the facts, or we think at least that the truth hasn't been explored. Young George Washington may have been incapable of lying, but the cherry tree incident was Parson Weems's invention. Abraham Lincoln emancipated American slaves, but only in the rebel states. Trademarks such as "The Greatest Show on Earth" and "The Ultimate Driving Machine" may express the opinions of their proprietors and satisfied clients, but fans of Wagner operas and Lamborghinis may demur. Sifting the legend of the Six Brown Brothers for its many grains of truth has been difficult and absorbing, but, at the end, it is clear that they occupy an eminent place in the history of American popular music. Though they didn't ignite the saxophone craze unaided, a strong case can be made that they were among those who ignited it, and an even stronger one that they fueled it, at the beginning, more than any other group or individual musician.

Whoever began the saxophone craze in America, we owe them a staggering debt of gratitude. Starting in the late 1910s, the instrument began to become standard in dance bands, until in 1926 the first book on orchestration for such ensembles declared that the "backbone" of the modern dance orchestra was a trio of saxophones and that "the saxophone individualizes the American dance orchestra,"[13] a judgment that stayed true as long as dance orchestras existed. As "hot jazz" styles became established in dance bands of the early 1920s such as those of Gene Rodemich, Fletcher Henderson, Ray Miller, and a host of others, soloists on jazz saxophone emerged, a development that culminated in the crowning of the saxophone as the jazz instrument par excellence. The sonic world of the twentieth century would have been vastly poorer without the great beauties created by Frank Trumbauer, Sidney Bechet, Coleman Hawkins, Johnny Hodges, Harry Carney, Lester Young, Ben Webster, Dexter Gordon, Charlie Parker, Stan Getz, and dozens of other artists who found their own voices on the instrument and channeled their genius through it.[14]

Exploring the legend of the Six Brown Brothers will take us on a trail through a near-panorama of show business in the late nineteenth and early twentieth centuries. Brass bands, minstrel shows, touring companies of *Uncle Tom's Cabin*, burlesque, vaudeville, phonograph records, musical comedy, sound movies, radio, and the dance-band business all figured in the group's history as it grew from two Brown Brothers in about 1903, to four around 1906, to the Five Brown Brothers in 1908, and finally to six from 1911 until 1933.

To begin exploring and assessing the legend, we need to know something about the place the saxophone occupied in the United States before and during the group's long birth. Adolphe Sax's new instrument, invented around 1838 and patented in 1846, was an immediate hit in French military bands, which adopted it universally and continue to use it today.[15] Its first known appearance in the United States came in 1853, when a French band led by Louis Jullien performed in New York City.[16] The United States should have been fertile ground for the introduction of the new instrument, since the 1840s and 1850s were decades when, "owing to the perfection and increased availability of keyed and valved brass instruments, enthusiastic musicians in communities throughout America were forming wind bands in their spare time."[17] Saxophones were, however, much more difficult to fabricate than the keyed bugles, cornets, alto horns, tubas, and so on favored by the emerging amateur wind-band movement. Had an enterprising American mechanic ventured to violate Sax's patent, the difficulty of manufacture would have resulted in a forbidding price. The price of saxophones from Paris, with transport costs on top of the expense of the goods, served as further discouragement to those who may have been attracted to the instrument. Perhaps for this reason, as so-called "brass bands," which often included non-brass instruments such as fifes, piccolos, and clarinets, and always included percussion, spread to most cities, towns, and villages in the country, saxophones were rarely used, except at the professional level, until the beginning of the twentieth century.[18] Even in professional bands, the instrument made its inroads slowly. Harvey Dodworth, a prominent figure in the New York music world, included a tenor sax in his Central Park concert band in the 1860s, and in the 1870s, the nationally famous band director Patrick Sarsfield Gilmore deployed a quartet of saxophones in his organization,[19] including the renowned and long-lived European alto saxophone virtuoso Edouard Lefèbre (1834–1911), who played with the group from 1873 until Gilmore's death in 1892 and then briefly with John Philip Sousa.[20] As director of the United States Marine Band in the 1880s, Sousa used three or four saxophones.[21] But not until the 1890s did saxophones become regular features of large professional ensembles.[22] Even as late as 1911, the instrument had not yet become a standard member of the wind band, on an equal footing with, for example, the cornet, clarinet, and trombone.[23] No doubt the professional associations of the instrument gave it a prestige that added to its intrinsic charms.

Another avenue of diffusion led through the ubiquitous touring minstrel shows, circuses, and theatrical companies that entertained the citizenry year round. In spite of the fact that every traveling show included some sort of musical ensemble, saxophones don't turn up in their pictures or rosters until the early twentieth century, with a few exceptions.[24] However, according to Clay Smith (1876–1930), an early fan and proponent of the instrument, in the 1880s "circuses and minstrels carried saxophone players to attract attention for advertising purposes as much as for their musical worth, for their uses were so limited that they were really a novelty. One of the first minstrel shows using the saxophone was Gorten's [sic] Golden Band Minstrels, and the crowd would usually gather open-mouthed and listen to the saxophone."[25] Doubtless the circus and minstrel ballyhoo saxophonists exploited the manifold comic possibilities of the instrument's sound as well as the unfamiliarity of its look in close-up. In the light of later developments, the humorous potential of the instrument seems to have been as powerful a motive for new musicians to take it up as was its prestige.

Musical ensembles within these traveling shows, which must have employed a large proportion of the professional musicians then working in the United States and Canada, had a strong braking effect on the introduction of the saxophone, but, at the same time, opened a way for the instrument's adoption in the context of specialty performances. The braking effect stemmed from the quasi-industrial organization of the musical portion of the entertainment business. Bands and orchestras were needed for the pre-performance parades as well as for accompaniment and interludes during the performances themselves. Each troupe invested in written music, which very rarely would have included parts for saxophones, and, in some cases, the troupe owned the instruments themselves. As a result, the economically wise move for a manager when a musician dropped out of an ensemble was to replace him with another who played the same instrument or instruments, rather than, for example, replacing an alto horn player with an alto saxophone player. Such a move would, of course, also preserve the characteristic sound of the ensemble, insofar as that was a consideration. The bands were like machines for producing music, and the musicians were the nuts and bolts, the levers and wheels. The loss of a part called for its replacement by a similar part, so musicians seeking work were motivated to play instruments already in common use.

Another economic factor counteracted the braking effect to some extent. Traveling shows promoted a culture of doubling in order to minimize the number of salaries they had to pay. The actor who played Phineas in *Uncle Tom's Cabin* could also play alto horn in the street parade before the show. The man who played string bass in the indoor orchestra might play tuba on the street. For this reason versatility was, in the ordinary case, a condition of employment, not just an option for the ambitious.[26] ("Doubling in brass," that is, playing in the street band besides one's other functions, came to be a familiar metaphor even outside of show business.) But there was another possibility for doubling (or tripling) besides street/indoor music and street/stage, for traveling attractions usually had a variety-show component as well. Circuses had "concerts" or "after-shows" after the main performance; minstrel shows and *Uncle Tom* companies had "olios." These provided an opportunity for the actors and musicians to do specialty acts in addition to their duties in the parade and the main show. Here versatility was indeed an option for the ambitious, and here the saxophone, exotic and prestigious, was given a place where musicians could explore its potential.[27]

A steady rivulet of variety or specialty turns using saxophones trickles through the pages of the *New York Clipper* (*Variety*'s predecessor as the most important show-business weekly) in the 1890s.[28] Josh Holbrook and Lizzie Hacking were the first, in 1891, "playing on a great variety of instruments, including Trombone, Cornet, Staff Bells, Clarionet, Saxophone, Hand Bells, Musical Glasses, Violin, Guitar, Sleigh Bells, etc."[29] The Elliotts, advertising their availability in 1892, informed the public that they not only played saxophones, cornets, and euphoniums, but also supplemented the music with a bicycle tournament, a "Grand Russian Quadrille on Unicycles," and hat spinning and throwing.[30] In 1893, Humphreys' Comedy Company bragged that it had "engaged noted special soloists on piccolo, clarionette, saxophone [*sic*], cornet, euphonium and trombone" for its tour in *The Lady of Chicago*.[31] Later that year, an agent listed Henry Kniep's Saxaphone [*sic*] and Mandolin Quartet among the acts he represented, while a couple of months later Kniep himself advertised his Saxophone and Mandolin Lady Trio.[32] Knox Wilson was also at liberty in 1893, offering German dialect comedy along with singing, dancing, yodeling, and performing on the concertina and saxophone.[33] Only one new act turned up in 1894, although J. H. and Lizzie Holbrook, evidently the Holbrook and Hacking of 1891, whose act still featured the saxophone, advertised their availability in the United States between tours of England.[34] The lone newcomer, Billy Young, the American Musical Tramp, rivaled the Holbrooks' multi-instrumentalism: he played alto saxophone, bassoon, trombone, bell lyre, sleigh bells, and mandolin, with a freight-car drop and campfire as accessories.[35] Traveling with the Sells Brothers' Circus in 1895 were Billy and Lilly Mack. Mrs. Mack opened with her singing specialty, and Mr. Mack joined her for duets on "calliopes, musical bottles, cow bells, funnels, sleigh bells, banjo, mandolin, Swiss 4 in hand bells and saxaphones [*sic*]."[36]

Whether these few vanguard saxophonists played in vaudeville as well as traveling shows is not known, but in the late 1890s, clearer signs start to appear that vaudeville performers had taken up the instrument, bringing its sound to an ever wider audience. Frank Mudge, at his death said to have been "the originator of the saxophone solo as a feature in vaudeville,"[37] first performed in vaudeville around 1896, and contemporary sources record the "cornet and saxophone solos and duets" of B. C. and Louise Linden Bent in 1897[38] and the saxophone solos of "Cliff" Farrell in 1898.[39] The brief notices of the two latter acts give little indication of their content, but acts from the next few years seem to have incorporated a fair amount of humor. In 1900, the "comedy musical act" of Harry A. Stone and Ben Wood featured saxophones as well as "violin, cello, musical glasses, mandolin, guitar, cornet and trombone."[40] The caption under a 1901 photo of Arthur H. Rackett, trap drummer and tenor saxophonist of Rackett and Hazard, notes that his act, "A Musical Trip Around the World," "has met with much success, the striking feature[s?] of it being 'The Chinese Theatre,' 'Hagenbeck's Menagerie,' with the Leedle German Band and singing dog finish."[41] In 1903, the "original Character Comedy Musical Skit" of the Majestic Musical Four featured a saxophone quartet along with quartets of brass, organ chimes, and xylophones.[42] The year 1905 brought Miss Graham, in Gray and Graham's "eccentric comedy musical act," doing "wonderful work on the largest saxophone in the world"; the Four Emperors of Music, who followed the comedy portion of their turn with a quartet of saxophones and brass; and Lew Wells, who chose to be photographed with his tenor sax, even though his repertoire also encompassed witty monologues, "piccolo solos, accompanied by mechanical birds, the beautiful rose bush, harmonious window blinds, [and] magic flower pots."[43] These and other notices in the musical and show-business press, more frequent each year, demonstrate the saxophone's spread in vaudeville circles without, unfortunately, providing a way to estimate how common it had become by the time Tom Brown started playing baritone sax around 1904.

At least one act touring vaudeville's higher-toned, self-improvement-oriented cousins, the Lyceum and Chautauqua circuits, also featured a saxophone quartet (one among several ensembles) early in the twentieth century—the Apollo Concert Company, founded by Clay Smith and Guy E. Holmes in 1905. These multi-instrumentalists eschewed the comic, concentrating instead on transcriptions of compositions such as the overtures *Orpheus in the Underworld* and *Light Cavalry* "without any cuts or simplifications" and selections from popular operas such as *Martha* and *Faust*.[44] Although the vaudeville audience overlapped with that of the Lyceum and Chautauqua circuits, the two latter probably reached more deeply into rural areas, especially in a broad band starting in Pennsylvania, widening as it swept westward across Ohio, Indiana, Illinois, Iowa, and Missouri, then petering out west of the Missouri River.[45] Thus Smith's and Holmes's missionary work probably recruited young people not otherwise reached. Smith and Holmes themselves thought that "the real inspiration that set thousands of youngsters marching forward" on the saxophone path was Edouard Lefèbre's series of coast-to-coast tours in the century's first decade with his saxophone quartet.[46]

After 1895, when the price of phonographs and gramophones began to fit the middle-class pocketbook, recorded cylinders and discs probably played a small role in the spread of the saxophone, although the extremely limited frequency range of the early recording process obscured virtually all of the instrument's distinctive character. The first known commercial recordings on the instrument, a series of twelve featuring the saxophonist Bessie Meeklens with piano accompaniment, came as early as 1892, when a listener was most likely to hear Thomas Edison's cylinders only on a coin-operated machine. In 1896, Columbia released a number of cylinders by the saxophonist Eugene Coffin, and in a December 1899 catalog, National Gram-o-phone listed fifteen solos and five duets featuring Jean Moeremans, Sousa's Belgian-born saxophone star. At an uncertain date in the late 1890s, Emile Berliner released a single disc recording of the Saxophone Quartet of Sousa's Band playing "Annie Laurie." Nine years passed before the next known saxophone recording was released, in 1908, a single side by Steve Porpora. In 1910, Edison marketed a number of cylinders by H. Benne Henton, another virtuoso in the Sousa stable.[47]

Slowly rising demand for the instruments in the 1880s, when they still had to be brought over from Europe, led to the C. G. Conn company's manufacture of the first American saxophones, in Elkhart, Indiana, around 1890. Not only were the Conn horns less expensive than comparable imported instruments, but they embodied innovations that made them easier to play. In 1893, the German-born F. A. "Gus" Buescher, the craftsman who had developed Conn's first instrument, launched a rival band instrument company in Elkhart, marketing a saxophone he had improved even beyond the Conn models and initiating a sometimes heated rivalry that extended well into the twentieth century.[48] Better and less expensive instruments facilitated recruitment to the slowly growing saxophone army.

In a culture that normally writes down music, a kind of symbiosis exists between the popularity of an instrument and the availability of printed music for it. In the United States, such music for saxophones was rare before 1900, occasionally found in scores for wind band, but almost never in the publication format called small theatre orchestrations, probably third in popularity after solo piano and wind band formats. A moderately schooled musician could play most cello or trombone parts from these theatre orchestrations on tenor saxophone, but the transposition of a ninth upward (and from bass clef to treble clef) could easily defeat most amateurs. The only saxophonist who did not have to transpose (before the easy availability of the C-melody saxophone) was the lucky player of the relatively rare and difficult soprano sax, who could read directly from B-flat cornet or clarinet parts, though some notes would be impossible to produce. The first prolific American composer-arranger of pieces specifically for saxophone ensemble was Guy E. Holmes, starting in the first decade of the century. By 1915, he reportedly had "the greatest number of compositions, and arrangements published especially for saxophone quartettes of any composer in the world."[49] Saxophone quartets of avid amateurs sprang up in response to the newly available music, and more selections were published in response to the expanding market.

All these engines of dispersion—brass bands, minstrel shows, circuses, vaudeville, Lyceum, Chautauqua, recordings, improved and affordable instruments, and pieces to play—help to explain the spread of the saxophone across the American landscape, but such gradual growth is not a craze. Smith and Holmes reported in 1915 that, "from a careful investigation made by visiting the various factories, we feel safe in saying that there were something over twenty-five hundred saxophones made and marketed in this country last year," and that another 800 or so were imported from Europe. They also estimated that annual production in the United States had increased 40 percent annually for the preceding ten years.[50] If purchase of the instruments more or less paralleled factory output, market growth from 121 (the result of applying the Smith-Holmes estimate) to 2500 in a decade is impressively large and gratifyingly steady, but perhaps not explosive enough to call a craze. For the Buescher company, at any rate, an explosion in sales may have come in the year before Smith and Holmes wrote the cited piece, when *True-Tone* reported that "the demand in the last twelve months [probably spanning 1913–14] for [Buescher's] True-Tone saxophones has increased over 200 percent. And the prospects for the future indicate that a still further increased demand will follow in the next similar period."[51] The prediction was borne out spectacularly. Although wholly reliable sales figures for the 1910s and 1920s are hard to come by, one source asserts that, at the peak of the saxophone craze, 1923–24, "100,000 saxophones a year were being made."[52]

What made the saxophone so attractive to the musicians of the era? Smith and Holmes offered the following analysis in 1915:

> The saxophone is probably growing in popularity faster than any other legitimate musical instrument. The reasons for it are two-fold: The sweet mellow, soothing tones that it produces make it a pleasant instrument to listen to. Then from the musicians' side, its popularity is partly due to the fact that greater progress is made and greater results obtained with a given amount of effort than upon any other instrument.[53]

They also noted the advantages that accrued to the members of a saxophone quartet, who could more easily find work than "a village or town band of twenty," and who would achieve a good ensemble sound faster because only four people, rather than twenty, had to be rounded up for a rehearsal. Clearly Smith and Holmes were talking about amateur groups, and there can be little doubt that reasoning like this led many amateurs with a thirst for ensemble playing and an acquaintance with human nature to adopt the instrument. Once one has become a saxophonist, Smith and Holmes go on, he "has a triple chance to be useful, for he can play in the saxophone organization, in the orchestra and in the band." At the professional level, they conclude,

> the bread and butter argument is all on the side of this instrument, for it is easier to get a position than on any other instrument. In fact, it is a common joke around old [American Federation of Musicians] local No. 10, here in Chicago, that if a flute, cornet or even a trap

drummer is needed in any organization, the first question asked is: "Can you double on a saxophone?"[54]

These were all good and even wholesome reasons for becoming a saxophone player, but perhaps what had been a swell became a craze because it had a less wholesome side as well. Calling something a craze, after all, is a sort of outsider's judgment, a categorization tinged with disapproval. The categorizer implies that there is something not quite right about people who invest their efforts and wealth in Mah Jongg or hula hoops or sport utility vehicles. Probably the instrument's potential for raising laughter provided some reason to disapprove of it, given the stiff attitude then current among lovers of the symphony and opera. But that kind of ground for disdain doesn't explain the almost moral cast that saxophone-bashing often had. When the saxophone craze was at its high point, it was a common joke to vilify the saxophone, as in this 1930 lyric:

> When noisy neighbors make you moan,
> Let's show you how to make them groan:
> One payment brings our saxophone—
> Send for our free booklet.[55]

For one early attacker, what was vile about the instrument was not the sound of a novice player, but that old enemy of Anglo-American society, sex. Isador Berger, a San Francisco musician and composer, explained his antipathy in a 1917 newspaper piece called "The Saxophone: Siren of Satan."

> One night, surfeited for the moment with grand opera themes and motifs, perhaps a half dozen musicians from the orchestra, myself among the number, sought refuge after a particularly trying opera in a cafe where a ragtime band enticed the patrons of the place to dance.
>
> Listening to the profane music which it played and noting the deplorable effect which these pagan strains and lawless rhythms produced in the dancers, I was prompted to analyze this appeal.
>
> Soon I became convinced that nothing was so much to blame as the saxophone, an instrument which seems to lead all the others in the dance music of the modern cabaret.
>
> Obviously, the saxophone, as an instrument is capable of producing pure, healthy music, and it can be employed in strictly legitimate fashion, but there can be no doubt of its immorality in the cabaret. In accompanying a dance it is so played that it preys upon the passions and emotions. It becomes patently suggestive, instinctly animallike.
>
> No other musical instrument can be so immoral. . . . The saxophone is guttural, savage, panting and low in its appeal. It achieves a peculiar whining, creeping mysterious sound.

As cabaret musicians play it a call insinuating and reckless comes from it—a call that possesses some strange psychologic power over the young dance devotees of America. The broken tempo in which it croons dance music is without principle or dignity.

The saxophone, breathing hurriedly, calling short and fast over and over again, adapts itself perfectly to the lure of ragtime. . . . The abstract immorality of the saxophone . . . is but an example of the power that gilded sin has for the moment over thoughtless minds. . . .

Some severe action must sooner or later be taken upon the matter of our dance music and measures enforced prohibiting the use of the saxophone in this connection or compelling musicians to play it in another fashion.[56]

Post-1917 listeners with the solos of Ben Webster and Dexter Gordon echoing in their minds' ears can only wonder what might have set Berger off in that anonymous cabaret musician's performance, what crude nuances he might have heard that proved to be initial footfalls on the path leading to the subtle erotically charged playing of the 1930s and later. For it can't be denied that the freedom of pitch contour and tone afforded by a saxophone makes possible a very sexy sound. And the possibilities of that freedom must have contributed to the saxophone's popularity among substantial numbers of listeners and musicians alike, leaving yet other listeners and musicians to label them crazy and their enthusiasm a craze.

To a greater extent than some biographies, the story of the Six Brown Brothers must be told from the outside. The Browns, like most of their associates, were people whose formal education ended early, who didn't keep diaries or write many letters, and whose personal lives are mostly preserved in the distant memories of their children and grandchildren and in brief recorded interviews with a handful of their friends. Newspapers and magazines, the main sources of information (and misinformation) about their lives and careers, are notoriously unreliable and tantalizingly silent on the details one would most like to know. Yet it is possible to reconstruct a fairly rich background for those lives and, combining it with the few available scraps of more personal material, to make plausible guesses as to what they were thinking and aiming for as they did the things that survived on public record. The wide background—war and plague, the decline of minstrelsy and then vaudeville, the rise of the movies, and the general economic wreck of the 1930s—affected the Brown Brothers in ways similar to those in which it affected millions of others. The narrower background—specific shows, business opportunities, and contracts—structured their lives in more particular ways, but still ways in which it would have shaped the fortunes of similarly talented individuals. Being constrained to rely so much on the background reveals, surprisingly, that the Browns are almost as interesting for their typicality as for their singularity—their undeniable place in the history of American popular music. To some extent they are the Everymen of early-twentieth-century show business and their story its Everystory. The beginning of that story lies in Ottawa, Ontario, and the quest of the brothers' cornetist father, Allan, for a position as director of one of those ubiquitous brass bands.

2

Father and Sons

1858–96

It always made a good story to say that the Six Brown Brothers were not really brothers, and at some points during the act's life, it was partly true. But there were six Brown brothers who performed under that banner at one time or another, and four who were with the group almost continuously from its birth until its death. Tom, the burnt-cork comedian who created and managed the act, used to tell interviewers he was the oldest sibling, but in fact he was the second. William, born first but the last to join the group, was the least able musician, relegated to keeping time in the background. Alec, Percy, Vern, and Fred followed Tom into the minstrel, circus, and vaudeville worlds where the troupe gradually coalesced, but around 1912 Percy finally settled into a career as a circus band director and gave William his berth on the boat to fame. Many other musicians passed through the ranks, but these Ontario boys inspired the enterprise.

The six and their sister Myrtle were the children of Allan and Maria Brown, part of the Irish diaspora that aided the settlement of Canada and the United States in the early nineteenth century. Little documentation, or even family tradition, survives about the early lives of Allan Brown and Maria Reid. Allan was born around 1858 in Richmond, Carleton County, Ontario, the second of ten children of an Irish Protestant immigrant, Thomas Brown, a blacksmith, and his Canadian-born wife, Eliza Jane. Maria was born in Dublin, Ireland, about a year later and immigrated to Canada at an unknown date with her parents, William and Ann. Allan and Maria married on November 11, 1878, in Ottawa, and the next year in the same city they had their first child, William. Allan first appeared in Ottawa city directories in 1881, as a Post Office messenger, and reappeared annually through 1886 variously as a musician, a civil servant, and an employee of the Geological Museum. There is reason, however, to think that the Browns resided for a time during that period in New York.

Allan was a cornetist who moved his steadily growing family around Ontario and northern New York state, evidently impelled by a strong drive to lead a brass band. From the middle of the nineteenth century until World War I, brass bands (sometimes called "military bands," even if they had no connection with the military) proliferated across the United States and the settled parts of Canada. Besides a gamut of brass instruments, from the small E-flat cornet to the bass tuba, these groups included various percussion and reed instruments. The fifteen-piece band that Allan led in Bowmanville around 1890, for example, included three B-flat cornets, a flugelhorn, two valve trombones, two alto horns, a baritone horn, an E-flat tuba, a piccolo, two clarinets (one played by his very young son, Tom), a snare drum, and a bass drum (see figure 1). As the ensemble's principal melodic voice, the lead cornet player occupied a position of respect and prestige. For the bandmaster, along with respect and prestige came the possibility of a steady income. "Almost every town and village of a few hundred population or more had its band of ten or twenty musicians who performed for almost all public gatherings: concerts, parades, dances, picnics, weddings, funerals." Despite all these performance opportunities, small-town band members were mostly nonprofessionals, except for the bandmaster, usually a multi-instrumentalist who could give his avid amateur bandsmen pointers on their instruments, select the music, and shape the performances into something the town could enjoy and even take pride in. "These local maestros . . . led the town band, organized string dance orchestras, and supervised the musical entertainment for grand celebrations. Almost without exception these musicians . . . supplemented their income by giving private lessons."[1] Whether Allan gave lessons or pursued some other line to support his family is not known.On March 27, 1881, Maria bore their second son, Thomas, and on September 9, 1882, their third, Allan Alexander (later called Alex or Alec), in a working-class neighborhood of Ottawa. Then the family began a series of moves. A year or so later, Maria, at least, was across the St. Lawrence River, in Potsdam, New York, only fifty-seven miles from Ottawa, where she gave birth to the fourth Brown brother, fair-haired Percy, probably on October 31, 1883.[2]

According to his recollection many years later, Tom learned to play cornet when he was four, so around 1885–86.[3] A family story, told by his son Tom Jr., says that someone first attempted to teach the child to play violin, but that, as Tom drew the bow back and forth across the strings, his lips, pursed in concentration, followed the bow's movement, making his teacher, parents, and brothers laugh, so he was switched to an instrument without, it was thought, the fiddle's comic possibilities. Although Tom continued to play the cornet from time to time, the instrument he specialized in as a boy was the clarinet, possibly taught by a man named H. G. Thayer.[4]

Tom's first music lessons may have taken place in Ottawa, but by 1887, the Brown family had moved to Toronto. There, on December 12 of that year, the Browns had a fifth son, Vernon, destined to be the first bass saxophonist on a phonograph record. According to an obituary in the *Toronto Telegram*, Allan had spent "three seasons in the Princess Theatre, Toronto, as cornet soloist" before relocating to Woodstock, Ontario, the county seat of Oxford County, 280 miles from Ottawa.[5] There Allan put down roots long enough for Maria to bear their sixth son, Fred, born November 18, 1890. For at least part of his time in Woodstock, Allan directed a brass band, but it wasn't long before he moved 133 miles east to lead a different band, in Cobourg, Ontario, on the shore of Lake Ontario east of Toronto. There the last of the family, Myrtle, was born on April 4, 1892.[6] Soon all the children, with the possible exception of William, were learning to produce music, as attested by a photograph taken about 1894, in which Tom and Vern hold clarinets, Percy and Alec cornets, and Fred and Myrtle violins (see figure 2). Forty years later, Tom used the photo in publicity for the Band School of the Tom Brown Music Company, his successful store in the Chicago Loop, with the headline "What an Early Start in Music Did For Me": "Clarinet player with a circus band—that was my first boy-job. Then one of my brothers joined me and we began to practice on the saxophone. Finally we and our four other brothers . . . started out in vaudeville as the 'Six Brown Brothers.'"[7] Only a casual viewer would think the photo depicted six brothers, however, since Myrtle's dress is a scaled-down version of a woman's dress, rather than the kind of baby dress a little boy would have worn.

After four moves in a decade (not counting Bowmanville, where Allan directed the band mentioned above, but may or may not have resided),[8] the now complete family made a fifth shortly after Myrtle's advent, settling down for five or six years in Lindsay, Ontario, the county seat of Victoria County, Ontario. There Allan organized and directed the Lindsay Citizens' Band, with three or four of his older sons among those under his baton. According to much later accounts, the boys also aggregated into an autonomous boys' band, entertaining at social functions such as picnics and fairs. Lindsay, sited on the Scugog River where there had been "almost impenetrable forest and swamp" in the 1830s,[9] was relatively new, having been incorporated about the time Allan was born. Like the Browns' ancestors, the first settlers, beginning in 1825, were Irish, and a special section, called "the Catholic village," housed refugees from the horrific Irish famine of the late 1840s.[10] The town, not very different from the others the Browns had passed through, had a population of 6081 in the 1891 census, about half of Irish descent. The 1890s saw Lindsay begin to flourish after a setback that had started in late August 1881, when a huge forest fire devastated most of Victoria County. The blaze destroyed crops and farm buildings, provoked a wave of emigration away from the farms surrounding Lindsay, and hastened the deforestation already begun by the region's logging operations. A similar fire in 1887 extended the barren district even farther.[11] Although the town's industrial base—lumbering, gristing, tanning, weaving, brewing, brick-making, iron-founding, and carriage-making[12]—was seriously compromised, Ontario had enough natural riches to fund a recovery and integrate the area into the general North American civic and technological progress of the late nineteenth century. A margin of wealth resulted that allowed the town to support small luxuries such as the Lindsay Citizens' Band, several athletic clubs, and a local theatre.

The Lindsay Opera House, begun in July 1892 (and still in use today, as the Academy Theatre), was "a four-storey building of red brick, 120 feet long by 55 feet wide," with a capacious stage and a 900-seat auditorium, "vaulted over with a magnificent domed ceiling."[13] Replacing a much smaller theatre from the 1860s, the grand new hall provided an up-to-date venue for both local productions and the many theatrical and musical groups that criss-crossed the United States and southern Ontario in those days, including perhaps the most popular form of theatrical entertainment, the minstrel show. The Brown boys were to spend substantial stretches of their future in minstrelsy, and Tom, in particular, was to form an emotional attachment to it that shaped his professional career and stage persona well after most of show business had left the genre behind. The importance of Tom's burnt-cork apprenticeship to the Brothers' story calls for a close look at the minstrel world when the Browns were growing up.

By the late 1880s, minstrel shows had reached an almost universal standard form. If a show was on tour, as the great majority were, it made its first, free public appearance around noon on the day of a performance, when the whole membership of the troupe put on as grand a parade as they could for their prospective evening clientele. Spectacularly clad drum majors strutted along the main street performing baton wonders, followed by one, two, or even three brass bands, made up of perhaps a third of the company. Most of the rest, dressed alike in suits of fine fabric and colors usually reserved for women, strolled and strutted between the bands and the wagons, brightly painted and laden with plantation props, that carried their colleagues, in blackface and ragged clothes, high above the crowd-lined street, giving tantalizing previews of their dancing, clowning, and banjo and fiddle playing. Locally recruited boys carrying banners often swelled the ranks, and the noisy, colorful, and thrilling spectacle stretched along the street to create the impression of a host even larger than its actual size of twenty to seventy. At intervals, the procession paused for a ballad or a comic dance from one of the stars. The parade ended at the theatre, where the troupe hawked advance tickets among the fired-up citizenry.

In the evening, the curtain rose on what was called the "first part," which used the full stage. The set suggested such locales as a ballroom, a cabin in the pines, or the deck of a battleship, as dictated by the imagination and financial resources of the troupe. Generally the small orchestra, which included instruments not represented in the noon parade, such as violins, bassoons, and even a harp, sat at the rear of the stage, behind a semicircle of chairs opening to the audience and ready for a small, select group from the company when the overture finished. The overture, which normally involved the whole cast, was usually a medley of choral songs with duets or solos interspersed, all accompanied by the orchestra.[14] Sometimes it would set out a theme for the rest of the first part, but often it consisted mostly of older minstrel songs, such as "Old Folks at Home" and "Dixie," calling on the audience's recollection of past pleasure to create good will and highlight the newness of the material to follow. At the overture's conclusion, one of the company, the middle man or interlocutor, commanded with a flourish, "Gentlemen, be seated!," and the chairs filled, with the interlocutor seated at the arc's central point. The chairs closest to the footlights were occupied by the end men—a minimum of two, but sometimes as many as four or six, depending on the company's size and comic talent. At one end sat the comedian or comedians called Tambo, who specialized in playing, spinning, and tossing the tambourine. The man or men at the other end, called Bones, played rhythmic patterns with long, hard, loud wooden sticks (bones) something like the claves in a twenty-first-century drummer's kit.

The nucleus of the first part originally coalesced on February 6, 1843, when four white men from the northern United States, who had been working separately as blackface entertainers in circuses, formed the Virginia Minstrels for a show at New York's Bowery Amphitheatre.[15] One played banjo, another fiddle, and the other two, seated at the ends, tambourine and bones. They wore burnt cork on their faces and hands and spoke in a synthetic dialect that had something to do with the speech of the slaves and freemen that their working-class white audiences probably hadn't heard much of, but that became accepted, largely because of minstrel shows themselves, as "the genuine dialect of the race."[16] Their evening's entertainment of instrumental music, songs, dance, and, above all, comedy, drawing on African American, Irish, and English sources, made an immediate hit and inspired a legion of imitators drawn from the ranks of saloon entertainers, circus clowns, and aspiring newcomers to show business. The original quartet went on to perform in Boston and then England, where they played Liverpool, Manchester, and London, finally disbanding before 1843 was out.

Public demand led to a flourishing business for the Virginia Minstrels' emulators, and competition for the public's attention led to countless attempts at novelty, but the general character of the first part was constant: a semicircle of musicians, dancers, and comedians, with at least one tambourine and one bones player at each end, trying to delight an audience with laughter and appeals to sentiment. The middle man, one of the early innovations, acted as master of ceremonies (hardly necessary in a quartet), an office he normally performed somewhat pompously, providing the end men with a target for many of their jokes and pranks. But he could also be a comedian or singer in his own right. In many minstrel shows, the interlocutor played in whiteface, that is, in the kind of stage makeup a white person would use for a "legit" drama, while the rest of the circle appeared in burnt cork, the end men distinguished both by cork and by bizarre costumes. But not all these features were universal, and they changed considerably over time. In all-white companies, the interlocutor sometimes appeared in blackface like the rest; or only the end men would appear in burnt cork; or the whole company might work in whiteface. An all-black company might appear either in burnt cork or in ordinary stage makeup. However, the interlocutor was virtually always distinguished from the rest by his clothing (for example, a white dress suit contrasting with the conventional black formal wear of the others) and elevated diction and elocution.

The gentlemen seated, the first part continued with the middle man inspiring the end men to make the audience laugh, either indirectly by a serious bit of speech (perhaps as simple as an attempt to introduce one of the group) or directly by inviting them to tell stories. Much of the humor turned on the stupidity or ignorance of the character played by one or both of the end men, but it often relied on making fun of the somewhat pretentious mannerisms, appearance, and speech of the interlocutor. Before the jokes had gone on for too long, one of the semicircle, now including those who were neither at the ends nor in the middle, would sing a sentimental ballad or a comic song, or dance a little, or astound the crowd with his prowess on the banjo. Generally, the entertainment in the first part was limited to verbal humor, song, small-scale instrumental solos, and dance. In the typical show of the 1880s and 1890s, the first part would end with a song and dance (something like a drill or a comic march) by the whole group, called a "walkaround."

Then came the second episode, called the "olio," where the artists presented their specialty acts. This could include almost anything: leaping acrobats, tightrope walkers, comic playlets, *tableaux vivants*, elaborate singing and dancing production numbers, cornet solos, banjo or mandolin ensembles, musicians who played several instruments serially or simultaneously, pantomime, female impersonators, animal acts, and more of the same sort of comic songs, sentimental ballads, and dances that were heard and seen in the first part. One of the most popular turns was the "stump speech," in which one of the company employed an urgent tone, high-flown language, malapropisms, pompous rhetoric, inscrutable reasoning, and (almost always) dialect to enlighten the audience on some topic of current import such as the temperance or women's rights movements or a recent or upcoming election.

The evening most often ended with an "afterpiece," a short comic play, usually satirical and frequently a burlesque of a piece at least dimly known to the audience, such as a Shakespeare play (*Othello* was an obvious favorite) or *Uncle Tom's Cabin*. Although the main business was physical clowning and verbal humor, the afterpiece could include an extra helping of singing, dancing, banjos, and tambourines. The curtain rang down after a final ensemble number involving the whole cast, usually to rise again for an encore, or a series of them for the company lucky enough to click with the crowd.

Making people laugh was the minstrel's main business, with occasional pauses to raise a tear or a sigh with a song of young love, broken hearts, forgiveness of prodigal sons, maternal concern, tragic death, and the other commonplaces of Victorian popular ballads. Although by the 1890s not all minstrelsy was done in burnt cork and grotesque dialect,[17] still the great preponderance of the laughter was created by exploiting cruel and demeaning stereotypes of African Americans. Minstrel blacks were always portrayed as uneducated, usually as pretentious in speech, and often as abysmally stupid. They fell comically short in their attempts to imitate white manners and institutions, and among their favorite pursuits was theft, especially of chickens and watermelon. During the 1880s and 1890s, in step with conservative white reaction to Reconstruction, the earlier minstrel stereotype had changed so that these laughable characters now acquired a set of sinister and menacing features as well. Writing of the so-called coon songs that began to appear early in those two decades, the historian James Dormon remarks that in their lyrics

> blacks began to appear as not only ignorant and indolent, but also devoid of honesty or personal honor, given to drunkenness and gambling, utterly without ambition, sensuous, libidinous, even lascivious. "Coons" were, in addition to all of these things, razor-wielding savages, routinely attacking one another at the slightest provocation as a normal function of their uninhibited social lives. The razor—the flashing steel straight razor—became in the songs the dominant symbol of black violence, while the "coon" himself became that which was signified by this terrible weapon.[18]

Although audiences saw this representation of the newly dangerous African American as a comic exaggeration, at the same time they likely accepted it as an exaggeration of some underlying reality or other. This acceptance reinforced or even created the belief that blacks constituted a genuine threat to the general social order:

> Blacks were not only the simple-minded comic buffoons of the minstrel tradition; they were also potentially dangerous. They were dangerous not only in the way that animals are dangerous if allowed to roam unrestrained, but dangerous as well to white bourgeois culture. . . . For this reason, they *had to be* controlled and subordinated by whatever means, so the coon songs signalled. The songs also argued, implicitly at least, for coercion, for lynching if necessary, to maintain control and the domination of white over black.[19]

Besides an implicit argument for coercion, the new image in the coon songs offered, just beneath the surface, a new vindication for the milder and more humane form of control constituted by ridicule, by making African Americans the butt of jokes, and the casual racism taken for granted by most whites became more deeply entrenched. Lynching itself could be joked about. In the sketch "Bones as a Traveler," after lying to cover up his bumbling attempts to make himself look important, meanwhile mispronouncing the names of several cities, Bones tells the interlocutor, Mr. Johnson, that he was once sitting under a tree reading a book,

> and just as I was gettin' into de best part ob de book, three big fellers comes up and taps me on de sholder and says: "*Look hyar, you great*

big nigger; I got you now." Well, I thought he *had* got me; I golly, you thought so if he got you de same way. Den he says again: *"Whar did you put my daughter, eh?"* Well, I just goin' to tell him dat I neber seen his daughter, nor him eder, when he asked me if I eber was at Short Branch? Den I told him no. [*To Mr. J.*]—Say, was you eber at Short Branch?

Mr. J. I told you before that I never was.
Bones. Well, you don't want to go. So dese three fellers dey showed me a short branch on de tree just whar I was settin'. *"Do you see dat?"* he says—I says "Yes, I see dat." Den I knowed wot was comin', for I seen one ob de fellers had a great big long rope. Dis place is in *Takeses.* Oh, I knowed just wat was comin'; so dey took dis rope, tied a knot, and den dey put it around my neck; yes, dey put de rope round my neck, just here, round my neck; and den dey told me to say my prayers, den sing a song, den roll over, and all de time I was skeered to deff. Den dey told me to stand on my head, and turn somersets, and whole lots of stuff; and den dey took de rope and passed it ober dat *short branch*, and den dey all took holed ob it, and what do you suppose?
All. What, what?
Bones. Dey took de rope down again.[20]

A particularly repulsive coon song, "I'll Make Dat Black Gal Mine," was sung by one of Tom's later patrons, the Canadian-born dancer George Primrose, along with "his Pickaninny Cake-Walkers," in Primrose and West's Minstrels, probably in the 1897–98 season:

A gal of mine, named Caroline,
Has promised fo' to marry me;
But her dad's got a dog named Spot,
Fo' to make me trouble, don't you see?
Dar's some swell coon, who's come to spoon,
And dat's the very reason why,
But I'll show them soon dat I'se a wicked coon,
Case [because] I'll win dat gal or die, Oh!

My, oh my, my coon blood will soon be boilin',
My, oh my, dat nigger must resign;
If he don't his good looks I'll soon be spoilin',
I'll make dat black gal mine.

I'll carve dat coon and place him soon
In de hollow of an old gum tree;
Where owls at night can scratch and bite
At his coal-black carcass, don't you see?
I'll take one shot at dat dog Spot

Den steal away my Caroline,
And coons will swear dar's hoodoos in de air,
When I make dat black gal mine, Oh!

My, oh my, my coon blood will soon be boilin',
My, oh my, dat nigger must resign;
If he don't his good looks I'll soon be spoilin',
I'll make dat black gal mine.[21]

Minstrel shows such as those described helped form Tom Brown's early consciousness of show business and later served as his training ground in the field. The stage persona he created and presented as the center of the Six Brown Brothers' comedy directly incorporated a panoply of details from minstrel tradition. The most important detail, too pervasive perhaps to be called a detail, is the very presentation of the performer (African American or Caucasian) as one of the imaginary types of black characters that minstrel practice allowed. Blackface performers developed an elaborate rationalization of their representations, based on a distorted view of their ultimate subjects. Dailey Paskman and Sigmund Spaeth's *"Gentlemen, Be Seated!": A Parade of the Old-Time Minstrels*, published in 1928 during the long twilight of minstrelsy, is explicit, though not self-conscious, about the derogatory stereotyping:

> [The Bones character] derives his name from the rhythmic noise producer that he manipulates. A "set of bones" was originally an actual pair of bones, used in the manner of castanets. The cannibals of Africa probably originated the idea when they wanted a little music after having feasted thoroughly upon their enemies.
> Malapropisms have always flourished in the minstrel show, particularly when imitating the speech of the negro, who loves big words and lots of them, and can mispronounce them and get their meanings tangled with grace, facility, and generally comic effect.
> It is to the negro that the white minstrel owes everything, for without the presence of the black race in this country American minstrelsy would never have existed. The pathos, the tragedy, the humour of the negroes, their heritage of superstition and of religious fervour, their music, their linguistic whims and fancies, have been the richest material for translation to the stage, and minstrelsy took its toll of all these elements.[22]

Clearly, the Bones explanation is supposed to be a joke, but, just as clearly, it reinforces the vague belief that the ancestors of African Americans were cannibals. The passage about malapropism merely projects stage practice back on to its supposed prototype. This is not to deny that badly educated African Americans who strove to impress others with a florid vocabulary sometimes mispronounced their words and tangled their meanings, but only to point out that uneducated people of any color are liable to such errors when they try that sort of display. And it would be hard to predict the outcome of a contest for the greatest degree of superstition and religious fervor between the ancestors of the African Americans, on the one hand, and their delineators of European descent on the other. We can concede to Paskman and Spaeth the stereotypes of pathos and tragedy, since nothing in the history of the United States is sadder or more tragic than the story of racial slavery and its long aftermath.

Around the turn of the century, some minstrel veterans complained that African Americans no longer fit the stereotype upon which the "darkey" portrayal was based. Frank Dumont, performer, producer, and one of the leading authors of sketches and afterpieces, said in 1899 that "minstrelsy is the one American form of amusement, purely our own, and it has lived and thrived even though the plantation darkey, who first gave it a character, has departed. The dandy negro has supplanted him, but the laughable blunders are still incorporated in the negro of the present time."[23] In 1902, Lew Dockstader, one of minstrelsy's best-known singers and comedians, was more pessimistic when he "told a [*New York*] *Sun* reporter that the Negro had so advanced that the dialects and material for the old-fashioned take-offs were already lacking, and so the 'Negro character' was being invalidated, bringing to a close one phase of Negro contribution to the American stage."[24]

Apparently absent from the consciousness of these writers and performers was the thought that the African American characters in minstrelsy were only to a small extent based on African American originals. Absent too was the thought that the blackface minstrel tradition nourished itself mostly on its own past, rooted as much in the musical and comic traditions of the British Isles as it was in the perception of African Americans, both slave and free, by whites mostly from the cities of the northern United States.

Burnt cork was only the first requirement for a minstrel "darkey." Distinctive minstrel costuming, central to Tom's later stage character, held equal importance. Formal dress was a frequent alternative for the first part, but the end men's clothing—either some extravagant version of formal dress[25] or a kind of thrown-together attire seen only on the minstrel stage—had to set them apart. And in the sketches and afterpieces, all the participants appeared in the latter sort of garments. An 1890 collection of minstrel humor specifies the following costumes for the two characters in "Dar's de Money," a burlesque of *Othello*:

> JAKE—*Blue swallow-tailed coat with large brass buttons—red vest— white trousers, not washed lately, rather full and too short—one boot, and one heavy shoe—battered hat. He is made up stout.* PETE—*black frock coat, with one skirt tattered[,] out at elbows, with buttons on breast and buttoned up to throat—no shirt collar shown at neck—dark trousers—a military undress cap.*[26]

In "Stocks Up, Stocks Down," the character Jeff appears in

> *short dark velveteen coat, patched with pieces of a light glaring color, the sleeves too short; check shirt, with broad collar, starched stiffly, turned down over the coat; black hat, battered, etc., with a fancy ribbon round it; shortcrop wig, with a tuft in the centre of the front over the forehead; drab trowsers, tight, patched; a large yellow bandanna handkerchief stuck in coat-flap-pocket with end half out.*[27]

Costumes such as these, which stemmed from those of circus clowns, emphasize the poverty of the characters portrayed, their childlike affection for bright colors and fancy clothing, and their inability to achieve, or even to approach, the coordinated ideal of "white" clothing. All these features afforded white audiences—who themselves fell short of the even higher ideal presented to them on the legitimate stage and in newspaper and magazine cuts—the comfort of believing that someone, indeed a whole "race," was inferior to them on that account. No doubt the audiences, or many of their number, didn't believe that the portrayal of African American dress was true to life, but the less sophisticated among them nonetheless must have come away with the impression that the presentation merely exaggerated what was actually worn.

Costuming plays an important part in one of the most often repeated legends of the business: the story of "Daddy" Rice (1808–1860), and his famous "Jim Crow" character, who lent his name to the repressive segregation laws in the United States of the late nineteenth and early twentieth centuries. According to an 1867 account, Thomas Dartmouth ("Daddy") Rice, an actor of no note, was working in Cincinnati, Ohio, in 1830 when he saw an African American in the street singing and dancing to a song with the refrain "Turn about an' wheel about an' do jis so, / An' ebery time I turn about I jump Jim Crow." The song and dance struck Rice as something to reproduce on the stage in African American costume. This he did when he got to Pittsburgh, Pennsylvania, later in the year, creating a sensation and beginning a long period during which the Jim Crow routine became his much-copied specialty. The legend includes the story of how Rice put together his costume for the first performance—borrowing (some versions say buying) the clothing of an African American porter at Griffith's Hotel, where Rice was staying, making up with burnt cork, and donning a black wig. "When the arrangements were complete, the bell [calling for Rice's entrance] rang, and Rice, habited in an old coat forlornly dilapidated, with a pair of shoes composed equally of patches and places for patches on his feet, and wearing a coarse straw hat in a melancholy condition of rent and collapse over a dense black wig of matted moss, waddled into view." The costume itself quieted the normally noisy house, and the combination of the appropriated clothing with the appropriated song and dance launched the mediocre actor Rice on a spectacularly successful career as a blackface entertainer.[28]

Another tale of appropriated clothing concerns J. W. McAndrews, a singer in Buckley's New Orleans Serenaders. On tour in Savannah, Georgia, another member of the troupe became fascinated by "a Negro vendor with a small donkey cart selling melons by calling his wares in a chanted song" and told some of his colleagues about it. "McAndrews found the vendor the next day, learned his song and routine, and bought his whole outfit—clothes, cart, and donkey," becoming "'The Watermelon Man,' a part he continued to play until his career ended in 1895."[29]

Both the bizarre costume of the stage darkey and the minstrel appropriation of African American clothing turn up in Tom Brown's later persona. A specific item that Tom adopted came from the ancient tradition of clowning, from which, like so many other properties and techniques, it was transmitted into minstrelsy: oversized shoes. Ebenezer Nicholson, a dwarf who went by the stage name "Little Mac," had become famous for his "Big Shoe Dance" in the late 1860s,[30] and Fred Stone, later an associate of Tom's for many years, did his early-1890s blackface song and dance with his brother Eddie in "long flap shoes."[31] The body part apparently too big to be controlled, along with the contrast between the feet's visual potential for clumsiness and the actual grace and cleverness with which they were used, gave an inventive performer endless possibilities for provoking laughs.

Although some minstrel troupes were all female (with male management)[32] and occasionally a female performer would appear in an otherwise male company, practically all the minstrel organizations were all male, and female impersonation was a feature of virtually every show. Right from the early days of George Christy with Christy's Minstrels (1847–53),[33] men portrayed saucy "wenches," shrewd, strong "mammies," hectoring landladies, and large, nagging wives. One very famous performer, Patrick Francis Glassey, known as "The Only Leon," made a long career (c. 1868–1903)[34] out of actually trying to look like a fashionable woman (in blackface), with beautiful gowns, studied movements, and "feminine" songs. But for the most part an impersonator's portrayal would be comic, raising easy laughs from the obvious contrast between the tall, heavy creature with a man's facial features and his woman's "face" and garb, falsetto voice, and padded breasts and buttocks.

Musical turns came in at the very beginning, with the Virginia Minstrels, and the banjo-fiddle-tambourine-bones combination survived in one form or another until minstrelsy was finally finished as a serious genre. Once the olio was added, the opportunities for instrumental prowess expanded, as long as the player could entertain the audience for the few allotted minutes. Solos on the cornet, the leading voice of the nineteenth-century brass band, were common, and the more visually arresting operation of the slide trombone helped make solos on that apparatus popular. An octave or so of tuned bells rung by four or five troupers produced ghostly melodies bound to please in a quieter way. Multi-instrumentalism was another possibility. Looking back over the halcyon days, a 1928 book says that "musical acts fitted in well with the second part of the minstrel show, particularly the kind that displayed unusual versatility, with one performer exhibiting his skill on ten or twelve different instruments."[35]

Tom Brown served his teenage apprenticeship in minstrelsy marching in parades, playing in the orchestra during the first part, and by 1903 joining the olio. Ultimately, he incorporated into his own act all the traditional features of minstrel practice discussed in the present chapter: burnt cork, outlandish costume, clothing appropriated from an African American, big shoes, female impersonation, and multi-instrumental musical performance, blending them into a famous stage character that outlasted most of minstrelsy.

One can only speculate about whether he also internalized the hateful attitudes toward African Americans embodied in the tradition. Although analyses such as Dormon's probably diagnose correctly the public attitudes that initially popularized and later sustained minstrelsy, they don't tell us what individual audience members or performers were thinking. Whether black or white, the performer could work in burnt cork, with all that it implied, only if his desire to be a part of that branch of show business outweighed his regard for the lives, safety, and dignity of black people. But the weight of that desire could be considerable. For nineteenth-century African Americans, minstrelsy was virtually the only point of entry into show business, and many paid the price of blacking up. For whites, it was one of the easiest points of entry. By the 1890s, the minstrel show was firmly in place. A newcomer to the field during that decade, if he thought about it at all, could tell himself that his recruitment added nothing to the general assault on black people, that they were no worse off for his participation. But that assessment would be naive, for he would be as much at fault as the last Roman senator to stab Caesar, or as a supernumerary member of a lynching party. Still, the stage called, and legions answered.

3

Darkest America

1896–99

Tom Brown recalled his early attraction to show business in some columns he wrote for the *San Francisco Call and Post* in the summer of 1923, when the Brothers were playing at that city's Granada Theater. "My earliest memory is that I wanted to crack into the show business. It was the one and only hope, aspiration, [and] ambition that my youth boasted."[1] "When I was a bit of a youngster I used to do mighty little other than to wait for the different shows to make the town. As soon as the troupe was off the train or the wagons 'lined' I'd up and brace the manager of the aggregation for a job peddling bills, toting a banner—anything, in fact, that would provide a ducat."[2] Late-nineteenth-century Lindsay hosted a wide variety of touring shows every year, including the *Uncle Tom's Cabin* companies and minstrel shows that Tom reminisced about. The former were his favorites, he reported, because they "generally meant a chance to lead the bloodhounds in the street parade and a session backstage helping to hoist Little Eva heavenward."[3]

Tom's first, brief professional engagement as a clarinetist came when he substituted for a member of the Guy Brothers' Minstrels band during one of their visits to Lindsay, sometime in the late 1890s. The regular clarinetist had fallen prey to drink, a constant threat on the road. Along with gambling, it was one of the few pastimes available to working show people on tour. Usually, their show was literally the only show in town, and small-town citizens tended to keep these strange outsiders at a polite distance, although membership in a fraternal organization such as the Elks (to which the Guy brothers and several others in their outfit belonged) opened local doors for banquets and parties.[4] Occasions of that sort, however, didn't exclude drinking to excess. However it had come about, the Guy musician was "most beautifully pickled"[5] by noon.

The year of the engagement is uncertain. If Tom was "going on for 18" when he joined the Ringling Brothers' Circus after his first stint as a minstrel bandsman,[6] he must have worked for the Guy organization before the summer circus season of 1899.[7] According to Tom's account, an unfortunate accident constrained him to play only in the midday parade, not in the evening's show. The Guy Brothers' parades in the late 1890s were typical of the period, gaudily costumed, full of music and spectacle, and guaranteed to capture a boy's imagination, especially if the boy was already stagestruck. The season of 1896–97 featured two bands and a drum corps, made up partly of the musicians who formed the twelve-piece orchestra at the evening performance, partly of those among the other eighteen or so performers who could "double in brass" for the street. "Thirty men dressed in silver plug hats and gold colored dusters, with red satin capes," participated in the noontime display, including the two eldest of the six Guy boys, George and William. Then in their thirty-fourth season as song-and-dance men and their twenty-seventh as managers of the Minstrels, they rode in a carriage drawn by two elaborately caparisoned horses. Three drum majors preceded the bands, and the heart-lifting, eye-filling procession included "a gun thrower, knife thrower, baton thrower" and "fifteen banner boys, dressed in uniform."[8] By the 1898–99 season, the company had increased from thirty to thirty-five, with a correspondingly grander parade, the troupe now dressed in "pink silk hats [and] pink dusters" and again featuring "gun jugglers, knife jugglers, baton throwers, drum corps, . . . [and] two bands." And they added "two buglers," perhaps in response to the recently concluded war with Spain, also reflected in the olio's Rough Riders marble statues act.[9]

In the parade remembered by Tom, the band played on "a regular circus bandwagon." He seated himself among the rest of the musicians, full of pride at having achieved his dream. But

> some roughneck had knocked the nubbin out of the pipe he had been smoking into the forward boot of the bandwagon, and there it smoldered until the right wind and the psychological moment arrived. We were driving down Main street.[10] There was a burst of flame and a cloud of smoke from under the front seat. The horses "rared," the driver tumbled off unceremoniously and a runaway was on.

Tom, experienced in handling horses, quickly replaced the driver without losing his grip on the clarinet. One by one the other bandsmen abandoned the speeding wagon, until Tom was alone, struggling to control the panicked horses. They shot past the fire department, not stopping until our brave clarinetist steered the team into the creek at Lindsay's edge. When the firemen got to the scene, he continued, "the fire was out, and so was the bandwagon, and the horses and I were in—up to our necks. Self and clarinet resigned."[11]

The evening's show offered typical minstrel fare. At the September opening of the 1897–98 season,

> the first part, entitled "The Huntsmen," was a grand sight; everyone dressed in scarlet coats and white tights, top boots and huntsmen caps. The eight end men were dressed in different colored silk jockey suits, and the new cut wood scene and green baze [sic] carpet made a

pretty picture. The olio consisted of all new acts. The Flood Brothers' acrobatic turn, the six marble statues, Harry Meyrick's monologue turn, Hamlin and Hamlin's knockabout turn, the banjo orchestra of ten soloists, Fitzgerald's club [juggling] act, the big musical act, and Arthur Guy and Billy Crawford's dancing specialty, and the grand finale of the big song and dance formed the best show the brothers ever carried.[12]

The orchestra had grown since 1896–97 from twelve to fifteen, and, by December, the marble-statues tableaux included twelve people, and Smith had joined Fitzgerald to form a two-man club-swinging turn.[13] Arthur Guy probably continued with his acclaimed and encored cornet solos,[14] and the choral singing of the six Guy brothers remained a feature until Arthur went out on his own in 1905.[15]

For the 1898–99 season, the marble statues portrayed Rough Riders, and the show added a "picture machine."[16] This was probably a magic-lantern show illustrating a singing performance, but it may have been an early motion-picture exhibition of the sort that had become popular in larger U.S. and Canadian cities and was traveling with the Ringling Brothers' Circus as early as 1897.[17] Other new attractions included Will Bensley—who wirewalked and balanced on rolling barrels—and, in the song-and-dance plantation finale, a "nigger band."[18] Starting in 1899–1900 and continuing for at least one more season, the olio also presented a pair of contortionists costumed as a lizard and a crocodile (or alligator—the difference didn't matter).[19] No matter which year or years of the waning century Tom caught the show, it must have been an electrifying and hypnotic spectacle for a small-town Canadian boy, a spectacle full of suggestion both about how he might break away from Lindsay's limited opportunities and about the many paths into that glamorous world: music, comedy, dance, even barrel-rolling. He was soon ready to leave.

Tom's childhood education in show business and attitudes toward African Americans wasn't confined just to minstrel shows. Although Tom's backstage job in the productions of *Uncle Tom's Cabin* that played Lindsay was to "hoist Little Eva heavenward," he must have seen at least part of the play itself, and he may have seen the show *Darkest America*, with its all-black cast, which played his hometown on May 18, 1896.[20] Harriet Beecher Stowe's renowned novel, the usually remote source for *Tom* shows, stressed the humanity of its black characters, Tom, George Harris, Eliza, and so on. However, the novel's message was primarily antislavery, and social changes in the United States since Emancipation—such as the collapse of Reconstruction and the advent of Jim Crow—potentially gave each version of the play a different message. Whether Stowe's message was generalized to the acceptance of free blacks as fellow citizens or as potential social equals depended on the specific production, and there is no way to know the details of the versions that Tom may have seen. By 1899, the *Dramatic Mirror* listed nearly 500 traveling *Tom* organizations,[21] and there is no reason to think that the list was complete. Some early versions of the play had ended with a plea for transportation of freed slaves to African colonies such as Liberia, bluntly contradicting the generalization I have suggested.[22]

> The play was never like Mrs. Stowe's novel, but native as a patchwork quilt. Bits of "business" from generations of Tommers [members of traveling *Uncle Tom's Cabin* companies] had developed the "sure-fire" stuff, the ad libbing making permanent the bristling lines. Some characters were built up into flesh and blood and sinew, others cut down to the grim essentials, or jettisoned. The original connecting passages were altogether cut and lost, but the scenes beat forcibly upon the heart and brain. Like Topsy, it "just grow'd"—giving us the true folk play.[23]

More important, the *Tom* shows of the 1890s were usually less concerned with the novel's plot and outdated message than with presenting a spectacular entertainment that overlapped in some particulars with minstrel shows. Some of the salient points of the spectacle were stage tableaux of the play's most exciting scenes—the brutal overseer Simon Legree whipping Uncle Tom; Eliza, the fugitive slave, fleeing the baying hounds that pursued her across the frozen Ohio River; saintly Little Eva dying in the presence of family and slaves. But *Tom* shows went far beyond the 1851–52 novel and its published dramatizations, into territory only hinted at by the latters' moral, social, and religious concerns. An 1896 *Clipper* ad for the Salter and Martin Mammoth Original Uncle Tom's Cabin Company, "THE GREATEST THING THAT EVER HAPPENED," proclaims that "for display in our great street parade we carry the following: Shetland Ponies, Siberian Bloodhounds, Burros, Mules, Horses, Donkeys, Oxen, Carts, Wagons, Floats, Phaeton Cart, Log Cabin, Eva's $1,500.00 Golden Chariot, BEAUTIFUL BANNERS, Magnificent and Dazzling Harnesses and Uniforms, All New." The parade's drum major, doubling as a buck-and-wing dancer onstage, was "A GIANT COLORED BOY," seventeen years old and allegedly eight feet tall, who led a parade including a sixteen-piece white band, "The Famous Alabama Whang-Doodle Pickaninny Band[,] and Malvina Moreau's Creole Ladies' Band." The two latter ensembles apparently also appeared onstage.[24] Individual Tommers sang songs appropriate to their characters—for example, the plantation owner St. Claire's lament at the death of his daughter, Eva, or the wild slave child Topsy's "I'se So Wicked," delivered as she danced a frenetic "breakdown." Choral singing by African American groups of "Jubilee Singers" was also a frequent feature.[25] The Peck and Fursman *Tom* company included the race between the *Natchez* and the *Robert E. Lee* in its 1888 production, and in 1897 the Barbour and Harkins troupe ended the spectacle with Abraham Lincoln reading the Emancipation Proclamation.[26]

A teenaged boy already in love with show business might easily fail to notice the play's partially submerged moral content in his infatuation with the lavish details of the medium in which it was drowning.

In May 1896, Al. G. Field's *Darkest America*, performed by an all-male troupe of African Americans under white management, played Lindsay near the end of its second year of successful touring, just before it was converted into a lavish stage pageant with a cast of fifty men and women, praised by the black press for its "delineation of Negro life, carrying the race through all their historical phases from the plantation, into the reconstruction days and finally painting our people as they are today, cultured and accomplished in social graces," a portrait that "holds the mirror faithfully up to nature."[27] From a surviving program for a performance[28] of the 1895–96 show, it is hard to tell whether the much smaller and less ambitious version aimed at the same target: "no straining at effect, no scenes of oppression, no striving to depict the woes of a downtrodden race, but a succession of scenes depicting the happy, humorous events of colored life, both high and low."[29] But that kind of aim is compatible with the program, which opens with a "Musical Melange" somewhat like a minstrel first part, though with no one in the roles of interlocutor or end man. An orchestral overture and chorus are followed by comic songs, ballads, monologues, and a two-man sketch, involving not only individual performers, but also the Magnolia Quartette and the Original Charleston Camp-Meeting Shouters. "Part Second" includes a trombone solo ("Tramp, Tramp, Tramp," with variations, a piece Tom recorded at one of his first recording dates in 1911); solo and duo comedy specialties; a twenty-man "March, Drill and Chorus"; "Suntaagg, the Automatical Enigma" (whatever that might have been); a dog act featuring balancing, pyramids, and acrobatics; and two playlets, "The Barber's Picnic" and "The Darktown Fire Brigade," complete with the drag characters Aunt Ann, Liza Hotfoot, Hannah Sayall, Mad Nance, Mother Goose, and Mamma Toodle. The cast included at least three actors who were then or later prominent in African American theatre: Lawrence Chenault, John Rucker, and Harry Fidler.[30] If the April 1896 version did present the "happy, humorous events of colored life, both high and low" without the grotesque and demeaning excesses of the minstrel show, a viewer used to burnt-cork distortions might well have tempered his view of what African Americans were like and how they ought to be treated. On the other hand, the weight of the minstrels' false testimony about black people may have seemed far greater than that of *Darkest America*. The revised 1896–97 version praised by the *Colored American* probably did not play Lindsay, since it was so large that it could turn a profit only if it traveled less and played only one-week stands,[31] something the small Lindsay economy could hardly support.

Besides Tom's first brief employment as a parade clarinetist with Guy Brothers' Minstrels and his participation in the Bowmanville 45th Battery Band and the Lindsay Citizens' Band, he reportedly created performance opportunities for himself, when, at age fourteen, he "organized [some of] his brothers into a band and they played for local engagements and at fairs."[32] But playing brass band music for small-town fairs must have seemed pretty insignificant compared to the excitement and glamour of a circus, a *Tom* show, or a minstrel troupe.

A successful forty-two-year-old Tom Brown recalled that

> finally there came a time when I decided that the shows were not coming along fast enough to suit me, so I tossed a pair of ice skates over my shoulder, tucked a pair of socks in my pocket and my clarinet under my arm and went away from the old homestead. Didn't have a dime—my capital consisted wholly of a sublime trust in Providence and a promise from the head of a minstrel show that he would stake me to a job if I ever needed one.

Although Tom didn't say which show he joined, it may have been the Guy Brothers', with which he later worked, in spite of the suggestion in his wording that it wasn't.[33] Tom set out for the long walk from Lindsay to Bowmanville, Ontario, where he knew the troupe was playing. "By the time I reached Jennetville [Janetville, Ontario] the cold wasn't the only thing troubling me. I needed food. There was a carnival on in the town and I lost no time in entering the skating races." He won first prize, a five-dollar coin, which he spent partly on food and partly for a ride on a bread wagon to Bowmanville. "Upon my arrival in Bowmansville [*sic*], I made a wild dash for the village opera house, found the minstrel man and, very much out of breath, stuttered, 'I've plumb run away from home. Do I get that job you promised me?' I got it and went to work tooting my clarinet at $8 a week and 'cakes' [room and board]."

Tom ends his recollection with the observation that "my fortune was made and I was on my way along the long, long road that has meant to me the fulfillment of a youngster's dreams—success of a sort in the glittering world of showdom."[34] A teenaged bandsman's life in a traveling show around 1898–99[35] must have been a difficult one, in spite of the glitter. The Guy Brothers' troupe seems to have been a "mud show," traveling from venue to venue in wagons, rather than in private railroad cars as did the larger Al. G. Field Big White Minstrels and W. A. Mahara's Minstrels, or even the smaller Barlow Brothers' company.[36] Extensive wagon travel on the primitive roads of the 1890s was not merely uncomfortable, but arduous and dangerous. If a vehicle got stuck, there was often no one to get it back in service besides the minstrels themselves. Horses had to be fed, watered, groomed, and led to and from night quarters, and chances are good that the younger and stronger members of the group were enlisted for such tasks, especially ones who, like Tom, had experience with the animals.

Disease and accidents posed special problems on the road, where victims would have to depend on the attentions of unfamiliar doctors and recover, if they did, without the aid of a nurturing wife or mother. Relatively sedentary theatre people, moving frequently in drafty wagons, chilled to the marrow in the winter and sweating buckets in the summer, consuming whatever food was at hand, and sampling new microbial communities at each stop, were especially prone to infectious diseases, from mild digestive disorders to the tuberculosis and syphilis that were epidemic at the end of the century. The constantly unfamiliar surroundings of life on the road offered plenty of opportunities for accidents on top of the special opportunities provided by the unusual activities of the minstrel life, such as, for instance, the runaway bandwagon that almost ended Tom's musical career at its outset. The sideshow band in the 1896 Buffalo Bill Wild West Show is a gruesome case in point. Their bandwagon was on parade behind a group of mounted cowboys, who moved to the opposite side of the street, with the wagon following, to avoid an oncoming streetcar. The horsemen easily passed under a bridge that spanned the street, but the more elevated musicians were "scraped . . . from their seats like ten-pins" as "screams and cries from the wounded men rent the air." Six were badly injured, two to the point where death was anticipated.[37] Lesser injuries constantly threatened any musician who played a wind instrument, in the form of the jabs, scrapes, bruises, and bumps occasioned by the necessary contact between instrument and mouth as the player marched or rode down the dirt streets, whether dry or muddy, of little towns.

Food and lodging for the performers, eating and sleeping in the wagons or even in small-town hotels and boardinghouses, must have been a good deal less attractive, on average, than what was provided in the Brown household. Alcohol was usually available as a solace, but, as illustrated by the temporary indisposition of the Guy Brothers' clarinetist, it could be a treacherous companion. Al. G. Field, a prosperous minstrel entrepreneur of the period, allowed in his autobiography that

> theatrical people with their peculiar temperaments and manner of life, are easily led astray but, I do not believe, comparatively speaking, there is nearly so much intemperance among theatrical people as some other professions. . . . We [managers] endeavor to dissuade them [performers] from all practices that will interfere with their duties. We take a great deal of pains with the younger ones, particularly as to the drink habit; do all we can with advice, and endeavor in every way to have them lead sober, moral lives. The general manager of one of the largest railway systems in this country, after twenty-five years' experience, has arrived at this conclusion. "Do all possible to rescue the man starting in on a drinking life. Bump the old soak and bump him hard; bump him quick. Never temporize with a man who has broken his promise as to the liquor habit. If he gets bumped hard, it will either cure him or cause him to drink himself to death. In either way society is the better off."[38]

Field was speaking in reply to an uncle's remark that "intemperance is the curse of the theatrical profession." He was not denying it, but only explaining why it was a curse—in practical rather than moralizing terms—and what was done to ward it off. Gambling posed a similar problem. Late-night card games, bets on sporting events, and wagers on the fall of the dice or tomorrow's weather provided easy and often exciting ways to pass the long months on tour, but they could quickly lead to financial problems, especially at $8 a week.

Accounts of the touring life during the period generally avoid mention of sexual matters, but an all-male troupe traveling through small-town Canada and the United States must have faced some problems in that aspect of life, especially those troupers who were heterosexual teenagers with the usual degree of lust. Local girls and women, except for prostitutes, would generally be unavailable for anything more intimate than flirtation, and their families would likely have discouraged even that because of the low social status of show people. Prostitutes, who were probably more easily available in small towns then than they are now, raised the specter of uncomfortable and potentially fatal disease, treatable only with poisons such as arsenic. Same-sex activity is known to have been common in such womanless nineteenth-century environments as mining and lumbering camps and West Coast Chinese ghettos, and it likely occurred from time to time in minstrel troupes, who shared the social attitudes of the theatrical profession, which were more tolerant than those of the general public toward "peculiar temperaments and manner of life." Homosexual liaisons would have the advantage over flirtation and commercial sex of including the possibility of relatively long-term affection. But, however individual members dealt with the predicament, it was a real problem, and it might have led a teenager, on his own for the first time, not just to want, but to long for a permanent union with a woman to be his companion in life on the road.

Despite the considerable difficulties of show business at this near-bottom level, it still glittered. It also offered a reasonable path for a boy who didn't want to work in Lindsay's shops and factories. Tom must have been aware of the difficulty of pursuing a musical career without getting into something like minstrel shows or the circus. He had before him the professional example of his father, moving from town to town for employment, and ultimately leaving Lindsay. The rank-and-file musicians of town bands were not professional musicians, but volunteers with day jobs to support them and their families. A move to a market with more employment for musicians, such as Toronto or Ottawa, both of which Tom's father subsequently tried before he too settled into a day job, would have involved more risk than signing up with a traveling show. So glamour and reason spoke with the same voice, even though Tom heard it as glamour's.

4

The Traveling City

1899–1909

Tom Brown, joined in sequence by at least four of his brothers, shuttled back and forth between minstrel companies and circuses between his flight from Lindsay and 1909, with a few attempts to break into vaudeville. But the circus offered a dependable income during the better part of the year, and there the Browns always returned until vaudeville began to pay. Traveling with the city of tents, Tom found his wife among the dancing girls, bought his first saxophone, and gathered his brothers into the nucleus of the future Six Brown Brothers.

Tom gave dozens of newspaper interviews during his sixty-nine years, many containing details of his early wanderings before he emerged in *Variety* in 1909 as the leader of the Five Brown Brothers, but the stories contradict each other in many respects, and independent evidence is sparse. Enough of the interviews mention Guy Brothers' Minstrels that the company was probably one of his main early employers. Two sources from early 1912 indicate that some of the Browns had worked for Lew Dockstader's Minstrels (which toured from 1903 to 1912),[1] and a clipping, unidentified but probably from the mid-1920s, that was preserved in Tom's scrapbook, adds two more minstrel troupes, saying that "The Brown Brothers have appeared with . . . Cohan and Harris, [and] Honey Boy Evans' Minstrels."[2] Much clearer documentation exists that the Ringling Brothers' Circus employed several of the Browns in 1906, 1907, and 1909, along with shakier documentation for 1905.[3]

Performers in those days commonly moved from show to show, as the Brothers did. Eighty-nine circuses toured the United States and Canada in 1901,[4] and each organization sent out a call for performers every year in early spring, opening up new possibilities of travel, adventure, and professional advancement to thousands of mostly young men and women. Tom and Percy answered the call, perhaps for the first time, at the outset of the 1903 season, playing the summer respectively as the clarinet and cornet soloists with the Walter L. Main Enormous Shows, one of the larger circuses. The move from minstrel orchestra to circus band was a step upward financially. Tom reported his first salary, around 1899, as $8 per week, and in an interview in the early 1920s, he recalled his Ringling Brothers salary around 1904 as $18 per week.[5] Overlapping seasons facilitated moves from minstrelsy to the circus and vice versa. The circus was a warm-weather creature, usually running twenty-eight weeks from the beginning of April until the end of October.[6] Minstrel shows, free from the production constraints imposed on a tent show by winter temperatures, had a much more flexible schedule, but normally stopped to rest and regroup during the summer. The Guy Brothers' 1896–97 season, for example, ran from August 28 until May 3—thirty-five weeks.[7] A talented and ambitious instrumentalist could easily work fifty-two weeks a year on the road. Tom and Percy left the Walter L. Main circus before the end of the 1903 season to seize new opportunities in Guy Brothers' Minstrels, where Tom became the leader of the orchestra for the 1903–4 season. But the more important opportunity, in light of what was to come, was the pair's debut as the Brown Brothers in the Guy olio. As far as the author knows, this event marks the beginning of the evolution of the act that eventually became the Six Brown Brothers.[8]

Besides the usual historiographical problems created by forgetful or unprepared witnesses, inattentive or lazy reporters, editors on deadline, and missing documents, the story of the act's development suffered under its own legend. The tale, created by an unknown press agent before Tom started giving interviews, is told in Roger Lewis's lyrics to the Brothers' 1913 hit "That Moaning Saxophone Rag":

> I'm going to tell you all about Tom Brown,
> A swell musician down in my home town;
> When but a boy he ran away from home,
> He didn't take a thing except his saxophone[.]
> We heard about him in a year or so,
> Somebody saw him with a minstrel show;
> He was the main attraction, there's no doubt,
> For ev'ry body raved about him going out.
>
> Oh, that moaning saxophone,
> Sweeter than a slide trombone,
> So surprising, harmonizing, emphasising ev'ry tone;
> Just a little silver home
> Where sweet melodies are grown,
> Oh, that groaning
> Oh, that moaning saxophone rag.
>
> Tom had some brothers, all musicians too,
> He wrote, "Come and join me and an act we'll do;—
> Draw out your money from the bank down home,
> For each of you will have to buy a saxophone[.]

> They're all together now, and when they play,
> The op'ra house is crowded ev'ry day;
> They've got their pictures up, like actor men,
> And ev'ry body hangs around and looks at them.

> Oh, that moaning saxophone [etc.][9]

The fully developed version of the legend made Tom, rather than William, the oldest of the brothers, and told of the brothers joining the group one by one as they finished school, finally ending up as a sextet, either with Ringling or with Guy Brothers' Minstrels.[10] Having circulated the legend, the Browns had to live with it and (sometimes, but not always) conform their published recollections to it. However, independent evidence and inconsistencies from interview to interview tell a much more complicated and much less linear story.

The Guy organization became somewhat unstable during the first few years of the century. The spectacle of six brothers—and, before his death in 1895, their father as well—performing together on the same stage, "an occurrence that had no parallel in minstrelsy,"[11] had been one of its big drawing points. But William (1853–1906) and George Jr. (1855–1942), the two oldest brothers, had to drop out for at least part of one season between 1901 and 1903, and in 1905, Arthur (1872–1937) left to form his own show, Arthur Guy's Novelty Minstrels.[12] William's death in 1906 was another serious blow to the organization. Nevertheless, the troupe seems to have flourished, and by 1903–4 and perhaps earlier, Percy had joined older brother Tom in the orchestra.[13] For a part of the relevant period, the troupe's musical director was Al Sweet, later the leader of the Ringling Brothers' band from 1906 to 1911.[14] Working with the Guy Brothers, Tom continued his passive apprenticeship as a minstrel, while Percy seems to have remained first and foremost a musician. By 1904, according to a number of sources, they had left Guy Brothers' for the Ringling Brothers' Circus.

The circus life, especially on a big show such as Walter L. Main's or the Ringling Brothers', was far different from the minstrel life. First, circuses were much larger, self-contained traveling communities that provided food, lodging, and society for their members. On the twenty-two railroad-carried shows among the eighty-nine touring in 1901, performers and workers alike slept on the trains, ate in the company's "cook top" (a tent erected at each stop to serve as a commissary), and socialized mostly with each other. Although there was a marked hierarchy among circus people,[15] a considerable amount of mixing across the boundaries took place, encouraged by the sheer numbers of talented people, drawn not only from all over the United States and Canada, but also from Europe, Asia, and Australia, available as potential companions. A person need not feel that he or she was part of a small group entering a series of possibly hostile larger communities; a citizen of the circus inhabited a moving city that had no need to interact (except through delegates) with the people it found itself among as it crossed the country.

Second, because circus troupes included women, young men like Tom could avoid many of the pitfalls of the all-male life. The lonely single minstrel, caught between sex with prostitutes or other men and chaste and fleeting (or nonchaste and perilous) relationships with local women, became the single circus musician, surrounded by attractive young women with whom he might have longer-term relationships. But of course there were trade-offs. Longer-term relationships could give rise to jealousy and conflict among performers, and unmarried couples could find themselves on the threshold of unwelcome parenthood. Circus management, aware of these dangers, forbade fraternization between unmarried men and women. Ringling Brothers' Circus, for example, had a rule that "male performers are not to visit with the ballet girls"—that is, the many low-salaried women, usually single and in their teens, whose function in the show was mostly decorative and auxiliary. Dressed as Egyptian princesses, they rode the elephants in parade. In biblical or medieval garb, they swelled the host in opening spectacles. They held hoops for acrobats, handed whips to equestrians or baskets of trained pigeons to the bird lady, and danced in the sideshows. For their protection, in part, but mostly for the welfare of the show, "the excuse of 'accidental' meetings on Sunday [when the show was idle], in parks, at picture shows, etc.," was not accepted. Moreover, ballet girls were forbidden to "dress in a flashy, loud style," directed to "be neat and modest in appearance," and "required to be in the sleeping car . . . not later than 11 P.M. and not to leave [the] car after registering." They were never to "talk or visit with male members of the Show Company, excepting the management, and under no circumstances with residents of the cities visited." They were never to stay in hotels.[16] Inevitably, the rules were broken from time to time, but, "after breaking the rules for a second time," reported Lizzie Rooney ("the star bareback rider of the Ringling show at the turn of the century"), "no further warning was given. The girl just found her trunk left on the lot and she was through."[17] (Such rules, and specifically a rule against swearing, had earned the Ringling Circus the nickname of the "Ting-a-Ling Show" in the more old-fashioned and rowdier segment of the circus business.)[18]

To continue making enough money to survive, a mud show—circus or minstrel—could travel only twenty or thirty miles between stands, precluding the greater profit and acclaim that might come from playing only in relatively large towns. A railroad show, on the other hand, had a range of about 150 miles overnight and 300 or more on a weekend, when blue laws prevented it from putting on a Sunday performance. Thus it could blossom, as the Ringling show had by 1900, into an enterprise employing a thousand people, and carrying "more than five hundred of the finest horses ever bred, some of them priceless[,] . . . hundreds of gorgeous chariots, dens, and tableaux, . . . a band of fifty solo musicians . . . and chiming bells weighing many tons, . . . hundreds of the finest artists and performers from every quarter of the globe, . . . four palace advertising cars, . . . tons of the finest lithographic paper, . . . a hundred busy advertisers, . . . [and] a million-dollar menagerie" to put on its extravaganza in "three large rings and mammoth elevated stages" under "a million yards of canvas that cover many acres," borne on "five large trains of railroad cars."[19]

Although the smoke and cinders of the railroad compared unfavorably with the fresh air of country roads,[20] train travel provided a much higher level of comfort than getting from place to place by wagon and staying in small-town hotels. Long hops in large sleeping cars afforded plenty of opportunities for getting to know one's colleagues off the lot, exchanging information, playing cards, reading, and entertaining each other with jokes and music. In the interval between the afternoon and evening performances— "the best loved hour of the performers' day," as described by the ballet girl Dixie Willson—"little groups gather around the back door [the private area from which acts enter the big top] to sew or read or write letters; the men discuss weighty problems, the price of eggs or the Einstein theory; there is tea; there are romps for the babies (though there are never many babies on the show), games of baseball or swimming parties, if a pool or lake is near."[21] The prohibition on Sunday shows afforded even longer periods of leisurely interaction.

> Never could there be lazier, happier days than those Sundays on the show train. During the morning there was always a two-hour stop to water and exercise the ring-stock [show animals]. Out in the sweet, open country, wild flowers crowding the fence, the drowsy song of insects in the grass, every one would come out along the tracks to visit and exchange magazines, to fill their arms with flowers, and make calls in the other cars. Very gay these Sunday stops: bright silk pajamas, Sunday lounging robes, informal ginghams; and up ahead the elephants, camels, zebras and beautiful ring horses unloading, going out across the meadow somewhere to water.[22]

During the 1904 tour, baseball games between Ringling clowns and acrobats snowballed into two leagues of eight teams each, playing daily and ending with a July championship game between the Acrobats of the Performers' League and the Canvasmen of the Working Men's League, the Acrobats winning 16-9.[23]

Circus trains arrived in a series. Days in advance of the rest, the advertising cars stopped briefly in the targeted town, laden with colorful posters, skilled billstickers, and publicists with fistfuls of complimentary passes to ease the way for the lithographs to go up, create enthusiasm in the local press, and recruit the platoons of local boys on which the show relied to perform such minor tasks as the proverbial carrying of water for the elephants.[24] Early on the morning of a performance, the train bearing canvas and poles arrived at the day's venue, and workers erected the cook top before the other tents in order to provide breakfast for performers coming later. As each train steamed in, parked on a siding, and disgorged its passengers, a new component was added to the ensemble, and by mid-morning, rails and weather cooperating, the traveling city had appeared on its new site: the big top, the menagerie, the sideshow, the auxiliary tents for dressing and eating, and the colorful, gilded parade wagons, some of them showcases for tigers, giraffes, gorillas, or hyenas, some of them mostly for pageantry, but several of them to display the Ringling musicians during the morning parade.

Photographs of the Ringling Brothers' parade during the 1904–9 seasons show at least four bands, including a group mounted on horses and three units playing high atop swaying tableaux wagons, two of them drawn from the big-show or concert band and the third a clown band. The 1912 parade included five bands of nine to fifteen pieces, including a ten-piece ticket-sellers band, a twelve-piece sideshow band, and a nine-piece clown band, along with four female and two male mounted buglers and, in the rear, a steam calliope.[25] Spaced evenly through the long line of march, the musical units supplied the rapid polkas, galops, and marches that underscored the visual spectacle and told the excited crowds on the sidewalk, in the most visceral way, that their excitement was the right response and that they needed to come to the tents for more of the same. For the musicians, parade work was physically the most taxing part of the performance day. Playing while seated on a moving wagon is tough on the embouchure even when the horses don't bolt, but the mounted musicians had it even tougher, playing on horseback with no wheels or springs to soften the ride.[26]

Once the last screams and hoots of the calliope faded from the street and the populace thronged the show ground, the musicians regrouped into specialized ensembles. The first to return to work were the members of the sideshow band, who alternated between playing in front of the tent to bring in customers and providing music inside the tent for such acts as the Streets of Cairo, an Americanized belly-dancing spectacle that had originated at the 1893 World's Columbian Exposition in Chicago. The sideshow opened for business at the end of the parade and, in some companies, including Ringling Brothers', continued even while the long series of displays unfolded in the big top.[27]

While the audience filed into the big top, the big-show band usually played a promenade concert, often featuring military-band transcriptions of highbrow orchestral material, such as overtures and suites drawn from the opera.[28] Once the audience was seated, a show such as Main's or the Ringlings', in the first decade of the twentieth century, began with the "spectacle," "a prodigious stage show" under the main tent, presented in pantomime and involving "hundreds of people, horses, camels, and elephants."[29] Main's spectacle for 1903, "Savage South Africa," recreated Boer War battles using

> sixty Boers, under Lieut. F. G. Mellon; eighty New South Wales Lanciers, under Corporal A. J. Roscoe; sixty Canadian scouts, under Corporal Clarke; two detachments of Naval Reserves, under Captain Henry Dugins; [and] one hundred Zulus, Matabeles, Swazas and

Bushmen. Over three thousand feet of panoramic scenery has been
painted for the spectacular production, and original oxen wagons,
vehicles, and the original Transvaal coach will be used.[30]

The Ringling spectacle of 1904, "Jerusalem and the Crusades," opened
before a painted backdrop of a French castle, "where the knights are mar-
shaled preparatory to their departure for the crusades. There were jousts,
sword combats and the blessing of the multitude," followed by "a garland ride
by twenty-four knights" as the scene changed to Jerusalem, "where fifty well
drilled girls dance before the emir. Mussulmans, Turks and Saracens stand by
and watch the festivities, which ends in the capture of the Holy City by the
crusaders."[31] In 1905, the Ringlings' "Field of the Cloth of Gold" purported
to recreate the festival surrounding the 1520 meeting of Henry VIII of England and François I of France, featuring more jousting and swordplay, along
with choral singing and "an intricate Dance on horseback, followed by a
Grand Ballet Divertissement of reveling, dancing girls in an artistic picture
of grace, color and movement, the scene culminating in a glorious feast of
mirth and merriment."[32]

After providing suitable accompaniment for the impressive opening display, which lasted about half an hour, the big-show band, seated opposite the
center ring, proceeded to spark the whole subsequent two and a half hours of
soaring aerialists, somersaulting bareback riders, waltzing horses, pyramiding
elephants, snarling tigers, rearing lions, gamboling clowns, and the rest. The
musical program, consisting sometimes of as many as 200 snippets,[33] from
graceful waltzes that turned the muscular strain of the trapeze artists into
effortless flight to drum rolls that focused attention and demanded suspense,
was planned down to the last detail. Yet the bandsmen had always to be ready
to change at a signal from the bandmaster, whose job it was to match the
music as exactly as possible to the imperfectly predictable progress of the
show. It was hard, exhausting work. "The circus bandsman had to develop
lips of iron and lungs of leather."[34]

Clowning pervaded the big show, sometimes as a feature in one of the
rings, but almost always as a wandering supplement to whatever might be
going on elsewhere. Massive clown ladies called for their missing children,
searching for them among the giggling audience. Tumbling clowns concluded a series of handsprings with a pratfall. Clown cars disintegrated
around their drivers while clown dogs dressed as lions jumped through hoops.
And the clown band plumbed the comic possibilities of their battered and
bent instruments. A clarinet can sound like water flowing over smooth
stones, but it can also shriek like a crow and cluck like a chicken. The trombone's majestic song is no more intrinsic to the instrument than its blats and
smears, and the very slide that makes those smears possible comes right off for
a surefire sight gag.

The three-hour extravaganza of trained animals, dazzling athletes,
capering buffoons, and constant music was presented twice at each venue,

afternoon and evening. But for some of the troupe, including many musicians, the work didn't end with the night's presentation. At the conclusion of both the afternoon and evening performances, the hardier members of the audience could stick around in the big top for the after-show or concert. An extra admission put the viewer in what had been the reserved-seat section to watch a variety show put on by a small group drawn from the troupe.[35] The entertainment resembled a typical vaudeville bill of the period, on a much smaller scale than the big show's overwhelming whirl of activity. Singers, dancers, acrobats, impersonators, actors in comic sketches, and musicians in specialties furnished a chance for the audience's overheated brains to cool down for a night's sleep and the next morning's reentry into the world of work and family.

A trouper's role in the circus was fluid to a certain extent. Sometimes in the smaller shows, "circus bandsmen had to perform nonmusical duties such as setting up tents, positioning benches, and distributing publicity notices."[36] And even on the Ringling show, the custom was "to help one another, to do any work that was necessary. The highest paid artist feels not the slightest hesitation about helping with the canvas, or doing any other work, if it is for the good of the show."[37] Dixie Willson tells of Ringling management offering a salary hike to any woman on the show, whatever her current function, who would become an "iron jaw" performer for the 1922 season, spinning by her teeth from a rope high in the tent rigging. She also relates that "there are always people learning to play musical instruments," no doubt not only to improve their position in the show, but also to increase their general mobility in show business.[38] And Tom Brown, in interviews, said that he and his brothers "doubled and tripled as clowns and ticket takers" and that one of them (Alec, by his own account) sold sweets in the stands as a "candy butcher."[39] Because of this fluidity, it is possible that Tom and one or more of his brothers at various times occupied not only the roles Tom mentions (including the big-show band, the sideshow band, a clown band, and a specialty in the after-show), but various others, down to cook crew and canvasman, that would have left their time free for a regular musical turn in the after-show.[40]

As noted, Tom said at various times that he was in the Ringling Brothers' big-show band, the sideshow band, a clown band, and the after-show. Tom himself said he was a Ringling musician in 1904, although no performers' ledgers or route books survive to document his presence or specify his role.[41] A roster of the big-show band from 1905 includes Percy on cornet, along with Tom and Fred (as "F. Brown") on clarinet.[42] Percy, Tom, and Vern are the only Browns listed as musicians in the 1906 and 1907 performers' ledgers, which also list the Brown Brothers as a separate after-show attraction, at an additional salary. The 1907 "Official Program" lists "T. R. Brown, saxophonist," as one of four featured soloists with the big-show band during the opening concert. Although Vern is listed in a couple of rosters of unknown reliability during the 1908 season,[43] vaudeville itineraries indicate that the

Brown Brothers toured in theatres that summer, at least three of them—
Tom, Vern, and Alec—returning to the security of the circus for 1909. No
documentation survives regarding the employment of other brothers as
candy butchers, ticket takers, or clowns, but the lack of documentation does
not indicate that they were not with the show. For example, the 1907 performers' ledger fails to name the members of the ten-piece sideshow band,
aside from its leader, William Markwith. (Markwith, also a saxophonist, was
to play an important peripheral role in the story of the Brown Brothers.)

According to Tom's accounts, it was on the Ringling show that he took
up the saxophone. A 1921 *Billboard* interview gives one version of the fateful
switch.

> More years ago than Tommie now cares to admit, 1904, while play-
> ing a clarinet with the Ringling Bros.' Circus he purchased a saxo-
> phone, a second-hand one, and he and one of his now famous broth-
> ers, together with Doc Healy [*sic*; actually George "Doc" Kealey],
> featured the saxophone at the big Ringling Brothers after show con-
> cert. The act was a success from the first.[44]

Another, enigmatically different and more detailed, appeared in a 1923
interview in the *San Francisco Chronicle*. The interviewer, George C. Warren, speaks first:

> Tom . . . was a clarinet player and he played for a time in the band
> with Ringling Brothers' circus. The leader wanted to have a saxo-
> phone solo and he proposed to put Tom in the center of the band if he
> would undertake the work. "That was 'duck soup' for me," he [Tom]
> told me, "for I had been taking all the work, the cadenzas and carry-
> ing the air with the clarinet. Then when we were in Kansas City one
> time and I was riding in the parade I saw the bass saxophone we have
> now in a pawnshop window, and I said: 'As soon as this parade is over
> I'm going to own you!' I went in to see the man and asked him how
> much he wanted. He said, 'I loaned $80 on it.' I told him I couldn't
> pay that much, but I would give him $60 for it. . . .
>
> "He refused my offer, so I went out, but I meant to go back. I
> trailed into a couple of saloons and then I found a man had been fol-
> lowing me. He said, 'Are you the man that wanted the bass saxo-
> phone?' I said I was and he said I could have it for $60.
>
> "I got Otto Ringling to lend me the money—I didn't have a cent
> in those days, for I was getting $17 a week until they raised me to $18
> for my saxophone solo.
>
> "I kept the bass instrument in an empty lion's cage for two or
> three weeks and then I sent for one of my brothers and he learned it
> and then I got hold of a tenor saxophone and another brother came
> on to play that, and then we made up the band and went into vaude-
> ville for a while."[45]

Although it seems impossible to combine these two versions into a single coherent story, some details match up nicely, especially the presence of three brothers in the Ringling troupe both at the end of the second story and in the evidence provided by performers' ledgers and independent testimony. This agreement makes it likely that at some point the nucleus of the Six Brown Brothers comprised (besides Doc Kealey) Tom, Percy, and Vern. The story of the purchase of the bass sax also fits with the fact that, during the better-documented 1909–30 era, Vern was always the ensemble's bass saxophonist, except for a brief period during World War I. One important detail fails to gibe with independent evidence, however, so that we must take the second story, as a whole, with a few grains of salt: the bass saxophone in photos of the Six Brown Brothers from about 1921 differs from the one that appears in earlier photos (and that is now in the collection of the National Music Museum at the University of South Dakota). So Tom's claim that the sax bought in Kansas City is the one "we have now" is wrong unless they kept it in storage for fifteen years or so. Since the early photograph described in the paragraph below shows Tom with a baritone sax, it is possible that the interviewer heard Tom wrong and that the instrument purchased in Kansas City was the baritone.

A photograph (see figure 3) in Tom's collection suggests that his first foray into vaudeville took place before Percy, at any rate, took up the saxophone, and so probably before the founding of the saxophone ensemble.[46] Taken in Chicago and bearing, alas, no date, it is inscribed on the back by Tom and Percy as a Christmas gift to their father. Tom, at the left of a space about ten feet wide, holds a clarinet, while Percy, on the right, holds a cornet. Tom stands in front of a splendid two-octave set of hanging orchestra bells, with a baritone saxophone near him, propped against the framework that supports the bells, and between them, closer to Percy, is a three-octave xylophone fronted with a floor-length banner reading "Brown Bros." This was clearly a publicity photo for a multi-instrumental act the two brothers had formed, possibly for the Guy Brothers' olio, possibly for the Ringling Brothers after-show, and in either case probably also for small-time vaudeville during the circus's winter hiatus.[47] The photo also suggests that Tom's first saxophone was a baritone, although he played alto (and occasionally soprano after 1919) once the Five Brown Brothers emerged as an enterprise in 1908.

During his circus years, Tom met and fell in love with his future wife, a beautiful dark-haired, hazel-eyed Italian American teenager, Theresa Valerio. She was one of eight children, six of them girls, of a show-business family who seem to have performed in variety theatre and the circus both in England and the United States.[48] Her parents and her three elder siblings had emigrated to the United States shortly before Theresa was born in Philadelphia in 1888.[49] By the time she was fifteen, she and her older sister and protector, Rosa, had become circus performers. The year of Tom and Theresa's first meeting is uncertain. They both told interviewers it took place in the

Ringling period, but some evidence points instead to 1903, when Tom, at least, was still with the Walter L. Main outfit.[50] Whatever the year in whatever circus, Theresa and Tom remembered their first encounter as happening on the Ringling show.

> One day, when Theresa tripped and fell during the act, she saw a young saxophonist in the circus band smiling sympathetically at her.[51] After that wonderful occasion, she glanced that way and saw the same smile at every performance. But the circus authorities didn't approve of love affairs among the actors, so the little dancer and the young musician would whisper in passing, "I'll meet you at the dog-cart," or "Meet me at the peanut stand," and thus the love affair flourished, unknown even to Rosa, until one night she heard a kiss—and found her little sister kissing the picture of a fine looking boy who was saving up his money so that he and Theresa could be married.[52]

Tom continued the story of the surreptitious meetings:

> We would have just time for a murmured confidence, a word of love, a quick, self conscious hug and away we'd scamper, delighted to know our secret was still safe.
>
> Why, at one time, Teresa [sic] used to climb into bed, wait until her sister Rosa had tucked her in and then hang her big braid out of the car window. I'd wait until the loading was finished and the lights were out, then I'd sneak along the side of the car, and tweak the braid. Teresa would wake, hang her head out of the window and kiss me goodnight. And that was the end of another day.[53]

According to the fully developed 1920 version of the Brown Brothers legend, Tom and his brothers formed a clown band within the Ringling show from 1904 through 1909.[54] Falsehood of detail aside, the claim suggests that some of their work was in clown costume, a permanent feature of the act starting with their Broadway debut in 1914. Perhaps the clown-band context led Tom to adopt the blackface persona that he had crafted from his minstrel apprenticeship and that was already a part of the act in 1909, when the other four members worked unpainted. Although we now picture circus clown makeup as involving an overall base of white, blackface clowns were common in the nineteenth century,[55] and a post-1919 photo of the massed Ringling Brothers and Barnum and Bailey Greatest Show on Earth clowns shows three of the forty-six in burnt cork.[56]

Another feature of the Brothers' costuming after 1909 dated back to the circus days—a pair of oversized shoes that Tom wore, continuing not only the minstrel and clown traditions of comically exaggerated feet, but also the minstrel appropriation of clothing found in the legends of Jim Crow and the Watermelon Man. As late as about 1926, Tom was still wearing shoes that he had acquired, as he put it, from a nigger giant on the Ringling circus lot, twenty years ago, and where I go, they go. I got 'em soon after I decided to do the clown act with my band. I saw this eight-foot nigger coming from the cook house and I said to him, "Boy, what'll you take for those shoes?" "Well, they ought to be worth six bits," he says. "Here's your money," I said, and when the giant saw the money he took off these shoes and walked in his stocking feet over to the side show. Those shoes are just part of Tom Brown now. I can buy new bow-legged pants, new pink neck-ties, but I keep these shoes.[57]

The rest of the brief article explains that Tom is "superstitious" about the shoes, the author commenting that "battered and patched so that little of the original leather remains, still Tom won't give them up," even though, as Tom's friends assured him, "shoes that size can be funny and new at the same time." If the author accurately assessed Tom's attitude, the shoes were for him much more than just a part of his costume. That extra, undiscussed aspect might well be the kind of guarantee of authenticity or of connection with real African Americans that "Daddy" Rice and J. W. McAndrews felt was provided by their appropriation of clothing, and that somehow made their impersonations legitimate.

Clowns, like minstrels, were in the business of making people laugh. When circuses were still small, one-ring affairs, talking clowns could employ the same kinds of verbal humor that minstrels did, even to baiting the pompous ringmaster in the way that end men baited the pompous interlocutor. But, as competitive pressure made tent shows balloon into the three-ring spectacles of the turn of the twentieth century, distances between performer and audience grew and noise levels rose to a point at which clowns had to create laughter without resort to jokes, which had to be heard by the audience. Pantomime, once a useful auxiliary resource, became the clown's main technique, helped along by the minimal indications of character and setting indicated by the clown's make-up and costuming. Much clown pantomime involves storytelling, "a small comedy or a slight drama . . . not only . . . action, but something to suggest an incident or a series of incidents."[58] Especially among the crowd of generally white-faced performers, a blackened face would suggest to the audience a range of possible characters contained in their cultural stereotypes of African Americans, leaving to the performer only the task of indicating with gesture the particular kind of "darkey" he represented: pretentious dandy, thief of chickens and watermelons, lazy slacker, ignoramus, believer in ghosts, or hunter of opossums; or, on the positive side, the raggedy but harmless poor man who sang and danced or converted a rich man's discards into treasures. The exaggeration intrinsic to minstrel make-up aided in an even more basic element of clowning, getting the audience to laugh as soon as they caught sight of the performer. As Jules Turnour, a star clown on the Ringling show during Tom's epoch, put it, "I had a good make-up, . . . and the people laughed as soon as they saw me. Laughter has a peculiar effect. If it ripples out as soon as you appear, you may be sure that you are succeeding, because if the people do not think you even look funny, they will not laugh."[59]

Some of Tom's later stage business—conducting the other musicians with comic movements of his hands and body—may also have come from an African American performer in the Ringling sideshow. This "veritable palace of amusement," with music furnished both by a ten-piece band and "an immense electrical orchestra" (possibly an Orchestrion, a player piano augmented by drums, xylophone, and various other instruments, all actuated by pneumatic valves following a program on a perforated paper roll), included on its 1906 roster "Mons. Geo. Levasseur, French Hercules; Cho Mah, Chinese pigmy; Prof. Leon Harto, magician and ventriloquist; Miss Verda Wren, athletic girl; Emil Millette, the 'bovine boy'; Chas. B. Tripp, armless marvel; Old Zip, Original What Is It?; The Scrantons, novelty entertainers; Lottie Rutherford, serpentine enchantress, and Dr. Bruce Miller's musical novelty, the Pneumultiphone."[60] Zip, the What-Is-It, "the doyen of all freaks," was an African American microcephalic from New Jersey named William Henry Johnson, who had begun his career in P. T. Barnum's American Museum in 1860 as the Wild Boy, wearing "an artificial topknot on his cone-like head, his body clothed in a suit of so-called gorilla hair." Barnum passed him off at first as an evolutionary link between humans and apes, reportedly paying him a dollar extra per day for refraining from using English before his public. His act mostly consisted in acting "wild," but "he had a knack for clowning and always got a laugh when he led the band as a ballyhoo [that is, an enticement on the platform in front of the tent] for the sideshow," and comic band-leading became one of his specialties. It was such an integral part of his persona that, when a group of sideshow performers visited him as he lay dying from pneumonia in 1926, they encouraged him by saying, "You must hurry up and get well, Zip. The band needs you to lead them."[61]

The circus furnished Tom and his brothers a show-business education probably not confined just to apprenticeships in variety acts and clowning, along with the wisdom imparted in conversation with the more experienced citizens of the nomadic republic. Given Tom's desire to improve himself, he likely took advantage of the circus's moments of relaxation to read "that masterpiece of invention,"[62] Alfred (Alf. T.) Ringling's *Life Story of the Ringling Brothers*, a very entertaining book published in 1900 and sold in the Ringlings' menagerie tent starting the following season. Not only did it give an easily readable and humorous account of Tom's employers' rise to fame with "the greatest amusement enterprise in the world's history," but it claimed to show "the true road to success."[63] Five of the seven Ringling brothers, sons of a frontier harness-maker who, like Allan Brown, had wandered from town to town in search of a living, initiated a traveling variety show in 1882, playing the small farming, lumbering, and mining towns of Iowa (where the family lived), Wisconsin, Minnesota, and Dakota. The oldest, Albert (Al), was thirty at the time, and John, the youngest, was only sixteen. During the first season they employed three non-brothers, but for the 1883–84 tour they decided to go it alone, presenting a "Carnival of Fun" in which nineteen-year-old Charles played violin and sang; twenty-two-year-old Alf. T. played cornet and organ solos and sang; John did blackface, Irish, and "Dutch" turns, including a wooden-shoe dance; and Al juggled and spun plates. In one turn, Charles and Alf. T. demonstrated their skills on twelve different musical instruments. Together, and now including twenty-three-year-old Otto, the show's advance man in charge of publicity, the brothers also staged a farce and an afterpiece.[64] By the summer of 1884, the brothers had saved enough money to start a traveling circus, and in 1890 they converted it from a mud show to a railroad-borne extravaganza with all the trappings of a modern circus, from aerialists and elephants to freaks and lemonade.

Alf. T. Ringling's map of the true road to success starts with the idea that the aspirant "needs a better and loftier ambition than the mere desire for gold." He goes on to point out a sine qua non:

> All worthy love for success has better ideals and nobler aims. The artist at his easel, the architect at his trestle-board, the minister in the pulpit, the author in his study, the farmer, the lawyer, the doctor, the statesman, the engineer—in short, the man of whatever profession or calling—only attains success when he loves the work of climbing each uneven step that reaches up and to it; and financial gain comes only as an incident, after all.[65]

Love of one's work, averred Alf. T., fosters patience and perseverance, carrying the aspirant through the inevitable hard stretches. His account of the little show's struggles stresses the brothers' "energy and push," their pluck, determination, zeal, and tenacity of purpose, their courage, hard work, economy, and ingenuity, all the established virtues of the heroes of nineteenth-century boys' fiction, and purports to illustrate the rewards of these virtues in charmingly funny set pieces. But the set pieces reveal that two unstressed factors played a substantial role in the brothers' early rise: luck and deception.

Sometimes the luck was bad, "But they knew not the meaning of the word 'fail,' and by ignoring the power of difficulties, and by a constant determination to overcome them, they vanquished misfortune and often made a disadvantage turn to their favor."[66] But sometimes the luck was good and proved pivotal, as when their first audience, in Mazomanie, Wisconsin, turned out to be friendly and uncritical and their second, in Spring Green, was swollen by a crowd that had come to town for a much-anticipated and unexpectedly canceled dance, leaving the disappointed revelers with no place to go but the Ringling Brothers' Classic and Comic Concert Company.[67]

The author presents his brothers' skillfully employed deception as "strategy" and "clever tricks." Right at the outset, the Ringlings, after some discussion, decided to bill their first season on the road as their fourth, in order to avoid the reputation of amateurs. Otto customarily avoided the embarrassment of the show's having only small fliers for advertising by telling local merchants that the large sheets at his disposal were too big for the town's bill-boards. When cash was short, the whole troupe sneaked its baggage out of a hotel and onto a train while Al distracted the attention of the proprietor. And a Missouri property owner reluctant to rent his lot for any purpose at all, but fond of boys, was tricked into signing a contract for it when young John (without actually lying) led him to think that the lot was wanted by a group of boys to play at circus.[68] A young man of Tom's intelligence must surely have understood the scarcely concealed inexplicit message along with the official one.

Loving his work and the climb so far, smart enough to use Ringling-style strategy on his future public, and possessed of the boys'-story virtues, all that Tom needed was good luck to follow the road to success. The examples of the five Ringling Brothers gazing nobly from 10,000 posters (not to mention the seven actually running the enterprise) and the six Guy Brothers performing together on the same stage must have resonated with Tom. It wasn't long before the Brown Brothers (two, then three, then four real Browns and an outsider) scrambled onto the next step on the upward climb.

5

Struggling into the Big Time

1905–11

By the end of the first decade of the century, vaudeville had attained a form that it would keep until its demise as a major field of show business during the Great Depression. Its immediate ancestor, variety theatre, can be seen in the Carnival of Fun that the Ringling Brothers staged in the early 1880s: an afternoon's or evening's entertainment composed of whatever was thought likely to amuse a paying audience. Variety differed from *Uncle Tom's Cabin* and its ilk by a lack of plot and from minstrelsy by its format—a mere series of turns rather than a tripartite framework of first part, olio, and afterpiece. An olio like the one in the Guy Brothers' Minstrels took a program one might have seen at a variety theatre (as well as in vaudeville) and compressed it into one segment of the presentation.

The switch from variety to vaudeville was a self-conscious one, spearheaded by the New York impresario Tony Pastor. The change was motivated by a commercial ideal in moral clothing: keeping the entertainment "clean" enough for nineteenth-century middle-class women and children to attend without being offended would result in a larger potential audience and better business. In the lore of vaudeville, a definite date marks the epoch: October 24, 1881.[1] At mid-century, the variety-theatre audience, at least in New York and other urban centers, was mostly male, except for the prostitutes who used the theatres as a market for their services. Performances were rowdy and sexy, the language was blue, and the general moral tone didn't measure up to the standards of church and hearth. Pastor's reformed institution insisted on well-mannered performers, dialogue and lyrics edited to avoid profanity, blasphemy, and vulgarity, and a moral decorum comfortably above the minimum expected in Victorian parlors. The commercial success of Pastor's innovations inspired a horde of competitors, so that, by the beginning of the twentieth century, variety as a separate institution had virtually ceased to exist, although many old-timers thought the label "vaudeville" pretentious and continued to call the purified institution "variety." Burlesque theatres still offered the kind of earthy, risqué amusement pre-Pastor variety theatre had provided, but burlesque had its own history, more or less independent of variety.

At first, the business end of vaudeville, like that of variety, was almost completely decentralized. Individual impresarios such as Pastor used separately owned or rented theatres to present programs built up from turns they hired themselves, and performers contracted directly with the impresarios. Following the general tendency toward consolidation in American business, however, chains of theatres began to form, constituted sometimes by ownership or leasing of multiple theatres, sometimes by agreements among independently owned theatres to use a common booking office. All these arrangements gave entrepreneurs greater control over their resources (the artists) and product (the shows), opening up avenues to larger profit margins. These "circuits," as they were called, appeared all across the country and ranged in size from a handful of small-town halls to the giant Keith circuit in the eastern third of the United States and its rival, the Orpheum circuit, which reached from its San Francisco cradle to Chicago. Concomitantly, performers were constrained to contract with the circuits, or sometimes with several circuits that shared a booking bureau, such as the New York–based United Booking Office, which made arrangements for the Keith circuit, the Percy G. Williams circuit, and several others, ultimately controlling performers' access to most of the country's leading vaudeville theatres. The major advantage furnished to the performer was that a circuit booking office could provide him or her with several months, perhaps even a whole season, of one-week stands.

As central to developed, big-time vaudeville as the existence of theatre circuits was the general practice of booking turns or acts as independent units ("spot booking") rather than as parts of whole troupes traveling together ("intact booking").[2] For a time, both ways of organizing bookings were common, and some theatres brought in integral traveling shows such as Florenz Ziegfeld's Trocadero Vaudevilles Company, while others made separate arrangements for comics, wire walkers, clog dancers, fire eaters, motion-picture exhibitors, and so on. But as the first decade of the century passed, spot booking became the norm. An abundance of entertainments still traveled whole: circuses flourished, and even minstrel aggregations and *Tom* shows continued to appear, though they were rapidly losing ground. By 1910, the principal form of "hall show" on the road as a self-contained unit was the burlesque show, and it was in that setting that the Browns made their first successful incursion into New York, then the undisputed capital of the American show-business world.

By the time Tom Brown and his brothers left the circus, most vaudeville theatres belonged to circuits, and circuits were loosely differentiated into the big time and the small time. Working conditions constituted part of the difference. On the big time, such as the Keith, Williams, or Orpheum time, a vaudeville bill would be presented to the public only twice a day, in the afternoon and in the evening, while on the small time, such as the Pantages or

Considine circuits, the bill could run continuously from an early matinee until late at night, repeating three, four, or five times depending on the length of the show. Small-time turns worked harder, were paid less, and were provided by the venues they played with less comfort and support, for example in regard to dressing rooms, stage machinery, and travel subsidies. From these differences arose a difference in performance standards, so that "small-time" became not just a job description for an entertainer who might very well ascend to a career in two-a-day, but a pejorative for the individual or group who didn't have the talent to please the discriminating audiences at the grand venues in major cities. Sime Silverman, the founder of the show-business weekly *Variety*, epitomized the difference in a 1914 review of the Four Rubes:

> Two views could be taken of the Four Rubes, a comedy quartet. It would depend where they were seen and in a way, exemplify the difference between big time and the smaller small time. The views might run like these:

> ### Small Time

> The Four Rubes could be called The Rube Minstrels, as it is a minstrel idea, fashioned somehow after the Crane Brothers and Belmont turn. Each of the men is in eccentric rural dress and make-up, going in somewhat for rough comedy, having plenty of jokes, and singing during the turn, which concludes with one of the men yodeling that gets over very big, earning an easy encore. The comedy talk and the characters will please in certain of the smaller houses.

> ### Big Time

> The Four Rubes got an idea and then ran away from it. It's a rube quartet with "gags," some of the oldest and the poorest that could be gotten for nothing. When the act thins down at any time and a laugh is needed, slapstick is indulged in by one of the farmerish men jumping at another's throat. All are grotesquely made up, have little natural humor, sing badly in the barber-shop way, and the finish, a yodel, sounds like a weak imitation of a steam calliope. For big time the turn never had a chance.[3]

The Brown Brothers, probably just Tom and Percy at first, perhaps then the Ringling after-show trio, growing in rough conformity with the legend, tested the waters of small-time vaudeville during the winter when the circus left the road. Four or five months without work could consume the savings of the thriftiest performer, so shifting from the tents to some form of "hall show" was a common practice.[4] For a musician, it also opened up the prospect of eminence and wealth far beyond what was available in the circus, where he would be limited to playing in one of the bands or presenting an after-show turn, never to attain the acclaim and high salary of an aerialist, equestrian, or lion tamer. The gamble required a considerable sacrifice in security. Away from the tent show's sleeping cars, cook top, fixed itinerary, and guaranteed seven months' work, a vaudevillian had to rely more on himself than did a circus "windjammer." Small-timers might have agents, but it was the performers themselves who most often arranged dates, booked travel, and found boardinghouses, hotels, restaurants, and laundries to supply their daily necessities. If they were lucky, they played enough dates to show a profit, or at least dipped less deeply into their savings than they would have without the tour. If they weren't, well, *Billboard* would be full of calls for circus performers by the following March.

Though less secure than the circus life, vaudeville life was also less hectic and taxing. For an act with steady bookings, moves took place once or twice a week instead of daily; each move provided the artists an opportunity to settle down briefly in a new hotel or boardinghouse, quite possibly more comfortable than a swaying bunk car with its smoke and cinders, and get acquainted with a new town in the intervals between stage appearances. A musician, even one involved in continuous vaudeville, would likely find the work less exhausting than that of a circus bandsman. "Ask any circus man when he sleeps, and he will say, 'In the winter time.'"[5]

The Brown Brothers' earliest documented vaudeville foray took them to Colorado, Utah, Wisconsin, Iowa, and Illinois from January to April 1905,[6] ending just as the circus season began. Although the photo (see figure 3) of Tom and Percy mentioned in chapter 4 is the only document of the early act, it suggests something of its probable character. The instruments (clarinet, baritone sax, orchestra bells, xylophone, and cornet), rather than being composed into a form that might catch or please the eye, are spread out across the picture plane like items in a catalog, as if to say, "We play lots of different instruments, and here they are." The brothers look almost relaxed and friendly—Tom with his feet apart and shoulders at ease, Percy with one arm behind his back—but their unsmiling faces, though not grim, betray not the least trace of humor. They wear only slightly fanciful bandsmen's jackets, tight to Tom's slim and Percy's husky body, topped with thick, jaw-high collars and horizontally striped across with six broad ribbons punctuated by three buttons each, the strong military/circus motif relieved only by almost-elbow-length cape sleeves bearing a device, repeated on the jacket peplum, of dots and an inverted tulip in silhouette. The double stripes on the fitted trouser legs disappear into knee-high gaiters that buckle over the tops of the brothers' highly polished (and correctly sized) shoes. Despite their slightly ridiculous appearance to our eyes a century later, the uniforms promise music, not comedy.[7] If that was indeed the character of the act, it was a mistake, since turns based entirely on instrumental music (except for occasional solo performers such as the ragtime pianist Mike Bernard and the accordionist Guido Deiro) seldom made more than a moderate hit. Vaudeville, like minstrelsy and the circus, was principally concerned with making people laugh. Amazing acrobats, graceful dancers, famous boxers, capsule melodramas, and highbrow violin solos could entertain audiences as a kind of relief from or complement to the laugh-provoking acts that anchored the bill, but without the laughs the bill was doomed.

At the end of the 1905 tent season, the Brown Brothers went into vaudeville a second time, perhaps still a duo, billed in the *Clipper* sometimes as "Brown Bros.," sometimes as "Browns, Musical," suggesting that their offering was still straight multi-instrumentalism. But small-town bookings in Dubuque and Burlington, Iowa, and in Peoria, Illinois, somehow led to an engagement at the Majestic Theatre in Chicago at the end of January 1906, where the act was renamed Brown Brothers and Hopkins, a billing that either added or recognized the addition of J. Frank Hopkins, who had probably played in the Ringling show band as far back as 1897, when that year's route book lists "J. F. Hopkins, musician." More significantly for the character of the act, newspaper ads for the Majestic billed them as "Brown Bros. & Hopkins, Musical Comedians,"[8] indicating that they had taken the first step in the direction that would ultimately bring them fame. A two-day booking in Milwaukee the following month billed them as "Xylophone Soloists and Sketch Artists."[9] The group may have been a quartet at this time, but it isn't known what made the act humorous, what the content of the sketches was, or what music they played. Perhaps they were already showcasing the kind of ragtime numbers they featured two years later. The billing weakly suggests that Hopkins was the comedian, a suggestion somewhat bolstered by the fact that, when the group later became the Brown Brothers and Doc Kealey, Kealey was the comedian. But a couple of sources state that Tom provided the laughs right from the beginning.

The Majestic, the newest of three Chicago theatres operated at that time by the Kohl and Castle organization, was a continuous-vaudeville house, presenting substantially the same fifteen acts (one of them a movie) over and over again from early afternoon until late at night. In March and April of the previous year, the Browns had announced upcoming engagements at all three Kohl and Castle houses (then the Olympic, the Haymarket, and the Chicago Opera House), but didn't perform at any of them, a sequence of events that suggests cancellations by management. If so, the 1906 engagement was a vindication as well as an opportunity to impress a big-city audience. They made almost no impression on the Chicago correspondent for the fledgling show-business weekly *Variety*, who commented favorably on nine of the acts, but only listed the Brothers among "others who shared in the applause," mislabeling them as "Brown, Bras, and Hopkins."[10] However, they made enough of an impression on theatrical management to pick up another Chicago booking right after the Majestic—at Sid. J. Euson's, a burlesque house, where they had the somewhat lighter task of playing in an olio of the sort found in minstrel shows. After a subsequent week in Milwaukee, they disappeared from *Clipper* listings, perhaps disbanding, perhaps taking March off in preparation for the 1906 Ringling season that was to begin April 5.

The source suggesting that the Brown Brothers and Hopkins were a quartet is an article by the circus-band historian Sverre O. Braathen. Braathen, however, places the origin of the Brothers' act in the 1906 season.

During the 1906 season this [Ringling] aftershow failed to attract sizeable audiences and was in other ways displeasing to Al. Ringling. It so happened that Albert C. Sweet was directing the Ringling band for the first time that year. Al. Ringling approached Mr. Sweet one day with the problem of the make-up of the aftershow.

Mr. Sweet mulled the matter over in his mind for a few days and then broached the subject to his first chair clarinetist, one Tom Brown. They discussed the matter at some length, making and vetoing a number of suggestions. Finally Tom Brown asked Mr. Sweet what he would think of a saxophone unit as the core of a new aftershow routine. They took the suggestion to Mr. Ringling who gave the green light to give it a trial.

Brown had a couple of brothers on the show and Tom knew they could give a creditable performance on saxes. He also arranged with a Mr. Hopkins to work in this unit, thus organizing a saxophone quartette. Together these men worked out a clever routine, with Tom acting as the black face comedian. After several rehearsals the group felt they were ready to appear in the concert after the main performance. Most of the circus performers were among the audience for that initial show, so it was a critical crowd the new sax quartet played to. They won a good deal of applause interspersed with much hearty laughter, so Mr. Ringling knew he was on the way to building an aftershow that would have audience appeal. He was right and business continued to improve for the balance of the season.[11]

The Ringlings' 1906 performers' ledger shows the Brown Brothers in the after-show as soon as the initial three weeks' stand at the Chicago Coliseum (during which there seems not to have been an after-show) ended, with a salary of $20 per week. The figure matches Braathen's report that Tom earned $5 per week with the Brothers, if they were a quartet that season. However, the ledger also shows J. Frank Hopkins dropping out of the big-show band on June 16. It isn't recorded whether he stayed in the after-show, but his presence is doubtful, given that it would have resulted in his total salary falling from $20 weekly (including the big-show stipend) to a mere $5.

Shortly after the end of the 1906 season, the Brown Brothers began their third vaudeville tour, now known as the Brown Brothers and Doc Kealey. Once again, they played Dubuque and Burlington, along with other venues in Michigan, Illinois, Iowa, Indiana, and Wisconsin, passing what must have been a cold week in Winnipeg, Manitoba, during January 1907. This time there was no Chicago booking. George "Doc" Kealey was both a clown and an elephant handler in the Ringling Brothers' Circus, directing "a Company of Intelligent, Agile Proboscidian Giants in Picturesque Pyramids and Displays" in Ring no. 3.[12] In 1901, he had been a member of the show's clown band. In the new act, Kealey was "the funny black faced comedian, always in trouble who gets in deeper at each step much to the amusement of the audience," according to an early review.[13] A print ad in December 1906 describes the act as a "Comedy Musical Trio, Black and White Face."[14] According to the 1907 Ringling performers' ledger, the group (as the Brown Brothers) was augmented for the circus tour, appearing in that season's after-show as a quartet.

After the 1907 Ringling season, the Brown Brothers and Kealey, now definitely a quintet, took to the vaudeville road again, but this time they didn't return to the circus family when the 1908 tents went up. Skipping Dubuque and Burlington, they began the tour in Minneapolis and headed north and west, through Winnipeg, Manitoba, and Butte, Montana, to Victoria, British Columbia, then south through Tacoma, Washington, and Portland, Oregon, to Sacramento, California. The San Francisco area, still enjoying a boom from the rebuilding necessitated by the disastrous April 1906 earthquake and fire, welcomed them in the best way, providing seven straight weeks of work (March 23–May 10) at various theatres in San Francisco, Oakland, and Vallejo and evidently erasing any thoughts of rejoining the Ringlings. An *Oakland Tribune* reviewer cheered them on at the Bell Theatre:

> There is a musical act at the Bell Theater this week that is a rare treat. It is furnished by four nice looking young men who call themselves the four Brown brothers, and by Doc. Kealey. All of them are musicians and Doc. Kealey is quite a bit of a comedian. They open their act with a blare of trumpets, which all goes to show they intend to do something, and then they proceed to do it. They succeed at everything they undertake, from playing on queer and peculiar instruments to the ever-difficult saxophone, and out of all they secure sweet and loud-applause music. They claim to have the largest saxophone in the world and it looks big enough to be all that is said for it. It toots loud enough and strong enough to speak for itself. The act is good, unusually so, because there is something doing every second. The audience is not kept waiting while clap-hard-and-I'll-come-back stunts are being pulled off, but these fellows keep the entertainment up all the time. They are deserving of all the good things that can be heaped into this one paragraph.[15]

For the balance of May 1908 and the early part of June, *Variety* listed only a Chicago address for the Browns and Kealey, with no engagements. But in mid-June, Percy began to be listed as a single on the East Coast while the renamed Four Brown Brothers and Doc Kealey appeared in the Midwest. Percy, who reportedly found it difficult to get along with Tom,[16] toured separately at least until the end of July, resuming during October. Meanwhile, the Brothers made their way to Kansas City at the end of June, apparently laid off during July, and played some very good venues from August through October, including the Temple Theatre in Detroit and two of the Kohl and Castle theatres in Chicago, the Majestic and the Olympic. Despite the apparent success of the Brown-Kealey combination, Doc Kealey left the group at the end of the 1908 circus season to take up the position of superintendent of elephants for the Ringlings at their Baraboo, Wisconsin, winter quarters. Kealey's departure cleared the way for the birth of the Five Brown Brothers, who took their first bows at the Lyric Theatre in Fort Wayne, Indiana, during the week of November 9–14. Percy's almost simultaneous disappearance as a single suggests that he was Kealey's replacement as a musician. But Tom, whether he had done blackface comedy before this or not, replaced Kealey as the comedian, and from this point on Tom and his burnt-cork persona were the focus of humor in the act.

At first Tom's character—"a black-faced corner-man with lots of patter," in Tom's phrase—relied heavily on verbal humor, probably minstrel or talking-clown stories and japes tailored to the musical nature of the act. A problem familiar to vaudeville comedians resulted: "I would arrive at a town and the stage manager would come to me and say, 'That joke is old. So-and-So told it here weeks ago.'"[17] Tom's response was not just to seek new material, but also to rely less on speech and more on pantomime, supplemented by nonverbal, extramusical sounds produced by the various instruments he and his brothers played. One early review commends the Brothers' "chicken music" as "deliciously funny, for anything more delicately absurd and at the same time ludicrously farcical . . . can scarcely be imagined," singling out Tom as "a genius in evoking comical effects,"[18] and Vern's bass sax ably portrayed a bullfrog on their 1911 recording of "The Bullfrog and the Coon."

Tom told an Australian interviewer in early 1925 that during the early years, the group "obtained an engagement in New York, and went right across the States to it, full of hope. But after a week's try-out they finished with us, so we had to go back West."[19] He was probably referring to a week at the Empire Theatre in Hoboken, New Jersey, starting March 1, 1909, announced as the group's "first eastern appearance," followed by a second week at the Empire in Paterson, New Jersey. The ad characterized the Brothers as "a Comedy Musical Offering With the Goods" and invited the audience to "let us prove it. Drop over and hear the Ragtime Saxophone Quintette."[20] A capsule review of the Hoboken program had a good word for almost every turn on the bill except the "Five Brown Brothers, musical act, fair."[21] The disillusionment of the Hoboken flop probably motivated the return of Tom, Alec, and Vern to the Ringling band for the 1909 season. But Tom persevered. "I made up my mind to make them like us in New York some day, and I re-arranged the act. . . . We appeared for a year in picture theatre orchestras and in burlesque shows. All the time we were building up the act, dressing it afresh."[22] He didn't give any details of the rearrangement, which may have included the creation of the minstrel character (literally *dressing* the act afresh) or a greater reliance on pantomime, but, when they returned, New York liked them.[23]

They arrived as a feature of a burlesque show traveling on the Western Wheel (also known as the Empire circuit, one of the two major burlesque circuits) called *Broadway Gaiety Girls*.[24] Burlesque shows shared with minstrel presentations the first part–olio–afterpiece format,[25] but with an emphasis on the display of female performers, especially chorus girls, in tights. Unlike our current stereotype drawn from the 1920s and later, 1910 burlesque did not go in for nudity, and the striptease hadn't yet emerged onto the stage from its probable whorehouse origins. But the atmosphere was sexy, the jokes occasionally blue, and the audience overwhelmingly male, as in the variety theatres of fifty years earlier. Western Wheel shows carried the reputation of being somewhat raunchier than rival Eastern Wheel (Columbia circuit) shows. As *Variety* put it, "Right along the Western Wheel managers have argued that the public wanted a real burlesque show, one of the old time sort, full of uproarious comedy, legs, and if need be, 'ginger.' The last word is interpreted by some Western Wheel managers (if their shows are to be taken for the opinion) as all grades of suggestiveness; from the subtle to the downright vulgar and coarse. These same managers, if they tell the truth, believe that their competitors of the Eastern Wheel are trying to turn out an imitation of the Broadway musical comedy."[26] Burlesque show olios featured the same sorts of acts found in vaudeville, and though a slight taint accompanied the lower salaries, burlesque functioned partly as a showcase in which agents and bookers might find a talented performer to transport into the more respectable world they represented.[27]

The *Broadway Gaiety Girls* company's tour began in Milwaukee in August 1909 and wound through the Midwest—Minneapolis, St. Joseph, St. Louis, Indianapolis, Louisville, Cincinnati, Chicago, and Cleveland—sometimes playing only three-day ("split-week") engagements, but more often weeklong stands, sticking to the larger cities, where there was more tolerance for slightly salacious fare. In January 1910, it reached New York, where *Variety* reviewed it in the magazine's trademark business-oriented fashion, praising without hyperbole what would draw an audience, offering suggestions for improvement, and evincing mild moral disapproval. The show, said Rush, "makes entirely satisfactory entertainment, being an adequate 'production.'"

Broadway Gaiety Girls, "uncommonly strong vocally" though "noticeably weak" in dancing, starred a number of now completely forgotten artists. May Strehl, the leading woman, conducted herself with "stately dignity . . . and impressed the audience with her generous figure and striking costumes." Kitty Pembroke, the show's best singer, created "real fun" as an eccentric comedian, though Rush scolded her for going "to great lengths in grotesque makeup, fairly plastering her face with flaming red paint." The review says little about the first part, except to mention Harry Brown, a member of the Five Brown Brothers, as a German comic and to praise the work of Frank Carlton, "an Irishman who gets a real, human type over the footlights," and the Brown Brothers' contribution to "a burlesque band affair." The olio offered song, dance, and verbal comedy, along with a routine in which "an inflated ball as big as a watermelon is kicked into the house and a general rough house follows." But the olio's high point was the act of the Five Brown Brothers, to which Rush devoted a separate, enthusiastic review (quoted later). The afterpiece, "The Retreat of the Pirates of Penzance," burlesqued the Gilbert and Sullivan operetta and featured a "mild" Isadora Duncan–like "Spirit Dance" by "a rather weighty chorister." Rush liked the cast's singing and May Strehl's abandonment of her earlier dignity in order to appear in tights, "thereby disclosing a set of curves and proportions unique in burlesque." Her "Amazonian figger" "startled the boys into rapturous applause." But he censured comedian Harry Antrim's "unmusical" feature number, "Foolish Questions," for its double-entendre banter between Antrim and some of the chorus. Until that point, the show had been "scrupulously clean in business and dialog."

Rush saved his closing paragraph for the chorus. "There are eighteen chorus girls representing both extremes of beauty and ugliness, the good looks being mostly in the possession of the eight or so 'ponies.' These ponies do a lot of lively maneuvering and keep the stage busy during the whole performance."[28] One of the beautiful ponies (a designation for the shortest dancers in the chorus, usually around five feet tall)[29] may have been Theresa Valerio, traveling with her future husband[30] and keeping him away from the temptations of the road, which must have been intensified by the sexual ambience of the *Gaiety Girls* company. In a 1924 interview, Theresa was said to have gone into "musical comedy" after leaving the circus, a possible description of pony-chorus work.[31]

The *Variety* review indicates that the Brothers worked harder in burlesque than they would have in vaudeville, not only appearing in their olio specialty, but also providing support (probably musical accompaniment) for other olio acts and contributing to the "burlesque band affair" in the first part. Perhaps the latter was an ancestor of a routine Tom did years later in which he directed the Brothers by such nonstandard means as pulling on his tie, counting his buttons, and using his feet.[32] The same issue of *Variety* prints Rush's description and evaluation of the Brothers' feature turn in the olio:

> The frame-up of the act follows more or less that of Waterbury Brothers and Tenny, inasmuch as four of the Browns work straight in military uniform and the fifth member affects blackface comedy in a quiet, effective manner. It must not be supposed, however, that the quintet have taken anything from the other act mentioned. The comparison is confined only to the general plan of the turn. They work entirely on the brass instruments, except for one selection on the bells (four using mechanical hand bells and the fifth accompanies on the bamboo chimes—a decidedly agreeable combination). The cornet numbers have the big, resounding quality that burlesque (and vaudeville) audiences like and a quintet of saxophones at the finish in "one" [that is, using only the front third of the stage, with a

drop concealing the rest] was a tremendous applause-getter. The comedian does just enough, getting incidental comedy points over without the common fault of "hogging" the stage. The act is a sure-enough winner.[33]

Shortly before the show's early January opening at New York's Eighth Street Theatre, *Variety* printed a two-column publicity blurb and photo of the Five Brown Brothers, naming them and briefly describing their act. Tom stands at the left in burnt cork, oversize painted lips, and a grotesque version of a bandsman's uniform, grinning and holding his alto saxophone. Brother Fred stands next to him, also holding an alto, and the line continues with Billy Markwith on tenor and brothers Alec and Vern on baritone and bass saxes respectively. All but Tom are standing like proper bandsmen, erect and unsmiling, unpainted and dressed in spiffy conventional band uniforms with elaborate arabesques appliquéd on the chest and lower sleeves. The old cape sleeves, tulip silhouettes, and gaiters have been left behind in the Midwest. The choice of saxophones for the photo visually establishes the group's difference from the typical musical act, likely to feature less unusual instruments, but the copy goes on to claim in addition that "they play a great[er] variety of instruments than other musical turns, and the numbers are enlivened with good comedy, which makes the act an ideal one for any bill. The instruments introduced in the act are: Saxophones, xylophones, steel organ chimes, novelty musical rattles, cornets, trombones and clarinets."[34] The more conventional instruments clearly get second billing.

Billy Markwith led the Ringling sideshow band in 1907 and appears in a photograph of the Ringling Concert Band in 1909, playing baritone saxophone alongside Tom on tenor, Alec on bass, and an unknown alto player (possibly J. Frank Hopkins; Vern is in the band's clarinet section; see figure 4). Other photographs indicate that Markwith was one of the Brothers on and off until as late as 1916, although in 1921 he stated in an affidavit that he had "worked with Tom Brown in his act for eleven years and was paid a salary."[35] Markwith's role may have alternated between that of a regular member of the Brothers and that of a standby substitute. The caption under the *Variety* photo marks almost the last time that the Brothers acknowledged that they were not all real brothers. In later years, except for a couple of 1919–20 pieces that exploited the incongruity that the real name of one of the group's members was Harry Finklestein,[36] the pretense of brotherhood was maintained by billing all the members as Brown, despite the likelihood that someone in the press or the audience might wonder why six siblings had ten or more first names among them. *Gaiety Girls*' Harry Brown, the German comedian at the Casino Theatre performance, may well have been Finklestein (1889–1951), who later adopted the surname Fink. Fink, born in Poland, would have found it easy to concoct an acceptably "German" accent for his role in the first part, and he begins to appear in datable photos of the group in the season of 1912–13, sometimes playing baritone sax, sometimes tenor.[37] It is not known which musician Fink replaced between the time the photo was sent to *Variety* and the night Rush went to the Casino.

The group's motivation for the pretense may have been the examples of the Guy and Ringling brothers, but there was a long circus tradition that, in their minds, may have taken away some of the flavor of dishonesty. Just at the time the Brothers opened in New York burlesque, the Ringling clown Jules Tournour explained that

> every great group of performers that you see in the circus or else-where, no matter if they perform on the flying trapeze, tumble, or ride on bicycles or horseback, is called a "family." They may be known as the Sensational Sellos or the Marvelous Revellis. Now the interesting thing about it is that they are not real families at all. They develop into groups simply because they take in young apprentices, train and develop them, and make them part of their troupes. Six or seven real families may be represented in one circus "family."[38]

The Brothers traveled with *Broadway Gaiety Girls*, playing stands in Montreal and Toronto as well as venues in the United States, until the season closed in early May 1910, then went into vaudeville.[39] In June, *Variety* announced that they were to open in big-time vaudeville July 17, performing on the prestigious Orpheum circuit,[40] whose theatres stretched from the San Francisco flagship Orpheum, newly opened after the 1906 quake and fire had destroyed its predecessor, to the Majestic (formerly a Kohl and Castle house) in Chicago. Beyond its value as a major forum for any act, the Orpheum circuit carried the advantage of affiliation with the predominant big-time circuits in the East—Keith, Percy G. Williams, and Hammerstein—via their common use of the powerful United Booking Office. If a turn met with success in the cities of the Midwest and Pacific coast, it could count on a tryout in the big-time venues of the Atlantic seaboard, a shot at lasting national prominence. The Browns' new booker was to be Chicago-based Jake Sternad, a successful veteran producer of vaudeville acts and an associate of one of the most influential American agents, Pat Casey.[41]

The act did well on the Orpheum circuit.

> Never, since the Orpheum has thrown open its doors to the public, has there been such thunderous applause as that bestowed upon the Five Browns, musical artists, last night. Their work is certainly swell and the spectators did not seem to be able to get enough of it. Time after time were they recalled and only stopped when they became exhausted. They have a large number of instruments upon which they not only play, but get good music out of. Their best work is probably done when the entire five play on saxophones [sic], and many a person has paid 50 cents to hear less than these people give.[42]

The Brothers' success west of the Mississippi propelled them eastward and landed them at Percy G. Williams's Greenpoint Theatre in Brooklyn the day after Christmas 1910. A page-wide one-and-a-half-inch strip ad touting them as the "World's Greatest Saxophone Players" heralded their arrival.[43] They were still doing a multi-instrumental act with comedy, but the saxophone quintet numbers that they saved for the act's finish drove audiences wild and even led reviewers to suggest that they dispense with the other instruments. Covering their appearance at the Alhambra Theatre in New York, *Variety* called them

> a big hit with saxophone playing. The rest of the musical specialty amounts to little. It is the work in "one" with the saxophones that makes them solid. The boys have wisely chosen selections and the way they can rip off "rag" on the instruments is a caution. The comedy is also good. They were forced to play themselves out before the audience was satisfied and even then they came back for three or four bows.[44]

> These boys put on a battle royal with some rag music in "one" that was right. They sparred with some comedy at first, but later scored a knock-out with those Saxophone "rags."[45]

> The Five Brown Brothers are a great [Hammerstein's] Roof act. Their handling of the rag melodies on the saxophones brought heaps of applause. The act could easily make good if they were to just do their specialty on the saxophones in "One" throughout.[46]

But another season was to pass before the Brothers gave up their other instruments.

The Brothers' tour of the East brought them back to the New York area three times after their initial hit at the Greenpoint. There could be no surer sign of vaudeville success. Audiences from Norfolk, Virginia, to Toronto, Ontario, shared Gotham's enthusiasm for the turn's virtuosity, minstrel humor, and ragtime on five saxophones. During one of their New York stays, they stepped out of vaudeville briefly to participate in a novel show-business experiment—for the United States, at any rate—the nightclub. They were booked to play the first two weeks of May on a bill at the new Folies Bergere, a restaurant and cabaret that had opened on Forty-sixth Street at the end of April. One of the two partners in the enterprise was Jesse B. Lasky, the pioneering film producer. According to *Variety*'s founder, Sime Silverman, the only similar attempt to combine dining and a French-style "revue" was the Shubert Brothers' Winter Garden, which had opened only a short time earlier. (The show component at both clubs owed something to Florenz Ziegfeld's *Follies* series, which had begun in 1907.) But while the Winter Garden was "altogether too large a playhouse for the purpose," the Folies Bergere was a "little hatbox of a pretty reception room" with "dainty furnishings, pretty coloring and a general tone which leads one away from the 'theatre' [and] gave the impression of a large house party." It seated 286 for dinner on the ground floor and in the front of the first balcony, and another 400 or so for the revue. Food (ordered from a menu written in French) and service were both first class, administered by waiters in grey suits who were in turn supervised by captains in black evening clothes with silver buttons. At the end of the evening, a call boy circulated among the patrons to determine who needed a taxi, distributing numbered cards to those who did. Two small string orchestras played for diners from 6:00 until 8:15, when the curtain rose on the first half of the program, two burlesques entitled "Hell" and "Gaby" separated by a ballet called "Temptations" directed by Alfredo Curti (or Corti), "the ballet master from the Olympia, Paris." "Better or more lavishly costumed productions have never been shown," opined Silverman. Nevertheless, he showed little enthusiasm for either of the short plays, the second of which featured the comedienne Ethel Levey (who had risen to fame in vehicles with her husband, George M. Cohan, whom she divorced in 1907) as the real-life vaudeville star Gaby Deslys and poked fun at Gaby's love affair with King Manuel of Portugal, "something long since forgotten." Silverman described the ballet as "conventional," noting that the ballet master "thought so well of his work . . . that he took a curtain call without being asked."

The second half of the program turned to vaudeville, six acts sandwiched into a little over an hour starting at 11:30. But it was vaudeville with a difference. As the singers sang and the dancers danced, two pianists accompanied them on a giant concert grand with two keyboards, while provocatively dressed young women posed in niches opposite the stage. Silverman found the piano insufficiently loud and recommended that the show use an orchestra instead. Although the opening-night audience was somewhat cold to the experiment, later crowds were more receptive, and the American supper club (though not the Folies Bergere itself, which closed later in the year) was assured of a future, as Silverman predicted: "If Messrs. [Henry B.] Harris and Lasky can whip their shows into shape before the novelty wears away, they will build up a formidable following, spread the fame of the Folies from coast to coast, and guarantee its future success."[47]

Following two weeks in the fledgling nightclub, the Brothers returned to theatre performances, remaining in the New York area for several weeks, during which they were to make their debut in yet another entertainment medium, sound recording. The series of New York appearances marked the beginning of the Brothers' rise to national recognition after three years as just another struggling vaudeville turn.

6

Beating the Competition

1909–12

The Brothers had many multi-instrumentalist rivals in the musical act category during the 1909–12 period, but only two that achieved any prominence as a result of incorporating a saxophone ensemble: the Four Cates (sometimes billed as the Four Musical Cates) and the Musical Spillers. In their advertisements, the Four Cates, billed as "America's Greatest and Most Meritorious Musical Act,"[1] often named three members of the group: Frank B., a cornet virtuoso; Walter H., allegedly the world's greatest saxophone soloist; and Fred O., who played "the largest saxaphone [sic] in the world," an E-flat contrabass said to encompass the unlikely chromatic range from "low B-flat to high G altissimo."[2] The mammoth instrument, "too large for any one to carry[, was] . . . mounted on a large frame."[3] The fourth member, never named in their ads, was probably Brinton J. Cate, the father of the other three, who wrote occasional letters to the editors of *Variety* on the group's behalf. Their repertoire was mostly music "of the classic order," but included "some catchy popular airs as well."[4] Nothing in their advertisements or reviews suggests that they did any comedy or tried to impress their audiences with anything other than their musical talent and versatility and the novelty of the world's largest saxophone (larger, it should be noted, than the "world's largest saxophone" used by the Four Brown Brothers and Doc Kealey in 1908, which was probably only a B-flat bass saxophone). The photo printed in more than half their ads during this period shows one of the group, probably still in his teens, standing stiffly at attention, wearing a conventional summer bandsman's uniform, with dark high-collared jacket, light trousers and shoes, and a light military cap. In his right hand he holds a diminutive curved soprano saxophone, and looming over him at his left is the contrabass saxophone, about a head taller than the man, and estimated by various reviewers to be six, seven, or eight feet high.[5] Their turn, similar to the Brothers' except for the lack of comedy and the emphasis on "high class" music, consisted of ensembles of different instruments, with one or another Cate coming to the fore. A quartet of saxophones played selections from

Bizet's *Carmen*, featuring a contrabass solo by Fred O., a quartet of large xylophones played Tchaikovsky's *Overture to 1812*, Offenbach's *Orpheus in the Underworld*, or von Suppé's *Morning, Noon, and Night in Vienna*, and an ensemble of two clarinets and two cornets provided a setting for Frank B.'s virtuosity on the "Cateasonian Polka-Fantasia."[6]

Small-town critics and small-time audiences liked them. A reviewer for the *Winnipeg Press* caught them at the Dominion Theatre in April 1910 and found them "well above the average not only in quality, but also because they are somewhat out of the ordinary. . . .The concerted work of the quartette on four smaller saxophones [sic] ranging from four feet down to a foot and a half in length is most tuneful. Their first selection on the xylophones, the overture, is very classical, and showed a high degree of proficiency."[7] The *San Antonio [Texas] Daily Express* praised the four-xylophone Offenbach in even stronger terms, as "a real interpretation showing a remarkable attention to the lights and shades of the delicate music" and "a revelation to music lovers."[8] Frank B., in his cornet display, was "the finest, beyond question, we have ever heard, with the exception of [Jules] Levy, now dead, who was the peer of all the world," according to the *Hot Springs [Arkansas] Daily News*.[9] At the Denver, Colorado, Pantages Theatre, "deafening applause was in order at the completion of the act."[10]

Unfortunately for the Cates, they never crossed over into the big time, despite heroic efforts to do so. One form their efforts assumed was an advertising campaign in *Variety* starting in April 1909 with a three-and-a-half-inch-high, two-column-wide announcement listing their specialties and footed with a notice: "AGENTS AND MANAGERS: If you do not book or play the best do not book this act. We will forfeit all claim to salary any time to any one producing this act's equal."[11] In their September 4 ad, they announced augmentations to the act: "Just arrived from Paris, France, Two Mammoth Bass Saxophones, One Bb Contra Bass, One Double Eb Contra Bass, absolutely THE LARGEST SAXOPHONE and the DEEPEST TONED bass instrument IN THE WORLD, also the only one of its size in the world. Height 6 ft. 8 in., tall."[12] (A few weeks later, however, the ad that made this claim ran on the page facing an ad and supporting photo for the team of Gray and Graham that pointed out that "Miss Graham featur[es] 'THE LARGEST SAXOPHONE IN THE WORLD,' and has been using this title for the past eight years. Size of Saxophone 6 ft. 8 in. Now, IMITATORS GET BUSY.")[13] Later ads in the series quoted the favorable parts of their reviews on the road, always stressing the "high class" nature of their repertoire and presentation.

Starting in August 1910, the Cates' crossover effort also included a series of challenges issued to other entertainers in which they offered cash prizes to anyone who could beat them at their game. The challenge idea seems to have come from a California musician, Harry Batchellor, who, in May 1910, ran an ad the same size as the Cates' and just below it. Billing himself both as "The Musical Rube" and "America's Supreme Musician," he appended a

"NOTICE—I hereby CHALLENGE WALTER H. CATE, any amount for tone and execution on the SAXOPHONE. Get busy; I mean business."[14] In November, B. J. continued the story in a letter to the editors of *Variety*:

> Walter H. Cate, who we claim to be the world's greatest saxophone soloist, and who we are willing to back against any saxophone player, was publicly challenged through VARIETY, May 7, 1910, by Harry Batchellor for any amount. Not to embarrass Mr. Batchellor, we accepted his challenge for the reasonable amount of $500. Since then we have heard nothing from him.
>
> We see in VARIETY that Mr. Batchellor is in or around New York. We are also in New York so we could easily get together on a day's notice. If he is conceited enough to think that he can play the saxophone equal to Walter H. Cate, we will gladly meet him in a friendly contest any time for five hundred or more.[15]

Although the stakes offered in the August ad, like those in the Batchellor challenge, were $500, in October 1910 the Cates upped the ante, envisioning something grander and potentially more exciting than just a *mano a mano* between Walter H. and Harry Batchellor: "FOUR CATES / World's Greatest and Best Musical Act / $1,000.00 IN CASH TO PROVE OUR CLAIM TO THIS TITLE."[16] Possibly a number of groups took them up, but the only one recorded in *Variety* was a group sponsored by the C. G. Conn Musical Instrument Company of Elkhart, Indiana. Despite the publicity-stunt aspect of the affair, *Variety* printed a short piece about it:

Terms of Musical Challenge

> The terms and conditions for the musical contest which may occur between the Four Musical Cates and representatives of C. G. Conn were wired to Mr. Conn last Sunday by B. J. Cate. The wire read: "It is necessary to have a stakeholder and judges for saxophone contest. We are satisfied to appoint manager of Prospect theatre stakeholder and leave the decision to the three following judges: Leader, Metropolitan Opera House orchestra, leader New York Theatre orchestra, leader New York Hippodrome orchestra. These four men to receive $50 each for their services $1,000 a side to be deposited and judges and stakeholder paid out of same before contest opens, leaving $1,800 for the winners. Wire answer." B. J. Cate[17]

Apparently the encounter took place around the turn of 1910–11, but the account provided by a subsequent Cates ad leaves the details unclear, to say the least: "Mr. Conn's Representative and party showed up after the appointed time for the Saxophone Contest to take place. They proved themselves to be very sociable fellows. They set up a fine banquet in our honor which we enjoyed immensely. We had all we could eat and drink. Now who is next? We are open for another Banquet."[18]

Almost precisely at this moment, the Five Brown Brothers reached New York with the *Broadway Gaiety Girls* company, announcing themselves in *Variety* as the "World's Greatest Saxophone Players."[19] Very likely aware of the Brothers' reputation as purveyors of ragtime on the saxophone, the Cates responded by repeating the challenge, but with a new twist aimed squarely at the Brothers: "Featuring Something New, 'The Championship Rag' Written especially for Saxophones By Frank B. Cate. Anyone can claim to be the world's greatest. We not only claim to have the World's Greatest Saxophone Soloist and Team, but we stand ready to back up our claim with One Thousand Dollars ($1,000)."[20] Apparently they received no response, for the Cates waxed even more assertive and insulting in subsequent ads. Referring to their self-conferred status as the world's greatest solo and ensemble saxophonists, they thundered that "infringers on any of the above titles who cannot or will not prove their claim to the same are not only pirates, misrepresenters and impostors, but are obtaining money under false pretenses."[21] Between late February and the beginning of May 1911, the Brothers toured outside the New York area, returning for the revue at the posh Folies Bergere. It's unclear whether they ever picked up the Cates' glove, but the final Cates ad directed clearly at them obviously tries to create the impression that they did, and that they lost the match:

FOUR CATES [each letter enclosed in a five-pointed star]

World's Greatest and Most Meritorious Musical Act.
Only a Mere Lunch
1. Baked Bluefish
2. Braised Beef
3. Blueberry Biscuits
4. Baked Beans
5. Brown Bread[22]

Whether or not the encounter ever took place, even if the Cates were triumphant, it would have been for the Brothers a battle lost in a war finally won. The Cates never made it out of the small time, while the Brothers were at the beginning of a stretch as one of the most popular acts in big-time vaudeville, and then as a featured turn in a series of successful Broadway shows. By August 1911, the Cates were playing with a circus in Holland; later they met with mixed success in Manchester, England, on a British tour of several months' duration.[23] After that, they virtually disappeared from *Variety*'s pages until the end of 1912, when an ad appeared for "Cates' Saxophonic Symphonic Band."[24] Although no recordings of the Cates are known, it is at least possible that they were better musicians than the Browns, who were very good, but are not documented as having attempted Tchaikovsky or Bizet (though they later recorded the quartet from Verdi's *Rigoletto*).[25] But musicianship wasn't what enthralled a vaudeville crowd. At the lowest level of critical response, the Browns had the advantage of playing a greater variety of instruments than the Cates. At a higher level, rather than creating a barrier between themselves and the audience by presenting their music in a solemn concert mode, as a precious commodity to be admired, the Brothers used comedy to put themselves on the same plane as their public, creating the quick rapport that stems from shared laughter at a common object of ridicule. And finally there was the music itself, a steady diet of "high class" sounds for the Cates, spiced by an occasional popular air, versus ragtime for the Browns. "Championship Rag" was too little and too late, whatever its merits as a composition and however impressively the Cates played it. *Variety*'s "Dash" summed up a similar contrast of styles in dance of the period:

> As for Ruth St. Denis [then appearing at Hammerstein's Roof], she might bring out a fashionable audience at the Carnegie Lyceum, but Ruthie will never fill a vaudeville want—or theatre. It's a great bunk for the highbrows, who insist that dancing is the poetry of motion, but My, Oh, My! you should see "Young Alabama" at the Folies Bergere do a "Grizzly."[26]

The vaudeville critic Caroline Caffin made the more general point a few years later, speaking of a vaudeville theatre manager's problems:

> Added to his other worries is a demon of which he lives in fear. He seeks it out in every act. He gazes suspiciously at every visitor for fear the latter has it concealed somewhere. I do not know, but I strongly suspect him of holding a ceremony of exorcism every Monday morning, sprinkling every crevice and cranny, every bit of scenery, every prop, "sealing unto himself" against its baleful influence every scene-shifter, limelight man and orchestra leader, and even then being worried and haunted with dread of it.
>
> And the name of this hideous demon—its dreaded name—is Highbrow! Of course it never has intruded. Occasionally some heretic manager has dared to take a chance and allow a suspect to appear on his boards. If the venture succeeded, we know for certain that it was free from the taint. For it is the first law of the cult of Vaudeville that "Highbrow Stuff Never Pays."[27]

An act much closer in character to the Five Brown Brothers was the Musical Spillers, formed by the former minstrel bandsman William N. Spiller, an African American from Virginia, around 1906. The Spiller group began the 1906–7 vaudeville season as the Three Musical Spillers, performing on saxophone, xylophone, and various brass instruments, and including in their repertoire both von Suppé's *Poet and Peasant Overture* and Tom Turpin's "St. Louis Rag." By spring, they had expanded to five. An April 1907 review of the turn at Bennett's Theatre, Ottawa, said they "played saxophones and xylophones like real musicians, and they introduced a little negro comedy into their act, which went well."[28] A photo (date unknown) of the Five Spillers shows a fashionably dressed woman playing alto saxophone and flanked by four crouching men in top hats, frock coats, and white spats, who play soprano, alto, tenor, and baritone saxes. By 1910, the troupe was touring the Pantages circuit as the "Six Music Spillers, Greatest and Only Large Colored Musical Act in the World," featuring "original 'rag time' music" played on "six saxophones, three cornets, three trombones and six hundred dollars' worth of xylophones. Three pretty women and three men with plenty of classy wardrobe. Play music, sing and dance."[29] Later reports and photos printed with Spillers ads indicate that they not only danced, but danced while playing,[30] a feat that seems to have been emulated later by the Browns. Early in 1911, very shortly after the Browns were picked up by the United Booking Office, the Spillers too had impressed show-business management enough that they started playing United time, which opened the door to steadier bookings, better venues and working conditions, and higher pay. In mid-1911, they were competing head to head with the Brothers in the New York area when Sime Silverman wrote a favorable, but neither detailed nor enthusiastic, review of their performance at Hammerstein's Roof, where the Browns had played only a week or two before:

> The Spillers are colored, mixed as to sex. They play musical instruments, with one of the girls singing a "rag" song. The act opens and closes well, with a little heavy stuff in between, as well as light material. There is a comedian in the turn, but he didn't overwork Monday evening. The position, "No. 3," on the Roof was against the act. In an indoor theatre, The Spillers, in the early part of a regular show, should do very well.[31]

Despite Silverman's lukewarm reaction, the Spillers went on to a long and successful vaudeville career, touring England in the winter of 1912–13 and returning to big-time United houses "full of life and ginger."[32] Around 1920, they expanded to seven, and they continued to tour until 1925. After a three-year hiatus, William Spiller formed a new Five Musical Spillers that toured Europe and South America from 1928 until 1939, when illness forced him to retire.

Like the Browns, the Spillers rode ragtime, "negro comedy," and saxophones into long-term prosperity, but, since they never made phonograph records, played Broadway, or got a contract endorsing musical instruments, they never achieved the Browns' level of fame. Unlike the Browns, the group seems never to have claimed to be the original popularizers of the saxophone, but such a claim is perhaps no less plausible in their case, given the vagueness and uncertain dating of the available documents. It would be tempting to attribute the higher ascent of the Browns to the American majority's racism. Very few African American artists recorded before the jazz craze of 1917–18, and, even then, white groups seem to have enjoyed an advantage out of proportion to their relative number. In spite of Bert Williams's success with the Ziegfeld *Follies*, it remained unusual to incorporate "colored" acts into "white" shows until decades later, and many white performers objected to Ziegfeld's employment of Williams. A number of shows with exclusively African American casts and mostly white audiences met with success during the 1920s, starting with *Shuffle Along* in 1921, but few black performers of that era achieved the wide fame and sustained prosperity of the Six Brown Brothers.

We should not underestimate the role of the Browns' very successful recordings in their overall rise to fame. The availability of recordings meant that their renown could spread to an audience beyond the reach of their tours in vaudeville or traveling musicals, as well as giving those lucky enough to hear the group in person an attractive souvenir to take home. Reciprocally, the discs created a market for the personal appearances. The welling wave of record sales in the 1910s had the potential to carry those who got there first higher and farther than those who followed. Not only were the Brothers the first saxophone ensemble to get there, but, partly for technological reasons, they were the only such group for six years.

The Five Brown Brothers recorded twice in mid-1911, on discs for the Columbia Phonograph Company and on cylinders for the United States Phonograph Company; both sessions were held in New York. The two American giants of flat-disc recording in the first decade of the century were Columbia and the Victor Talking Machine Company, but Columbia was a distant second.[33] The third recorded-sound giant of the era, Edison, began to make disc recordings only in 1913.[34] Columbia had issued a few saxophone recordings before, in 1896, 1901, and 1908, but a quintet was something new. The announcement in the company's October 1911 supplement read, in part:

> One of the finest and most uniquely attractive novelties we have offered in many months. The peculiarly mellow and beautiful tone of a single saxophone is most impressive at all times, but a quintet of these instruments, forming a combination from which all orchestral harmonic effects can be obtained, forms one of the most delightful sources of musical entertainment imaginable. The Brown Brothers Saxophone Quintet is an organization practically unique and has been heard everywhere throughout the United States in vaudeville in one of the most successful musical specialties now on the boards. . . . Such perfection in saxophone playing has seldom if ever been recorded before.[35]

There were good reasons why nothing like the Brothers had ever been recorded. Chief among them was the narrow frequency range achievable on early acoustical recordings, roughly 168–2000 cycles per second, or from the E below middle C to the C three octaves above middle C. The fundamental pitches of the bottom octave and a fifth of the bass sax literally could not be heard on an acoustic recording. Similarly, the fundamentals of the bottom fourteen notes on a baritone sax and the bottom eight on a tenor were inaudible. Even the alto was deprived of its three lowest pitches. Fortunately, acoustic recordings could still "reproduce the auditory sensation of a musical note whose fundamental is below this [lowest actual pitch captured], even though the fundamental and one or two of its harmonics have been eliminated in the reproduction." The illusion exploits the fact that the timbre—the characteristic sound—of the instrument depends not only on the fundamental, but also on the higher, but softer, frequencies produced along with it. The loudness of these higher frequencies relative to each other and to the fundamental forms what is often called the complex note's harmonic profile, and it differs from instrument to instrument.[36] A note played, for example, on a bass saxophone is still identifiable as such, even in the absence of the lower frequencies of its harmonic profile, by a kind of projection the auditory faculty makes on the basis of the frequencies that can be heard. At any rate, it's identifiable as something different from a note played on a banjo, or even on a baritone or tenor saxophone. Nevertheless, early recording companies generally avoided trying to catch the sounds of low-pitched instruments, giving up altogether on string basses and cellos in favor of tubas, bass clarinets, and other instruments with a more forgiving harmonic profile.

A second pervasive mechanical problem in acoustic recording stemmed from loudness. A recordable sound had to be loud enough to cause vibration of the diaphragm that moved and modulated the engraving needle, but not so loud that the needle would "blast its way right through the wall of the record groove."[37] Too much "light and shade" of the kind exemplified in the Four Cates' *Orpheus in the Underworld* resulted inevitably in inaudibility on the one hand and disaster on the other. Once a group's sound had been tested and found to avoid both risks, often at the cost of having the musicians spread out around the studio, some of them facing away from the recording horn and therefore from their collaborators, there was no choice other than to stick to the approved narrow dynamic range for the duration of the recording.

On June 26, 1911, the Browns and Columbia's technical staff rose to these challenges in a creditable manner. They attempted four titles but achieved issuable results only with two. The instrumentation sounds like that in the 1909 *Variety* photo: two alto saxophones, probably played by Tom and Fred; a tenor and a baritone saxophone, one (though which one can't be determined) probably played by Alec and the other by Harry Fink; and a bass saxophone, played by Vern. The two rejected titles were "That Beautiful Rag," a ragtime song by the highly successful publisher and songwriter Ted Snyder, and "Tramp, Tramp, Tramp—Theme and Variations," probably the Civil War song rather than a 1901 Victor Herbert composition of the same name.[38] Columbia had released a solo version of the second title, by the saxophonist Eugene Coffin, on cylinder in 1896 (the same year Tom had a chance to hear *Darkest America's* Fred W. Simpkins play it on trombone), but Coffin's version had dropped out of the catalog by 1911.[39] In its October supplement, Columbia offered the two successful titles, "American Patrol" and "The Bullfrog and the Coon—Medley."

"American Patrol" is a march (given renewed life by Glenn Miller's swing version during World War II) that, in addition to one strain of its own, incorporates "Columbia, the Gem of the Ocean," "Dixie," "The Red, White, and Blue," and "Yankee Doodle." The simple orchestration begins with Tom playing the first strain's melody solo while Vern marks the 2/4 beat and the rest play afterbeats with a lively oom-pah effect. In the second strain, Fred adds a harmony line below Tom's melody while the other three maintain the oom-pah. The side is peppy and exuberant and was bound to please the gramophone public as a new twist on the march sound that formed so much of the disc repertoire then available. The alto saxes, their frequency range fairly well matched to that of the gramophone recorder, come off with a certain degree of "realism" considering what was possible at the time.

"The Bullfrog and the Coon—Medley" begins with Tom playing a low-register solo on "Chicken Reel," with clucking-chicken effects, as the other Brothers provide an oom-pah backup. The second segment, "Cubanola Glide," alternates four- or five-part organlike harmony led by Tom with oom-pah passages and brief interjections by Vern's bass sax. The other two pieces in the medley, "When the Moon Plays Peek-a-Boo" and "The Bullfrog and the Coon," are scored almost entirely in the form of a solo lead by Tom over an oom-pah background. "Peek-a-Boo" creates a tiptoe effect with soft staccato. On the last selection, Vern foregrounds a repeated pickup-downbeat figure in his bullfrog role. His bass sax is somewhat more prominent on this side than on "American Patrol"—probably an indication that the Columbia technicians were experimenting with the sound. The overall effect is sweet and amusing, and many customers undoubtedly chuckled with delight at Tom's chicken and Vern's amphibian.

For reasons now unknown, neither disc bears much of the Browns' acclaimed ragtime. "Ragtime," in 1911, referred primarily not to wordless, multistrain syncopated compositions such as Scott Joplin's "Maple Leaf Rag," but to peppy, sometimes only mildly syncopated popular songs such as that year's "Alexander's Rag-Time Band," by Irving Berlin.[40] Although the four selections in the "Bullfrog" medley have their syncopated moments, they lack the exuberance that would put them squarely in the ragtime category. Later, the Brothers recorded a number of rags (such as "Chicken Walk" and "Smiles and Chuckles") and ragtime songs (such as "Walkin' the Dog") that probably furnish a better idea of what it was that drove their audiences wild.

Columbia was not satisfied with the sound its engineers were able to achieve. After waiting almost six years to release further saxophone recordings (by a group emulating the Browns), the company included this statement in the catalog copy:

Announcement of saxophone recordings by the Columbia Company has been delayed until this time owing to its principle to issue no records until practical perfection is reached in reproducing the instrument or voice in question. In all recording experience no instrument has presented the difficulties of the saxophone. . . . [The] singular, dim, rich tone of the saxophone has at last, and we believe for the first time, been absolutely reproduced in all its fidelity on the initial records by the Saxo Sextet.[41]

The United States Phonograph Company, a small-scale, short-lived manufacturer located in Cleveland, Ohio, listed three U-S Everlasting Non-Breakable cylinder recordings by the Five Brown Brothers and one by Tom Brown in their October 1911 catalog. Probably recorded in New York about the same time as the Columbia disc, two-minute versions of "Tramp, Tramp, Tramp" (Tom's solo, no. 407), "Bull Frog and Coon Medley" (no. 408), and "Independentia and Billboard Medley March" (no. 409), and a four-minute version of "American Patrol" (no. 1321) preserve a clearer and brighter impression of the quintet's sound, to judge from "American Patrol."[42] The cylinder recording process had two advantages over the lateral-cut disc process that are still audible in their products today, when they are not worn out by ninety or more years of use. First, the motion of the needle engraving the hard-wax master—up and down rather than from side to side—made possible a somewhat greater dynamic range, since the needle couldn't "blast through the wall of the record groove." Second, since the cylinder whirled under its engraving or reproducing needle at the same linear speed from beginning to end while the disc's speed with respect to the needle slowed drastically toward the end, a cylinder's frequency response remained the same throughout instead of narrowing as the selection went on.[43] (The innermost groove of the Browns' 1914 Victor recording of "That Moaning Saxophone Rag," for example, moves past the needle only a little more than half [13/24] as fast as the outermost groove.) The Everlasting "American Patrol" shows both these advantages, especially in the "dogfight"[44] section before the second strain reprises, where Tom plays appreciably louder and with a much more extravagant vibrato than would be possible on a disc recording of the period.

With big-time vaudeville success and national projection in a new medium under their belts, the Browns, perhaps emulating the Spillers, expanded their ranks and their musical potentialities at the beginning of the 1911–12 season. As of August 3, at least eight months after the addition of a sixth Spiller, there were Six Brown Brothers, once again touring on the Orpheum circuit, but newly handled by a very well-connected agent, Pat Casey.[45] A photo in the Christmas 1911 issue of *Variety* shows Tom and Fred on alto saxophones, a tenor player (very likely Billy Markwith), Alec and Percy on baritones, and Vern on bass.[46] The extra instrument made possible a new kind of orchestration that appears on the Brothers' later recordings. The two harmonizing alto saxes and three-man rhythm group (Vern's "oom" and two more for the "pah") were now supplemented by a second baritone sax, freeing the tenor sax to play, among other things, decorative phrases and countermelodies to create a more complex ensemble texture. Whether this texture appeared before the Brothers' next recording sessions, in 1914, is not known, but, when it did, it considerably improved the musical interest of their recorded performances.

The photograph also provides a first look at the costume Tom was to wear, with only small variations, for the rest of the Brothers' career: white pants stiffened to make him appear bowlegged; a short, tight bellboy jacket with three downwardly converging rows of fourteen or so small buttons; a shirt with a detachable stiff collar attached only at the back so that it splays to both sides; and a huge bow tie. On one side of his head, atop a ratty Afro-style wig, Tom sports a small, smashed pillbox cap, decorated with a long feather shaped like a question mark, on his hands he has black gloves, and on his feet he wears the Ringling giant's shoes. The other five wear uniforms more or less the same as those in the 1909 photo.

The group's new agent, Pat Casey, "a close personal chum of [*Variety* founder Sime] Silverman's" and an associate of the theatre owner Percy G. Williams, hailed from Springfield, Massachusetts, where he had belonged to the Elks chapter, founded by George Guy Sr., that counted the Guy Brothers as members. As noted earlier, he was also an associate of Jake Sternad, the Browns' agent during the 1910–11 season. In ways now unknowable in any detail, these personal connections must have aided the Browns in their accession to Casey's roster, "one of the broadest" of the time.[47] No doubt it was also an advantage to have their agent headquartered in New York, then the center of American show business, rather than Chicago.

Variety's John J. O'Connor ("Wynn"), in a review of the Brothers' season opener at the Orpheum chain's Majestic Theatre in Chicago, didn't remark on the group's expansion, but he gave them a very strong endorsement: "One of the big hits of the evening was the Six Brown Brothers, who appeared rather early. The sextet blew ragtime out of saxophones in such a fashion the house refused to allow them to leave until their repertoire had been exhausted. Most of the comedy has been dropped to advantage. The act as it now appears runs up with the best in the line."[48] The curtailing of "the comedy" may correspond to Tom's 1925 reminiscence about his response to theatre managers' complaints that the Brothers were using old jokes: "Then we went and paid highly for others to write our humor, and after a fortnight or so we would find other performers had stolen it and were using it. So I cut out the talking altogether, and got the humor another way."[49] Reviews and United Booking Office managers' reports from later in the season indicate that, as in the previous year, the encore-provoking saxophone feature was consistently saved for last.[50]

After the Chicago opening, the Brothers started a six-month trek through Orpheum theatres as far west as San Francisco and as far east as Detroit before returning to the Majestic for a week's stand in mid-February 1912. En route, Tom and Theresa got married on January 30, the second day of a week's stand at the Majestic in Milwaukee, Wisconsin.[51] One of the witnesses was Billy Elliott, who was on the same bill as a part of Billy Elliott and Four Folies Bergere Girls (perhaps from the New York nightclub). A version of the Guy Brothers' Minstrels, reduced to vaudeville-turn size, opened at the Milwaukee Empress, a small-time venue on the Sullivan-Considine circuit, the following week. Perhaps the two groups' stays in the city overlapped enough that some of the old Guy colleagues were able to attend the ceremony or at least to celebrate together.

A Chicago review gives such a nice sense of the return engagement at the Chicago Majestic and the Browns' triumph that I quote it at length:

> The Browns are in town—six of 'em—occupying that strategic position on the Majestic bill which is neither too close to nor too far from Eva Tanguay [who had been held over from the previous week]. Yesterday afternoon's audience promptly elected them headliners despite little Eva and her $3,000 a week. Vaudeville audiences move in mysterious ways their wonders to perform and that of yesterday was no exception. The Browns were, so to speak, the dark-brown horse of the bill. . . . They were disguised under the innocuous announcement "versatile comedy musicians."
>
> Some of the audience had settled down for a comfortable five minutes browse through the program for vicarious rides to California in trains de luxe or to sample mentally various bourbons and lagers urged for domestic consumption. In came the Six Brown Brothers in all the glory of silver cornets and trombones. The audience was prepared for the worst. It didn't come. The Browns discarded conventional instruments for the mirambaphone [sic], a sort of super-saw horse with a resonant sounding board. Upon this the Brown family concentrated, wooing melody as deep and mellow as that of Belascoan chimes. The sixth Brown brother clowned in black face at the end of the strange instrument. He was funny. The house fired solid applause across the footlights. But the Browns had not yet begun.
>
> Their number took on its real color when the Brown family became the Saxophone [sic] family. To begin with, the saxophone is, unaided, a humorist. It looks like a sea horse and sounds like a canned fiddle. One, alone, gnaws at a funny bone, but six, ranging from a little one, with the voice of a deflating rubber bladder, to a paternal one that croaks like a musical bullfrog, are too much for any audience. The Browns raked the house with saxophone ragtime, with popular ballads, with tunes from the musical comedies of the hour. They had unnumbered encores. They bowed and bowed and then played again. It was a great afternoon for Anglo-Saxaphonophobes.[52]

Eva Tanguay, the notoriously temperamental "I Don't Care" Girl, had risen swiftly in the preceding seven years to become the highest-paid performer in vaudeville with her song-and-dance routines, partly improvised on the spot and always wild.[53] Beating her out for headliner status, even on what may have been an off day, was an aspiring act's dream.

Leaving Chicago, the Browns appeared mid-continent from New Orleans to Montreal, finally moving to the Keith circuit for a successful Philadelphia stand and arriving in the New York area at the end of May, where they reestablished their credentials in the eyes of the movers of show business with three solid weeks in Percy G. Williams theatres. After a week at Keith's in Boston, they returned to New York to close the season. Among the accolades was *Variety*'s opinion that "Tom Brown is one of the funniest blackfaced comedians on the stage."[54] Enough people shared that opinion that the Brothers' next career move went in tandem with a solo move on Tom's part to minstrel end-man status with the newly regrouped Primrose and Dockstader's Minstrels. For the next two years, Tom was to embody the classic Tambo character as well as his own saxophone-playing blackface pantomime clown, and the other Brothers were to join him under burnt cork.

7

Primrose and Dockstader's Minstrels

1912–14

From September 1912 until April 1914, the Six Brown Brothers continued to strengthen their rapidly growing stage reputation by starring in the olio of Primrose and Dockstader's Minstrels, America's last top-quality touring minstrel show. Vaudeville became only a fallback for periods when minstrel bookings failed. Two eminent burnt-cork veterans whose careers stretched back to the 1860s and 1870s headlined the spectacle: George Primrose and Lew Dockstader.

The dancer George Primrose, born George Delaney in London, Ontario, almost sixty years before the Six Brown Brothers' Chicago triumph, had debuted as "Master Georgie, the infant clog dancer," in Detroit just two years after the end of the Civil War. After a decade of hoofing in variety, minstrelsy, and after-show circus concerts, Primrose became a star performer and co-proprietor of Barlow, Wilson, Primrose and West's Minstrels, a company that endured from 1877 until 1898, through two subsequent changes of name. As Primrose and West's Minstrels from 1889, it grew in size and popularity until it fissioned into two separate companies, one headed by Primrose, the other by West, for the 1897–98 season, and then dissolved. From 1898 until 1903, Primrose headed "the premier minstrel organization" in the country with his new partner, Lew Dockstader, who had been featured in Primrose and West's in 1890 and 1891.[1] From the breakup of Primrose and Dockstader's Great American Minstrels until 1912, Primrose alternated between working in vaudeville and heading his own minstrel troupe until a joint billing at a Friars' Club Frolic in June led to the rebirth of Primrose and Dockstader's company.[2] "One of the most graceful dancers in the profession," Primrose was also "concededly one of its best business men."[3]

Lew Dockstader, fifty-six as the 1912–13 season opened, had started in minstrelsy at age seventeen under his real name, George Alfred Clapp. Three years into a promising career, he inherited enough money to open a theatre in his native Hartford, Connecticut, but sold it after four months and headed for California in search of adventure. When his money ran out in San Francisco, he became an end man in variety and worked his way east to New York, where he acquired his new name upon teaming with Charles Dockstader for five years (1878–83) as the Dockstader Brothers in variety theatres and a number of touring minstrel companies.[4] Following a break with Brother Charles and three successful years (1883–86) as a comedian in other managers' troupes, Lew opened Dockstader's Theatre in New York to provide a permanent home for his own new aggregation, "surrounded at all times with the luminaries of the minstrel world."[5] Unfortunately for Dockstader, resident minstrel shows were on their way out of the metropolis, and Dockstader's, the last of any consequence,[6] closed at the end of 1889. After eighteen months on the road as a "principal comedian" with Primrose and West's, he founded his own touring company, which lasted four years before he once again gave up management for the relative security of vaudeville, where his minstrel fame, comic songs, and topical monologues made him a headliner from coast to coast.

The 1898–1903 Primrose and Dockstader's Minstrels, capitalizing on two of the profession's best-established reputations, clicked with the public from the start. The company did "phenomenal" business in major population centers such as Detroit, Cleveland, Pittsburgh, and Chicago, eclipsing smaller companies such as Guy Brothers' and making its proprietors the "most widely known team in minstrelsy."[7] As the popularity of minstrelsy declined, Primrose and Dockstader prospered, finally splitting up, perhaps because of management tensions, after five acclaimed seasons. Dockstader wasn't ready to give up the road, however, and revived Dockstader's Minstrels for the nine years between the two versions of Primrose and Dockstader's, continuing both to showcase the best minstrel talent of the nineteenth century and to develop new stars for the twentieth, among them the singer-comedian Al Jolson. As noted earlier, two 1912 sources predating the Brown Brothers' stay with Primrose and Dockstader's placed them in Dockstader's troupe as well, at an earlier date not specified.[8]

The reborn Primrose and Dockstader's Minstrels, a company of fifty, opened in September 1912 somewhat smaller than the original, but "both stars were in the best of form," and they put on "a genuine old-fashioned minstrel show," with no white faces, no women, and no attempt to emulate musical comedy. In at least one city (Providence, Rhode Island), the troupe even staged a minstrel parade at noon on opening day, with "the resplendent white silk hats, the uniform overcoats and other evidences of the sound old tradition, just as they used to appear in 1885." The cast included five comedians besides Primrose, Dockstader, and Tom Brown, along with thirteen vocalists to complement the efforts of the four comedians who also sang. The Six Brown Brothers were the principal feature of the olio except for Primrose and Dockstader themselves. According to one source, Tom was also the musical director and bandmaster of the entire show, at least for the first season.[9]

The curtain rose on the traditional semicircle and orchestra, in a set described as "spectacular"[10] and "of unusual splendor." The comedians and singers, "gorgeous in dress suits of white, yellow and blue,"[11] alternately convulsed the audience with quips, jokes, and rapid-fire exchanges with the interlocutor, Harry Sievers, and amused, amazed, and moved them with music, emphasizing "songs that will be welcomed as old friends; songs made famous from ocean to ocean by George Primrose and Lew Dockstader in seasons past."[12]

Tambo and Bones were incarnated twice in the first part, at the outset by Tom Brown and "Happy" Naulty (later in the tour replaced by "Happy Jack" Lambert), and, once the audience was warmed up, by Primrose and Dockstader. In spite of the unavoidable comparison with his senior colleagues, Tom's "quaint humor"[13] received accolades from reviewers: he "made good in emphatic fashion";[14] he "takes life seriously and is funny, in his quiet way, by contrast."[15] "His method," according to a later account, "was to preserve an air of deep gloom as he sat on the end during the entire first part, never cracking a smile, which always engaged the attention and resulted in the merriment of the audiences."[16] Besides baiting the interlocutor and telling his share of funny stories, Tom sang one of the "old friends," "I'm Hungry."[17]

Although the *Chicago News* reviewer felt the show, then on the boards for about two months, needed more rehearsal and a stronger orchestra, he praised the individual performers:

> All the wit and humor in the banter between the end men and the interlocutor was capital. . . . Some of the best and cleanest end stories in ten years . . . surprised both by newness and worth. The comedians are talented and good dancers, fine singers and all around quick witted actors. Happy Naulty is original and amusing and has a big voice in a quaint little body. Frank Farron is interesting with a singular falsetto voice tacked on a deep range register. . . .
>
> The sensation of the entire entertainment was a radiant soprano voice, which preened itself exquisitely in the throat of a youth named Raymond Wylie.[18] He is a tall, quiet youngster, with a heavenly voice ranging from rich barytone [sic] into bird-like loveliness in the top notes. Not a falsetto voice at all, but an adorable boy soprano, kept clear and jubilantly pure through the change of voice. [Among other selections, he sang the "Miserere" from *Il Trovatore*.] . . .
>
> Then came the expected treat of beholding Lew Dockstader and George Primrose once more hand in hand. Prim [Primrose], natty, graceful with that eternal promise of jog steps as long as he lives in his heels, bantered the long young interlocutor brilliantly and sung [sic] the prettiest song on the bill, "When I Waltz with You," and then he danced and they made him speak and he tenderly congratulated himself. Perhaps the new generation did not know why. George is just as many years old again as he looks and then some. But he danced nimbly, sung [sic] sweetly, spun through a witty dialogue gayly and made the evening enjoyable.

Early in the season, Dockstader, "the king pin of them all," with his "natural brilliancy, clean, bolting wit, great spontaneity and a grip on his audiences, which he never loses,"[19] sang in the first part, including two of his signature songs from the 1890s, "Everybody Works but Father" and "And Dat's No Lie." But by spring, he "contented himself with a delivery of 'Dockstaderisms,' in which his recital of an experience with an automobile provoked spasms of mirth. The first part ended with a chorus in an exceptionally effective rag-time rendition of the 'Lucia' sextet."[20]

After intermission, the olio opened with a musical sketch by the Four Harmonists, in the fall of 1912 entitled "Memories of the Battlefield at Gettysburg" but later changed to the more contemporary "Camp Life in the Philippines." The quartet "appeared in the guise of Philippine soldiers," exploiting a growing tendency in the United States to lump all darker-skinned non-European groups together, "and dispensed vocal harmony with very good effect."[21] Dockstader's feature turn followed. At the beginning of the 1912–13 season it had been a short play, in two scenes, called "The Bull Moose Dream," that lampooned Theodore Roosevelt's 1912 presidential bid and the woman suffrage movement. The program copy suggests the involvement of opium:

Lew Dockstader's Political Satire

The Bull Moose Dream
It's a pipe in two scenes
Scene First—The Suffragettes addressed by Teddy.
Scene Second—White House. The dope in evidence.

Dockstader, "Happy" Naulty, and unnamed members of the company appeared in drag as "Theodora (alias Teddy)," "Dane Jadams," and "Bluffragettes, Stuffragettes and Guffegettes," while the interlocutor and vocalist George Thurston impersonated Woodrow Wilson and William Howard Taft. No script, if there was one, is known to have survived, but later reviews indicate that the sketch was dropped after the November election in favor of a Dockstader monologue, still built upon his already famous Roosevelt impersonation, jokes about sexual equality (aimed at both its advocates and its opponents), and the topical and local gibes his audiences had come to expect from him.[22]

Dockstader's portrayal of Roosevelt, in blackface, garbed in a "misfit dress suit," but without the minstrel version of African American dialect,[23] was "a work of mimetic art"[24] that was said to have made the former president himself "laugh until his sides ached" at the "travesty of his admitted and well-known foibles."[25] Newspaper and magazine articles occasionally ran pieces typifying Lew's satirical style. Here he does Roosevelt:

La-dies and gentlemen, I am dee-lighted. I wish to speak to you of the greatest theme in the wide world—myself. And when I say

myself, I am not egotistical. What does the word mean, gentlemen
and ladies? Look it up in the dictionary. The dictionary is a great
book; it should be on every table, alongside with Shakespeare and
the Bull Moose platform. . . . Egotistical, according to the dictionary,
means thinking too much of one's self. Then I am not egotistical,
because neither I nor any other man could think too much of
Teddy.[26]

Here, no longer in the Roosevelt character, he organizes male opposition to
women working for social parity:

The male sex is in great danger of being submerged, of being forced
into a condition of abject slavery, eternal thralldom, and right here I
wish to shudder with dread at the coming of that fateful day when
women have the vote. . . .

Well, I am going to fight. I do not want to reform any more than I
have already been forced to. I do not want to try any experiments in
happiness. I want to preserve and save for my fellow men such privi-
leges as they now possess; such happiness as they now enjoy. Therefore I am going to organize the National League of Herogettes [so
called because a man must be a hero to oppose his wife]. . . . For one
thing, they [women] will demolish our clubs. We will say adieu to
the jovial life of the clubman, to all our little joys, masculine com-
forts, and relaxations.

After quips comparing marriage to jail, strangulation, and poisoning, Dockstader goes on:

Things have come to a pretty pass and we are surrounded by suffra-
gette spies. You call up your wife, tell her sweetly that you are going
to the club for dinner, give every legitimate explanation, and some
female Benedict Arnold rings her up and informs her that you are at
Jacks or Churchills [expensive New York Restaurants] with "a certain party." That is the situation all men have to confront today.
Again, I shudder with horror!

I claim that the married man gives his wife more liberty to-day in
the United States than he receives from her. If the wife goes out in
the evening she always insists on hubby accompanying her, but does
hubby always insist on wifey going along with him when he peram-
bulates in the stilly night? No.

Then again, if wifey goes out to do some shopping at a bargain
counter in the afternoon, she does not want hubby to go along, but if
hubby goes she will insist on escorting him.

Dockstader continues with comic descriptions of men doing housework,
women holding down office jobs, and the substantial power that pre-suffra-
gist women already have over their husbands and swains, concluding with a

puff of conventional sentiment to indicate that he doesn't fully subscribe to the attitudes espoused by his philandering comic persona:

> If the ladies obtain the right to vote and make laws calculated to repress and restrain the liberties of man, which I think they mean to do, all these laws will not be as effective in keeping hubby at home in the evening as a wife's love and children's caresses. Take this from a merry minstrel man. And by the way, I will make a bet that the famous suffragette leader, Mrs. Catt, is afraid of a mouse.[27]

The monologue "kept the audience in a roar throughout"[28] at the Brooklyn Majestic and even "made some of the audience hysterical"[29] at the Providence Opera House. As Dockstader's ovation subsided, Primrose resumed the stage in a turn with his disciples, John Foley and John Murphy. Billed as "America's Most Graceful Dancer," he performed his signature soft-shoe dance, and Foley and Murphy pitched in "spiritedly," doing "buck and wing and the waltz clog of olden days,"[30] "backed by fine scenic effects."[31] "It is hard to conceive of a man 60 years of age doing such graceful dancing as does George Primrose," said the *Brooklyn Daily Eagle*'s reviewer. Perhaps because of the Ontario connection, the *Ottawa Citizen*'s reviewer praised him in even more enthusiastic and affectionate terms:

> The warmest place in the hearts of those who filled every (or nearly every) seat from orchestra to "gods" [the cheapest section of the gallery] was reserved for George Primrose himself. It must be upwards of forty years since he first tripped the light fantastic toe on the boards of an Ottawa theater; much water has flown [sic] down to the sea since that time, and yet seemingly age cannot wither his infinite versatility. As a quick-step dancer, George Primrose was at all times a marvel; at his age such a performance as he gave last night is little short of miraculous. . . . His wonderful instinct for what is graceful, combined with a bewildering rapidity of footwork earned him thunderous applause.[32]

The Six Brown Brothers, in serious peril of being overshadowed by the performances of their legendary employers, finished the olio, now no longer as a multi-instrumental turn, but just as a saxophone sextet.[33] But they were equal to the challenge. The *Chicago News* writer called them "the real music of the show. Good, sweet, cultivated music, uttered on silver saxophones delightfully." The *Ottawa Citizen* cited them as "worthily upholding the city's reputation as a nursery of musical talent" and described some of their comedy:

> They possess a perfect mastery of their special instrument, the saxophone, and can draw from it grace, tenderness, and humor in abundance. If their performance was a delight from a musical point of view, it was none the less deliciously funny, for anything more deli-

cately absurd and at the same time ludicrously farcical than their chicken music can scarcely be imagined; we could see the great Dr. [Richard] Strauss introducing them cunningly with telling effect in some of his more bizarre pieces of orchestration.[34] Tom Brown in particular . . . showed himself a genius in evoking comical effects.

The afterpiece, "Way Down South," featured eight comedians and vocalists as Trenton Sambo, Rebecca Allup, Clinton Quimbo, Peter G. Washington Green, Georgia Carolina, Florida Alabama (Tom Brown), Cloe ("the belle of all Dixieland"), and Slow Joe ("the troublemaker"), along with the rest of the cast as "singers, dancers, cotton pickers and drivers of 'dat mule.'" Its four scenes "gave a vivid representation of the mirth and melody and joys and sorrows of the cotton worker at New Orleans and in the field and at home"[35] and provided the company an "opportunity for various plantation songs and dancing numbers, with a little comedy thrown in on the side."[36] From the second scene, which included the stage effect of a steamboat approaching from afar, already a cliché of minstrelsy and *Tom* shows, the *Chicago News* reviewer singled out "the great shout 'Waitin' for de Robert E. Lee'" for praise, opining that it had been "for the first time . . . given its full musical significance." Staged in a "very lavish and tasteful manner," with "lighting effects [that] aroused great admiration," the show-closer's reassuring picture of African Americans firmly occupying the place wishfully assigned to them by the white majority rounded off "an evening's entertainment of laughter and song, unmarred throughout by any vulgarity or indelicacy, such an entertainment as paterfamilias might treat his wife and children to with perfect propriety."[37]

Near the beginning of the Brothers' two-season tour with Primrose and Dockstader, just after their appearance at the American Music Hall in Chicago, Theresa Brown gave birth in that city to Tom Jr. The date, November 17, 1912, just five days after George Primrose's sixtieth birthday, may have led his parents to give him the middle name "Primrose," later a source of adolescent embarrassment.[38] Theresa may have been traveling with the show up to that point, but the advent of the new family resulted in her temporary residence at 2525 Jackson Boulevard in Chicago, the city that later became headquarters for four of the Brothers, including Tom.

The Brown Brothers' personnel shifted at least once before August 1913, when two photos show the group newly consisting of the real Browns Tom, Fred, Alec, Vern, and William, along with Harry Fink, who may have been with the group in 1910.[39] Percy spent the circus season of 1913 as the assistant director of the Hagenbeck-Wallace organization's band and probably never returned to the Brothers. The career up to this point of the oldest brother, William, is unknown, but he moved in and out of the act until at least 1930. This same lineup is pictured on the piano-sheet cover of Tom, Harry Cook, and Roger Lewis's "That Moaning Saxophone Rag," published in 1913 and announced as "Originally Introduced in Primrose and Dock-stader's Minstrels." From this point until about 1921, Tom, Fred, Vern, Alec, and Harry Fink appear in all clear and datable photos of the group that the author has seen, although Fred and Vern were absent for a few months during World War I. During this same period, a few undated photos show a substitute for William, probably Billy Markwith. The "Moaning Saxophone" distribution of instruments has Tom and Fred on alto saxophones, Harry on tenor, Alec and William on baritones, and Vern on bass. About 1914, Harry and William swapped instruments, and later, probably starting in early 1916, they both played tenor.

"That Moaning Saxophone Rag," Tom's first published composition, was brought out by Will Rossiter, a leading Chicago publisher with a national reputation. The Browns had had some prior connection with Rossiter, having lent their name to a 1912 advertisement as one of four "Good-Luck Star" turns endorsing Rossiter's "Good-Luck songs,"[40] and Rossiter later published numerous pieces associated with the group, many of them bearing photos. The photo on "Moaning Saxophone" occupies the whole cover, with lettering superimposed. Such a design made the sheet somewhat unusual for the period, when artists' likenesses were more typically placed in drop-in windows that could be changed from printing to printing to cater to market forces. The piece, a pleasant but unremarkable ragtime song consisting of a short introduction followed by a sixteen-bar verse and sixteen-bar chorus, doesn't quite amount to a rag of the Scott Joplin sort in formal terms, although the version recorded by the Brothers in 1914 does, since it includes a third sixteen-bar strain. The third strain might have been a new addition for the recording, but more likely the piece as played in Primrose and Dock-stader's already had three strains, one of which was dropped in order to create a conventional verse-chorus ragtime song for publication.[41] Scott Joplin had similarly truncated his 1908 "Pine Apple Rag" (dedicated, incidentally, to the Five Musical Spillers) to accommodate lyrics, omitting one of its four strains, combining two others into a verse, and employing a third as a chorus. The lyric of "That Moaning Saxophone Rag," cited in chapter 4, marks the apparent beginning of the Browns' official public-relations legend, the story of Tom bringing his five brothers one by one into the circus and starting them on the saxophone.

Another strand entered the legend's fabric around this time, one that named the Brothers as the original popularizers of the saxophone. It peeks through in a January 20, 1914, *Brooklyn Daily Eagle* review of Primrose and Dockstader: "The six Brown brothers, in their saxophone sextette, with Tom Brown furnishing the comedy, furnish a novelty. . . . Incidentally, the Browns are saxophonists from away back yonder at the head of Saxophone creek, and even if Tom did not rouse the risibilities that act would be warmly encored."[42] The claim that they were the first didn't gain much prominence in their press encounters until some years later, when audience memory of groups such as the Cates and the Spillers had faded a bit. But by the mid-1920s, it had become almost as important to their public image as Tom's minstrel clown character.

Primrose and Dockstader's March 1913 performance at Ottawa's Russell Theatre occasioned a private closing-night reception at the Russell's café, hosted by E. B. Eddy, a prominent local businessman who had published "In the Firelight Glow," a ballad featured in the show (see figure 5). Besides honoring the two headliners, the gathering paid tribute to the "Ottawa boys"—Raymond Wylie and the Brothers. The dinner "started with blue points and ended just before the golden exhalations of the dawn began to kiss the crests of the eastern horizon, with general expressions of good fellowship." Toasts were drunk to King George V, President Wilson, and minstrelsy; George and Lew offered a little comedy; and Wylie, the Brothers, and several others "entertained the company with short appropriate addresses."[43] Among the revelers was the Brown boys' father, Allan Brown, who had become the leader of the Russell Theatre's orchestra.[44] Just about the time Tom left Lindsay, Allan had apparently spent a very short time in 1898 as director of the Governor General's Foot Guards Band in Ottawa, which was followed by a period as a cornetist in that same group under the direction of his much younger brother, Captain Joseph Miller Brown, who led the organization from 1900 until 1923. At some point before 1899, he had separated from Maria and moved to Toronto and Detroit in pursuit of musical opportunities, finally settling in Ottawa around 1906, where he worked as a draftsman for the Canadian Department of the Interior until his retirement in 1925.[45] He must have seen a reflection of his own struggles and wandering in the slow evolution of the two small-time Brown Brothers into six traveling in the company of minstrelsy's most famous partners. Despite being a justifiably proud father, he must have felt to some extent the mixture of envy and self-satisfaction that a part-time musician divided between his music and a day job feels in the presence of a successful full-time musician: envy that someone else has really made it in a tough business and satisfaction that he himself has steady employment to fall back on when the gigs fail.

Allan's sons moved on to Toronto with the Minstrels after the Ottawa stand, and the company wound its way back to the East Coast, playing fairly short but reasonably successful engagements until recessing for the summer in early June "after forty-one profitable weeks." The season ended with a gratifying validation of the up-and-coming Brothers by their eminent elders:

> Instead of making straight for the country, Messrs. Primrose and Dockstader tarried over in New York yesterday for the express purpose of attending the opening performance of the Six Musical Browns, of the minstrel organization, at Hammerstein's [Hammerstein's Victoria Theatre, New York]. The sextette of versatile musicians, which had been one of the big features of the minstrel show

throughout the season, have been re-engaged for the Fall. Strangely enough, however, neither of the owners had ever seen the act in its entirety, as both were engaged in making up while the Browns were on the stage. Yesterday they stood in the foyer and applauded their colleagues. Also they laughed boisterously at the antics of the comedian of the sextette.[46]

During the previous week, another act called the Brown Brothers (a duo) had opened at New York's Union Square Theatre to a very weak *Variety* review that called it "a mild and poorly executed Cabaretish turn, with an equally poor comedy roller skating bit for a finale." The reviewer closed with an acknowledgment of the Six Brown Brothers' solidly established reputation: "The work brought recollections of Mullen and Coogan, Jeter and Rogers, and a few others, and the name—well, the original Browns should worry!"[47]

Neither the season past nor the one to come was free of troubles for Primrose and Dockstader's. Bookings for such a large show were difficult to secure, and at least once (March 1913) a hiatus was filled with a vaudeville stint for Primrose and Dockstader, the Brothers, and the Four Harmonists as separate turns, while the rest of the company lay idle.[48] Before the opening of the 1913–14 tour, Primrose briefly played with the company under his name only. An early-season review of the full show (August 15, 1913) called the effort "fair," complaining that it "drags in spots" and concluding "6 Brown Bros., hit of the show."[49] With Dockstader back on board, the organization managed to get by for almost eight months before management was constrained to invoke a contract stipulation that reduced cast salaries by 50 percent. The entire troupe went on strike, including Primrose's dancing protégés, and the tour ended on April 19 in Willimantic, Connecticut.[50] Fortunately for the Brothers, their reputation was now at a high point, and Pat Casey was able to book them on the vaudeville circuits for the remainder of the season.

Without knowing it, the Browns had been present for the death throes of the last first-class touring minstrel company. The decline of minstrelsy had been a topic of discussion for some time. The *Providence Journal's* reviewer sounded the note in March 1913:

> When Primrose and Dockstader's Minstrels appeared in their street parade yesterday noon there was a revival of hope among some who had been inclined to the pessimistic belief that the real minstrel show was a thing of the past. . . .[But] the purity of the real thing was preserved intact, and from the enthusiastic applause and the unrestrained hilarity it appeared that Providence had been hungering for minstrels for a long time.

Though he harbored doubts, the reviewer took the view that minstrelsy was not only not dead, but not even moribund:

Minstrels, like the circus and "Uncle Tom's Cabin," and several other estimable institutions, have become a connecting link with a popular entertainment of a past generation. But that is by no means equivalent to saying that minstrels are obsolete, or even that they are to be classed with the Uncle Tommers and the circus. It means merely that the entertainment is a type that has survived, and without the radical changes that have been noted in legitimate drama and the various brands of musical performances. A good minstrel show is essentially the same to-day that it was 25 years ago. It has long since reached its culmination in point of numerous performers and spectacular magnificence, and it will never discount the excellence attained by the famous old company headed by the present Mr. Primrose and Mr. Thatcher and Mr. West, or that other brief-lived organization conducted by Willis P. Sweatnam, Billy Rice and Barney Fagan. Various experimental efforts have been made to modernize the form of entertainment, such as the introduction of a first part constructed along the lines of an easy-going musical comedy, in place of the conventional circle of black-face singers and end men, and of white-face acts familiar in the vaudeville houses, but the experiments were discountenanced by the public. And wise managers have found it safer to stick to the old minstrel traditions and to discard rash innovations.

Thatcher, Primrose, and West's, which flourished from 1882 until 1889, furnishes a prime example of "rash innovations." The minstrel historian Robert Toll notes that they were one of the first American companies to switch to a predominantly whiteface cast, in one season wearing "'Louis XI [sic] court dress': white satin coats, vests, breeches, silk stockings, low-cut white satin shoes with diamond buckles, lace collars, and white wigs." Later, "concentrating on refined singing and dancing and inoffensive material, they focused on lavish productions of current fads. Lawn tennis, baseball, bicycle riding, yacht racing, polo on skates, and fox hunting furnished them with subjects for their balletlike dances and their light musical comedy skits."[51]

Despite the *Providence Journal*'s opinion about the policies of "wise managers," the minstrel mogul Al. G. Field offered a rationale for following Thatcher, Primrose, and West's example in his 1912 autobiography:

The basis of minstrelsy will always be that which it is and has been, but you can't hand them [the audience] the same things they've been accepting the past forty years and expect them to enjoy and buy it. The farce comedy, the musical show are virtually minstrel shows. Based upon music and dancing, they produce about the same stuff the minstrels do. . . .

Every manager that has endeavored to present an old-time, black-face minstrel show in late years has failed. . . . Two friends were responsible for my decision to put on a simon-pure, old-time minstrel show. I engaged the best talent procurable, costumed the show in conformity with the ideas of my friends. It was the least profitable of any season since my first year; or it would have been had I continued. I changed my entire show in the middle of the season, going back to the black-face comedians, white-face singers. . . .

I can fully understand why a minstrel, an American minstrel, singing a plantation melody to his dusky dulcinea, should have a blackened face, but why a man blackened as a negro should sing of 'My Sister's Golden Hair,' or 'Mother's Eyes of Blue,' is too incongruous for even argument's sake. . . .

I had opposition [i.e., appeared simultaneously in the same city] with one of those so-called old time minstrel shows a short time ago. Our company was making money every night. They were barely paying expenses. And yet the greater part of the press work was devoted to informing the public that we were not genuine minstrels, our singers wore white wigs, flesh colored stockings and satin suits. They were really advertising one of the attractions of our exhibition. We copied that notice and had it sent broadcast over the sections where the companies conflicted. I watched the press closely and but one paper that came under my observation endorsed their idea.[52]

Field was not the only manager who thought along such lines. In the 1899 *Witmark Minstrel Guide and Burnt Cork Encyclopedia*, Frank Dumont (who headed what may have been the last metropolitan resident minstrel company)[53] offers programs for and drawings of several first parts that all but eliminate blackface. In "Our Boys in Camp," for example, the entire company is in whiteface and the four end men are Rough Riders; in "Congress of All Nations," the end men are a Japanese, a Negro, a Scotchman, and an Irishman.[54] An advertisement added in the 1905 edition touts a script for an all-Japanese first part.

Dockstader had long been engaged on the other side of the debate, sticking with burnt cork, coon songs, and plantation spectacles, although he felt that he was innovating or at least keeping pace in other ways, for example, in the "dignity" of the songs and humor, the large size of the company, and the use of elaborate settings. "Formerly a minstrel show didn't carry any scenery. I carry two carloads with my show. And you will find people who will tell you that the minstrel show of today is just the same as the old show of 30 years ago, when I first broke into the field."[55] In response to Thatcher, Primrose, and West's innovations, he said, "Minstrelsy in silk stockings, set in square cuts and bag wigs, is about as palatable as an amusement as a salad of pine shavings and sawdust with a little salmon, lobster, or chicken."[56] When Primrose teamed with Dockstader from 1898 until 1903, the dancer too became an adherent of the old-time camp, and he seems to have stayed with it after their first breakup, judging from a 1905 program for his Big Minstrel

Company, which puts the cast in blackface for at least half (maybe all) the first part, some (probably not all) of the olio, and all of the afterpiece. But, like the first part in the 1912–14 show, Primrose's 1905 opening contrasted the old time with the present spectacle (actually purporting to recreate the original 1843 Virginia Minstrels), probably as a way of reassuring the audience that they were seeing something up to date or, to quote the program, "Minstrelsy in its Highest State of Development."[57]

But neither the old-time presentation nor the new style espoused by Al. G. Field survived at the higher levels of professional entertainment. Primrose announced in May that he "had permanently retired from the stage," explaining, "'My health has been none too good this last while.'"[58] Although he returned to vaudeville during several seasons before his death in 1919, the 1914 closing was indeed his farewell to the minstrel show. Dockstader too continued as a single, nine years later taking to the road again with Tom Brown, but never again attempting to assemble a troupe. In retrospect, what killed the big-time traveling minstrel show was probably the combination of factors Field had cited: first, other forms of entertainment were becoming more and more difficult to distinguish from minstrelsy except for the blackface, and second, the public was growing tired of the old blackface formulas. Burnt cork in itself was no handicap in show business, as the subsequent fame of such entertainers as Eddie Cantor, Bert Williams, and Lew's protégé Al Jolson attests, but a whole evening of it could no longer fill enough big-city theatres to finance a long tour by a first-class company.

About a year after Primrose and Dockstader's ignominious Connecticut collapse, Brander Matthews, a theatrical scholar from Columbia University, mulled "the rise and fall of Negro-minstrelsy" (referring to the all-blackface sort) in *Scribner's* magazine,[59] finding "more than one sufficient explanation" for "a decline and a degeneracy and a decay which seem to doom it to a speedy extinction." One was the lack of women entertainers, "necessarily depriv[ing] it of the potent attractiveness exerted by the members of the more fascinating sex." Another was recognizably Field's reason: the narrowness and monotony of minstrelsy's material made it unable to "withstand the competition of the music hall, of the variety show, and of the comic musical pieces, which satisfied more amply the same tastes of the public for broad fun commingled with song and dance." But the reason to which Matthews devoted most attention was, oddly but interestingly, the genre's "failure to devote itself lovingly to the representation of the many peculiarities of the darker people." Oddly, because Matthews himself acknowledged that only a small portion of minstrel song, dance, and humor was, even at the beginning, derived from African American prototypes, and that minstrelsy's pretended dedication to "the humorous reproduction of the sayings and doings of the colored man in the United States" was "often only a hollow mockery"; such a reason raises the question why minstrelsy didn't fall immediately upon rising. Interestingly, because Matthews saw some measure of love in what to twenty-first-century eyes is for the most part thinly masked hatred, fear, and contempt. It would be comforting to think that love rather than the latter attitudes were what motivated otherwise attractive entertainers such as Primrose, Dockstader, and Tom Brown—that they were not just blind or indifferent to the oppressive consequences of their collective efforts, but were actually proceeding under the assumption, on the conscious level, that burnt-cork caricature was a kind of harmless and affectionate teasing. After a lifetime of exposure to the caricature, these men may have believed that it had some robust basis in fact (rather than mainly an existence within the stage tradition) and that African Americans should join them in chuckling at such "foibles" as stealing chickens, fighting with razors, mangling English, and dressing either in rags or in gauche finery. Such beliefs made it possible for shreds of minstrelsy to hang on, even to flourish, for decades after the Primrose and Dockstader's performers' strike of April 1914.

8

All American Vaudeville

1914

Vaudeville theatres generally closed for the hot summer months, and artists either vacationed or signed on with circuses or outdoor pleasure-garden and "hippodrome" shows. The Brown Brothers, back on the circuits after the April 1914 collapse of Primrose and Dockstader's Minstrels, were incorporated into a novel undertaking that kept took them to the British Isles for July and most of August before they returned to the United States and a decade in musical comedy.

In 1914 American entertainment was enjoying a vogue in England. The previous year's American hit *Hullo, Ragtime* had inspired a successor song-and-dance revue called *Hullo, Tango*, starring Ethel Levey, who had become famous in the States in vehicles written by and co-starring her prodigiously talented husband, George M. Cohan (whom she divorced in 1907). Individual Yankee turns such as Con Conrad and Jay Whidden's ragtime piano-violin duo met success in theatre after theatre. The bookers of Moss and Stoll's Music Halls, a leading variety chain in England, Scotland, and Wales, decided to cash in on the craze by staging an All American Vaudeville show at their Finsbury Park Empire Theatre in London, with the idea of putting it on tour if it scored. The headliners were to be the Avon Comedy Four, two of whom were Joe Smith and Charlie Dale, later to become even more famous as Smith and Dale, the subjects of Neil Simon's play *The Sunshine Boys*. The Avons were already touring Moss and Stoll houses, but the other acts, including the Brown Brothers, were to be imported directly from the States.

The Brothers, along with Theresa Brown and Gertrude Fink, Harry's wife, sailed on the *Aquitania* on July 1, 1914,[1] leaving Tom Jr. behind with Theresa's mother in Philadelphia. They were to be billed second, ahead of four other acts with big reputations in the United States and two that were just beginning to gain some notice. Although an overseas booking was not ipso facto prestigious (remember the Cates), the idea of being on a bill represented as a distillation of American vaudeville must have been a source of pride, even for someone born in Ontario, Poland, or (in the case of the singer Josie Heather) Scotland. Besides the Avons, the Browns, and Josie Heather, the bill included two husband-and-wife comedy turns, Dooley and Sales and Charles and Fannie Van; a phenomenal gymnastic troupe called the Four Bards; a violinist, Ethel Mae Barker; and the Stanleys, an act that told amusing stories with shadow puppets. Stage direction was in the able hands of the renowned choreographer Ned Wayburn, whose thirteen years of acclaim in New York and Chicago working with such major producers as Lew Fields, Klaw and Erlanger, the Hammersteins, and the Shubert Brothers had recently brought him to London,[2] where his work on *Hullo, Tango* had "put the piece over to a success."[3] Musical direction was shared between Louis Hirsch, a prolific composer whose "My Tango Girl" was featured in *Hullo, Tango,* and the pianist, singer, and composer Melville Gideon, who later became a star of the English musical stage.[4] The All American Vaudeville was bound to be a production of the highest quality.

On opening night, July 13, the eagerly expectant audience included numerous vacationing Americans, including the top vaudeville personalities Al Jolson, George Jessel, Eddie Cantor, Jack Norworth, and Will Rogers. Rogers, an old friend of the Avons, contrived a gag to rattle them: giving the ushers a thousand pieces of chewing gum to pass out to the public with instructions to start chewing when the headliners took the stage. Management agreed with Rogers that gum, a trademark of the cowboy monologist and a current fad in the States, would give the occasion an appropriately American touch, and it was distributed for the remainder of the run.

The playing order of the show is unknown, but a good conjecture can be made on the basis of a surviving description of the playbill[5] and a 1916 magazine article by George Gottlieb, the head booker for the Palace Theatre, New York's leading vaudeville house. In the article, Gottlieb explained common practice for arranging a program and rationalized it in terms of audience psychology.[6] A good show opens with an "act that does not depend on its words being heard," one "that makes a good impression and will not be spoiled by the late arrivals seeking their seats." Each succeeding act in the first half is intended to capture and reward the audience's attention more than the one before it, with the second-billed turn of the whole performance appearing just before intermission, to give the audience "something really worthwhile to talk over." The first post-intermission spot has to bring the audience "once more into a delighted, expectant attitude" without eclipsing their memories of the first-half closer; this spot, too, is sometimes filled by a nonverbal or "dumb" act. Then follows an even more entertaining act, often by a big name, and then, next to closing, the bill's headline attraction, the one that most of the audience is most excited about seeing. When the closing act takes the stage, says Gottlieb, "we count on the fact that some of the audience will be going out," so again a "dumb" act is a good candidate, but one that will create a big impression and "send . . . the audience home pleased with the program to the very last minute."

Since the Avon Comedy Four headlined the playbill, with the Brothers second, it is likely that the Brothers were in the number four spot, concluding the first half, and the Avons in the number seven spot. The three "dumb" acts, namely the Four Bards, The Stanleys, and Ethel Mae Barker, probably appeared in the number one, number five, and number eight slots, and perhaps in that order, since that is the order in which their names appear on the playbill. Again following the order on the playbill, we can put Dooley and Sales in the number two slot. Since common practice, as described by Gottlieb, discouraged putting two acts of a similar character one after another, it is unlikely that Charles and Fannie Van, another husband-and-wife comedy team, followed them, leaving the singer Josie Heather as the only candidate for number three and placing the Vans at number six. On with the show.

The original Four Bards were four real brothers, Ed, Harry, John, and James, but the Finsbury Park group probably included only three of those plus a replacement.[7] They certainly would have been good attention-getters—four handsome and muscular young men in tights performing feats of acrobatics and hand-balancing seldom equaled. In Sime Silverman's weighty opinion, "They will have to go some, and yet go some more to beat the Four Bards."[8] In one of their simpler moves, "one of the brothers leaps from the shoulders of his supporter, turns a half somersault and alights with one hand only on the head of a third performer and maintains his balance."[9] In another three-man trick, Ed started center stage with two of his brothers (the pitcher and the catcher) facing each other from opposite sides; he ran toward the squatting pitcher, stepped into his clasped hands, and, propelled by the quickly rising pitcher, flew backward in a high arc to land in a hand-to-hand stand on the upraised arms of the catcher. (At New York's American Theatre in January 1911, this stunt "brought a wave of applause that drowned all other sounds of the evening.") A maneuver combining features of the first two featured a Bard flung through the air to alight in an even more difficult hand-to-hand stand, in which the flier used only one hand, gripped by both the catcher's hands.[10] Two four-man tricks described in reviews are just as breathtaking. In one, devised by the Bards during the 1909–10 season, two pitchers stood on either side of a face-down flier, swinging him back and forth by his arms and legs in growing arcs until enough momentum was developed to launch him head first into the air, where he executed one and a half somersaults and a half twist of his body before landing in a hand-to-hand stand with the catcher at trajectory's end.[11] The other, added as a finish in 1911, began with the Bards spaced evenly across the stage, two facing each other on the left and two facing each other on the right. On a single cue, each outside man ran toward the crouched inside man facing him, stepped into his clasped hands, and was cast ceilingward in an arc, passing the other flier in the air, into a hand-to-hand stand with the other inside man.[12] After such a riveting exhibition of seeming impossibilities of strength, poise, control, and teamwork, the audience must have cleared its mind of anything that would distract it from the entertainment about to unfold.

A *New York Morning Telegraph* review several weeks into the run named J. Francis Dooley and Corinne Sales "the most popular turn" on the bill[13] in their skit "That's Silly," "a mixture of good-natured nonsense of the 'nut' variety."[14] They had polished their ensemble technique by working together since about 1907, although Dooley had also played as a single during the period, most notably during Sales's long recovery from a serious automobile accident in the Catskills in 1911. Married since New Year's Eve, 1911, they were popular headliners on the U.S. big time. Dooley was known for his improvised comedy. "Indeed, he himself says he has no act but that [working as a single] he makes up a new one every time he goes up on the stage just from things that happen after he has made his entrance."[15] Sales complemented and anchored Dooley's wildness with her warm stage personality, sense of humor, "stunning appearance," and "infectious way of laughing."[16] Although no description survives to give the details of their 1914 routine, it probably followed their usual pattern of comic songs and dances framing and punctuating a hilarious, partly impromptu dialogue, during which they would josh with the orchestra, the audience, and each other. Whenever the non sequiturs reached a particularly grievous point, Dooley would utter his signature line, "That's silly—there's no sense to that."[17]

Josie Heather was the one European on the All American bill. A dainty, graceful, and beautiful Scots singer in her mid-twenties, Heather had "blue, blue eyes that twinkle, dimples that come and go, . . . a smile that pouts and beams by turns," and a "pleasantly sweet and charming" voice.[18] Specializing in Scottish tunes and humorous topical songs, she made a hit at the Empire singing the new and slightly risqué American song "Who Paid the Rent for Mrs. Rip Van Winkle?"

> Oh, oh, many years ago,
> Lived the wife of happy Rip Van Winkle,
> One day, she drove poor Rip away,
> As the little stars began to twinkle.
> All that he had, he had under his hat,
> And she was glad to see him go,
> So, over the hills he went,
> Left her without a cent,
> One thing I'm anxious to know:
> Who paid the rent for Missus Rip Van Winkle, when Rip Van Winkle went away?
> And while he slept for twenty years,
> Who was it kissed away her tears?
> She had no friends in the place, had no one to embrace,
> But the landlord always saw her with a smile on her face;
> Who paid the rent for Missus Rip Van Winkle, when Rip Van Winkle went away?[19]

The *Times* reviewer selected the "merry comedienne" for special praise.

Minstrel humor had been popular in England continuously since the first visit of the Virginia Minstrels seven decades earlier. Tom Brown's eye-catching costume and expert pantomime, the novelty of six saxophones wonderfully played, with occasional displays of their capacity for imitations of chickens, bullfrogs, and deflating bladders, and a playlist of the latest American song successes that probably included "That Moaning Saxophone Rag" must have driven the audience to the accustomed cheering and calls for repeated encores before the curtain fell for intermission. The Brothers were the public's "something really worthwhile to talk over" during the break-time drink, smoke, or snack.

The Stanleys and Ethel Mae Barker, the two acts on the bill about which the least information has survived, were among the three singled out by the *Times* of London as "among the most artistic (and least tumultuous) numbers." (The third was Josie Heather.) The Stanleys opened the second half of the program with "Fun in Shadlowland,"[20] "a delightfully fantastic display of shadow marionettes."[21]

The audience having been restored to the desired receptive attitude, the Vans took the stage. Charles and Fannie Van had presented a series of sketches written by Charles, going back to the beginning of their partnership around 1898, each one evolving from the previous one and all featuring Fannie as an actress and Charles as the Stage Carpenter. In the first, he was looking for work as a stagehand. In "A Case of Emergency," the second, he had the job.[22] By October 1913, the team had begun doing a third, "From Stage Carpenter to Ackter," in which he and Fannie decide to team up, leaving her ex-partner behind.[23] Although their eighteen-year-old son, Fred C., was in the November 1913 version and may have come with them to England, they went back to the two-character "Case of Emergency" for the Finsbury Park engagement. The skit began with Charles by himself, pretending to be an actual stagehand. "A great deal of fun sometimes results from the audience failing to grasp the fact that the man in overalls is the well known comedian, that is, until [he] gets started in his work."[24] After some funny solo business, he is joined by Fannie, playing a "loquacious soubret"[25] who "has had a row with her regular partner."[26] The Carpenter's bumbling attempts to help her out result in a comic quarrel during which the actress gets some "rough handling" from the stagehand.[27] The resolution of the playlet isn't recorded in surviving reviews, but journalists regularly found the turn "a great big laughing hit."[28]

Charles illustrated the verisimilitude of his Carpenter getup with an anecdote:

> It is well known that Eva Tanguay is much addicted to tantrums when anything goes wrong, and she takes it out on the unfortunate stage hands, who are obliged to humor her. One week in New York we were both playing on the same bill and I came on the stage just in time to find the crew lined up against the wall getting a liberal dose

of "what's what!" Spying me across the stage laughing heartily she marched me over to join the others, and rather than spoil the joke I lined up and took my medicine with the rest. Later when the mistake was discovered she apologized and joined me in a good laugh.[29]

The Vans' special drop now disappeared into the flies to reveal the schoolroom set for the whirlwind comedy of the Avon Comedy Four: Joe Smith, Charlie Dale, Irving Kaufman, and Harry Goodwin. Smith and Dale, the nucleus of the group, had been doing a version of their skit "The New School Teacher" since 1901. The teacher, pinch-hitting for his sick brother, is to suffer the fate of all substitutes, starting with a spitball as he calls the roll (absent students being told to answer "absent") and continuing with persistent wisecracks and mischief from his three pupils, the "Hebrew type" Isidore Fitzpatrick, the tough Irishman John L. Sullivan McGovern Sharkey, and the "sissy" Reginald Redstocking. But he gives as good as he gets, knocking heads for insolent answers and revealing, in the process, that he knows as little about geography, history, and spelling as his surly charges. He rejects Sharkey's proffer of "Atlantic and Pacific" as two of the world's principal oceans: "No, that's a tea company." But he seems happy with Sharkey's report that Abe Lincoln was born in a log cabin that he helped build. The situation provided a loose framework for manic stereotype-based comedy, solo and ensemble singing, and energetic dancing.[30] To give the occasion an American touch, the Avons sang "All Aboard for Dixie,"[31] one of dozens of songs then popular that expressed the supposed nostalgia of African Americans for rural life in the South. "The outstanding feature" of the Avons' Finsbury Park performance, according to an early August review, was "the capital acting and dancing of Joe Smith."[32] A contemporary vaudeville critic, Caroline Caffin, described Smith's dancing that same year:

> His style is the traditional step-dance, allied to the buck-and-wing. When once he gets started there seems to be no stopping him, and he jigs along, back and forth across the stage, executing one after another of a variety of steps, like a specimen of perpetual motion. His arms hang loose in the traditional manner of the step-dancer, but they are by no means inexpressive. Some slight alteration in the pose of them, and he has imparted a new character to his dance; or a slight gesture, and he has let you into the joke at which he has been smiling all the time his feet clicked out and shuffled their ever changing tattoo.[33]

They closed, as always, with a rousing close-harmony treatment of their signature song "The Wearing of the Green."

After the storm of applause for the Avon Comedy Four abated, Ethel Mae Barker appeared onstage for the sometimes thankless task of closing the show, even as some of the audience were "hurrying off to their after-theatre supper and dance."[34] Barker, "an accomplished violinist,"[35] was

> A petite little Miss who deals almost exclusively in classics and who handled the most difficult spot of the Columbia [Theatre, New York, November 29, 1914] bill with no evidence of nervousness nor extra effort, corralling one of the hits. She doesn't sing, confining her time to four selections on the violin. . . . With proper handling Miss Barker will eventually reach her goal, for she carries all the requirements—appearance, ability, personality, and all.[36]

Overall, the production "met with a good success and honors were rather evenly divided among the turns decorating the program." Someone, probably Ned Wayburn, whose reputation was partly built on his famous stage pictures, was inspired to round out the All American conceit with an uplifting patriotic finish. "At the conclusion of the first performance, all the artists gathered upon the stage, when the orchestra, led by Lou Hirsch, struck up 'The Star Spangled Banner' for them to sing. None knew the words."[37]

The show remained at the Finsbury Park Empire for at least three weeks, "a distinct success. Crowded audiences, largely composed of American visitors to this city, have almost cracked the welkin with their deafening applause."[38] Among the visitors may have been the prominent New York producer Charles B. Dillingham, a Florenz Ziegfeld associate who managed the massive 5000-seat Hippodrome and the smaller, newer Globe Theatre, both in Manhattan.[39] Dillingham had been vacationing in Europe since late May, but both the diversion and his sideline search for new talent had been dampened by an unspecified illness that had led him to Carlsbad to take the curative waters at one of its luxurious spas. By late July, he was back in London where he had started, much improved in health and ready for the tonic of the All American Vaudeville[40] and a look at the latest efforts of Wayburn, who had worked on Dillingham productions during the previous three years.[41] According to a story Tom Brown told twenty-six years later, Dillingham was especially impressed by the Brothers:

> Dillingham . . . saw us in London, and because we did only pantomime and music, thought we were a continental troupe. He asked us to come to the United States. We had just come from there, but I put on an accent, and said that he would have to see our agent. I cabled our agent to raise our price, and by the time Dillingham got to him, we were able to hold out for more money. We had been on big bills in the States, but we hadn't been headlined, so he didn't recognize us.[42]

As amusing as the tale of trickery may be, its main features can't be true, since the Brothers had already signed a contract with Dillingham in April, after he had heard them with Primrose and Dockstader at Hammerstein's Victoria Theatre in New York, just a week before the minstrel company disbanded forever.[43] The contract marked the beginning of nine years during which Dillingham would direct their fortunes.

The producer reportedly had them in mind for *Watch Your Step*,[44] a lavish revue planned for the fall season in New York, with a score by Irving Berlin, at that time America's most sought-after popular songwriter, and starring Vernon and Irene Castle, the country's best-known ballroom dancing couple, who were fast becoming Manhattan's criterion for youthful beauty and modern deportment. An opportunity to move from vaudeville success (somewhat attenuated by two years, albeit successful ones, in minstrelsy) to a Broadway venture promised much more in benefits than in risks. If the show flopped, as the great majority did, the Brothers could always go back into vaudeville, with only a small loss in time before the public outside New York. If the show prospered, as seemed likely with the team of Dillingham, Berlin, and the Castles, the Browns could avoid the inconveniences and frustrations of life on the road for what might turn out to be a long run, and they would gain the subsequent advantages of association with one of New York's most powerful coalitions, the Dillingham-Ziegfeld partnership. As things developed, the Broadway break also gave Theresa a chance to return to show business, as a chorus girl.

But present clouds somewhat dimmed the bright future. More than four decades of peace among the major European powers had been imperiled, even before the Browns boarded the *Aquitania*, by the assassination on June 28 of the Austrian Archduke Franz Ferdinand in Bosnia-Herzegovina. Failed diplomacy, complicated treaty commitments, and national pride led inexorably to England's August 4 declaration of war against Germany after the latter's unprovoked invasion of Belgium. Almost immediately, war fears caused music hall patronage to fall off badly, and salaries, reduced by 50 percent,[45] were paid in paper money instead of gold. By government order, theatres on the seacoast shut down altogether.[46] A large number of American acts, including the Brown Brothers, balked at working for half salary. In mid-August, now in Liverpool after a stand in Glasgow, the Brothers refused to open without a guarantee of the full contractual amount.[47] Matters were complicated by their having booked an August 26 return voyage to the States on the *Kronprinz Wilhelm*, as all German reservations were canceled at the rupture of relations between the kaiser and the English crown. In spite of keen competition among fleeing Americans for transatlantic berths made scarce by the loss of the very large German commercial fleet, the Browns managed to return to the States by early September.[48]

9

Three Years with Montgomery and Stone

1914–17

The Six Brown Brothers' lucrative nine-year association with C. B. Dillingham extended their renown farther than ever, both because he featured them in three tremendously successful shows and because the group's first Broadway triumph opened the door to a renewed recording career. As thousands rushed to take up the saxophone in 1914–17, the Brothers were its most visible champions and their sound its most widely audible manifestation.

Besides the prospects of fame and leaving the road for a while, the Brown Brothers had an additional reason to be glad for an opportunity to move out of the vaudeville arena. The Orpheum circuit, their meal ticket for the two seasons before they joined Primrose and Dockstader, had gotten stingier, largely in response to the movies' burgeoning success in competing for the public's entertainment dollars. Through the 1910–11 season, the circuit had helped performers making the long hops through the Midwest and West by paying their rail fares. In the next three seasons, having reconsidered their generosity, Orpheum bookers paid travel subsidies only on routes west of Omaha, and in the fall of 1914, dropped them altogether.[1] In addition, both the Keith and Orpheum circuits had effectively lowered performers' salaries. Of the normal thirty-nine weeks' booking on the eastern circuit, only nineteen were to be at what used to be the turn's standard fee, the other twenty being "cut weeks" at reduced salary; of the normal twenty-five weeks on the Orpheum time, eight were to be cut weeks, and another four weeks would be lost in unpaid traveling, with the result that only seventeen of twenty-nine weeks on the road would bring full pay. Finally, starting a trend that would accelerate through the 1920s, fewer theatres planned to adhere to a big-time policy of only two performances a day, so that vaudeville artists would be working more while being paid less.[2]

The Browns began a tour of eastern vaudeville theatres in September, waiting for the call to join *Watch Your Step*, which didn't open until December. Meanwhile, one of Dillingham's other projects, *Chin Chin*, started a try-out run at the Forrest Theatre in Philadelphia on September 30. The extravagantly staged and boisterously funny show "was pronounced an instant and unusual hit by a capacity audience." Though billed as a musical comedy, it came across as a revue. "The book is extremely 'thin' and serves only in a slight degree to connect the various scenes in which is incorporated one of the best and finest vaudeville shows ever seen," said *Variety*'s critic.[3] Despite the show's enthusiastic reception out of town, Dillingham, like any successful producer, continued to reshape it during the tryout, but, since it had a vaudeville/revue format, reshaping wasn't limited to corrective dramaturgy. Dillingham had the Brothers up his sleeve, and when he "discovered that there was a spot in the second act which needed brightening, the Browns were rushed to Philadelphia to fill the gap." "This accidental booking settled their fate,"[4] at least for the next nine years, by linking them up for that stretch with Fred Stone, half of the famous Broadway team of Montgomery and Stone, managed by Dillingham since 1906. It also settled the group's look for the rest of its life, divesting the Brothers other than Tom of the military-band uniforms they had worn for five years and putting them into white clown makeup, tall pointed hats, and Pierrot costumes.[5] Tom retained his minstrel persona (see figure 7).

David Montgomery (born in 1870) and Fred Stone (born in 1873) had formed a blackface comedy song-and-dance duo in 1894 or 1895, while both were in their twenties. They scored an early hit in Haverly's Mastodon Minstrels, one of the largest and most famous companies of the 1880s and 1890s. Their stage characters were variously described as "dandy coons," "swell coons," or "real gallus coons," caricatures of northern urban blacks (in "mulatto makeup")[6] dressed in loud, mismatched clothing and given to bumblingly pretentious speech. They spent the rest of the decade wowing variety audiences in the United States and Europe until they were blacklisted by the major circuits in 1900 for being among the seven founders of the White Rats, a pioneering vaudeville artists' union formed primarily to create a workers' counterforce to the excessive power of the Keith circuit magnates B. F. Keith and Edward Albee. But they did very well without the major vaudeville circuits, starring in a series of hit Broadway shows. *The Girl From Up There* (1901) established them as musical comedy stars, and *The Wizard of Oz* (1903) was the biggest hit of its New York season,[7] with Montgomery as the Tin Woodman and Stone as the Scarecrow. ("The Bullfrog and the Coon," recorded by the Five Brown Brothers in 1911, came from the latter show.) *The Red Mill*, a 1906 production with a Victor Herbert score, began their long association with Dillingham. It was followed by *The Old Town* in 1910 and *The Lady of the Slipper*, again with music by Herbert, in 1912.[8]

Their dancing received enthusiastic praise in a 1912 book, *Dancing and Dancers of Today: The Modern Revival of Dancing as an Art*:

For the mixture of the humorous and grotesque it is impossible to imagine anything that could surpass Montgomery and Stone. Not only are the physical contortions of which both, and especially Stone, are masters, subjects of constant astonishment and a refutation of all theories of anatomy, but everything is done with a deftness and artistic touch which raises it far above mere eccentric contortion. They have invented and perfected a language of quaint caricature which is as complete as that of any pantomimist and whose vocabulary is constantly growing.

The authors went on to speculate that these "artists of undoubted equipment" might develop "a subtlety of suggestion . . . , a display of human feeling, a tenderness for the child spirit," already shown in *The Wizard of Oz*, into "something of more exquisite . . . appeal than caricature,"[9]—in other words, into a higher sort of art.

Fred Stone entertained audiences not only with his singing, dancing, and acting, which he had polished over the years since a childhood appearance as Topsy in a *Tom* show,[10] but also with athletic feats stemming from his youthful training in the circus, which he and his younger brother Eddie had joined when Fred was thirteen. His loyal public had come to expect expert wire walking, trapeze work, rope twirling, and tumbling from him, and in each show he added some new specialty, such as ice skating or sharpshooting. He aimed not just to dazzle, although he always did, but also to find the comic possibilities in all this physicality.

By 1914, Montgomery and Stone had dropped blackface. In *Chin Chin*, among other roles, they played Chinese characters Chin Hop Lo and Chin Hop Hi, but no African Americans. The *New York Times* ran an anonymous, effusive opening-night review headlined "Rapid Fun Makes 'Chin Chin' a Go":

To attempt to do justice to "Chin Chin," the extravaganza which came into the Globe Theatre last night, with nothing but a Mergenthaler machine and a press turning out 40,000 papers per hour, is out of the question. The only device capable of keeping up with the speed of the new Montgomery and Stone production is a moving picture outfit—and the camera man would have to be replaced by a motor at that.

"Chin Chin" is far and away the biggest show of its kind, which is hardly the way to express it, as it stands in a class by itself, that has ever come to Broadway. It is every sort of an entertainment rolled into three tremendous, smashing acts, and it provides enough laughter to establish the success of half a dozen more Broadway shows. There are girls and girls and girls, circus clowns, circus horses, and circus performers. There are moving pictures and dancers and singers and vaudeville artists galore, and then there are Montgomery and Stone, who are on the stage most of the time.

The show's minimal plot afforded plenty of opportunities for barely related interpolations. Violet Bond (played by Helen Falconer) is "a young American girl who is touring China with her father." In a Chinese toy bazaar, where Montgomery and Stone first appear as porcelain figures, Violet meets Aladdin (played by Douglas Stevenson), and they fall in love. "By the aid of Aladdin's magic lamp he becomes a prince of China, and everything goes well until the lamp is stolen and the girl taken thousands of miles away." The porcelain figures, now come to life, team with Aladdin to follow Violet and the thief, recover the lamp, and ensure a happy future for the young lovers.[11]

The first-act specialties included a dance for three teddy bears, one of whom was Theresa Valerio. It consistently pleased audiences, and one reviewer lamented that the petite dancers with the attractive legs didn't remove the teddy-bear heads for their bows. Chin Hop Lo and Chin Hop Hi did some verbal comedy and a song titled "Go Gar Sig Gong Jue" in nonsense "Chinese," and, in the "Chinese Honeymoon" number, Montgomery portrayed Stone's wife, to whom Stone made "ardent love." Finally, Stone's character performed a burlesque of modern dance with Fan-Tan (played by Violet Zell, "The Human Rag-Doll"). One reviewer called this "Danse Poetique" "perhaps the most laughable" of all the interpolations. Zell, "who weighs 70 or 80 pounds if she weighs an ounce, was carried upon her partner's feet, was whirled about like a wand, and disappeared by a flight through the air which was one of several effective touches of extravaganza."[12] "Stone does everything with his dancing partner except break her neck," said another reviewer.[13]

The second act introduced the circus motif, with David Montgomery and the Six Brown Brothers among the clowns (and seventeen-year-old Marion Davies as a bareback rider). The Brothers' usual mix of comedy and music elicited a strong response from the New York Evening Journal's Stella Flores: "The six Brown brothers are one of the biggest features—they are the funniest clowns I have ever seen, and their music simply sets you quivering to get up and join them in their antics. All the thrill and tingle of the most stirring bands you have ever heard come rolling out of their great horns."[14] A newspaper cartoon of the Brothers in the show portrays them as capering or dancing while they played. Waving ribbonlike in the background of the drawing are the first few bars of "When You Wore a Tulip and I Wore a Big Red Rose," a 1914 Jack Mahoney/Percy Wenrich hit that was not part of the score (by Anne Caldwell, James O'Dea, and Ivan Caryll), indicating that the act interpolated currently popular tunes to engage the audience.[15]

Stone joined the circus in a tutu and tights as Mlle. Fallofski, a bareback rider who found it comically difficult to stay on her mount. "Four thousand sides ached (counting both sides of the 2000 present) when Stone finished his . . . bit in the circus scene. For robust hilarious comedy and punk acrobatics this act has no equal in any part of the vast amusement business."[16] In his two remaining solo turns, Stone first portrayed a ventriloquist whose dummy (named Eddie, like Stone's late brother) turned out to be alive and deserted his master, then Ignace Paderewski, who, after eliciting spectacular music from his piano, walked away from it a little too soon, since it then went on playing by itself. Both turns were "interesting as studies in the psychology of amusement. Nine-tenths of the fun, in each of these cases, lay in the growing suspicion of the audience that it was being fooled."[17]

Reviews didn't give Montgomery nearly as much attention as they did Stone, a situation that reflected the degree to which he took second place except in their duet numbers. Besides the "Chinese" song in the first act, they sang the timely soldiers' favorite "It's a Long Way to Tipperary," replaced later in the run by a fake "Irish" number called "Bally Mooney and Biddy McGee."[18] They also appeared together in short films featuring special effects of "cloud-soaring and moon-tumbling."[19]

Although it charged Broadway's highest ticket price ($2.50), Dillingham's Globe Theatre housed the longest-running show to open in 1914. It lasted 295 performances against competition such as Watch Your Step, which finally opened on December 8 for 175 performances; an Al Jolson vehicle titled Dancing Around; The Girl from Utah (with music by Jerome Kern); and Ziegfeld's Follies of 1914, whose outstanding cast was headed by Ed Wynn and Bert Williams.[20] Variety's December review of box-office receipts reported Chin Chin "getting around $17,000 weekly. Enormous drawing powers of this show not diminished. While speculators have been caught with a few tickets now and then box office is turning an overflow nightly into other musical comedy theatres. Front seats still bringing high premiums."[21] The same issue ran a feature story about Chin Chin having inspired a producers' rush to stage revues instead of the more usual kind of musical comedy. The story names five major production companies, and the writer goes so far as to venture that the revue format "bids fair to succeed the customary 'musical comedy' New York has grown to know so well."[22] Two weeks later, after the revue-style Watch Your Step had opened with scalped tickets priced even above those for Chin Chin, another piece along the same lines appeared, warning that "the rush of revues is going to tighten up the local vaudeville market. Any number of managers and agents are out scouting for vaudevillians who will fit into the various pieces."[23]

The Browns became the subjects of valuable free publicity during the show's New York run. The New York Times's opening-night review singled them out for mention, and the New York Evening Journal ran a photo of them in costume flanked by dignified vignette portraits, without makeup, of Alec, Tom, Fred, Vern, William, and Harry Fink, echoing the Ringling Brothers' posters of an earlier era.[24] At least three newspapers printed caricatures of them, and the one already mentioned ran above a doggerel tribute by Archie Gunn:

> Six little brothers came to town
> > To seek renown;
> Their names were Brown;

Five of them wore a dress like a clown,
    And one as a coon paraded.
Now Dillingham saw a chance to win,
So he cornered the bunch for his play, "Chin-Chin."
A plan very wise,
As I surmise,
    To stimulate appetites jaded.
These six little Browns are full of fun—
    Whatever they get they earn the mun.
In a classy show
They make things go,
    With a bang! and a whoop-ta-ra-ra!
And they seem to elicit most marvellous tones
From strange looking things called saxophones.
And their melody sweet
Is really a treat,
    Like the harp in the halls of Tara.
And the popular tunes these brothers play
Seem fresh and bright in a different way;
For the tone and the moan
Of the saxophone
    Brings out the airs so sweetly.
"When You Wore a Tulip and I Wore a Rose,"
As played by these comical, clever, Pierrots,
Just fills out the bill
With a kind of a thrill,
    And catches you completely.
You can talk as you please of the slide trombone
Or laugh yourself sick at funny Fred Stone,
But the brothers Brown
Have caught the town
    With their melodies saxophonic.
And if ever you feel the least bit blue,
And you want to laugh, or you think you do,
See merry "Chin-Chin,"
With the clown band in,
    And you'll find it a wonderful tonic.

Despite the teddy-bear disguise in her feature number, Theresa too was brought to the attention of the newspaper-reading public during the New York run when her photo, along with those of chorus members Rose Cayle and Florence McGuire, was printed under the headline "3 Pretty Chins in 'Chin Chin.'" Theresa's image is the most alluring of the three. Rose Cayle turns her head forty-five degrees to look directly at the camera with a sober, almost melancholy expression; Florence McGuire is shot in profile with her eyes lowered; but Theresa looks over her partly bared shoulder, lips slightly parted in a knowing smile.[25] Later, when the show went on the road, she appeared in a full-length portrait, identified as "Mrs. Tom Brown," on the sheet music of Tom's 1916 composition "Chicken Walk," a rag the Brothers featured in the show.[26] Gaining a reputation for her exotic Italian beauty, she was to achieve more celebrity as a performer in 1917, when, costumed as a human, she was given a feature song in the next Stone-Dillingham collaboration, *Jack o' Lantern.*

Less than two weeks after *Chin Chin* opened, the Brothers were honored by an invitation to appear in the olio of the White Rats' third annual minstrel show, among such stars as New York's hottest composer, Irving Berlin, and one of vaudeville's best-paid and most versatile singers, Belle Baker. The October 22 bash, enjoyed by all, was declared to have "excelled by far the two others."[27] (By the following July, Tom and Alec had both become life members of the short-lived entertainers' union.)[28]

Thanks most likely to the success of *Chin Chin*, the Brothers also attracted the attention of the Victor Talking Machine Company. Victor records were America's most prestigious and best-sounding discs and far outstripped the products of its main rival, Columbia, which had recorded the Brothers in 1911. Concluded less than two weeks after opening night, the contract offered $300 for four "complete and perfect master records" and gave Victor the option of recording more at the same fee.[29] The group went to Victor's New York recording studio twice in November and once each in December and February. It repeatedly attempted to obtain good takes of five titles but in the end succeeded with only three. This prima facie low ratio of successes to attempts probably resulted from technical obstacles in the underexplored territory of recording saxophones, and especially groups of saxophones. Although phonograph technology had undergone rapid refinement during the 1911–14 period, Victor engineers must have faced most of the same problems as their Columbia counterparts had, especially with respect to limited dynamics and frequency response. But their efforts bore fruit, and the Victor discs provide a much clearer image, even today, of the Brothers' sound than the Columbia recordings. For the next two years, the Six Brown Brothers would be the only saxophone ensemble making records.

Victor seems to have chosen repertoire partly with an eye to supplanting Brothers discs and cylinders already released. "Chicken Reel Comedy Medley," attempted at both November sessions and at the one in February, was a cousin to Columbia's "The Bullfrog and the Coon—Medley" in that both include "Chicken Reel" and end with "The Bullfrog and the Coon." Similarly, "Independentia," attempted in November, December, and February, but not successfully recorded until June 1915, was substantially identical to the shorter U-S Everlasting cylinder version. The group waxed some more up-to-date numbers as well. Unreleased versions of the "Chicken Reel Comedy Medley" included Grant Clarke and Irving Berlin's "He's a Devil in His Own Home Town" (1914), and an unreleased version of "Independentia" included "When You Wore a Tulip and I Wore a Big Red Rose." "Chicken Reel Comedy Medley," incidentally, is one of the few discs that display any of the Browns' comedy. It begins very seriously with a stirring passage from von Suppé's *Poet and Peasant Overture*—a piece that would have been familiar to middlebrow Broadway audiences—only to segue abruptly into the bucolic lope of "Chicken Reel." An attempt from February was released on Victor 17799.

The other three pieces tried were Sebastián Yradier's well-known habanera "La Paloma," which had been copyrighted in the United States in 1883; "That Moaning Saxophone Rag"; and Charles L. Johnson's "Dill Pickles Rag," from 1906. Victor and the Browns made releasable takes of the first two titles at the second November session, although they tried to make a better "La Paloma" in February. But "Dill Pickles" was given up after many trials.[30]

Except for the *Poet and Peasant* opening, "Chicken Reel Comedy Medley" uses the same orchestration techniques as the 1911 recordings. "Chicken Reel" and "The Bullfrog and the Coon" are indistinguishable from the earlier versions, and the melody of "Virginia Lee" is harmonized in three parts over an oom-pah accompaniment. Three-part harmony pervades "La Paloma" as well, over an habanera figure that requires only one bass-saxophone "oom" per bar. Tom employs a very emotional vibrato on this piece, as wide and almost as rapid as Sidney Bechet's, though less regular. In one strain of the piece, where the habanera figure is presented with no further melody, there is an apparent struggle over what tempo to use; perhaps it was this awkwardness that led Victor to ask for another attempt in February.

The arrangement of "That Moaning Saxophone Rag," on the other hand, innovates in a number of ways. Although the first strain (the verse, in the song version) predominantly presents a solo melody played by Tom over the usual oom-pah figure, one of the lower voices offers a few discreet decorative phrases in the background. A second strain (not in the song version) follows, in which the meter drops a half beat in a confusing but rhythmically exciting way. The two passes through it are orchestrated differently, contrary to normal practice at the time, which was to vary the repeat only to the extent of changing the loudness. The first time through, the lead is in the first alto sax; the second time, it is taken by one of the lower voices while the two alto saxes play a sort of sighing figure over it. After a reprise of the first strain, the trio (the song's chorus), in two-part harmony with oom-pah, appears twice, with a dogfight (not in the song version), in thicker harmony, interposed between the first statement and the repeat. The repeat, which ends the record, is the most innovative passage. Not only is the alto saxophone lead taken an octave above the initial statement, but Tom plays a slight variation, not too distant from qualifying as jazz, on the written melody, while another saxophone (perhaps Fred) plays an even freer melody in the background. Although the duet is not wild enough to count as a foretaste of the jazz that Victor would record in 1917, it clearly presages the (once-) famous saxophone duets of Clyde Doerr and Bert Ralton on the 1919 Columbia recordings of Art Hickman's Orchestra, often credited with starting the vogue for saxophone sections in dance orchestras.[31]

Perhaps because its title promised something new to record buyers, Victor released "That Moaning Saxophone Rag" first, on the B side of a disc whose A side augured good sales: "The Original Fox Trot," played by the Van Eps Trio. Banjoist Fred Van Eps was one of Victor's most solidly established artists, and the fox-trot was the new dance craze of 1914. "Chicken Reel Comedy Medley" was issued second, this time as the A side, again paired with a Van Eps Trio selection. By the time "La Paloma" came out, a June 1915 session had yielded a good take of "Independentia," and the two were issued on the same disc, a tribute to the commercial success of the earlier recordings.[32]

The Brothers' success as Victor artists led to another source of revenue for Tom, who on May 1, 1915, signed a contract with Will Rossiter, the Chicago publisher of "That Moaning Saxophone Rag," whereby Rossiter was to pay Tom half of any royalties it received from sales of any Victor disc by the group. On top of that, Rossiter agreed to pay him half the royalties accruing from any other artist's Victor record if the music involved was "played or sung by other parties through the influence of Mr. Tom Brown." In effect, he became an agent for Rossiter, though an agent with no obligations to the company he worked for. It is likely that this contract was a lucrative one, even on the sole basis of returns from the twenty-six Brown Brothers sides Victor ultimately issued, six of which were Rossiter numbers. "That Moaning Saxophone Rag," for example, sold 200,638 copies before it was discontinued.[33]

On June 11, with *Chin Chin* beginning its ninth month of near-capacity business, the Browns returned to Victor's New York studio for another five tries at "Independentia"; the fourth one finally met the company's high standards and fulfilled the October 1914 contract. The lively march is mostly written for two alto saxes in harmony over the usual oom-pah foundation, but the first strain features interjections by Vern's bass sax, and, in the second strain, Vern plays the melody in octaves (or perhaps even in unison—it is hard to be sure) with one of the baritone saxes, while the alto saxes join the others in marking time. The lead on the "Bill Board March" section of the medley returns to Tom, who plays the reprise an octave higher, far up in the alto's top register. The Victor engineers changed the recording balance considerably from the winter sessions, foregrounding Tom to a point at which the other five sound as if they are in an adjoining room. The overall sound is less attractive than that on the earlier sides.

Victor, probably elated by the mounting sales of "That Moaning Saxophone Rag," offered an enhanced contract on June 23, raising the fee for four marketable sides from $300 to $500.[34] Two days later, on June 25, the Brothers ventured three takes each of two new titles: "American Patrol," their old Columbia hit, and Wilber Sweatman's "Down Home Rag," the latter of which had already been successfully waxed for Victor by James Reese Europe's Society Orchestra, resident band of Vernon and Irene Castle's Castle House dance studio, on December 29, 1913. None of the Browns' six takes was satisfactory, although a master of "American Patrol" was made and kept for a few weeks before it was destroyed.[35]

After almost forty weeks of acclaim, with the gruesome heat of a New York summer coming on, Dillingham recessed *Chin Chin* on the Fourth of July, giving cast and crew a welcome six weeks' break. The Brothers spent a day at each end of the vacation (July 8 and August 13) at Victor. Both times, though, they failed to produce a satisfactory version of Abe Holtzman's "A La Carte," and in August they essayed a single rejected take of Harry L. Alford's 1912 march "The Hustler." "Down Home Rag," however, came out well at the July session and was issued shortly after the "La Paloma"/"Independentia" coupling, in tandem with Fred Van Eps playing "Dance of the Bugs." "Down Home" consists of four melodically repetitious strains, each only eight bars long instead of the usual sixteen, here played (each strain being designated with a letter) AABBAACCDDCC, with a modulation between the fourth A and the first C. The short strains and relative poverty of melody, along with a recurring rhythmic figure of dotted eighth notes followed by sixteenth notes, give the piece its "down home" fiddle-band flavor. Recording quality and balance make it difficult to tell whether the first strain is harmonized in two or three parts, but at any rate, it adds nothing new to the Brothers' practice. The B strain features Tom playing solo over a metric background and taking rhythmic liberties (slightly retarding and anticipating) with the written melody, but not embellishing it as he had on "Moaning Saxophone." The effect brings to mind African American blues singing recorded a decade later, but without doubt already to be heard in theatres after the success of W. C. Handy's "Memphis Blues" (1912) and "St. Louis Blues" (1914). After two uneventful reprises of the A strain and a modulation in six-part harmony comes C, which is played at the same tempo, but in a sort of slow swing; Tom's solo melody is complemented by a countermelody in two-part harmony led by the second alto. The dissonant D strain, now clearly in three-part harmony against an oom-pah background, appears twice, followed by two statements of the C strain that are indistinguishable from the earlier two. If only A and D had risen to the level of B and C, this disc could have passed as a harbinger of jazz.

For the next ten months, the Browns were absent from the recording studio but still busy with *Chin Chin*. "The best blend of melody, comedy, and good taste that New York has seen in a number of years" reopened at the Globe on August 16 for a planned three weeks' engagement prior to "a long stay" in Chicago. "From the size and enthusiasm of the audience that welcomed this remarkable entertainment back the performance might have been its premiere and the night a cool September one instead of the beginning of the play's forty-fourth week at the end of a far-from-perfect day." The company had been somewhat reduced in anticipation of the road trip, and

Allene Crater, Fred Stone's wife, had joined the cast. "When Fred Stone and David Montgomery came bounding down the stairs of the toy bazaar for the first time the applause stopped the proceedings for several minutes while the comedians bowed and grinned."[36] The three weeks stretched into eighteen before *Chin Chin*, still doing good business, closed in New York on December 18, 1915, and moved on, not to Chicago, but to the Colonial Theatre in Boston for a highly profitable run of over a month. The show finally opened at the Illinois Theatre in Chicago on January 31, 1916, packing the auditorium right through the nominating conventions for both the Republican and Progressive Parties in early June and closing on June 11, just in time to avoid the steam bath of an Illinois summer.

In a May letter, Dillingham asked Tom to stay in *Chin Chin* for 1916–17 and alluded to an earlier conversation with Tom about the possibility of a "stunt" for 1917–18, apparently a theatrical venture with Tom and/or the Brothers as the leading attraction. Tom replied with thanks, along with a clear implication that he would be able to keep the act together only if Dillingham increased their pay for the following season.[37] The resulting contract covered two years, with a 10 percent increase to a weekly $550 for 1916–17 and a more gratifying jump to $650 for 1917–18.[38] The two-year renewal shows Dillingham's confidence in the act's future and perhaps also his shrewd determination to control that future.

Billy Markwith, the leader of the 1907 Ringling sideshow band, who had appeared in a 1909 photograph as the tenor saxophonist in the Five Brown Brothers, resurfaced in *Variety* during *Chin Chin*'s return to the Globe, leading the Saxo Sextette, which seems to have been an effort to copy the Six Brown Brothers' act. The Saxo Sextette is one of a number of groups pictured in a full-page ad for the music publisher Jerome H. Remick, all endorsing various new Remick songs. Personnel is given as the "Four Markwith Bros., Meade and Lewis," and Billy, probably the central figure in the photo, distinguished from the others by his blackface and top hat, is mentioned as the group's comedian. Although the ad says they "have just started their season at the Fifth Avenue Theatre," they don't appear in contemporary *Variety* reviews of the New York theatre by that name.[39] About fifteen months later, a Saxo Sextette, which could be the one in the Remick ad, recorded for Columbia, sounding quite a lot like the Brothers. From this meager information, it seems likely that Markwith was trying to parallel Tom Brown's path, an attempt that would result in a couple of collisions in later years. Meanwhile, following a widespread practice of bandleaders with more offers for work than they could accept in person, Tom had authorized two satellite groups to appear under the aegis "Tom Brown Presents." It is not known whether the two groups, called the Symphonic Sextette and the Six Harvards, copied the Brothers' routines or were straight musical acts.[40]

A little over a week after the Chicago closing, the Brothers repaired to Victor's studio in Camden, New Jersey, for five straight days of recording (Monday, June 19, through Friday, June 23), trying to make up the three-side deficit from their 1915 contract while getting a start on the further sides called for under their new agreement.[41] The fee had climbed again, to $1000 for six usable masters. Their efforts enjoyed a much higher success rate than before, eight issued sides out of forty-four takes of nine titles. Even the unissued title, "Tambourines and Oranges," was good enough that Victor scheduled one of the three takes for release and kept the master until October 1926 before discarding it.[42] The constitution of the Brothers may have shifted by the time of these recordings, since a photo of the group (without stage makeup) appears in the September 1916 Victor Supplement showing someone other than William on tenor sax,[43] probably Billy Markwith, but possibly Guy Shrigley, who is credited as co-composer on "Bull Frog Blues" (with Tom Brown) and "Walkin' the Dog" (with Shelton Brooks), two of the selections recorded. Both "Walkin' the Dog" and "The Darktown Strutters' Ball" (recorded in May 1917) originally appeared as songs with Shelton Brooks named as sole composer, then reappeared in purely instrumental versions (recorded by the Brothers) with an extra sixteen-bar strain and additional credit for Shrigley. Perhaps the added credit points to Shrigley's presence on the two selections. On the other hand, Victor may have printed an old photo.

A notable addition to the Brothers' forces at this time was F. Henri Klickmann, an outstanding arranger on the staff of the McKinley Music Company of Chicago, who appears in the Victor recording book as the orchestrator of at least six of the nine pieces and as the composer of "Tambourines and Oranges." Klickmann had already produced a theatre-orchestra arrangement of "That Moaning Saxophone Rag" that Will Rossiter had published in 1915 (which, by the way, included a transcription of Tom's proto-jazz variation on the third strain). Although his writing didn't alter the group's established sound in a radical way, it was noticeably more sophisticated and helped them avoid some of the muddy voicing they had occasionally fallen into previously.

Klickmann's arrangement of "Pussyfoot March (In Fox Trot Time)," the first selection recorded in June, differs subtly from the Brothers' older charts. In the first strain, Tom plays the melody over sustained chords by two or three of the others, and although Vern marks the beat, there are no answering afterbeats (no "pah"). The second strain reverts to the old pattern of a melody harmonized in two parts over an oom-pah accompaniment, but Klickmann gives the bass line more punch by having one of the baritones double Vern's three-note runup to the first note of bars 1, 3, 5, 7, 9, and 11. Like the first strain, the trio or third strain is rhythmically grounded on Vern's "oom" with no "pah," while three- or possibly four-part harmony couches the songlike melody. When the trio repeats, one of the higher saxophones overlays a quiet countermelody, again presaging the interplay of Clyde Doerr and Bert Ralton in Art Hickman's Orchestra. The piece ends with an unchanged reprise of the second strain.[44]

The recording book does not indicate that Klickmann orchestrated "Chin Chin—Medley Fox Trot," which was successfully laid down on Tuesday, although there were further trials on Wednesday and Friday. Nevertheless, the arrangement deploys some new techniques. The performance begins and ends with "Pretty Baby," a song by Tony Jackson, a popular African American cabaret entertainer then working in Chicago, with melodic additions by the Illinois songwriter Egbert Van Alstyne (and sanitized words, not sung on the present disc, by the much-published lyricist Gus Kahn). Between the two choruses of "Pretty Baby," the Brothers play "Chin Chin, Open Your Heart and Let Me In," not part of the original *Chin Chin* score. It's very likely, however, that both tunes were interpolated into the road presentations of *Chin Chin*, in line with the Brothers' policy of keeping their repertoire current. "Pretty Baby," by the way, was very up to date, having been registered for copyright only on June 21, a day after the released take was made.[45] The opening introduction and verse of "Pretty Baby" feature a three-part harmonization of the melody over a background that alternates between oom-pah and sustained chords. In the chorus, there is a discreet figure in either the tenor or one of the baritones that almost amounts to a countermelody. This bright and refreshing first outing for the Brothers on a song with the *aaba* structure that was to become ubiquitous in the 1920s must have whetted many an arranger's appetite for a saxophone section, something that had not yet appeared in American dance orchestras. The languid twenty-four-bar melody of "Chin Chin" is divided in a way not heard on earlier Brothers records, stated the first time by the tenor sax with a faster-moving obbligato for alto, then on the repeat passed back and forth between the tenor-alto combination and two altos and ending with all three saxes involved. Although the reprise of the chorus of "Pretty Baby" that closes the record is the same as the initial statement, it gains in liveliness through contrast with the slow-moving melody of "Chin Chin."

Klickmann's arrangements of "Saxophone Sobs" and "Walkin' the Dog," both from the Thursday session, don't add anything new to the established Brown style. It is disappointing that the former, whose title is probably intended to recall "That Moaning Saxophone Rag," doesn't include any of the sobbing sounds that the Brothers probably were using onstage but that reviewers mention only later in the Brothers' career. "Bull Frog Blues" and "Chicken Walk," on the other hand, respectively furnish musical versions of bullfrog sounds from Vern and clucking from Tom. "Bull Frog" transforms some of the melodic material from "The Bullfrog and the Coon" into a three-strain composition. The first has the harmonic plan of a twelve-bar blues, but the melody is more cheerful than not. The second strain, although sixteen bars long, starts as if it is going to be another twelve-bar blues, but then turns into two eight-bar phrases that begin alike but end differently. The first reaches the dominant in its eighth bar, while the second goes to the supertonic minor in the fourth bar and resolves the mild harmonic crisis by a tiptoeing figure in three- or four-part harmony and an alto saxophone arpeggio back to the dominant of the key. The third strain alternates between the kind of smooth, singing melody associated with march trios and a skipping, dotted melody like the one in the first strain. Tom and Guy Shrigley managed to update "The Bullfrog and the Coon" in a sweetly comic way. It was the first of the June waxings issued, paired with "Pussyfoot March" and released on August 28. Victor's copywriter opined that "these numbers can be fully described only by pronouncing them 'corkers.'"[46]

Tom's composition "Chicken Walk," on the other hand, uses the familiar format of a rag with three strains, although the second one uses the very unusual length of twelve bars (unusual, that is, for a strain that, like this one, doesn't use a blues harmonic progression). The piece doesn't achieve the melodic beauty and surprise of contemporary rags by masters such as Scott Joplin or Joseph Lamb, but it has its moments of delight. The melody of the first strain moves quickly for four bars, more deliberately for four more, returns to the first four bars, and ends with a two-bar break for the two alto saxes in harmony and a fast-moving resolution. The second strain teases the seasoned listener by beginning with a four-bar phrase made up of two very similar two-bar segments, then repeating the first two bars so that we expect another, related two bars to bring us to the middle, if the strain is to be sixteen bars long, or the end, if it is to be eight. Instead, we hear a quizzical, chickenlike two-bar break from the alto saxophone that seems to take us to the relative minor, followed by two bars of an ascending arpeggio (again suggesting the relative minor) by three saxophones, followed by the first two bars of the strain over again. The piece toys with and frustrates our expectations three times: first when bars 7 and 8 fail to bring a cadence or half-cadence, second when bars 9 and 10 continue the interruption begun in 7 and 8, and third when bars 11 and 12 present what sounds like the final cadence. But is it? When the repeat begins (with those same two bars), we don't know where we are—nearing the end of sixteen bars or starting over. The trio, which comes as a relief from the pleasant confusion, is thirty-two bars long and for most of its length sounds like the trio of a military march, or even a polka. A solo break for the alto sax just before the midpoint (bars 15 and 16) is all unsyncopated eighth notes (in 4/4 time), in contrast to the syncopated figuration of the first and second strains. But at the climax (bars 24 to 32), the earlier syncopation returns to let us know that this "Eccentric Fox Trot" is a rag after all. Klickmann employs a technique on the trio not heard before on Brothers records, in that the first time it is played, the tenor sax plays the lead, with harmony played above the lead by the two altos. On the repeat, the lead is split between the tenor and Tom's alto, the latter of which ends the piece.

The other two June 1916 pieces contrast sharply with the ebullient, raggy nature of the first six. "Passion Dance (La Danza Appassionata)" carries the subtitle "Parisian Fox-Tango," but rhythmically it is another habanera like "La Paloma," played slightly faster. Tom plays the melody with heavy vibrato, over two harmony parts and the habanera rhythm of the other three saxophones. The sinuous minor melody could well have inspired passionate dancing among Victor's customers.[47] Victor management chose to market this piece (after the others had all been released) on a disc coupling it, not with one of the Brothers' hotter selections, but with their "Rigoletto Quartet," a straight reading of Guy E. Holmes's transcription of the quartet from Verdi's *Rigoletto*. There is not a whiff of comedy on the recording, but, on the contrary, very operatic passion helped along by extravagant vibrato from everyone involved. It shows a serious side to their work, but one that, unlike the Cates, they chose to show only after their public knew that the highbrow stuff was a minor part of what they could do.

Thanks to records such as these, we can still hear something of what the Browns were doing. Had Dillingham agreed to a 1916 proposal by bandleader Uriel Davis, a spokesman for Webb Talking Pictures, a company which seems to have made films to exhibit synchronously with already existing phonograph discs, we might have been able also to see what they were doing. Unfortunately for posterity, Davis was informed that the act (already on the road) was not available at that time, and the proposal seems to have been dropped.[48]

Two music publications mark 1916 as an important year for the Brothers' reputation. The mid-size St. Louis firm Buck and Lowney brought out a piece by a young African American composer and musician later famous as a Chicago bandleader, Charles L. "Doc" Cooke, called "Tom Brown's Trilling Tune," dedicated, above the title, to Tom. And the Chicago firm of Will Rossiter published, along with piano sheet music of "Bull Frog Blues" bearing photos of the Brothers in costume and Tom in civilian clothes, Klickmann's small-theatre orchestration of "Chicken Walk" including parts for saxophones (alto and tenor), one of the earliest uses of saxophones in that format.[49] Above the title on each part appeared the words "Six Brown Bros," to let the user know who had made the piece worth publishing. Since small-theatre orchestrations, previously written for eleven to thirteen instruments, were the standard medium for publishers to disseminate their music to most professional ensembles (and probably many more amateur ones) of whatever size, the inclusion was historic, a gesture toward a future soon to come, in which a choir of three saxophones would become the norm in the dance orchestra arrangements that largely supplanted small theatre charts in the 1920s.

Shortly after Alec, Tom, and Theresa attended the baptism of Alec's first child, Myrtle, in Newark on August 13,[50] *Chin Chin* went back on the road. The 1916–17 itinerary was more arduous than the previous year's, a long series of short stands in larger cities, including Washington, Baltimore, Pittsburgh, Cleveland, Cincinnati, Buffalo, Detroit, and St. Louis.[51] Two years of advance publicity from New York, Boston, and Chicago, along with the nationwide sales of the Brothers' Victor discs,[52] assured its continued success. In Washington, Tom and Theresa's son Tommy made his stage debut a week after his fourth birthday with a walk-on in Chinese garb, Montgomery and Stone holding his hands.[53]

One evening during the Cleveland engagement, Tom and Theresa dined with a group that included Fred Stone and the Indians outfielder Tris

Speaker. "For some reason, Stone chose to speak in the Italian dialect which he used in the 'Goodaby John' number in 'The Red Mill,' and Miss Valerio, a daughter of Venice, responded in kind. It was Speaker who suggested an Italian revival" in Stone's next show. Stone promised to put in a good word with Dillingham. This resulted, finally, in a feature number for Theresa, no longer a dancing teddy bear, in *Jack o' Lantern*, the Dillingham show that followed *Chin Chin*.[54] Meanwhile, Will Rossiter decorated the cover of the piano sheet of "Chicken Walk" with a large full-length photo of Theresa, billed as "Mrs. Tom Brown." Her posture and facial expression make her look sexy, but neither vulgar nor immodest, and tough, but not at all aggressive. She stands in contrapposto, hands on hips, her head slightly lowered to her right, casting a knowing look at the camera, but without a smile on her beautiful face. Her dark, high-waisted, long-sleeved dress, the kind a woman of 1917 would wear to shop for fine clothing, ends at a fashionable length midway between ankle and calf. The dress's wide, white collar, softly covering her shoulders, finds echoes in a strand of pearls and her white, high-topped shoes with Louis heels. Her dark, round hat, with a circlet of flowers at the base of the crown and a long, narrow ribbon that drapes from the back over her left shoulder and down to her waist, angles forward to touch her right eyebrow. She is pictured as a young, modern woman of the city, on the model of Irene Castle, protected by the "Mrs." label from appearing too forward (see figure 8).

When the company reached St. Louis, two and a half years of good luck ran out. A nagging illness brought Dave Montgomery to a St. Louis physician whose diagnostic probe injured tissues near the bladder. A three-week return engagement in Chicago opened on March 11 with Montgomery in that city's Presbyterian Hospital, where his continued illness and X-rays revealing the damage done in St. Louis led his doctors to forbid him from performing.[55] Surgery failed, and his condition worsened. The company moved on to St. Paul, Minnesota, and then to Montreal, canceling further bookings after its April 14 closing, as Fred Stone and Allene Crater rushed to Chicago to be with their old friend as he fought for his life. Stone's visit awakened Montgomery from a five-day coma,[56] but he died, with the Stones at his bedside, on April 20, just a day after the anniversary of the men's first partnering.[57] About an hour before he succumbed, Montgomery responded to Stone's self-reproach for not having ended the tour in Chicago, praising his loyalty and the sacrifice of a possible brilliant solo career to the career of the team. "I know that you've been the whole show for a long time—that the people went to see you, and that I've been simply paid as part owner of the old trademark."[58] Stone was devastated by the loss of his closest friend.

> For twenty-two years we had been together. We had built our careers together, so closely that they seemed like one career. We had in common a whole lifetime of shared experiences, and deep-rooted friendship and trust. We supplemented each other, as is the case with all enduring partnerships. He had a gayety and sparkle and love

of life that aroused a response in his audience and his friends. No one will ever know how I missed him. The most difficult thing I ever had to do was to go ahead alone. For one thing I decided—I would never take another partner. No one should have Dave's place.[59]

Most of the *Chin Chin* cast attended Montgomery's funeral in New York three days later, along with Dillingham, George M. Cohan, Elsie Janis, Leon Errol, Will Rogers, and hundreds of lesser lights of the show world and veterans of the countless audiences he had entertained.[60]

Figure 1. 45th Battery Band, Bowmanville, Ontario, c. 1890.
Cornetist and bandmaster Allan Brown is seated behind the
bass drum, with son Tom, holding a clarinet, next to him.

Figure 2. Six Brown children in 1894. Left to right, Percy,
Fred, Tom, Myrtle, Vern, and Alec.

Figure 3. Tom and Percy Brown, c. 1904–5.

AL SWEET'S CONCERT BAND — RINGLING BROS. SHOWS · SEASON 1909.
Pre-eminently a Conn Band which during the Summer Seasons delights countless
thousands. Behold the majestic proportions of the Tuba Grands and the Giant
Conn Sousaphone BBb Bass in the background, flanked by Conn Artist Model Slide
Trombones on the right and all Conn Mellophones. Trumpets and Cornets.

Figure 4. Ringling Brothers' Circus Band, 1909. Director Al
Sweet is seated front and center. The four saxophonists just
behind him, left to right, are an unidentified tenor (J. Frank
Hopkins?), Tom Brown, Billy Markwith, and Alec Brown.
Vern Brown is sixth from left in the clarinet section.

Figure 5. Primrose and Dockstader's Minstrels at the Russell
Café, Ottawa, Ontario, March 28, 1913. At the extreme
left is Lew Dockstader. Clockwise around the table from
him, the first seated figure is Tom Brown and the third and
fourth standing figures are Harry Fink and William Brown.
Standing at the far end of the table are George Primrose
(fifth from right) and Vern Brown (second from right).
Counterclockwise from Dockstader, the second figure
(closest to the camera) is Raymond Wylie, the third Allan
Brown, the fifth Alec Brown, and the seventh Fred Brown.

Figure 6. Six Brown Brothers, c. 1912–16. Left to right,
Tom, Fred, Billy Markwith (?), Alec, Harry Fink, and Vern.

Figure 7. Six Brown Brothers
in *Chin Chin*, 1914. Front and
center, Tom; left to right on
the pedestal, William, Harry
Fink, Vern, Alec, and Fred.
(Courtesy of Mal Sharpe.)

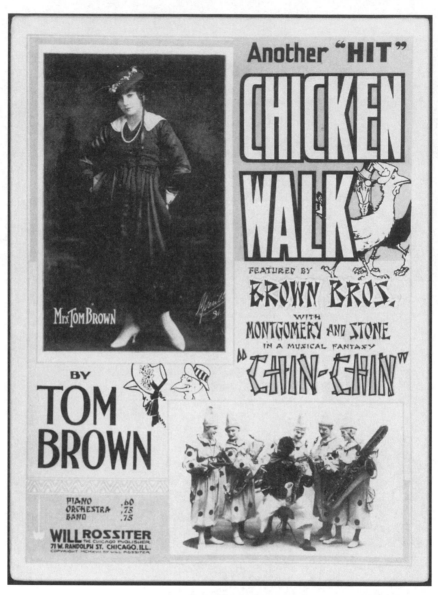

Figure 8. "Chicken Walk" cover, 1917. Theresa Valerio in
the top photo. Left to right in the bottom photo (from the
same 1914 series as Figure 7) are Fred, William, Tom, Alec,
Harry Fink, and Vern.

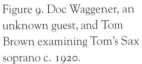

Figure 9. Doc Waggener, an unknown guest, and Tom Brown examining Tom's Sax soprano c. 1920.

Figure 10. Fred Stone and Theresa Valerio in a program photo for *Tip Top*, 1922.

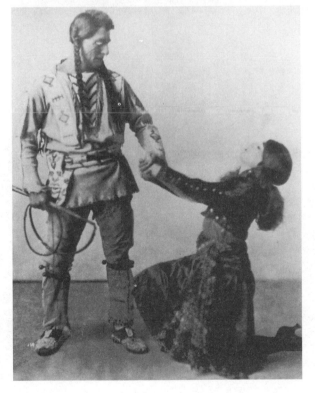

Figure 11. Tom in semi-drag on the SS *Buford* voyage, 1923.

Figure 12. Six Brown Brothers in parkas, Alaska, 1923. Left to right, Fred, two unknowns, Tom, Alec, and Vern.

Figure 13. Six Brown Brothers serenade a whale carcass,
Akutan, Alaska, 1923.

Figure 14. Alec Brown with his daughters Dorothy, Helene, and Myrtle, c. 1924.

Figure 15. The Six Brown Brothers with their thirty (don't count 'em)-piece saxophone orchestra, 1924. Front row, left to right: Fred, unknown, Tom, William, Alec, and Vern. The figure at the right end of the second row may be Billy Markwith.

Figure 16. Tom Brown and His Merry Minstrel Orchestra, 1925. Tom is seated in the center, with Will Morgan just to the right. On the far left is Ted Morse and on the far right, Jack Carpenter. The man with the mustache may be Thurlow "Ponzi" Cranz.

Figure 17. Tom Brown himself, probably in the mid-1920s.

Figure 18. A family gathering c. 1930. Alec Brown is in the foreground. Left to right behind him are Tom, Burr Elliott (sister Myrtle's husband), Tom Jr., William, and Fred.

10

Jack o' Lantern

1917–18

Besides establishing Fred Stone as a musical comedy star on his own, the next Stone/Dillingham extravaganza, *Jack o' Lantern*, brought the Six Brown Brothers back to the tough Broadway market for a second test. They passed it with high marks. During the long recess between Dave Montgomery's funeral and September 1917, when rehearsals began for the new show, the Six Brown Brothers made more discs and played a prestigious Chicago gig, but they also lost their six-year position as the only saxophone ensemble on records. Looming over the whole 1917–18 Broadway run of *Jack o' Lantern*, the war in Europe threatened to snatch the two youngest Browns away to distant fields of battle.

The Brown Brothers' twelve issued Victor sides had sold so well that the company invited the group back to the studio a couple of weeks after Montgomery's funeral, increasing the per-side stipend by 25 percent, to $2,500 for twelve sides.[1] Victor had released the numbers from the June 1916 sessions one or two at a time, from August through February,[2] and the many Victor dealers who had experienced good sales were clamoring for additional titles. On Monday through Thursday, May 7–10, 1917, the Brothers attempted twelve selections, seven of which were released. Besides arranging, F. Henri Klickmann figured as composer or co–composer of four of the pieces: the wonderful "Smiles and Chuckles (A Jazz Rag)" and three fox-trots, "Ghost of the Saxophone," "My Fox Trot Girl" and "Saxophone Sam" (the last two in collaboration with saxophonist Paul Biese). The other three numbers eventually issued were Shelton Brooks's "The Darktown Strutters' Ball," an ebullient successor to his "Walkin' the Dog," Gus King's one-step/march "Comedy Tom," and a medley of George Meyer's "For Me and My Gal" and Irving Berlin's "From Here to Shanghai." The selections never released included two waltzes, "A Wonderful Thing" and "Tom Brown's Saxophone" (the latter composed by Tom), an Ernie Erdman piece called "Saxophonology," a march called "Daughters of the American Revolution," and "The Aunt

Jemimas [*sic*] Slide." After two to six takes of each title, Victor mastered one of each. Four of the five unissued masters were good enough that the company retained them for nine years before destroying them. "The Darktown Strutters' Ball" and "Comedy Tom," incidentally, were Will Rossiter publications, yielding Tom a royalty kickback.[3]

Klickmann's arrangements for the May 1917 sessions didn't introduce any new techniques, but they sustained the very high level of the 1916 Victors. The billing of "Smiles and Chuckles" as a "jazz rag" probably had less to do with its musical content than with Victor's desire to link it to the newborn craze for jazz. In New York the preceding winter, the Original Dixieland Jazz Band, a group of five young white men from New Orleans, had become enormously popular at Reisenweber's Restaurant, playing high-energy rags, one-steps, and blues in a loose, noisy, parade-band style that inspired hordes of looser and noisier imitators. Victor capitalized on the fad quickly, recording the ODJB (as it is usually called) in February of 1917, rushing the discs into stores perhaps as early as April,[4] and realizing massive sales across the United States. "Smiles and Chuckles," a more sophisticated cousin of "Chicken Walk," is formally the most traditional rag the Brothers ever recorded (except for the unreleased "Dill Pickles"). They played it faster than any of their previous efforts, giving a breathless quality to its flying syncopations. The third strain of the piece is crucial to its supercharged sound, violating listener expectations in that it's not the songlike trio customary in marches and less inventive rags, but a kind of perpetual-motion repetition of one raggy rhythmic figure (♫♫ ♫♫) with varied melodic material until near the end. (The first strain of Henry Lodge's very popular "Temptation Rag," from 1909, was built on repetition of the same figure.) Speed, energy, repetition without monotony, and up-and-down chromatic and scalar breaks create a marvelously humorous three minutes, but not a performance one would then or now categorize as jazz, lacking as it does a 1917 jazz band's earmarks of variations on the melody, pounding drums, trombone glissandi, wailing clarinet, and flutter-tongued cornet.[5]

Three of the sides, simple, buoyant two- or three-strain pieces in fox-trot arrangements, look forward to the dance music that was to become typical of the 1920s. Combining a singable melody with a steady fox-trot rhythm, "The Darktown Strutters' Ball," "My Fox Trot Girl," and the "For Me and My Gal" medley are almost as far from the Brothers' earlier prevailing rag/march pattern as "La Paloma" and "La Danza Appassionata." The 1916 discs had already been pitched at the lucrative dance-record market, with all the titles except "La Paloma" and "Rigoletto Quartet" designated on the label as fox-trots, "in fox trot time," or, in the case of "Passion Dance," as a "Parisian fox-tango." The two unreleased waltzes from the 1917 sessions may have been an attempt on Victor's part to open up a larger segment of the dance market for the Brothers. The company acted as quickly in releasing the first fruit of the May sessions as they had in issuing the initial ODJB disc: it hurried a pairing of "For Me and My Gal" and "My Fox Trot Girl" to the market in July, for the first time listing a Brown Brothers disc under "Dance Records" instead of "Miscellaneous Instrumental Records."[6]

Just about the time of the May sessions, Victor's rival Columbia announced its first saxophone recordings since the Brothers' 1911 dates.[7] Waxed in January and February of 1917, the Saxo Sextette's (or Sextet's; the spelling varies) ten selections included "American Patrol" and "Bull Frog Blues," along with a blues medley, popular songs from recent Broadway shows, and a couple of marches.[8] Clearly Columbia was aiming to capture a part of the market that had been created by the Six Brown Brothers. A small photograph of the Sextette (in dress suits and without makeup) accompanied the Columbia catalog listing, but it is hard to identify any of the members, although clearly none of them was a Brown brother. It seems likely that the group is somehow connected with the Saxo Sextette that appeared in a Jerome Remick advertisement in 1915, which included Billy Markwith, and indeed the second alto saxophone player from the right bears a resemblance to Markwith. Their sound is less polished than the Brothers', as well as somewhat lighter, partly because of their use of three, rather than only two, alto saxes, along with tenor, baritone, and bass. They also play more softly than the Browns, perhaps because of some limitation in Columbia's recording technique, so that the overall aural impression lacks the vigor of the Brown sides. Despite Columbia's engineers having made considerable progress since 1911, the discs lack the clarity and brightness of the Victors.

The Pathé company chose April to enter both the saxophone-ensemble and jazz markets, releasing two discs by Wilber ("Wilbur" on the label) Sweatman and His Jass Band. The badly recorded group consists of Sweatman on clarinet and a very hot backup saxophone quintet of an alto, two tenors, a baritone, and a bass. From a twenty-first-century perspective, the Sweatman group, though far from emulating the sound of the ODJB, produces something a lot closer to jazz than the Brothers did. The announcement in the Pathé Frères Phonograph Company catalog for May 1917 indicates that the Jass Band was a working group, but nothing else is known of its career. A year later, Sweatman was recording with his Original Jazz Band, whose constitution and approach were much closer to those of the ODJB.[9]

Later in the year, Columbia announced the first solo saxophone disc it had issued since 1908. Mystery still surrounds the August 1917 release of Columbia A2099, which paired "The Sunshine of Your Smile" with "Somewhere a Voice Is Calling," nominally played by Fred Allen, but actually by Fred Brown. Fred had recorded the two pieces almost a year earlier, on August 19, 1916. Three days later, he recorded two more numbers, "Kiss Me Again" and "Love, Here Is My Heart," finally released under his true name in October 1917.[10] It isn't known why the sides were held from release for such a long period. Normally, record companies attempted to issue their product while the music was still current, and a year far exceeds the life expectancy of most popular songs. Perhaps both the long delay and Fred's use of a pseudonym were motivated by Tom's desire not to have under his wing a competitor for saxophone-record dollars. But that guess leaves unexplained the marketing of "Love, Here Is My Heart" and "Kiss Me Again" under Fred's real name. None of the four titles competed directly with anything the Brothers were doing on disc, as Fred's alto saxophone slowly crooned the two fox-trots and two waltzes to orchestral accompaniment. The rubato and rallentandos of Fred's treatment clearly suggest that the records were intended for dreamy listening rather than dancing. Victor, apparently aware of Fred's Columbia connection, had added a new stipulation in the Browns' 1917 contract. Not only did it guarantee Victor the usual exclusive rights to recordings by the sextet, but it extended the restriction to the individual members as well, from May 1, 1917, to May 1, 1918. The letter of acceptance was signed by Tom, Fred, Harry, and Vern.[11]

None of the Browns was a match for the saxophone virtuoso who arrived on Broadway in February 1917. Californian Rudy Wiedoeft, billed as "The Kreisler of the Saxophone," combined unprecedented technique and speed on the horn with an ability to improvise that gave him a place in the swiftly growing market for jazz. While the Six Brown Brothers were entertainers who made music, Wiedoeft was primarily a musician who entertained in order to make a living. A few saxophone sextet recordings in 1919–22 brought him into direct competition with the Browns, but otherwise his career seems to have had little to do with theirs.[12]

Despite the competition of the Saxo Sextette and Wilber Sweatman's Jass Band, as well as the beginning of Wiedoeft's rise, the Six Brown Brothers stayed on top of the saxophone hill during 1917–18, fortified by their record sales and their appearances in *Chin Chin* and *Jack o' Lantern*. Carl Fischer, one of New York's largest music publishers, boosted the Browns' prestige by another means. The Fischer organization was well known for recasting successful music in new molds—transcribing selections from nineteenth-century opera for military band, orchestrating popular songs for mandolin ensembles, or producing concert versions of African American spirituals. In early 1917, Fischer brought out arrangements for saxophone quintet and piano of three of the Brothers' Victor hits, "Bull Frog Blues," "Pussyfoot," and "That Moaning Saxophone Rag."[13] The arrangements, while generally following the Browns', couldn't be mistaken for them, even without the piano. Great fun for the Brothers' admirers to play, the new charts, perhaps the first ragtime published for saxophone ensemble, helped fuel the accelerating amateur saxophone movement.

From mid-July until mid-August, the Browns played at Chicago's Bismarck Gardens, the elegant and expensive dowager of the city's cabarets, reportedly for dancing.[14] Such an engagement, with a dance band's commitment to providing three to five hours of music loud enough to be heard over the patrons' sliding footwear, would have been grueling compared to the twenty-minute performances the Brothers had become used to during the *Chin Chin* tour, although the work would have been light compared to a circus bandsman's. Perhaps the report is based instead on a series of appearances in the "elaborate, colorful, skilful, and decorous" floor shows at the Gardens (later in 1917 renamed the Marigold Gardens).[15] The after-theatre crowds who repaired to the North Side for a few drinks and a turn around the floor must have been thrilled to have one of the country's foremost recording groups guiding their steps.

While the Browns ameliorated the sweaty Chicago summer for the fox-trotters at the Bismarck Gardens, Fred Stone practiced ice skating, his new specialty for *Jack o' Lantern*, the Dillingham show that was to open in the fall, using the shuttered Hippodrome in New York for his workouts. Stone had contacted Dillingham during the previous winter's tour about the possibility of a skating turn. The producer having given the high sign, Stone began learning fancy moves on the abundant ice of Chicago and St. Paul. The Hippodrome, managed by Dillingham, had featured an ice rink in the show that had just closed, so providing practice space was just a matter of the manager lending one of New York's largest venues to his favorite star for his private use.

Rehearsals for *Jack o' Lantern* started in September, in anticipation of a short run at Philadelphia's Forrest Theatre prior to a Broadway bow on October 16 at the Globe Theatre, scene of *Chin Chin's* 1914–15 triumph. The score came from the pens of Ivan Caryll and Anne Caldwell, two members of the trio that had furnished the music and lyrics for *Chin Chin*. The production team of Ned Wayburn, Joseph Urban, Homer Emens, and Robert Burnside was nationally famous for its Broadway work, especially in Ziegfeld productions such as the *Follies* of 1914 (Emens), 1915 (Urban), and 1916 and 1917 (Wayburn and Urban).[16] Once again, the Brothers and Theresa had boarded a hit vehicle, with the sweet promise of continued acclaim complemented by the sweet actuality of a substantially higher income, the sextet raised from a weekly $550 to $650 (see chapter 9) and Theresa, now a featured player, raised from an unknown, but undoubtedly tiny, chorus girl's salary to a decent $35 [17]

Like *Chin Chin*, the show's elaborate fantasy existed mostly as a showcase for Fred Stone, but this time the book was a nursery story, centered upon the children Bobby and Babby, a sister and brother in the care of their Uncle George, who schemes to kill them for their money. One day as the wicked uncle is driving the children in a wagon, John Obadiah Lantern (Fred Stone), a rover from Zanesville, Ohio, emerges from its load of hay and is mistaken by George for the assassin he has hired from New York's Bureau of Crime, Inc. Jack, seeing a chance to rescue the innocents, exploits George's error by demonstrating his skill at disguises. He "appears with giddy swiftness as a Spanish don, a braw Scot with a Harry Lauder burr, a Cossack dancer, an English music-hall comedian and an Italian organ grinder," singing and dancing in each new character, with a different beautiful chorus girl as a foil in each episode. "As the Cossack, [Stone] does feats of dancing which seem incredible until he reveals the apparatus with which he keeps his balance, and defies gravity with a device which enables him to hang out, with no visible means of support, almost horizontally over the orchestra pit."[18] In his organ grinder guise, he is joined by the Italian nurse, Zingarella (Theresa Valerio), to sing and dance an Irving Berlin number, "I'll Take You Back to Sunny Italy," and conspires with her to save the children. At the conclusion of the act, policemen arrive to detain the suspected assassin, but Jack runs up an inclined tree trunk, does a backward somersault over the heads of the three cops, and escapes "on a bicycle that jumps through a barn window, landing him in the loft, from which he falls bouncingly from the load of hay to the stage, where he becomes the hub and spokes of a hollow wheel, and finally gets away by jumping through a signboard and emerging as a sheeted jack o' lantern."[19]

The second act opens on Joseph Urban's set of a medieval-style banqueting hall at Jack's villa, where he is entertaining the rescued Bobby and Babby, feeding them lavishly and reading them stories after dinner. After falling asleep, they visit the Cave of Dreams, where (probably with the aid of animated film) they relive the banquet as a nightmare. "The fish leaps from the plate into a bowl and splashes about in the water, the bottle of wine decants itself and the beverage flees from one glass to another, the lobster arises and bites the Comedian's finger, . . . the turkey springs from its platter to do a double shuffle,"[20] and "the bologna sausage develops a head and a tail and barks until Stone shoots it with a toy pistol."[21]

A rapid change of scenery transports the trio to Candyland, where "the houses are made of bon-bons, the roofs are tiled with caramels, the posts of the porches are barber poles, and the chimneys are peppermint sticks. The chorus is dressed to represent all kinds of sweetmeats and confections. Three candy boxes open, and forth trip the Lilliputian Princesses Nougat, Caramel and Marshmallow," portrayed by the Hoy Sisters, a song and dance trio, variously described in reviews as midgets or dwarfs.[22] Jack "arrives, dressed as a troubadour, and from a window Violet Zell tumbles into his arms for a 'nightmare dance.' This is an incredible display of elastic bodies and muscular suppleness, Stone whirling his partner about like a rag doll, and ending with circus stunts which can hardly be believed until it appears that Miss Zell is supported by a wire."[23]

Jack next appears as an aviator stationed at Camp Nowhere, surrounded by "maidens in the garb of a dozen nations,"[24] to sing "Along Came Another Little Girl," a big comic/patriotic dance number, during which one of the guaranteed laughs of the evening is elicited by a baby (one of the Hoy Sisters) in a perambulator who bums a cigar from Jack and lights up.

After a special Joseph Urban curtain falls, screening the back of the stage for scene shifting, the Six Brown Brothers enter for their specialty, Clowntown. Fragmentary descriptions in reviews portray it as a turn very similar to the one in Chin Chin. "These artists on the saxophone, whose syncopation is the steadiest and jazz the smoothest of the entire brotherhood, brought the house down with their music and comedy in an act which they had all to themselves."[25] With "the same crisp rhythm and breezy style that . . . made them famous,"[26] they played "new music that permits of an even better demonstration [than in *Chin Chin*] of the musical possibilities of this instrument in the hands of expert musicians."[27] Their repertoire consisted mostly of popular hits of the day not written for *Jack o' Lantern* (including "Comedy Tom"), and they closed with George M. Cohan's audience-rousing war anthem "Over There." On the comic side, they carried on a musical dialogue "in scraps of popular song hits which the audience easily recognized."[28] In another bit, Tom was "excruciatingly funny,"[29] as he "led the group by queer movements of his hands and feet, tugging at his tie, and counting the buttons on his coat."[30] Reviewers were unanimous in praising the Brothers in glowing terms, and audiences consistently encored them. On opening night in Milwaukee, the act "was applauded so long and so insistently that the snowstorm in the succeeding . . . scene was almost over before the audience consented to let the performance proceed."[31]

The succeeding scene was Fred Stone's pièce de résistance, the Ice Carnival, for which he had been preparing since the dark days of Dave Montgomery's final illness. The Brothers' drop rises on a mountain resort, where a snowstorm is falling on an ice rink that covers most of the stage. Costumed in "blue silk set off with white fur,"[32] a beautiful young woman (Ellen Dallerup during the 1918–19 season, Katie Smith in the following year) enters, a "marvelously graceful and brilliant skater who pirouettes and whirls all over the ice, who dances and leaps and glides as though skating was the easiest and most natural game in the world."[33] The audience dazzled, a master of ceremonies announces the next act, the world's greatest skater, Charlotte Russe (whose name recalled for the audience, rather bluntly, the exhibition skater Charlotte [Oehlschlaegel], the star of Dillingham's *Hip, Hip, Hooray* in 1916–17, on the very Hippodrome ice where Stone had worked up his routine). Stone then glides on, "arrayed in a white velvet ballet costume with his face framed in blond curls,"[34] to present in a new medium his trademark combination of awe-inspiring athletic ability and physical comedy. Mingled with his comic falls and graceful figures are handsprings and somersaults, which he comes out of "landing surely on the blades every time,"[35] and "a rag skating dance to 'Walking the Dog' that no one else has done."[36] His "exhibition on the ice . . . was such as to cause a general craning of necks to make sure there was no faking,"[37] such as the apparatus that supported the Cossack or the wire that aided Violet Zell in her flight. Completing the turn with some spectacular duet skating, Fred and his partner retire for a few moments as Uncle George repents, Bobby and Babby are returned to their father, and Uncle George's daughter is finally permitted to marry one of the other characters, resolving a subplot that almost none of the reviewers mentions.

Onstage throughout except for the Clowntown scene, Fred Stone was the show. "As a comedian [he] stands supreme. Every movement of his lithe body has a meaning, every grimace has a purpose. It is clowning, but it is the clowning of a man who gives to the results of hard toil and careful study the appearance of spontaneity that few are able to impart."[38] But Theresa came in for praise in nearly every review. After her duet with Stone on "I'll Take You Back to Sunny Italy," "probably the best sung, as it is certainly the best-acted number on the program,"[39] "there was a rustling of programs by the audience to determine for themselves who this dark-eyed, graceful girl might be—she with the patois of Italy in her tones, and the fire of the Southland in her speech and eyes."[40] Theresa's striking beauty inspired the dramatic editor of *Town and Country*, a magazine for the affluent, to invite her to pose for a color photo in her costume for the Italian number. Published in the April 10, 1918, issue, the portrait, shot from shoulder level, shows her from the waist up, her body in profile, her face in three-quarters view, and her eyes looking directly at the viewer. Her back, left arm, and shoulder are provocatively bare, and the top of a camisole peeks through the low-cut armhole of her dark dress, but her left hand rests demurely on her chest. Above her slightly lowered eyelids and arched eyebrows, a green scarf with a painted rose encircles her dark curls. A beaded hoop earring disappears into dramatic shadow to complete the gypsy effect. The caption maintains the publication's old-money, Anglo-Saxon pretense and only slightly patronizes the emerging stage beauty: "Miss Teresa [sic] Valerio. One of the 'Jack O' Lantern' Company, who has a right to that kind of name and to the emerald-green kerchief turban effect. She not only sounds and looks Italian but, by all that's curious, she is Italian-descent." Theresa's talent and increased prominence were rewarded with a raise of almost 150 percent for 1918–19, to $85 per week.[41]

Disrupted by World War I, the personnel of the Brothers during the three years *Jack o' Lantern* ran (1917–20) is not known. But it is likely that Tom, William, Alec, and Harry Fink were on hand for the whole stretch. Just three weeks before Dave Montgomery's death, the European war had become an American war. The United States decided on April 1, 1917, to enter the conflict and quickly passed a conscription bill that required all able-bodied men between the ages of twenty-one and thirty-one to register for the draft. Fred Brown, now twenty-six, was one of the first in New York's theatre district to sign up, arriving at the Precinct 10 registration booth in the early morning of June 5 and leaving with card number 6.[42] Vern registered as well (at an unknown date), but the other brothers (besides being British subjects) were too old. Although he was twenty-seven, Harry Fink already had two daughters, so would probably not have been accepted as a draftee. It is unknown whether he enlisted. Fred was accepted for the draft in August 1917, just as the Brothers returned to New York from Chicago.[43] But he remained a civilian for a little more than a year, benefiting from the government's gentle treatment of entertainers, whose presence on the home front was regarded as important to the war effort. He probably played the whole 1917–18 season and the first few performances of the second season before being drafted into the navy in early September 1918. Vern may have been inducted even earlier.[44] It is uncertain when Fred and Vern returned from the service. There is some evidence that they were back by the summer of 1919. An Emerson Records catalog for November 1919 gives a personnel for discs made the preceding summer identical with the 1914–15 personnel, although the tenor player, called Harry in the catalog copy, is not specifically identified as Harry Fink.[45] Perhaps, then, Fred and Vern were both back for the 1919–20 season, or even a few months earlier, since an article published at the beginning of the Philadelphia run weakly implies that by late April 1919 the group consisted of five blood Browns and an unnamed non-relative. Neither is it known who replaced Fred and Vern. Percy could have substituted for Vern in the spring and summer of 1918. During the 1915 season (perhaps only for a part of it), Percy was the bandmaster of the Hagenbeck-Wallace Circus, but by the 1916 season, Fred Jewell had replaced him, and it is not known whether Percy stayed with the organization during 1916–18.[46] At the beginning of the 1918–19 Broadway season, Percy was in Tom Brown's Clown Band in another Dillingham production, *Everything*, at the Hippodrome.[47] A very likely substitute for Fred or Vern was Matthew Amaturo, an Italian-born musician who later performed and recorded (for Victor) with the Benson Orchestra of Chicago.[48]

Despite these shifts in constitution, the Six Brown Brothers remained an entity with its own personality, firmly guided by Tom. *Jack o' Lantern* had renewed the act's New York cachet. The two succeeding years on the road, with summer engagements in Manhattan, would do even more for their reputation.

11

On the Road with *Jack*

1918–20

During the period bracketed by the end of *Jack o' Lantern*'s Broadway run and the 1920 opening of the next Stone/Dillingham musical, *Tip Top*, the Six Brown Brothers and Theresa Valerio spent most of their time in national tours with *Jack*. But the Brothers had reached a new show-business elevation in the 1917–18 Globe season as the act neared the high point of its trajectory. Florenz Ziegfeld canonized them by putting them into his *Midnight Frolic*, not once but twice, where they mixed with top-echelon entertainers such as Bert Williams and Will Rogers. Sousa added a saxophone sextet to the concert programs of his internationally famous band. And a new record company, Emerson, briefly captured the Brothers to add their glamour to its roster of stars. But fear and frustration were constant themes. The draft took Vern and Fred Brown, then expanded to threaten the older brothers, and an epidemic brought home by repatriated troops disrupted the theatre business and killed Percy Brown. The war crippled the Victor Talking Machine Company, a strike closed the *Midnight Frolic*, and Tom Brown's ambition to headline his own show met with frustration. By the end of 1920, unreadable signs of coming descent were all around.

Jack o' Lantern could probably have played well into the New York summer, as *Chin Chin* had in 1915, but Fred Stone closed the show on June 1, 1918, in order to make a film, *Under the Top*, in California.[1] After resting for a couple of days, the Brown Brothers spent June 4–7 recording for Victor, rested for a few more days, and on June 10, at Florenz Ziegfeld's personal request, joined his *Midnight Frolic*, already in its seventh week at the Danse de Follies (also known as the Amsterdam Roof and the Ziegfeld Roof) atop the New Amsterdam Theatre on Forty-second Street.[2]

The Brothers' new Victor contract was signed at a difficult time for the company, which had cut record and phonograph production when a substantial portion of its capacity was converted to the manufacture of armaments. Instead of announcing forty or so new releases in each month's *Talking Machine World*, as it had from January to November of 1917, Victor listed an average of barely more than fifteen per month for the next two years, not counting two months (November 1918 and July 1919) when not a single new Victor disc came out. Nevertheless, only five months into the long emergency, the company made the Browns its handsomest offer yet: $6,000 for fifteen selections, with an option for more at $250 per side.[3] Perhaps because of the cutback, five titles from the May 1917 sessions were still awaiting release (which never came).

After multiple takes, all sixteen pieces recorded in June 1918 were mastered, but only seven of the masters were kept for more than a couple of months. Of those, only two were finally issued, on Victor 18476. One side was billed as a one-step (James "Slap" White's "When Aunt Dinah's Daughter Hannah Bangs on That Piano")[4] and the other as a fox-trot (Raymond Walker and Abe Olman's "Chasing the Chickens"), following a common practice in the dance-record market that gave the purchaser a choice of steps. Neither piece offers the Brothers fan anything new except for the compositions themselves. "When Aunt Dinah's Daughter Hannah" is a simple verse-chorus song, played at a brisk tempo, with a brief dogfight section featuring the bass sax just before the third and final statement of the chorus. "Chasing the Chickens," with three strains like a march or a rag, offers more melodic and textural variety. Although the title recalls earlier Brothers' "chicken music," the piece avoids the clucking and crowing effects of "Chicken Reel" and "Chicken Walk." The only touch of comedy peeks through in the trio, where bars 5 through 8 come out just slightly shorter than they should be as the lead tenor sax plays a slow-moving melody accompanied by an agitated responsive figure in the two altos and other tenor. Two of the rejected selections, "Cry Baby (A Jass Fox Trot)" and "Play It Again (One Step)," were composed by Tom Brown with the collaboration of Ernie Erdman, a well-known popular tunesmith. "Cry Baby," which the Brothers were to attempt again the following May, is said in the recording book to be from *Jack o' Lantern*. Given what is known about the way in which the Brothers varied their onstage repertoire, it's likely that most of the pieces had been played in the show, even if they weren't written for it.

Ziegfeld's *Midnight Frolic* was the sixth in a series of successful Amsterdam Roof revues so named. The Roof had opened for dining and dancing in 1914, launching its first floor show in January 1915. Soon after, Joseph Urban added one of its most famous features, a plate-glass runway over the first row of tables, where interested patrons could view the legs and undergarments of Ziegfeld's renowned chorus girls from a vantage point normally reserved for lovers and physicians. With the 1917 edition of the *Follies* about to open in the big house downstairs on June 12, the *Frolic* cast was changing, so it is impossible to determine who appeared along with the Brothers out of the original cast, which had featured Fannie Brice, Eddie Cantor, and Will Rogers, all slated for the new *Follies*. *Variety* reported, however, that Joe Frisco remained in the Roof show and that Bert Williams joined the cast in mid-July after settling a contractual dispute with Ziegfeld.[5]

Variety's review of opening night, seven weeks before the Browns joined, had found many flaws, pointing out that, in their solo turns, Rogers presented very little new material and Cantor none and that their turn as a duo, impersonating local figures such as Ziegfeld, Dillingham, and *Follies/Frolic* songwriter Gene Buck, though funny, was too long. Lillian Lorraine's "voice, never very strong" in the *Follies*, was even worse on the Roof, and she seemed "unable to get a song over." Two of her three numbers "did not look to have been staged with any care or thought," and, in general, the previous *Frolic* had been "a much faster and better performance." Some performers were praised, including Bird Millman, a circus wire-walker who had risen to fame with the Ringling Brothers show. Chorus girls engaged the men in the audience in a ring-tossing game, with four or five vertical canes on a stand around each dancer's waist as the target, and the cane ringed as the prize. Later they sang a song about automobiles, "with six or seven girls wearing the familiar radiator fronts of the better known cars. Dolores was handsomely gowned as a Rolls Royce, while the 'Ford' girl appeared in overalls."[6]

The trademarks of Joe Frisco, "one of the big hits" of the show, were a derby, a cigar, and a stutter. Known professionally as "the Jazz Dancer," he did an up-to-date version of the kind of soft-shoe and eccentric dancing that George Primrose was famous for, perfected at Chicago's Lambs Cafe and the Montmartre nightclub in New York.[7] The April–August 1917 *Frolic* was his second, and *Variety's* reviewer approved: "Frisco jazzes his cigar and his dancing as he pleases, doing whatever he wants to up there and getting away with it. He has added a jazz 'waltz clog' with 'posing' and puts that over also. Frisco is a creator of something really odd in dancing."[8]

Bert Williams, a brilliant pantomimist, storyteller, and sketch actor, who delivered comic songs, many of his own composition, in a half-sung, half-spoken style, joined the cast on July 15. He was already internationally famous when he broke the Ziegfeld color line in the 1910 *Follies*. Mixed European and African ancestry had given the tall, handsome West Indian too light a complexion to fit show business's stereotype of a black man, so he worked in burnt cork right from the beginning of his career in the 1890s, teamed with song-and-dance man George Walker as "Two Real Coons." In response to criticism of their "'good-time' Negro" stage personas, Williams and Walker had written to a professor at Western University, an African American college in Kansas, that they aimed to strike an "average" between "such characters as remind him ['the colored theatre 'goer''] of 'white folks'" and "the ante-bellum 'darkey'" who "might please the non-sympathetic, biased and prejudiced white man." They felt they were delineating "characters most familiar to-day," "draw[ing] from the mass and not from the few," and so reaching a much larger audience than would be possible if they tried to inspire young people of "our race" with portrayals of the "Oxford, Yale, Harvard and Cambridge graduates of color" that their critic, Professor Albert Ross, would have preferred. Their answer appeared narrowly professional and seemed to ignore Ross's taunt that "making money is not the greatest thing in life. Bettering mankind, uplifting your fellowmen, bring a far greater joy and personal contentment of mind and life spent in this world." But the answer clearly stemmed from the fear that, if they didn't black up and conform to the established pattern, not only would they lose the "tremendous influence" Ross credited them with, they would hardly be noticed, and whatever potential they may have had for bettering mankind would become negligible.[9]

Williams had worked solo since just before Walker's death in 1911 and by 1918 had become one of vaudeville and Broadway's greatest box-office draws, a successful recording artist, and a film actor. One wonders what a man trapped in blackface as the price of success, as Williams regarded himself, thought of Tom's burnt-cork routine. In some ways, Tom's persona was less objectionable than the minstrel prototypes it drew upon. Although the exact content of the act at this point is not known, in slightly later versions the humor depended on the blackface character's being easily frightened, sexually "loose," and bizarrely dressed, but it did not add to those features the razor-fighting, chicken-stealing, dice-throwing coon-song caricature. Moreover, the act depended as much, if not more, on music as on comedy for its effect on audiences, to judge from reviews, so an observer could appreciate the former aspect separately from the latter. Tom's reliance on pantomime rather than verbal humor may even have made the stage character less repulsive to Williams, since it could have been seen as the end of an ameliorating process by which the caricature was made less damaging—stage-darkey dialect giving way in the 1890s to standard English, then English to the nonverbal.

Midnight Frolic was still doing good business when the Brothers arrived in Chicago to open in the road version of *Jack o' Lantern* at the Colonial Theatre in Chicago on August 31, 1918, where it was a "sweeping success."[10] Very shortly after the opening, Fred Brown was obliged to leave the group, summoned by the draft to Pelham Bay, New York, for induction into the navy.[11] Since brother Percy was in Tom Brown's Clown Band in *Everything* (which had opened August 22) at the New York Hippodrome and Vern was probably already in the navy, the Chicago version of the Brothers likely included only three Browns—Tom, William, and Alec—along with Harry Fink and two unknown replacements, one of them probably Matthew Amaturo. But, as of the end of the preceding July, a new threat hung over the heads of the three remaining brothers, in the form of a law decreeing that on September 28, all British subjects between the ages of eighteen and forty-five (the limits for conscription into the king's armed forces) who resided in the United States and had not enlisted in the empire's service would become subject to the American draft, regardless of the fact that American citizens were liable only between the ages of twenty-one and thirty-one.[12] Tom and Alec, married men with children, must have been less nervous about the edict than William, but the prospect must still have been dreadful. It is not known how they dealt with the problem, but none of them enlisted. Fortunately, the war lasted only a little more than six weeks after the American deadline.

Another threat appeared in the fall. The so-called Spanish influenza, which was to prove the deadliest plague of the twentieth century, had been carried by returning soldiers from the trenches of Europe to the East Coast of North America. By early October, the fear of contagion had inspired emergency measures in many of the urban areas affected: closure of schools and churches, mandatory wearing of masks on the street, and strict quarantine of those infected. Show business was hard hit as theatres were shuttered in step with the moving front of the epidemic. Vaudeville and burlesque, dependent on complicated touring schedules among cities, were almost completely disrupted, since closures en route laid artists off unexpectedly, sometimes leaving them without means to arrive at the next engagement. By the beginning of October, all theatres in Massachusetts had been closed, along with those in major cities of Maine, New Hampshire, Vermont, Rhode Island, Connecticut, and upstate New York. Theatres that remained open often found themselves with insufficient business to cover expenses.[13] And many performers were among the twenty to forty million who perished and the millions more who suffered and recovered.

As the disease gripped Chicago, Jack o' Lantern was the only show that continued to do good business, but, over a period of a week in early October, attendance dropped sharply even at the Colonial. On Tuesday, October 15, performances were suspended altogether as all theatres in the Loop were ordered shut. At that point, Variety estimated that 90 percent of U.S. theatres were closed. Downtown Chicago remained dark for a little over two weeks, but a frightened populace bought few tickets through all of November. Finally, in December, as the first wave of the epidemic receded, Jack o' Lantern slowly returned to capacity business for a good finish before moving on to the Colonial Theatre in Boston for a Christmas opening.[14]

It is puzzling that, although the plague raged in New York as elsewhere, its theatres, those natural reservoirs of infection, never closed. In its October 11, 1918, issue, Variety began to run a weekly list of "Epidemic Casualties" in show business, including among the first victims Everything's "best male voice," Arthur Geary, forced by illness to leave the show on October 5.[15] Dozens more show people followed. Geary's fellow cast member Percy Brown fell ill about December 9, contracting pneumonia, a common Spanish influenza complication, on December 17 and dying what was probably a horrible death at New York's Misericordia Hospital on December 21. Allan Brown came south from Canada to accompany his son's remains back to Ottawa for burial on the day before Christmas.[16]

Jack o' Lantern played to packed houses in Boston except for a brief slump late in February, when theatrical business faltered throughout the city. A planned closing in mid-April was put off by continued capacity attendance until almost the end of the month, when the company returned to its tryout theatre, Philadelphia's Forrest, on April 28 for three successful weeks.[17] Shortly after the Forrest opening, Tom received a handsome gift from an admirer in Omaha, Dr. H. A. Waggener, an amateur saxophonist and collector of musical instruments.

Perhaps when *Chin Chin* played Omaha during the 1916–17 tour, Waggener, who led a group that emulated the Brothers, had made Tom's acquaintance, and the two began corresponding.[18] In early April of 1919, Waggener bought a soprano saxophone, manufactured around 1863[19] by the factory of Adolphe Sax himself, from Olaf E. Pedersen, a musician from Norway. Before Pedersen immigrated to the United States around 1890, he had played the instrument in the Royal Norwegian Band and the orchestra of the National Theatre. Waggener sent the instrument to Tom as a "token of . . . esteem and friendship." The pioneer saxophonist Clay Smith reported that

> the invincible Tom says it is the finest playing instrument . . . he has ever played on. Says it is in more perfect tune than any modern instrument, but the key action is not so perfect. Notwithstanding the fact that he has always been prejudiced against the soprano he intends using this old instrument instead of his E flat alto in making all his records.
>
> Tom went into ecstasies telling the writer about it, "Why Smithy, a fellow can attack a tone as softly as a violin and increase the tone to fortissimo without a waver. I never saw such a sensitive little thing in my life."

Tom reciprocated by coming to Omaha to appear with Waggener's saxophone octet in "an exact duplicate of the act [Tom] has been doing for the past two years," in a show staged by the Knights of Ak-Sar-Ben, a Nebraska businessmen's fraternal organization. Presented before an all-male audience, the "three-act extravaganza" was a men-only burlesque of the reform movement called "The Wandering Juice, or The Trail of the Lonesome Wine," in which "Terpsichore, the Goddess of Dancing; Nicotena, the Princess of Smokes, and Old John Barleycorn," were chased from earth to Olympus to Hades, finally finding a haven at the bottom of the sea. The Brown/Waggener interpolation, the hit of the show, ended with "as many encores as the stage hands would stand for."[20]

Despite Tom's enthusiasm for the Sax instrument, he didn't use it on any of his later discs released by the Victor or Emerson companies. He did, however, play it as a feature of his stage presentation from fall 1920 onward, and it was heard on a privately issued recording, of unknown date, of "Rosy Cheeks" and in a Vitaphone film short he made in 1927.[21]

Just before *Jack o' Lantern*'s May 17, 1919, closing in Philadelphia, the Brothers traveled to Camden for a two-day series of recordings for Victor, since they hadn't yet produced the fifteen complete and perfect master records called for in their May 1918 contract. Seven of the nine selections attempted were mastered, though only two were released by the still beleaguered company. "Peter Gink" and "Egyptland" came out in August on Victor 18562. A note in the recording book indicates that the master of Vincent Rose's "Oriental Fox Trot" was destroyed because Joseph C. Smith's Orchestra, Victor's top dance band, had already recorded the tune. "Missouri Blues," though mastered, may have been left on the shelf because the Brothers soon after cut it again for rival Emerson Records. It isn't known what determined the fate of the other three mastered numbers, "Off Again, On Again, Gone Again, Finnegan," "Cry Baby," and "Sweet Jazz o' Mine," but Victor may have been reacting to the Brown Brothers' defection to Emerson later in the summer.

"Peter Gink," George L. Cobb's rag constructed out of themes from Edvard Grieg's *Peer Gynt*, is presented in an unusually intricate arrangement. "Anitra's Dance," "In the Hall of the Mountain King," and "Morning Mood" are stretched and syncopated in a way that reportedly filled contemporary lovers of Grieg's music with horror.[22] Tom plays up to the top of the alto saxophone's normal range, ending both the second and third strains on a concert A-flat above the staff. Some discographers have claimed that there was a soprano saxophone in the ensemble, perhaps on the basis of these notes. But the timbre seems clearly to be that of an alto rather than a soprano, and, toward the end of the piece, Tom seems to be straining a bit for the note, which he wouldn't have had to do on a soprano. James W. Casey's "Egyptland" (arranged by Klickmann) is a verse-chorus song, taken at a fast tempo, with a sixteen-bar dogfight between the second and third statements of the chorus. The four-bar introduction in five-part harmony, with the baritone doubling the bass, leads to the "oriental" verse in F minor, written as a solo for Tom over a very active rhythmic hubbub. The first statement of the chorus (in D-flat major) is given to the first tenor sax over a marchlike rhythmic figure played by the two altos, while the other three provide an oom-pah foundation. The second statement is led by Tom in harmony with the second alto and first tenor; he plays with a passionate vibrato, but passes up a chance to play a high A-flat in the middle of the chorus. The dogfight goes abruptly to B-flat minor, with two short breaks by the baritone and bass in octaves, then modulates back to D-flat for the final statement of the chorus. Tom plays it with more abandon this time, bending the pitch on many notes (something he hadn't done on records since "Down Home Rag" four years earlier) and emphatically hitting the mid-chorus high A-flat.[23] The excitement of the variation is almost enough to overcome the monotony of three repetitions of the same slow-moving melody.

On June 6, after a little less than three weeks' liberty, the Browns joined the cast of the 1918–19 edition of *Midnight Frolic*, which had already been running for almost six months. The original cast had included the Ziegfeld veterans Fannie Brice, Lillian Lorraine, Bert Williams, and Bird Millman, along with the Ringling trapeze artist Lillian Leitzl, "without a doubt the greatest woman gymnast in the world," and Georgie Price, a teenaged boy who did blackface imitations of Al Jolson and Eddie Cantor. A shimmy-dancing theme ran through the show, Bee Palmer vibrating her shoulders as she sang "Let Me Shimmie and Be Satisfied" and Bert Williams responding with "You Cannot Shake Your Shimmie Here."[24] Williams, however, had left the show by June, and Will Rogers had joined the shifting *Frolic* roster.[25] Whoever the other June 1919 principals may have been, the spectacle, according to Sime Silverman, consisted of "numbers and songs, songs and numbers, clothes and women."[26] The Brothers "scored one of the biggest triumphs of their career."[27]

Ziegfeld was trying to boost Roof profits that summer by running an early show, the *Nine o' Clock Revue*, concurrently with the *Follies* and charging separate admissions for the *Revue* and the *Frolic*. The experiment worked, enduring several years until the national prohibition of liquor sales sent the hard-drinking nightclub crowd into speakeasies. Silverman complained about the $3.30/$2.75-per-show admission and the $10-per-bottle wine at the same time that he recognized the great advantage to Ziegfeld of the house's 35 percent share of the added sales.[28] Roof business improved even further when the new *Follies* brought after-show crowds to the *Frolic*.[29] In order to encourage repeat customers, a new *Frolic* edition was planned to open around August 20, perhaps with the Brothers in the new cast, but a strike by the Actors' Equity Association, beginning on August 7, forced a postponement.[30] At first the strike did not directly affect Ziegfeld, since there were not many Equity members among his artists, largely drawn from vaudeville and burlesque rather than the dramatic stage. However, on August 17, the New Amsterdam stagehands walked out in sympathy, causing the *Follies*, the *Nine o' Clock Revue*, and the *Frolic* to fold.[31]

Perhaps impatient with Victor's inability to produce and the ten still unreleased sides from 1918 and 1919, the Brown Brothers signed with the upstart Emerson label, which released their first efforts in mid-October.[32] Victor's exclusive option on their services had lapsed May 1, 1919, and, when a new contract was offered on July 25, it didn't include an exclusive-artist clause. At any rate, Tom didn't accept the contract until October 15, giving the Brothers ample time to perform for Emerson without violating the clause forbidding them to become exclusive artists for any other company.[33] Emerson had been founded in 1915 by Victor Emerson, "a major figure in Columbia [Graphophone Company]'s growth" in the two preceding decades.[34] At first the firm had marketed only six- and seven-inch discs, but in June 1919 they went into the ten-inch field, attempting to compete with the industry heavyweights, Columbia and Victor, both by signing well-known recording artists and by getting their versions of new song hits into the public's hands "one to five months in advance of the competition." "While other manufacturers take *months* to release a new number," said an August 1916 ad, "we take *weeks*. Broadway's stamp of approval [on a song] is our cue to act." Emerson succeeded in capturing a substantial share of sales in the short run. Among their early signings for the new ten-inch series were the Six Brown Brothers. Although Brian Rust's estimate of a July 1919 recording date for the two Brothers discs announced in October would be about right for a Victor issue—June's "Peter Gink"/"Egyptland" (Victor 18562) was announced in August—Emerson's claim of a minimum "3 Weeks From Broadway to Your Store" makes an August or even September waxing possible.[35] Emerson first announced the signing, "during the past few weeks," of the Brothers in the September 15 issue of *Talking Machine World*.[36]

Since Emerson documents comparable to the Victor recording books are not known to exist, information about which and how many titles were attempted, like information about recording dates, is lacking. Five sides were issued, including a literal repeat of the Victor "Peter Gink"; "Carolina Sunshine," the Brothers' first released waltz; "The Concourse March"; "Missouri Blues," a number Victor was still holding from the May session; and a medley of three popular songs: "I'll Say She Does," "I'm Forever Blowing Bubbles," and "Smiles," the last of which had been a Lillian Lorraine feature in *Midnight Frolic*.

"Peter Gink," Emerson's gauntlet across Victor's cheek, offers a chance to contrast the two firms' recording qualities. The Emerson sound is warmer, probably owing both to a studio with more reverberation and to an emphasis on the reproduction of midrange frequencies at the expense of higher ones (very similar to Columbia's sound). Victor's sound, both more brilliant and deader, makes it easier to hear the individual instruments, while Emerson's makes it easier to identify their timbres, for instance on the "Dawn" theme, which sounds as if it could be carried by either a tenor or a baritone on the Victor version, while it is clearly being played by a tenor on the Emerson. "Carolina Sunshine" is a pleasant and unremarkable three-strain number, obviously designed for the dance market, and played in two-part harmony with fleeting countermelodies in the tenor over a muffled background. The joyful circus flavor of "The Concourse March" recalls "Independentia" more than "Pussyfoot March." Marches in 6/8 meter, such as "Concourse" or Sousa's "Washington Post," had once been popular as music for two-stepping, but by 1919 big-city dancers had abandoned the two-step for the foxtrot, so it is hard to imagine what Emerson had in mind for this number's commercial exploitation. Two features lend some excitement and interest to what is otherwise a run-of-the-mill march. First is the Brothers' punchy though familiar effect of the bass and baritone saxes playing in octaves, used here both in the second strain, played twice, and in the dogfight between statements of the trio. Second is a delightful alto sax obbligato over the second and third statements of the trio, coming as both a surprise and a relief after the first, unadorned statement in three-part harmony over a modified oom-pah background. "Concourse," incidentally, was not released until December.

The most interesting of the Emerson recordings are "Missouri Blues" and the "I'll Say She Does" medley. The former is a simple three-strain composition in medium tempo, whose third strain is a 4/4 paraphrase of the 1901 perennial "Missouri Waltz." The melodies of the other two strains follow the older, raggy tradition of "The Darktown Strutters' Ball" and "Walkin' the Dog," rather than the smoother, less syncopated, current popular-song model exemplified in "Smiles," one of 1918's biggest hits.[37]

The medley is remarkable for several reasons. First, it presents a condensed version of part of the Brothers' stage routine, starting with a few 6/8 bars of "Hail, Hail, the Gang's All Here" as an introduction before leaping into the three up-tempo 4/4 fox-trot hits. ("Chicken Reel Comedy Medley" has a similar structure: a few introductory bars of *Poet and Peasant*, followed by a medley of popular tunes.) Second, after fast-moving harmonized statements of "I'll Say She Does" and "Smiles" comes a surprise in the form of an impressive virtuoso cornet or trumpet obbligato over a reprise of "Smiles," in a style that mixes an approach like that of the concert soloist Herbert L. Clarke (long featured with Sousa's band) with syncopations and fluttertonguing from the bag of the Original Dixieland Jazz Band's cornetist Nick La Rocca. The cornetist gets no separate credit either on the record label or in the Emerson catalog, but, since the saxophone background doesn't audibly change between the first and second times through "Smiles," it is possible that the player is an unnamed guest artist. (It could also be Harry Fink, whose photographs in the Vincent Lopez Hotel Pennsylvania Orchestra, which he joined after leaving the Brothers, show him with a trumpet among his array of instruments and whose November 3, 1951, obituary in the *New York Times* mentioned his notable talent as a trumpet player.) A 4/4 paraphrase of the waltz "I'm Forever Blowing Bubbles" follows the "Smiles" pattern, the saxophones playing it twice with a difficult and astonishingly poised cornet obbligato laid over the repeat.

For reasons now unknown, Tom found the Emerson discs unsatisfactory and expressed doubt whether the Brothers would make more of them, although they went on to make several over the next year. He also felt that his contract with Victor amounted to little from a financial point of view. Dillingham suggested that a Columbia contract would be more lucrative and offered to act as an intermediary.[38] Unfortunately for the scheme and probably unknown to Dillingham, Columbia might not have been receptive to such a proposal, since they had just begun releasing the first in a long series of recordings by the Columbia Saxophone Sextette, organized by the energetic musical entrepreneur Harry A. Yerkes.[39] It is not known whether Dillingham ever approached Columbia about the matter. At any rate, the Browns did not pick up a Columbia contract.

In apparent tribute to the Brown Brothers' star status, John Philip Sousa began in the summer of 1919 to feature a saxophone sextet in the concert tours of his internationally famous band, as encores to the solo work of H. Benne Henton. Among the "popular syncopated melodies" played by the new ensemble was George L. Cobb's "Russian Rag,"[40] a Rossiter publication endorsed by the Brothers in *Variety* shortly before Sousa's tour started.[41] This emulation (if it was that) by the best-established figure in American popular music marked the Browns' new importance as clearly as Ziegfeld's recognition had, and for a national audience that might never travel to New York or be able to afford the Amsterdam Roof's high prices.

Jack o' Lantern's demanding 1919–20 tour took it to thirty-one cities (Baltimore twice) in thirty-six weeks, ranging as far west as Kansas City and Omaha and ending with return engagements in Boston (three April weeks, again at the Colonial) and the New York area (this time at the Montauk in Brooklyn for a week in mid-May).[42] Success greeted the show at every stop, despite the high ticket prices (a top $3 on the road plus the 10 percent war tax, raised to $3.50 plus tax in Brooklyn).[43] New Year's Eve found the company in St. Louis (at the American Theatre), where they celebrated the holiday with a midnight cast party featuring a travesty of the show, called Jack o' Lantern Upside Down, "presented by members of the company as a testimonial to Mr. and Mrs. Fred Stone." All the actors cross-dressed, with Theresa as Jack, Stone's longtime stage manager Charles Mast as Zingarella (Theresa's character), and the Brothers as interpolated characters May, Gladys, Bessie, Tessie, Nora Marks, and Iona Mann (respectively Tom, Vern, Harry Fink, William, Fred, and Alec). The program credits include the note, "The theater perfumed by the East St. Louis Stock Yards," and the warning that, during the post-performance meal, "to prevent pie being taken from the table, there ain't going to be any pie." In the small hours, Tom Brown and His Jazz Band played for dancing.[44]

In spite of the way the act had prospered under Dillingham's control, Tom was growing restive. As early as 1916, he had gotten assurances from Dillingham that some unspecified "stunt" would headline Tom or the Brothers in the 1917–18 season, but they appeared in Jack o' Lantern instead. At some point in 1919, Tom again put in a bid for "something big, that would be our life's opportunity to get some 'real' money," this time specified as a minstrel show with the Browns as the main attraction. After an interview with Dillingham, Tom thought he had a promise for such a production in 1920–21, but Dillingham wrote him that he had misunderstood and that the agreement was for 1921–22. A new Stone show was in the works for fall 1920, and Dillingham made it clear that he intended the Brothers to be in it. A revival of minstrelsy, said the producer, would be "no good" if it were like minstrel shows of the past: "It must be so different and so entertaining that we could not possibly get one up in a few months." Being in New York for the first season of the new Stone show, Dillingham assured him, would give Tom an opportunity to get the new venture together. Disappointed but powerless to change his boss's decision, Tom acceded but asked for a hefty raise to $950 per week for the 1920–21 season.[45] In the event, he got a raise to $1,000, but he didn't get the minstrel show.

Once or twice during the tour, the Brothers were in New York long enough to make more records for Emerson, which were announced in the May, June, and July 1920 issues of Talking Machine World. One of the sides, "Twelfth Street Rag," bears the matrix number 4688, placing it somewhat later than the 1919 numbers (4437 through 4441), but the other five bear the numbers 41105 through 41109, suggesting that they were waxed within a day or two of each other. The best recording opportunities would have been the week of March 8–14, when *Jack o' Lantern* played Newark, and the week of March 28 through April 4, when the company laid off between stands in Springfield, Massachusetts, and Boston. Fred Brown, at least, was in New York during the Newark stand long enough to marry Leita Randall, a beautiful member of the *Jack o' Lantern* chorus, with Fred Stone acting as "master of ceremonies" at the Little Church around the Corner.[46]

The orchestrations on the 1920 Emersons (possibly by Klickmann, since he is the composer of one of the selections, "Lazy Jazz Waltz") are more intricate and display a more varied texture than the Brothers' earlier charts. Perhaps the new style was adopted in response to the competing recordings of the Columbia Saxophone Sextette, the first of which had been issued in May 1919.[47] The Columbia group had a much lighter and more florid sound and frequently featured extra instruments, like the cornet or trumpet on the Brothers' "I'll Say She Does" medley. Tom's alto still carries the melody most of the time, but there is much more sharing with Harry's tenor and the team of bass and baritone in octaves. Movement in the inner voices appears more often, perhaps emulating the polyphony of the early jazz bands, where cornet, clarinet, and trombone each went its own way. The resulting sound, however, is much more orchestral than jazzy.

Two of the numbers, "Alexandria" and "Fatima," fall into the same "oriental" category as "Egyptland," but both offer a lot more musical interest. "Egyptland" is a straightforward verse-chorus song with a dogfight, and the arranger does little to differentiate the three statements of the chorus. "Fatima," however, has three strains, and, although the first strain is played three times, the repetitions are separated from each other and from the initial statement by other strains, a strategy that avoids the monotony of a single theme played over and over. Klickmann gave the first statement of "Egyptland"'s chorus to the first tenor sax and the other two to the first alto, but the arrangement of "Fatima" introduces more voices more often, passing the lead from tenor in the first strain to alto in the second and from alto to the baritone-bass duo in the third. Two of "Alexandria"'s three strains are dominated by the alto sax, but movement in the inner voices and the first strain's unexpected length of thirty-six bars, rather than the conventional thirty-two, keep it interesting, and in the third strain the melody is traded back and forth between the higher and lower saxes.

Klickmann's composition "Lazy Jazz Waltz" (puzzlingly subtitled "Sweet Hawaiian Moonlight") features prominent countermelodies in the tenor sax almost throughout, giving this medium-tempo waltz much more life and interest than the previous year's "Carolina Sunshine." Klickmann also varies the voicing between the first and second statements of the first theme, first splitting the melody between tenor and alto, then giving it entirely to the alto with a tenor countermelody. (Even considering the many different ways in which the word "jazz" was used in 1920, it's difficult to guess at the motives of the person who gave this piece its title. "Lazy Jazz Waltz" has only a few bars of syncopation, its limited polyphony doesn't recall that of early jazz bands, and it has neither the speed nor the energy of the 1917 "Jazz Rag," "Smiles and Chuckles." But it does end with a two-bar cadential tag characteristic of the ODJB's records.) "Rainbow of My Dreams" is a vigorous and unremarkable fox-trot played in a medley with "Norse Maid" to lend a little thematic variety to the performance. After the last four bars of "Rainbow"'s chorus are deployed as an introduction, the altos and first tenor play the melody of its habanera verse in three-part harmony over the usual rhythm, yielding, at the chorus, to Tom's solo statement over a bubbling background. The next two choruses are a straightforward rendering of the chorus of "Norse Maid," again for a three-saxophone choir in harmony, after which the chorus of "Rainbow" returns, indistinguishable from its first appearance. Although a cornet is sporadically audible in the ensemble, it stays in the background.

The flip side, "Jazz Band Blues" (a "Slap" White composition), provides more interest and excitement than "Rainbow," but, like "Lazy Jazz Waltz," would have been a disappointment to a purchaser expecting jazz, even by the vague and evolving understanding of the term current in 1920. In form, the piece is an AABBCA rag with an introduction at the beginning and another just before C, rounded out with a one-bar tag that repeats the final cadence in ODJB fashion, and all strains are the expected sixteen bars long. Rhythmically, its pattern of dotted eighths and sixteenths sounds stiff compared to the "swung" patterns that were creeping into the sound of jazz bands. Melodically, it invokes the blues by using a familiar motif from W. C. Handy's "St. Louis Blues" and "Joe Turner Blues" in the A strain (the phrase that goes "Got the St. Louis Blues"). But what makes it interesting is the roving presence of a saxophone that sounds a little drunk, "laughing" in the A strain and bending his pitch in bars 5–6 and 9–10 of the B strain—the sort of thing that could have been exaggerated and accompanied by stage business in live performance. It is hard to tell whether the featured saxophonist is Tom (playing in his lower register) or the tenor player, but in the C strain the tenor is clearly a prominent solo voice.

The most elaborate and interesting side is "Twelfth Street Rag," where inner-voice movement pervades the arrangement and the melody often moves from instrument to instrument. The first strain, not heard on most recordings (for example, the famous and long-lived 1928 Victor disc by Bennie Moten and His Kansas City Orchestra), features some call-and-response figures for the high and low saxes, and the second strain's melody, played mostly by Tom, is punctuated by brief responses from the second alto and first tenor, with a longer break by the bass and baritone at the strain's midpoint and background glissando figures in bars 25–28. The fourth strain pits a strong and simple tenor-sax countermelody against the repeated three-eighth-note figure that dominates the melody (a simple inversion of the second strain's) and again heads off monotony by complicating the texture.

These six sides were to be the Brothers' last for Emerson. "Overexpansion, lower-than-expected sales, and an unhealthy level of debt forced the Emerson organization . . . into receivership on December 10, 1920."[48] As the company staggered onward under a series of new owners before succumbing in 1927, its subsequent releases continued to emphasize current hits, while relying less on expensive recording artists to make its offerings more attractive than those of its rivals. The firm's advertising, on the other hand, still featured rosters of its heyday artists. As late as 1923, these included the Six Brown Brothers, though the 1919–20 discs that had once sold for a standard 75 cents had been discounted to 50 cents.[49]

The Emerson sides were almost the last records the Browns made, but they still had obligations to Victor under their very generous 1919 contract. Tom had agreed to make eighteen records over three years for $9,000, an increase of 25 percent per master over the 1918 fee. Since at least six were to be made each year,[50] the Browns were already behind by six when they returned to the Victor Recording Laboratory on November 22, 1920, a few weeks after their next Fred Stone show, *Tip Top*, opened. Only a single day was devoted to the effort, during which all three titles attempted issued in good takes, though Victor released only two of them, a medley from *Tip Top* and another from *Tickle Me*, another new Broadway attraction, but one with which the Brothers had no connection. Perhaps Victor was emulating Emerson in its unusually quick announcement of the result (Victor 18714) in the January 1921 number of *Talking Machine World*. Giving the title "Tip Top—Medley" to the first side and "If a Wish Could Make It So (Intro. Tickle Me)" to the second, thus invoking the names of the shows from which the tunes came, may also be seen as a response to Emerson's emphasis on the connection between the recordings and their Broadway sources.

The medley from *Tip Top* opens with a brief introduction, followed by the verse and two choruses of "Wonderful Girl, Wonderful Boy," then the verse and two choruses of "The Girl I Never Met," and ends with a reprise of the chorus of "Wonderful Girl, Wonderful Boy." Both songs have an appealing sweetness and bounce, helped along by a cheerful countermelody from the tenor on the first song's chorus and some graceful three-voice polyphony on the second song's verse. The other medley is taken at a slightly slower tempo, so there isn't time for the verses of both songs. We hear the verse and two choruses of "If a Wish Could Make It So," two choruses of "Tickle Me," and a reprise of "If a Wish Could Make It So." The arrangement on this side is somewhat less complex than the one on the other, but very much in the same joyful, danceable style. The Victor engineers put Vern closer to the recording horn for this side, so that he is louder throughout and well positioned for his brief featured spots. The resulting disc is an excellent dance record, soon to become outmoded as the dance-band revolution initiated by Art Hickman (who made his own successful Columbia disc of "If a Wish Could Make It So") and Paul Whiteman took over the market.

The title not released by Victor, George L. Cobb's "Shivaree," was mastered, held, and finally destroyed in 1926, when the new electrical recording technology had rendered the disc's sound obsolete and unsuitable for release on a major label (although smaller labels continued to issue acoustically recorded discs for several years). A test pressing from that master, however, is the probable source for one side of a privately issued disc bearing a "Six Brown Bros. Saxophone Records" label in the National Music Museum.[51] "Shivaree" is one of the oddest pieces the Brothers recorded. Perhaps that was the reason it was withheld from release, since its fast pace and impeccable playing make it exciting listening. In this ragtime adaptation of Schubert's "Serenade," Cobb went a step beyond "Peter Gink" (and his better-known "Russian Rag," featured but never recorded by the Brothers, based on Rachmaninoff's "Prelude in C-sharp Minor") in that, instead of trimming Schubert's amorous lament to fit the sixteen- or thirty-two-bar strain lengths[52] of a normal rag, he used A and B strains of twenty-four and twenty bars each, with a trio or C strain of the customary thirty-two bars, in the overall familiar structure of a four-bar introduction followed by AABBACC. The first two readings of the A strain throw the listener off balance with an *aa'b* form, each section of which is eight bars long, so that, when the strain is repeated, its *a* section starts out seeming to be the end of the first statement rather than the beginning of the second. The B strain starts out with an eight-bar section, then surprises the listener with an extended twelve-bar second part. Both the A and B strains begin in minor mode, itself somewhat unusual in ragtime, but the B strain ends in major, compounding the strangeness. After all this contravention of audience expectation, the trio comes as something of a relief, an easy, songlike strain in comfortable eight-bar chunks and Sousa-march *abac* form with only a little weirdness in the harmonic progression at the beginning of the *b* section. Tom's strong, wailing lead is set off by lots of contrasting figures in the other voices, including clean chromatic runs and Vern's pumping bass.

The end of the Six Brown Brothers' recording career found them playing at the highest level they had reached. One wonders why they never recorded again (except for a couple of soundtrack discs for the Talking Picture Company and Vitaphone), and in particular why they failed to fulfill their lucrative Victor contract. Perhaps some forgotten dispute with Victor, together with the failing fortunes of Emerson and a precipitous general decline in the record business in 1921, left them without a label willing to pay the Brothers' fee of $500 per side. Or Perhaps Victor took advantage of the group's violation of the contract to cancel it, given the changing taste of record buyers (although the sextet's final Victor disc ultimately sold a very healthy 199,453 copies).[53] The Browns could provide neither the small-band hot jazz that had been popular since the ODJB's 1917 shellac debut nor the newer "sweet jazz" that catapulted Art Hickman's and Paul Whiteman's Orchestras to the top of the dance-record heap in 1920 and 1921.[54] Whiteman's 1920 coupling of "Wang Wang Blues" and "Anytime, Anyday, Anywhere" on Victor 18694, for example, sold 457,080 units.[55] The Brothers' unique sound, so engaging in the stage context of Tom's clowning, may have come to seem old hat on the Victrola in the postwar living room, where the young people gathered to dance. The period from 1917 to 1920 had seen a small flood of recording by saxophone ensembles, but their days were numbered, even as discs with saxophone solos and the developing sound of dance-band sax sections welled into a new and vastly larger flood.

12

Tip Top

1920–23

When the long-lived road company of *Jack o' Lantern* dissolved in May 1920, the future plans of the Six Brown Brothers were unclear. Although Tom, on the act's behalf, had signed a contract in March to appear in *Tip Top*, the new Fred Stone vehicle projected for the fall, rumors circulated that Tom was organizing a 150-piece saxophone band for another of Dillingham's autumn spectacles, the new Hippodrome show, ultimately entitled *Good Times*.[1] The idea of an oversized saxophone ensemble had been floated three years earlier, when a *Variety* piece announced that "Tom Brown is to organize a saxophone band of 60 pieces for the next Hippodrome show, probably with the brothers as a nucleus."[2] No such group seems to have emerged, however, and the fall of 1917 found the Brothers in *Jack o' Lantern*. A similar idea surfaced again in April 1920, when Tom advertised in *Variety* for "(60) Real Saxophone Players (60) for Summer Engagement," warning that "Only the Best Need Apply."[3] Whether the summer project materialized or not, neither *Variety* nor *Billboard* took notice of it, and the Brothers themselves were otherwise engaged.

After appearing at New York's Hudson Theatre in a May 23 benefit for the Relief Fund of the Treasurers Club of America, along with Ed Wynn, Eva Tanguay, and more than two dozen other acts, the Brothers laid off for a few weeks.[4] Perhaps it was during this hiatus that they reportedly made an experimental sound-movie short (now lost) for the Talking Picture Company of New York.[5] Tom traveled to Omaha for the June 7 opening of that year's Ak-Sar-Ben show, *Sky-Low*, where he was featured with H. A. Waggener's saxophone octet.[6] By mid-June, the Brothers were reunited for their summer gig, headlining a revue at the Marigold Gardens in Chicago that also featured, along with the usual singers, dancers, comedians, gymnasts, and shimmy-dancing chorus, a fashion show exhibiting "everything from sable coats to lace underwear."[7]

When *Good Times* opened on August 9, neither the Brothers nor the rumored saxophone regiment was on the bill.[8] The Brothers seem to have stayed at the Marigold until late August, when rehearsals began at the Globe in New York for *Tip Top*,[9] which was to be their main showcase for the next three years. The new Stone/Dillingham collaboration began a two-week pre-Broadway run at the Forrest in Philadelphia on September 22. *Variety's* Sime Silverman reported a negative anticipatory buzz among competing New York producers:

> "That Stone show is a terrible thing," said one. "Guess Dillingham has gone off his nut," said another. "He thinks he can get away with murder just on the Stone name." "Have you seen the Stone show? What a show! Cost a lot of money? You're crazy. I could duplicate the entire production for $12,000." "Well, it's sure to run a few weeks on the Stone draw." "Say, if I tried to put over one like that they would drive me out of town."

Nevertheless, the musical opened to enthusiastic reviews. In Silverman's opinion, "Dillingham and Fred Stone turned out a great show. . . . You will want to see it, and your kiddies will make you let them see it. It's another 'Jack o' Lantern' and better than that."[10] Alexander Woollcott called it "just such a show as 'Chin-Chin' was, and 'Jack-o-Lantern,' just such another extravaganza of sound and color as gives a wonderful and ageless clown a fresh chance to provoke the still unanswered query, 'Say, is there anything that Fred Stone can't do?'"[11]

Different reviewers take different views of exactly what *Tip Top's* plot is, so much so that the differences might have to be explained by actual changes in the plot from season to season, or even from venue to venue. In a script in the Billy Rose Theatre Collection of the New York Public Library, the action turns on the behind-the-scenes attempts of the Fairy Justicia, whose supernatural mission is to ensure that love affairs go well, to patch up two relationships she has so far managed badly. The two pairs of lovers are Tipton Topping (Fred Stone) and Jinia Jones (Theresa Valerio), and Dick Derby (Scott Welsh, later replaced by the Arrow collar model Roy Hoyer) and Alice Barker (Gladys Caldwell, later replaced by Marie Sewell). Justicia is to be aided in her campaign by two lawyers (actually cats disguised as humans), and her reward for success will be an end to her exile from Fairyland. Since the script covers only the first act, the original dénouement is unknown, but reviews and programs indicate that most of the stage events have to do with Stone's efforts, in various disguises, to inform Dick of the latter's unexpected $5 million inheritance, simultaneously trying to save the money from pursuing villains. One reviewer referred to "what may, for purposes of analysis, be called the story. It is hardly a story, though it gives to the performance a certain continuity and it lapses, with easy facility, into moments of mirth, melody and maidens, backgrounded against settings that reflect the usual Dillingham taste."[12]

After the overture, the curtain rises on a courtroom populated by human-sized cats, where the young and attractive Miss Puff is on trial for an obscure offense. The Globe Theatre chorus girls constitute the jury, four of the Brown Brothers (William, Vern, Alec, and Harry Fink, listed as "Harry Brown") are Court Attendants, and Fred Brown is the Court Clerk (with a very brief speaking role). The opening chorus and dialogue are as full of low puns and silly jokes as a minstrel first part. When Miss Puff begins to faint, Judge Tiger, "gazing amorously" at her, says, "Give that cat - a - piller." When she complains that her hair is mussed, he says, "Give the cat - a - comb." Judge Tiger interrogates Miss Puff's rough alley-cat fiancé, Charlie Youngcat:

> Judge Tiger: You took her out in your car.
> Charlie: Yes.
> Judge Tiger: What make was it?
> Charlie: A Catallac.
> Judge Tiger: Didn't you swear to be true to her all her life?
> Charlie: Yes—but she had nine lives.
> Judge Tiger: Wasn't she a kind loving cat to you?
> Charlie: No, she treated me like a dog.
> Judge Tiger: When you made love to her didn't you promise to marry her?
> Charlie: No, I was on the fence.

At this point, Miss Puff invokes Justicia, who appears, explains her status as an overseer of romance, and produces Dick and Alice as an example of her failure.[13] A black curtain drops for Justicia's specialty song, "Little Fairy in the Home," a comic homily on the advantages of having children. The song continues as another curtain is revealed, this one with fourteen small, proscenium-framed openings for the chorus's "Doll Girls" number. Each frame contains a dancing, singing little-girl doll, whose head is that of a chorus girl and whose legs and feet are her arms and hands. The scene closes with yet another black drop providing a background for a dance by the Blue and Red Cats.

The second scene is laid in the shop of Alice's stern father, Mr. Barker, with the chorus attired as shoppers in silk shoes, lace dresses, and oversized straw bonnets with flowers on the brims and ribbons trailing almost to their knees. Alice and Dick take the opportunity to dance to "The Girl Who Keeps Me Guessing," soon joined by the shoppers, and Alice's two mischievous younger twin sisters, Bad and Worse (the vaudeville team Vivian and Rosetta Duncan) appear, exchanging insults. The action is interrupted by the sound of an explosion and the sight of Fred Stone, his head covered with foam, catapulted onto the stage, a result of Tip Top's having put one too many raisins into the home brew he was making in the cellar of Barker's shop. After explaining, he jokes and flirts with the shoppers, sings his recurring signature number, "I Want a Lily," dances both solo and with the chorus, and rescues Jinia from Mr. Barker, giving Theresa and Fred an excuse to sing and dance their big duet number, "I Don't Belong on a Farm." Barker fires Dick and forbids him to court Alice any longer, somehow providing a chance for more ensemble dancing with Fred, Theresa, and the chorus, followed by the arrival of a letter announcing Dick's inheritance. The scene closes with one of Stone's physical-comedy set pieces as he makes a getaway with the letter: "he did a bewildering acrobatic stunt with a barrel, leaped as nimbly as a gazelle from one piece of furniture to another and ended by bounding over the footlights onto a bass drum, from which he bounced back among the chorus as easily as if he had been made of India rubber."[14]

Now that the main continuity device has been introduced, interpolations only very loosely related to the plot proliferate. The third scene takes us to the exterior of a school, where another chorus, the London Palace Girls, imported from England by Dillingham for the 1920 season, does the "Dance of the School Girls," carrying slates and clad in white socks and knee-length plaid school dresses with matching bonnets and white aprons. They "are not, of course, as beautiful as the American ensemble," remarked one critic, "but they do dance infinitely better."[15] Other reviewers praised the precision of the young Englishwomen, "whose lefts kick as one, their rights the same, whose heels tap together, and whose every movement is in unison—a sweep and dash of melodious motion that captured the house."[16] "And how the London Palace Girls can dance, with the accuracy and uniformity of so many shuttles on a row of spinning machines!"[17] Once the scene behind the schoolhouse-exterior drop has been shifted, we see the schoolroom, where part of the Globe chorus concentrates on lessons until the Duncan Sisters enter and do a vaudeville turn (with Vivian at the piano) of little-girl jokes and close harmony on jazzy current tunes such as "Left All Alone Again Blues" and "April Showers," along with parodies of antiquated favorites such as "Darling Nelly Gray" and "Oh, Dem Golden Slippers."

During the schoolhouse scene, the audience learns that Dick has gone west to Red Canyon, with Tip not far behind and the audience only a little farther. The Red Canyon setting and costumes are mentioned by most reviewers as the most spectacular of the show. The Globe chorus, as "Sixteen Indian Girls," dances to Broadway's idea of Native American music, soon joined by the London Palace Girls as "Sixteen More Indian Girls." Tip Top, disguised as a southwestern indigene in braids, buckskin, and beads (see figure 10), enters to sing "Keewa-Tax-e-Yaka-holo," a satirical song partly in a made-up language, partly in English, backed by the thirty-two spear-carrying women in feather headdresses and long skirts split to the knee. Then begins what the audience has been waiting for most, Fred Stone's new bag of tricks for the season. First is a demonstration of Australian whip cracking, in which the "snapping end [of the lash] flicks a cigar from an assistant's face, snips paper, uncorks a bottle and snatches the wig off the assistant's head,"[18] besides "cutting an apple in two while another man holds it in his fingers, lighting a match . . . and . . . extinguishing it."[19] Amazed by the whip turn, the cheering audience then sees Charles Mast, as the Squaw, throw a hundred resin balls in the air one by one while Stone, dancing, blasts them to pieces with a .22 rifle. Stone later estimated that he averaged ninety-seven or ninety-eight successful shots per night,[20] but many reviewers stated that he shattered every ball. The finale of both scene and act brings back the thirty-two chorus girls and adds a spirited show horse on a treadmill for some acrobatic bareback riding by the star.

The second act opens at a beach resort, the latest stop in Tip Top's pursuit of Dick, and the site of a family vacation for Alice, her father, and her sisters. Both the Globe chorus and the Palace Girls appear in beach attire, though nothing as sexy as the audience would see in a Ziegfeld show. The Londoners wear Louis heels, long dark stockings to show off their attractive legs, loose mid-thigh-length striped trunks, beribboned middy blouses, and gypsy head-scarves, while the Americans sport more provocative loose tank tops over short, curve-hiding polka-dot bloomers; white stockings and soft caps complete the visual contrast between the two ensembles. After the Globe chorus's opening song and dance, Alice and Dick meet unexpectedly to sing a tune together, then with the chorus, and then to dance to it. The Duncan Sisters do another kiddie number before Tip Top arrives, clad in a linen summer suit with an enormous chest and oversize collar that allow him to retract his head, turtlewise, for quick changes of facial appearance, such as adding a mustache. Following some plot-advancing dialogue, Stone sings a song about bathing beauties ("The Wild, Wild Waves"), and closes the scene dancing both solo and with the London Palace Girls.

Act 2, scene 2, "Melodyville," belongs entirely to the Six Brown Brothers, who work in front of a shimmering gold drop[21] as the scenery behind is prepared for the finale. They enter one by one, "marching around the stage"[22] in new black-and-white costumes with their newly gold-plated instruments moving up and down in unison, with Tom in the forefront playing Irving Berlin's current hit "All By Myself." Then comes a medley of popular tunes (plus a bit of *Poet and Peasant*) that changed to keep up with the song market over the three years' tour. In March 1921, it included "Whispering," "Margie," and "Love Nest,"[23] but by February 1922, those tunes were all out, replaced by "Twelfth Street Rag," "Wabash Blues," "The Sheik," and others. The Brothers wowed the audience as always with their punchy, exciting versions of the latest melodies. But the costumes, gold plating, and playlist were not the only new features. Tom had worked up a novel comedy routine using elements documented earlier, such as his Sousa burlesque (from perhaps as early as 1910), his moaning and sobbing on the sax (from at least 1913 and 1916), and a musical "conversation" between Tom and the other five using phrases from songs the audience was sure to recognize. Reviewers began to mention the conversation format in early 1920 during *Jack o' Lantern*'s last year on the road, but they didn't mention the device that gave form to the *Tip Top* version: Tom's impersonation of a pregnant African American woman whose husband-to-be fails to show up for their wedding. Instead of the wigs, dresses, and padding of minstrel days, Tom chose the barest indication of femininity, a long, unmistakable bridal veil added to his familiar stage outfit. The abandoned-bride episode would become the

Browns' centerpiece for as long as the act endured. Tom described the routine in a letter to Waggener five months into the run: at the end of the opening medley, Tom is seated on a stool at center stage with the other Brothers standing around him in a semicircle,

> finishing with the last strain of Ghost dance with the clowns creeping as close as possible to the stool to appear as though they were trying to frighten the nigger. This gets big applause and nigger EXITS. Then the clowns move over to the left stage and play HERE COMES THE BRIDE. I walk in slowly [wearing the bridal veil] and stand in the centre of stage for a second with a long staring look in my face (which gets a laugh) and play, There was I waiting at the church, (CLOWNS) WEDDING MARCH. (I PLAY) ROCK A BYE BABY (CLOWNS) OH WHAT A PAL WAS MARY. (I PLAY) NOBODY KNOWS AND NOBODY CARES. (CLOWNS) HAIL HAIL THE GANGS ALL HERE. (I PLAY) WHAT THE HELL DO I CARE. (CLOWNS) HOOCHY COOCHY (I PLAY) YOU MADE ME WHAT I AM TODAY I HOPE YOUR [sic] SATISFIED. Then I walk as though I was going to leave them when I hear them start to play SWEET ADELINE I turn back smilingly and do the DIRECTING to SWEET ADELINE (which is a big success) then at the finish of the directing after I do the scratching (Which gets a big laugh—) I run off and take off the bridal veil and get back in time to line up for the RUSSIAN RAG which is the finish of the act. Of course we do the dance with the rag which helps to put it over.[24]

Tom's schematic account omits the aspect that transformed a simple comic idea into a routine that convulsed audiences and led Gilbert Seldes to call the Brothers' work exquisite and Alexander Woollcott to call Tom "funny beyond words." The bride doesn't simply say "Rock-a-bye, baby": she says it with a mixture of courage and diffidence. Her "What the hell do I care?" is defiant at first, but then is repeated in a way that makes it clear that she cares profoundly and that her heart is broken. Tom inflects every line like a Barrymore until the lyric scraps give way to sobbing and wordless speech that oscillates between complaint and helpless grief. The poor woman's suffering becomes comic—becomes bearable—only because her delineator is a clown and her voice comes out of a saxophone. The subtle detail of Tom's exit and reentry without the veil may seem unimportant, but it can be seen as reassuring the audience that the "real" world of Melodyville contains only music, dancing, and laughs, and that the bride's plight is only make-believe. At some point in the run, the finale was changed from "Russian Rag" to a medley featuring Tom playing the soprano Waggener had given him. In Boston programs (December 1921–March 1922), it is billed, in good Ringling fashion, as "the first instrument made by the inventor, Mr. Sax, and . . . the oldest saxophone in existence."

On one side of a 78 r.p.m. disc in the collection of the National Music Museum, what could be a scrap of the Browns' Melodyville medley survives: an acoustic-era recording (of unknown provenance) of Tom playing the medley's 1922 finale, "Rosy Cheeks," on the soprano, backed by the Brothers. The four-bar introduction, eight-bar verse, and sixteen-bar chorus are played with pervasive rubato at the dramatically slow average tempo of about one beat per second. Tom leads throughout, wailing the hymnlike melody with his emotionally charged circus vibrato right through to a final high D-flat, the highest note (faking aside) on his antique Sax instrument. The listener can imagine Tom as Tom Jr. described him seventy years later, encircled by the spotlight, eyes closed, his blackface clown persona set aside for two minutes of nothing but music. The Sax soprano angles farther and farther from his body until the finish, when he raises his right arm to point at the ceiling and projects the last note of the soprano, held in his left hand, to the back of the highest balcony.

The play's final scene takes place in the Land of Heart's Desire, where the Dick-Alice and Tip Top–Jinia couples, along with two other pairs, are finally united, giving each of the four twosomes an opening for its own brief specialty number after the villains have been foiled and Dick has been apprised of his inheritance. The scene's first big specialty, however, is a new version of the now familiar acrobatic dance of Stone and Violet Zell, this time costumed as Punch and Judy. The flexible Zell once again dances on Stone's toes and is tossed about like a puppet, as is a life-sized doll that surreptitiously replaces her for the parts involving Stone's roughest treatment. The London Palace Girls display their uncanny precision in a red-costumed "Dance of the Valentines" before the Fairy Justicia returns to remind the audience of the supernatural plot line, which has been thoroughly obscured by the legacy story since the cat courtroom scene. A gigantic production number follows deploying all the principals, the Six Brown Brothers, the Globe chorus (divided into contingents of Cupids, Brides, and Pages), and the London Palace Girls. At the conclusion of the swirl of joyous music and breathless dancing, Stone, now in fancy eighteenth-century attire, asks the audience, "Is everybody happy?," and its unanimous, full-throated affirmation is rewarded with a reprise of "I Want a Lily" and a final ensemble dance by the whole company, now including the Duncan Sisters.

The musical opened at the Globe on October 5 to excellent business. Alexander Woollcott's review of opening night in the New York Times made special mention of "our old friends, the Six Brown Brothers, or, what is more important, . . . those five saxophone players and Tom Brown, the melancholy one who stands apart and sobs with a saxophone and is funny beyond words."[25] Besides this endorsement from the top of the Broadway critical establishment, Tom had an extra reason to be happy as the prospect of another successful season stretched ahead. The Saturday after opening night, he wrote to Waggener:

Really a MIRACLE has happened to me—Last month it was so hot in New York—that I was forced to take off my TRUSS—it became so uncomfortable—and I haven't had it on for "FOUR WEEKS" excepting when I do the act—I can COUGH—SPIT—SNEEZE—JUMP—and—???????????—FIGHT AND FOOT-RACE—without any thought of the HERNIA coming out—You can try and imagine how good it has made me feel—Outside of that everything is O.K.[26]

Fred had time to spend with his new bride, chorus member Leita Randall, and Alec was close once again to his Irvington, New Jersey, home, where he could occasionally drop in on his wife, Edith, and his two- and four-year-old daughters, Dorothy and Myrtle.

Billed in Buescher Band Instrument Company ads as the country's "Highest Paid Musical Act,"[27] the Brothers had signed on for the first eight weeks of the run at $900 per week, with an agreement that, in the ninth week, they would either be given "a roof engagement" (probably in *Midnight Frolic*)[28] as well or receive a reward for success by being assigned exclusively to *Tip Top* and raised to $1,000 per week. Dillingham retained control over the Browns' other performance opportunities, having Tom agree on their behalf "during this engagement not to render any services for any other party, than myself or to appear at any other theatre, whether at private or public entertainment, or otherwise, including acting or posing for motion pictures, without my written consent." Finally, he contracted for the option to extend the agreement for 1921–22 with the Brothers' weekly salary pegged at $1,000.[29] It was a pretty good deal for the Brothers and a great deal for Dillingham. Theresa's new contract kept pace with her rising star status: her pay jumped from $85 per week in 1918–20 to $125 for 1920–21, and the agreement gave her an option to renew at $150 for 1921–22.[30]

Tom probably continued to chafe at the bit in spite of Dillingham's generosity, but he was not the only restive Brown Brother. At some point during the winter of 1920–21, Harry Fink began to moonlight at Thomas Healy's, a fashionable and sumptuous restaurant at Sixty-sixth Street and Broadway that offered ballroom dancing, cabaret entertainment, and an ice ballet in addition to steaks and chops. It is not known whether Harry figured in the dance orchestra or the cabaret entertainment. Advised of Harry's new employment, Tom reported to Dillingham's secretary, Bruce Edwards, that he had "warned Harry about playing at Healy's and explained to him that it was wrong and against the rules of my contract. His answer was that he didn't think it wrong and intended to continue, so I immediately started to look for someone to take his place. . . . I shall dismiss him as soon as I have the new man ready."[31] Thus abruptly ended the partnership that reached back to *Broadway Gaiety Girls* and the Five Brown Brothers' breakthrough success in the crucial New York market. Harry may have continued to play at Healy's, but by the following spring he had taken up a chair in the Vincent

Lopez Hotel Pennsylvania Orchestra.[32] The orchestra's New York base kept Harry closer to his wife and two daughters in New Jersey than the wanderings of the Fred Stone troupe would allow, and the rising tide of dance-band popularity was about to lift Lopez to national prominence. Harry's replacement, probably Harry Young,[33] easily assumed the Harry Brown musical identity, although, even under clown makeup, he could hardly be mistaken for Fink.

The season rolled on, with *Tip Top* filling the Globe most of the time, and a run until late June was anticipated.[34] Then, on a Tuesday in April, while doing one of his less athletic dances, Stone broke a toe. For the first time in fifteen years he was forced to miss a performance.[35] After shuttering the Globe for a couple of nights, Dillingham tried replacing Stone with Harland Dixon, of Dixon and Doyle, a team that had played road versions of Montgomery and Stone vehicles for many seasons,[36] but box-office receipts fell off disastrously. Contrary to press releases promising Stone's imminent return,[37] the star's doctors projected a long period of healing and kept him at home. After two money-losing weeks, Dillingham closed the show in early May.[38] The Brothers, suddenly high and dry, had been refused Dillingham's permission to play the summer season at the Marigold Gardens, on the theory that a long engagement there would diminish their commercial value when *Tip Top* hit the Chicago boards around Labor Day. It was rumored that their alternative plan was to join *Midnight Frolic* again, but, if it was, they were disappointed, since slow Prohibition business and high postwar prices led Ziegfeld to close the show at the end of May,[39] after a short three and a half months. (The last of the *Nine o' Clock Revue* series had opened at the same time, but closed even sooner; the new *Frolic*, opening in November 1921, was to be the last.)[40]

Beginning June 9, the Browns were part of the entertainment on the Detroit Board of Commerce's annual cruise, headlining the show on the SS *Noronic* as it parted the waters of Lake Huron and Ontario's Georgian Bay for four jolly days and nights.[41] Just afterward, Dillingham, now with veto power over all the group's engagements, arranged a short tour over the Keith circuit, the Brothers' first vaudeville outing since just before *Chin Chin* opened in 1914. From mid-June until July 24, by which time the rehearsals for the road version of *Tip Top* had begun, they appeared in New York, Philadelphia, Boston, and two theatres in Brooklyn, including what was probably their first and only appearance at vaudeville's highest temple, the Palace on Broadway.[42]

Billboard[43] and *Variety* both reported that the Brothers scored a hit at the Palace, but *Variety*'s reviewer, while conceding the high quality of the act, stressed the fact that it hadn't changed much in its seven years away from vaudeville: "Second after intermission Six Brown Brothers scored a comedy and musical hit with their playing. The turn remains practically the same in construction as when last seen in two-a-day houses . . . .. They are the same sterling musicians with the same sure assortment of musical comedy and popular song melodies that left the varieties for the legit attractions."[44] The end of the tour, a week at the Brooklyn Orpheum beginning July 18, was to be the Brothers' final appearance in North American big-time vaudeville. The Palace gig had marked a real apogee, though the descent from it would be long and complicated.

The summer hiatus for the Fred Stone company turned out to be shorter than usual, probably to make up for Dillingham's lost revenue. After rehearsals at the Globe in New York,[45] the road version of *Tip Top* ran for a successful shakedown week at the Powers Theatre in Grand Rapids, Michigan, before moving to Chicago's Colonial Theatre on August 7. Ticket sales were excellent despite torrid weather and a public unaccustomed to summer openings.[46] The local press gave the show plenty of coverage besides the usual reviews, and the cast spread goodwill as the cat courtroom scene was staged for children at Marshall Field's downtown department store[47] and the Brothers played on "professional night" at the Friar's Inn, a resurgent Loop cabaret.[48] Theatre business slumped citywide in late September, however, a decline attributed by *Variety* to high ticket prices and bad weather, and, although the Stone show briefly returned to sold-out houses in October, by November it had yielded its leading position to the Eddie Cantor vehicle *Midnight Rounders*, one of four musical comedies that had followed it into the City of Big Shoulders.[49] After roller-coaster business ranging from "disastrous" to standing-room only, Dillingham paid a visit to the Colonial and decided to move the show to Boston three weeks earlier than planned, on December 5.[50]

Although Tom had had previous ties to Chicago extending back to the Wabash Avenue business address of Brown Brothers and Kealey in the summer of 1908, in 1921 he made decisions that strongly committed him to the city. One fateful step was lending his name to the Tom Brown Saxophone Shop, a musical instrument store at 17 West Lake Street in the colossal State-Lake Building, which had recently replaced the Majestic Theatre Building as Chicago's center of show business. Another was settling his family in the city, with the Near North Side's Ambassador Hotel as their residence and the exclusive Thorpe Academy in nearby Lake Forest as a boarding school for Tom Jr., now nine years old. Before 1921, the Brothers' business address had been the Globe Theatre, New York, and Tom and Theresa had left Tom Jr. in the hands of Theresa's mother when they were on the road, sometimes renting a whole building near the Globe as a residence and rehearsal space when they were in New York.

Martin Beck, mogul of the Orpheum circuit, headed a consortium of theatrical entrepreneurs (including Caroline Kohl, widow of C. E. Kohl of the Kohl and Castle Theatres) that financed the construction of the State-Lake Building on the commercially neglected north edge of the Loop, and he moved the circuit's headquarters there shortly after its 1919 opening. The other main tenants were the Chicago operation of the United Booking Office and an enormous 3100-seat theatre, whose policy of interspersing feature movies with short vaudeville programs (called "the State-Lake policy") was to contribute materially to vaudeville's eventual extinction. Leading entertainment agencies, such as those of Pat Casey and Jake Sternad, packed most of the remaining offices in the twelve-story building designed in gray-granite-faced "modified French Renaissance" style.[51] The inevitable confluence of show people on the site made it a prime location for a music store, and Tom's name would help ensure such a store's success, even without his active participation in the business. Sales were so good that, after a little more than a year, the business was incorporated as the Tom Brown Music Company, with Tom as president, George M. Bundy, the president of H. and A. Selmer Company (a major manufacturer and importer of instruments) as vice president, and William H. Lyons, manager of the Saxophone Shop, as treasurer. Tom's stake as majority shareholder in the enterprise, by 1925 capitalized at $150,000, promised a substantial supplement to his show world income.[52]

Tip Top's Chicago run also provided the setting for a long-impending collision with Billy Markwith, the 1907–9 Ringling colleague who had played tenor saxophone with the Brothers at various times from at least 1909 on and whose 1915 Saxo Sextette had mimicked the Browns. According to *Variety*'s report, affidavits submitted to the United States District Court in Chicago stated that

> Markwith worked for Tom Brown in his act for eleven years and was paid a salary. That during 1918 or 1919 when Tom Brown was appearing at the Colonial Theatre, Chicago, with Fred Stone in "Jack-o-Lantern,["] C. L. Brown was introduced to him by one Al. Sweet, and at the time C. L. Brown informed him that he was a member of the circus band with the Sells Floto Circus. At the time he is said to have told Tom Brown that he was crazy about the act of the Six Brown Brothers, and that he went up to the gallery of the Colonial Theatre every night to see the act.
>
> Shortly after that meeting Tom Brown alleges that C. L. Brown appeared in an act known as the American Saxophone Sextette and started playing the smaller theatres in and about Chicago. That shortly after that time C. L. Brown produced an act known as "Brown's Saxophone Six" and represented himself to agents and managers as "Tom Brown." The complaint charges that he dressed the act in direct imitation of Tom Brown's act, with one black face comedian, wearing duck trousers and five other men in clown makeup.

Variety went on to say that Tom had confronted C. L. Brown "some time ago" about his infringements and that C. L.'s agents had relayed a promise that the impostors would change their costuming and presentation.[53] But evidently they had not done so. On November 29, the Court granted Tom a permanent injunction against Markwith and C. L. Brown, in which the judge agreed with Tom that the defendants had been deceiving managers and the public alike with their publicity material and costumes and restrained Markwith and C. L.

> from using the name of SIX BROWN BROTHERS in connection with any billing, advertising, letterhead, stationery, cards, contracts, lobby displays, cuts, photographs, lithographs or any other form of advertising and from advertising or displaying or stating that BROWN'S SAXOPHONE SIX are of Victrola fame or have played for the Victor Talking Machine Company or in any way inferring [*sic*] or intimating that BROWN'S SAXOPHONE SIX have played for the Victor Talking Machine Company or are of Victrola fame.[54]

However, the judge did not forbid the Brown/Markwith groups from giving performances similar to those of the Brothers, and they continued to do so, setting their course for another collision a few years down the road.

Tip Top ran its full projected fifteen weeks at the Boston Colonial and emerged as the most profitable show of the Hub City season, despite box-office downturns owing to a February cold wave and monster snowstorm.[55] A return engagement at Philadelphia's Forrest Theatre ran four weeks in March and April, starting out with poor business but ending up doing better than any other stage attraction in town.[56] Brief stands at the National Theatre in Washington, D.C., Ford's in Baltimore, and the Shubert Majestic in Providence brought the tour to an end on May 21.

The slow, slight, but steady decline in the popularity of Stone/Dillingham shows since the overwhelming New York success of *Chin Chin* must have been obvious to all concerned. Despite continuing profits overall, the familiar old vessel had clearly sprung a leak.[57] Although newspaper reviews almost always singled out the Brown Brothers for separate, and sometimes extravagant, praise, they said little about the content of the act, which had changed only in details during their whole association with Stone. When Alexander Woollcott referred to the act as "our old friends," the effect was flattering, but there may have been a slight edge in similar critical remarks such as that "they are as popular as ever, although (or rather, because) they have varied their entertainment little," that "these minstrels of the saxophone are the same as ever, and still several shades better than any of their numerous imitators," or that "the Brown Brothers make their familiar appearance and awaken the familiar enthusiasm."[58] In becoming a standard act, the Brothers had run up against a familiar show-business dilemma: on the one hand, the presentation must remain the same, since that's what the public has grown to love and to expect; on the other hand, the presentation must change, or it will begin to seem like a relic, as outmoded as *Uncle Tom's Cabin* or a minstrel show.

Although the sextet relied on its veteran comedy formulas, it continued to replenish its repertoire of popular songs with the latest material. At some point they seem to have quit commissioning their arrangements from F. Henri Klickmann, since the mammoth arranging offices of Harry L. Alford bragged in the January 1922 number of their house publication *Sharps and Flats* that they were supplying orchestrations for the act's *Tip Top* feature. Alford's staff, five floors above the Tom Brown Music Company in the State-Lake Building, wrote at least nine charts for the Brothers, including ones for two songs composed by Tom Brown (in collaboration with Jack Frost), "Finders Is Keepers" and "Sweet Baby Mine."[59] Although reviewers seldom noted the up-to-date playlist, it seems to have been an important feature of the act. On one notable occasion when the list was made up of slightly stale tunes (the October 1922 New York opening of *The Bunch and Judy*, described later), audience and reviewers noticed and disapproved.

In the middle of the Chicago stand, Tom had signed a contract committing the Brown Brothers to eight weeks of performances in the chain of Chicago movie palaces owned by the Balaban and Katz organization, to commence at the end of *Tip Top*'s run.[60] The Brothers wasted no time, opening at the Riviera Theatre only two days after the Providence curtain rang down for the last time. The Balaban and Katz Theatres were presenting only films and the Brothers, not vaudeville bills, and the contract called for more effort than the two shows a day demanded on the Keith circuit a summer earlier. By 1922, big-time vaudeville had practically vanished from Chicago, represented clearly only at the Orpheum circuit's Majestic, and in an attenuated form at the State-Lake. At the gigantic new 5000-seat Chicago Theatre, across the State Street from the State-Lake, the Browns agreed to present four shows on weekdays and five on weekends and holidays, while at the smaller Riviera (near the Marigold Gardens), Central Park (on the West Side), and Tivoli (on the South Side), they were to do only three shows weekdays, boosted to five on weekends and holidays. Fortunately for the group and their public, all four houses were air-conditioned. Working much longer hours than they had in the Stone show, the Brothers earned a much lower $785 per week for sharing the stage with the flickering images of such opulently wealthy, semidivine stars as Gloria Swanson, Rudolph Valentino, Jackie Coogan, Wallace Beery, and Richard Barthelmess.[61] It must have begun to seem to them, as it seemed to many vaudeville veterans, that they were in the wrong business. But a practical technology for sound films still lay several years in the future, despite the experiments of Webb Talking Pictures, the Talking Picture Company of New York, and several other concerns.

The 1922–23 road season began with cast changes, as Violet Zell dropped out and the White Sisters, Thelma and Marjorie, capably replaced the Duncan Sisters. "Sister acts have been a la mode for several seasons. . . . Every well arranged musical show has a pair of cuties who can at least pass for 'kiddies,' but few with as much success as the White girls. One, of course, is pretty and has a voice—the other comic and almost dumb—perfect complements."[62] But a more drastic change waited in the near future, resulting in a two months' absence of the Brothers. In early November, Dillingham was grooming a new show for the Globe season that featured a Jerome Kern score (with lyrics by Anne Caldwell) and the sensational dancing team of Fred and Adele Astaire. The musical, *The Bunch and Judy*, opened at the Garrick in Philadelphia on November 6 to lukewarm reviews. *Variety* reported that the audience for the premiere, "composed largely of hard-boiled and blasé first-nighters or show people," loved the first act, which had featured Adele Astaire (as Judy) in a hilarious operetta parody, followed by a banquet scene during which Judy's theatrical friends (the Bunch) hoisted the table into the air to create a platform for the Astaires' "wild, rhythmic soarings."[63] The fresh songs, expert comedy, and graceful Astaires made the playgoers think "that this was one of the snappiest and most promising shows of its kind seen here in several seasons. Unfortunately," the reviewer continued, "after the final curtain, the general high estimation of the play took a tumble. Whether this second act can be whipped into real shape is the problem which Dillingham is facing. Otherwise he has only half a hit."[64] The planned two weeks at the Garrick stretched into three as various remedies were applied, and at the last minute matters were made worse when Joe Cawthorn, a comedian whose bit in the operetta parody had been one of the highlights, tore ligaments in his knee in a backstage fall.[65] By the time of the November 28 move to the Globe, Dillingham repeated the remedy he had administered to *Chin Chin* in 1914 by exercising his contract power over the Brothers to pull them out of the *Tip Top* tour and interpolate a cabaret scene into the second act featuring them and vaudeville singer Grace Hayes. Together with the new comedy provided by Cawthorn's replacement, Johnny Dooley, and his sister Ray Dooley, the alterations ultimately resulted in a viable show. (The Brothers were replaced in *Tip Top* by the Famous Clown Band, a group managed by Tom and led by Harry Voltaire, who later gave saxophone lessons to future swing-band leader Charlie Barnet.)[66]

But opening week on Broadway was a shambles. Cawthorn's role had been rewritten quickly to fit Dooley's style and incorporate his sister, leaving them only two Philadelphia performances to polish their presentation for New York. In Sime Silverman's opinion,

> The Brown Brothers got the worst of the entire deal . . . . Out with the Fred Stone show and the hit of that troupe, other than its star, the Browns, with their saxophones, had a routine of pop melodies made up for the road. Called back to Broadway and without sufficient notice to rehearse anything newer, they were forced immediately onto the stage that but a short while before had housed the entire [Paul] Whiteman Band in the [George] White's 'Scandals.' It was a pretty tough assignment, and before the wise first-nighters who did not take into account any of the surrounding circumstances, the Browns were no riot.

Silverman's point about Paul Whiteman was probably twofold: not only had Whiteman been playing the latest New York hits rather than a medley of somewhat older tunes that were recognizable by the less up-to-date road audiences, but Whiteman's approach to the material, which had gained a national audience (via Victor recordings) two years earlier, represented the vanguard of dance music as against the long-familiar sound of the Brothers. Silverman noted, however, that at the performance he was reviewing, ten days into the stand, the Browns "seemed as big as ever before a regular audience, and received an applause reception on their appearance."[67]

Once it recovered from its bad start, *The Bunch and Judy* turned a profit. But it never did the volume of business that Dillingham had hoped, so he sent it on the road (to the Colonial in Boston) after only eight weeks,[68] freeing the Brothers to return to the *Tip Top* tour.

Dillingham had directed the career of the Six Brown Brothers for almost nine years. With his help they had risen to stardom and modest wealth, but the price was surrender to his control. At least twice, he had dangled the prospect of a show with Tom as the leading attraction, and twice he had snatched it away. His veto of a pleasantly stationary summer engagement at the Marigold Gardens in 1921, coupled with his approval of a Keith circuit tour instead, had kept the Browns away from their new Chicago base for most of that summer. Although there is no record of Tom's reaction, the embarrassment of being thrust unprepared into *The Bunch and Judy* must have been something like a last straw. The time was near when Dillingham and the Browns would part ways and the Browns would head unprotected down a difficult path. They were now a standard act in vaudeville, where an army of imitators—many more than just the C. L. Brown groups—both enhanced their prestige and diluted their impact. But vaudeville was shrinking rapidly as the moving-picture business, with lower production costs, cheaper admissions, and the advantage of novelty, turned vaudeville into a sideshow. Tom Brown's next big move would be an attempt to headline his own revue. But first he would take Theresa and the Brothers on a party cruise.

13

Something New and Different

1923–24

After the Six Brown Brothers completed the *Tip Top* tour, their break with Dillingham came quickly. Free from his control, they scrapped an elaborate summer plan in favor of a curtailed series of Chicago performances, followed by a festive expedition to the Alaska Territory in the company of San Francisco businessmen and their wives. Once back in California, Tom finally mounted his own show, *Black and White Revue of 1924*, starring, among others, himself, the Brothers, and Theresa. The realized dream of independence amounted to considerably less than they had hoped for.

Except for *The Old Town* in 1911,[1] Dillingham had sent road versions of Fred Stone vehicles only as far west as Kansas City and Omaha, but in the third season of *Tip Top*, the troupe made it to the Pacific Coast, with stands in Vancouver, Seattle, San Francisco, and Los Angeles, before returning to the eastern states via Salt Lake City, Cheyenne, Denver, and Detroit. The Six Brown Brothers rejoined the show by the middle of February 1923 and perhaps earlier. Theresa may also have been out of the show for a while, since one reviewer noted that Fred Stone's seventeen-year-old daughter, Dorothy, was listed in one evening's printed program for the Jinia Jones part, though it was in fact filled by Theresa.[2] As early as March, Dillingham and Stone let it be known that they were thinking of taking a new direction in their collaboration for the fall of 1923, since some press reports mention that Dorothy Stone was to be his co-star during the following season.[3] And indeed she was, in *Stepping Stones*, a Jerome Kern–scored production slanted much more toward dance and song and away from athletics than was the Fred Stone norm. Its cast did not include the Six Brown Brothers.

Near the end of the *Tip Top* tour, the Brothers, now "under the personal direction of Arthur J. Houghton," Fred Stone's longtime manager, announced their summer itinerary in a full-page *Variety* ad. The plan was to open May 21 at the Chicago Theatre, move on June 16 to Sid Grauman's Million Dollar Theatre in Los Angeles for a six-week stand, and return to New York on September 1.[4] But after a few weeks in Chicago, with Dillingham no longer in the background to tell the Browns what to do, they abandoned the plan and headed instead for San Francisco and Siberia.

Their string of engagements at the Balaban and Katz theatres was shorter than it had been in 1922, just a week each at the Chicago, the Tivoli, and the Riviera. In their "New Creation 'Land of King Tut,'" Tom's character made his entrance in Tutankhamen garb, joining in American pop-culture enthusiasm for the discovery of the boy king's tomb the previous November. Their June 10 closing gave them time for the long trip to San Francisco, where they opened on June 16 for two hit weeks as the between-movies attraction at the palatial Granada Theatre on Market Street.[5] There they temporarily replaced the bandleader Paul Ash (later known as "the Rajah of Jazz"), one of the pioneers of what was called the "presentation," a sort of abbreviated revue especially designed to replace vaudeville bills in movie-house service, and a form of production that lay not too far in the Browns' future.

During the Granada engagement, Tom was treated like a celebrity by the San Francisco press. Some of his reminiscences and stories were published sporadically in the *San Francisco Call and Post* as "Stage Tales On and Off," a series announced with the headline "Yeh, Tom Brown; He's the Bird That Gave the Saxophone Its Start; Now He Can't Stop It."[6] The articles, which dealt with Fred Stone's recent turn to religion, Tom's own history, and show-business anecdotes, were lively and generally good for a chuckle. The *Chronicle* ran an article that offered a peek at the Brothers' offstage lives:

> The Six Brown Brothers . . . are running wild just now, for their mother left 'em flat to go to the Shriners' convention in Washington. This is the first time she has left her boys unchaperoned since they began their public career, and that was some years ago.
>
> They really are brothers, and there were originally six of them. One died during the epidemic of the "flu" and another is ill just now, suffering with a nervous breakdown. So, somewhat like the "nine little darkies in the peanut shell," the ranks of the simon pure Browns have been decimated and two other players have come into the band, which is unique in the amusement world. . . .
>
> "Our mother always travels with us," Tom, the leader and chief comedian of the band, said yesterday, . . . "She sees to it that we are all in bed before she goes to her own room, too, and if we are staying at different hotels she makes the rounds.
>
> "She looks after us just as though we were still youngsters needing a mother's care. She feels the sheets to be sure they are not damp, and watches over us with the greatest care.
>
> "One of the boys, the one who is sick, is a pretty consistent drinker and has always been, but mother doesn't know this and thinks that her boys are all temperance advocates. In a group of women one night she said, speaking of this brother, 'I know he

never drinks anything. Why, I have seen him drink a whole pitcher of ice water in the morning, and if he were a drinking man he couldn't do that!'"[7]

The consistent drinker suffering a nervous breakdown was probably William, absent from the group's roster a few weeks later, replaced by a "Brown" whose first name was Cecil. It is not clear how much of Tom's story about his mother was a tall tale, since Theresa and Leita Randall, Fred's wife, were also traveling with the group.

At the end of June, a train ride down the coast took the Brothers to two weeks (July 1–14) at Grauman's Metropolitan Theatre in Los Angeles, where they brought down the house on at least one Saturday night. "The audience was determined that the famous saxophone artists should give them another encore after they had completed their turn. The house was darkened and the feature film started. But the spectators would have none of it until the musicians again appeared. The first reel must have been nearly run when the management decided the applause must be considered. The film was stopped and the sextet brought out. Even after this additional number, the clapping continued for several minutes."[8] Buoyed by this evidence of their continued popularity, the Browns returned to San Francisco, not for another theatre engagement, but for seven weeks of occasionally working vacation on the SS *Buford*, departing the Golden Gate on July 20.

The opportunity for the cruise may have arisen because Tom and Fred, and possibly Vern and Alec as well, were Shriners. The San Francisco Chamber of Commerce had organized a six-week trip to Alaska to promote business ties between California and Alaska, with a secondary mission of bringing Shrine ritual to the isolated lodges of the territory, particularly Nome, where a number of "eligibles . . . desired to see the 'True Light,'" according to Illustrious Potentate Walter N. Brunt, who wrote an entertaining doggerel narrative of the trip.[9] About twenty-two Shriners joined the cruise, half of them Nobles of the Islam Temple (San Francisco) of the Ancient Arabic Order, Nobles of the Mystic Shrine. Somehow, probably during the Brothers' San Francisco visits in spring and summer, officials of the chamber had asked them, as well as Theresa and Leita, along on the trip. The Brothers played for dancing in the evening,[10] performed on the forward deck as the *Buford* came into port, and occasionally entertained on shore, but for the most part they were passengers like the rest, enjoying a leisurely trip to the temporarily thawed frontier of the American empire. The Brown contingent treated the excursion as a long party, an apparent celebration of their release from Dillingham's control. The trip was chronicled in some detail both by Brunt in "The Buford Trip," and by a sixty-odd-year-old E. B. White, the novelist and journalist, looking back on his twenty-four-year-old self with wry humor.

White joined the expedition in Seattle, where he had recently lost a steady job as a reporter. Although he paid his passage as far as Skagway, he was gambling on getting a position on board from no later than that point on, since by then he would be out of money. According to White's memoir, the general mood of the passengers was boredom. When visible, the majestic shoreline varied little from day to day, and for long intervals it was hidden behind a uniform curtain of fog, pierced only by the ship's plaintive foghorn.[11]

The Browns were the chief purveyors of relief from the monotonous grandeur of the Alaskan coast. Snapshots show them seated on the deck, swathed in heavy overcoats and performing on instruments other than saxophones: two clarinets (one of them played by Tom), trumpet (played by one of the tenor saxophonists), trombone, baritone horn, and bass tuba. A minute or so of surviving home movie shows a slightly larger group taking turns clowning as they play on deck. A bass drum bearing the legend "Six Brown Brothers with Tom Brown" and a snare drum have been added, and instead of a second clarinet, there is an alto horn. The players, standing in a semicircle and hidden by brass tubing and layers of wool, are difficult to identify, but the bass drummer is probably Tom's valet, Eddie Kennedy, who had once been a dancer in George Primrose's troupe, and the trombonist looks like the younger of the two tenor sax players. The trombonist executes a couple of tap steps before he pivots 360 degrees on his left heel, Tom baby-steps up to the camera and back, and the bass drummer, puffing on a cigar, paces in a small circle. But the snare drummer (identified by Alec's children as their father) takes up the bulk of the time, pansy-walking toward the camera and flipping up his coattails as he returns to his place, then repeating the back-and-forth three times, first with an Irish jig, then with Charleston knee-wagging, and finally with a limp as he approaches and a crouch as he retreats. Such a performance may be the subject of a journalist's description of their arrival in Juneau:

> [The] Browns . . . organized a six-piece band, and when the Buford arrives at any town to be visited, this band, which can make more music than the average 16 or 18 piece band, serenades from the forward deck. When the Buford came into port yesterday afternoon, the Brown Brothers were on deck and their band was liberal in selections which were applauded by the hundreds on Admiral dock.[12]

In the ship's ballroom, the Brothers played what White describes as "sweet jazz"[13] (probably up-to-date fox-trots) for frequent dances and parties, and one snapshot shows Tom on deck doing what is apparently his abandoned-bride routine, in blackface with a flowered straw bonnet and the kind of undergarment that supports a hoopskirt, worn over his usual bowlegged white trousers (see figure 11). On one grave occasion early in the trip, the group was pressed into service for a different sort of music. President Warren G. Harding, who near Seattle had waved his wife's handkerchief at the Buford from the deck of the Henderson, on which he was returning from Alaska to San Francisco, died at that city's Palace Hotel on August 2. The news reached the Chamber of Commerce expedition at Cordova, and a memorial service was quickly organized. As the ship approached Seward, the Browns prepared an appropriately funereal set of tunes. White "felt bereft. Mr. Harding is not greatly mourned these days, but we of the *Buford* blew him a heartfelt tribute from Seward that night, on six jolly saxophones hastily converted to solemnity."[14]

The *Buford*'s first sight of Alaska was the Inside Passage, the waterway between the Territory's long, narrow southern strip of coast and the sheltering islands of the Alexander Archipelago. At the vessel's stop in Juneau, the capital, the Brothers put on an outdoor concert for about a thousand in the town's Triangle Square, then went to the residence of the territorial governor, Scott Bone, to serenade him. The governor responded graciously with an invitation for them to come inside, where the group continued to play for another hour.[15] Farther north along the coast, at Skagway, the passengers were treated to a train ride through White Pass to Bennett Lake in British Columbia for a day of breathtaking vistas. Out of Skagway, the *Buford* left the relatively peaceful waters of the Inside Passage for the heavy seas of the Gulf of Alaska, en route to a call at Anchorage, at the north end of the long Cook Inlet. Between Anchorage and Kodiak, the big waves were augmented by a violent storm that confined everyone to quarters as the ship began to follow the long beard of the Alaska Peninsula southwestward to the Aleutian Islands.

At Akutan, in the Aleutians, a delegation that included the Brothers visited a large butchering operation where whales were reduced to their commercially valuable components of oil, bone, meat, and ambergris. The Browns reacted to the grisly sight of a flayed leviathan by serenading the carcass as they capered in a circle around it and grouping in front of it for a photograph (see figure 13)[16]

After a stop at Unalaska, another of the Aleutians (where White became messboy for the ship's firemen), the company turned north into the Bering Sea, calling at several of the Pribilof Islands, including vast seal rookeries on St. Paul and St. George Islands. Theresa posed for snapshots amid the teeming animals and declared the pups "adorable." Anchored off St. Lawrence Island, the *Buford* welcomed a delegation of twenty Inuits from the village of Gambell who came to sell items crafted from ivory and sealskin. During the visit, "the six Brown brothers unlimbered their horns, and the Eskimos danced, with surprising frenzy. None of them had ever heard a sax, and the sound made them drunk."[17]

Eastward from the Pribilofs lay the next port of call, Nome, "the gateway to the top of the world," in White's phrase.[18] As the party tried to debark, "The stormy wave would not behave, / And the barge dashed 'gainst our ship," reported Brunt. The voyagers had to be lowered into the landing vessel in a rope cage,[19] and many of them vomited when they reached terra firma. White speculated that the town "must have been a particularly heavy shock" for "San Francisco's business giants," with its single street of dilapidated houses, their backs to the beach, and the beach itself heaped with discarded food tins.[20]

Nevertheless the Nome visit turned out to be lively. Once on shore, said Brunt, briefly shifting to the historical present, "troubles for time are o'er."

> H. Delbert Snow[21] gave African show,
> We heard Brown Brothers' Band
> And Chamber Commerce gave Nome a promise
> To send best in the land.
> Next day the Shrine parade in line,
> Ceremonial and eats,
> Eighteen benighted were all true lighted,
> Performing wonderful feats.
> We had all sorts Esquimaux sports,
> Toss, jump and race canoe,
> We saw wolves prance in sacred dance
> That nearby hall put through. . . .
> The dance that night proved great delight,
> Next day a smoker came 'long,
> Speeches were made 'bout 'Laskan trade,
> I gave resume in song.[22]

At the Shrine induction ceremony on August 15, Tom acted as Second Ceremonial Master and Fred as Marshal as Nome's "Sons of the Northern Desert became Nobles of Islam Temple."[23] At the smoker, staged by the Nome Chamber of Commerce to honor their San Francisco counterparts, Tom "entertained with an inimitable line of funny stories," while the businessmen drank and pledged commercial solidarity into the small hours, before being called home by a delegation of wives showering pebbles on the Log Cabin's windows.[24]

The brief Nome respite gave everyone a second wind for the leg of the trip that would carry them through the Bering Strait into the Arctic Ocean, with landfalls in Asia. On the way, Captain Louis Lane anchored the ship for a few hours at the edge of pack ice, descended to the floes, and shot seven walruses, which were then hoisted to the *Buford*'s deck. Theresa, Tom, Alec, and numerous others were photographed with the carcasses, a decaying and unwelcome presence for the balance of the cruise. On August 23, the expedition reached Asia, landing at an Inuit village at Cape Serdze. South and east along the coast, the North Americans were allowed to visit the squalid settlement of Uelen, after bribing the Soviet officials with "Twelve dollars cash, . . . spuds to mash, / Coal oil and sugar and gum,"[25] then set off for a return visit to Nome before making the long run back to Seattle with only one stop, at False Pass in the Aleutians. In the northern Pacific, the ship encountered a gale that converted the badly behaved waves of Kodiak and Nome into fond memories. For three days, violent winds and enormous seas fought with Lane and his crew for control of the *Buford* as seasickness laid low the preponderance of seamen and passengers alike, and provisions and cargo, including several souvenir sled dogs, were tossed and battered.[26] But recovery was quick, and the first-class passengers celebrated the tempest's end with a masquerade that ran until midnight the evening before they made Seattle. After a night in port, three days' steam returned the sojourners to the safety and comfort of San Francisco on September 8.[27]

Tom, Theresa, and the rest had returned to California laden with souvenirs: mukluks, elaborate parkas in which the Brothers had had their pictures taken with the Inuits, a hand-carved ivory gavel destined for the St. Cecile Lodge of the Shrine in New York,[28] and even a sled dog. The husky had been bought as a pet for Tommy, back in Chicago, but his parents realized that it would be difficult for him to keep a pet at either the Ambassador Hotel or his boarding school, so it ended up in the care of Eddie Kennedy. During the brief hiatus between docking in San Francisco and opening in *Black and White Revue*, Alec spent several days in Long Beach, California, where Edith, expecting a child, had brought their two daughters across the country from New Jersey to see him. It was a joyful reunion for the family, but Alec left on *Black and White*'s West Coast tour before their new daughter, Helene, was born in October.

After the summer's cold vacation, Tom Brown for the first time in his life found himself masterless. Since his childhood, a succession of tutor-benefactors had ruled his professional development. His father, the Guy Brothers, the Ringling Brothers, Primrose and Dockstader, and, for the nine years just previous, C. B. Dillingham had nurtured his abilities like the show-business monarchs they were, knowing that their own glory and prosperity depended on the fame and well-being of their subjects. But the price of fame was obedience. Although Tom and the other Brothers had flourished within the limits set by their bosses, the yoke must have chafed on their talented and ambitious necks. Dillingham in particular, in treating them as the valuable commodities that they were, made a series of decisions that kept their profiles and salaries rising, but at a slower rate than Tom dreamed of, repeatedly putting off that "something big," that "life's opportunity to get some 'real' money."[29] The producer eased them into their second and third Fred Stone shows after leading Tom to think he would get his own,[30] forbade them to play the summer of 1921 at Marigold Gardens, sent them out to play between movies in the summer of 1922, and patched them ill prepared into *The Bunch and Judy*. Tom must have been relieved at his 1923 parting from his benefactor-master. Tom's time had come to be the principal in a full-length production, not just a vaudeville topliner or a featured attraction in someone else's show. And the time had come to stage his long-deferred minstrel show, or something like it.

Tom heeded Dillingham's 1919 warning that a minstrel show with hopes of success could not be like those of the past. *Black and White Revue of 1924*, which toured from California to the Midwest between late September 1923 and March 1924, was not even billed as a minstrel show. Although it had a few blackface characters and a first part ending with a walkaround, it also had lots of women, a jazz band, and famous performers in the olio who had built solid reputations outside the confines of the minstrel stage. It isn't known when Tom (possibly with Dillingham's help) started making the contacts that led to the mounting of the *Revue*, but the opportunity may have presented itself in March 1923, when *Tip Top* played San Francisco's Curran Theatre while, a few blocks away, Julian Eltinge, America's most renowned female impersonator, headlined the bill at the still all-vaudeville Orpheum. Eltinge and Brothers bookings overlapped again in July, when the impersonator played the Los Angeles Orpheum as the Browns entertained at Grauman's Metropolitan.[31] Eltinge had just returned to vaudeville after the failure of his starring vehicle *The Elusive Lady*.[32] Its producer, Jacques Pierre, may have met with Tom during one of the overlaps and convinced him to join Eltinge in the *Black and White* project, which, at any rate, Pierre ended up producing. Just below the well-known names of the co-stars Tom Brown and Eltinge, the programs would feature those of Lew Dockstader, Tom's old friend and patron, and Theresa Valerio.

In the previous year, as the Brothers closed their series of appearances at Chicago's Balaban and Katz theatres, Dockstader was sharing topliner status at the Orpheum circuit's showplace Majestic Theatre, still doing his monologue number but now probably satirizing Harding and flappers instead of Roosevelt and suffragists. Perhaps ties were renewed that led to the *Black and White* partnership. Dockstader, about to turn sixty-seven in 1923, needed hope. In January 1920, only a few months after George Primrose's lingering death from intestinal cancer,[33] Lew's wife Julien had died after a week's illness. Lew, busy on the road, arrived home too late to see her alive. The next day, as he made the funeral arrangements, their Long Beach, New York, home burned. Although he and a neighbor were able to rescue Julien's casketed remains while firemen saved the Dockstaders' three-year-old grandson Eugene Stevenson, nearly everything else was lost.[34] Not too long after the fire, Lew broke his leg in an onstage fall. These blows had given him ample reason to be discouraged about the future. Minstrelsy's near-death and vaudeville's sharp decline added to the burden of melancholy by drastically narrowing his work opportunities. Although he had portrayed the blackface title character in the 1914 feature film *Dan*, the role had not resulted in a crossover to the screen.

Julian Eltinge, by 1923 a nationally known star of the comic stage, film, and vaudeville, had built his reputation mostly outside New York. Born William Dalton in Newtonville, Massachusetts, in 1881,[35] he had toured the country in plays written to show off both his impressive ability to portray women and his comic and vocal skills in male guise. The profits from *The Fascinating Widow* (1911 [opened out of New York in 1910]), his first successful play on Broadway, helped build the Eltinge Theatre on New York's Forty-second Street, said to be the first (or perhaps only the third) New York theatre named after an actor.[36] *The Crinoline Girl* followed in 1914, *Cousin Lucy* in 1915, and *The Countess Charming* in 1917. Although most of his plays opened in New York, none of them had long runs there, prospering (or, in the case of *Elusive Lady*, foundering) instead on the road. He was introduced to a potentially wider audience in a series of three films that appeared in 1917–18: *The Countess Charming*, *The Clever Mrs. Carfax*, and *The Widow's Might*, followed in 1922 by *The Isle of Love*, apparently a scissors-and-paste job that mixed some leftovers from an earlier Rudolph Valentino vehicle with new Eltinge footage.[37] Intervals as a vaudeville topliner bridged the gaps between plays and movies. If the Brown Brothers were, as reported in one source, part of the short-lived Cohan and Harris Minstrels company, they might have gotten to know Eltinge during his 1908–9 tour with that troupe.[38]

Eltinge's act tiptoed along a fine line drawn by American attitudes toward men who dress as women. He successfully avoided the imputation of homosexuality, which would have been a heavy liability at the beginning of the boy's career in the 1890s, when the Oscar Wilde scandal was fresh in public memory. Typical of critical reaction are a 1911 review that mentions Eltinge's "fine manly self," one from 1914 that praises Eltinge's "ability to wear women's clothes without being offensive," and the 1921 opinion that he was "the manliest man off-stage and the girliest girl on-stage."[39] In response to interviewers' inevitable questions about the woman of his heart, he would always say he was waiting for the right woman (meanwhile living with his parents). The act's content would also reassure audiences that they were not watching a "sodomite." In his vaudeville appearances, where there was not time to change from his elaborate gowns into male dress, he would whip off his wig and speak in his reassuringly virile baritone. His plays and films were epitomized in a review of *Cousin Lucy*:

> An Eltinge show is an Eltinge show. And there you are. The recipe for such an entertainment must be fairly simple. Take a plot concerning the fortunes of a rough-spoken, devil-may-care fellow and puzzle your brains till you have devised some situation wherein he must don feminine finery as a disguise. Add one suggestion that his cheek is incongruously rough and another that he must not be left alone with the girls lest they tell him things he ought not to hear. Flavor from time to time with guarded drinks, smokes, curses, and fist clenchings, just to indicate that all this is not at all to his liking. Stir briskly and serve in a hurry.[40]

The vaudeville historian Anthony Slide says that, when out of character, "Eltinge went to extraordinary lengths to stress his masculinity; there were endless stories [offered by Slide's informants] of his beating up stagehands, members of the audience, and fellow vaudevillians who made suggestive remarks about his sexual preferences."[41] Slide also reports that two of his informants were, nevertheless, "of the opinion that Eltinge was homosexual."[42]

By 1923, aged forty-two, Eltinge was past his prime as a woman, no longer "an ingenue that you would find yourself making eyes at," "a girl . . . any man would rave over," or "the perfect man-woman."[43] His body had thickened as his soprano register grew less reliable. As early as 1909, he confessed to a *Variety* interviewer that his tight corsets, once bearable, were "disorganizing my digestive apparatus. Try as I may to diet and exercise the curse of weight threatens my every waking hour. I manage to keep under 178 always, but I realize that it is not for long. After that? Well, I will find some other sort of specialty to do."[44] Fourteen years, many pounds, and at least two retirement announcements[45] later, his specialty was substantially the same and continued to be so until his death in 1941.

Black and White Revue opened to enthusiastic tryout audiences in Santa Barbara on September 20 and San Diego on September 21. By the time it reached Los Angeles's Philharmonic Auditorium for a week's stand starting September 24, it had been shaped into ten "Episodes," four in the first act and six in the second, beginning and ending with the whole singing, dancing cast onstage, but without the least suggestion of a book to tie the production together. One of the earliest reviews called the show "a glorified vaudeville," and the phrase recurred on entertainment pages all along the route. It seems to have been an accurate characterization. Although the casual, vanguardist program lists the members of the cast, under the rubric "those who will offer entertainment," it says little about the content of the episodes, aside from giving the names of the principals in each one: Dockstader, Theresa, the four singers of That Quartet, Eltinge, and Tom. With Brechtian directness, the copy reads "Time—Present / Place—This Theatre" and provides a brief foreword: "It is the aim of Messrs. Eltinge and Brown, of the Black and White Revue, to offer the audience something new and different in the way of amusement. With this in view, the form, routine and detail of a theatrical programme will be omitted."

Episode 1 during the Los Angeles run was a minstrel first part with Aubrey Pringle (of That Quartet) as interlocutor, Tom Brown and Lew Dockstader as end men, and a majority of women among the participants.[46] Reviews and the Philharmonic Auditorium printed program suggest that the entire company participated in the walkaround at the end of the episode. Although a New Orleans review said that the show was "unsurpassed in the theatrical world of today for beauty, splendor of costuming and scenery, novelty of acts, and excellence of musical talent,"[47] none of the forty or so reviews available to me described the scenery in this or any other episode, except for occasional mention of the Egyptian setting of the Brown Brothers' turn. Brown and Dockstader's humor seems not to have broken new comic ground. Reviewer Grace Kingsley said, "Some of the jokes are so old we had forgotten them, so they are as good as new, and anyhow, who can get them off as can those two boys?"[48] A less receptive journalist in New Orleans three months later, after Dockstader had left the cast, characterized Tom's endman routine as "rusty minstrel wheezes,"[49] while Henry Segal, covering a

January 1924 performance at Cincinnati's Grand Opera House, estimated that "some of [the comedy] is as old as Tom Brown's saxophone (1856)" and complained that "some of the jokes are off-color."[50] The denizens of the time-honored semicircle took turns performing; they included (in the words of the unreceptive New Orleanian) "a male soprano with a voice as soothing as a calliope."[51] Julian Eltinge, "athletic of frame, in dinner jacket and flannel trousers," delivered a sentimental song called "Absent" in his natural baritone and "exchange[d] fizzling pleasantries with Tom Brown over the latter's prospective marriage to a 413-pound girl."[52]

The second episode on the Los Angeles bill was entitled "The Golden Terrace," but early reviews fail to distinguish it by name or description, so it was either negligible in content or so similar to the opening that reviewers assimilated the two. Probably it was the one of the original ten episodes dropped after the first month or two. (By March, in Madison, Wisconsin, there were only seven.)

Dockstader, in blackface and tattered formal dress, with a sparking antenna mounted on his top hat, followed with his solo turn, treating the audience to his end of conversations over the "Radio-Phoney" with public figures such as President Calvin Coolidge, Henry Ford, and William Jennings Bryan, telling Ford "that if he wanted the presidency he'd better run for it—that he could never make it in that car of his," and Bryan that he "was the best president we never had."[53] He ended his routine with a eulogy, familiar to reviewers, of John Barleycorn, who had passed away some three years before.[54] Though Dockstader was "the same old Lew,"[55] one journalist opined that he "might quicken his delivery a bit."[56]

Audiences and reviewers were particularly enthusiastic about the next episode, called variously "Dancing Mad" and "Dancing Fiends." The presentation changed in detail as dancers moved in and out of the cast, but at various times its perpetual motion included an exhibition waltz, an eccentric solo, an adagio, the Virginia Essence (an old minstrel standby) rendered by Theresa Valerio and Eddie Kennedy, an acrobatic dance in which "two slim Valentinoish men in soft white silk shirts and velvet trousers each whirled a maid about as if she was an inanimate object," a Bowery dance by the choreographers June and Jack Laughlin, and an array of "slim, dainty ankles . . . flashing across the stage and toes . . . tapping in mad dances." A popular feature often mentioned in reviews was Spark Plug (from the "Barney Google" comic strip), "a sad and dejected horse with gifted front and hind legs [who] ambled in for an hilarious episode"[57] that ended as "his hindquarters tried to bow individually to the applause . . . with the result that his exit was rather informal, as the forequarters proceeded abruptly off the stage."[58] The music was provided by Eddie Pomeroy and the Black and White Jazz Band, sometimes billed in print ads as a "Symphonic Jazz Orchestra." (For many potential customers, the group's name probably evoked recent memories of Ray Miller's Black and White Melody Boys, who had made a series of popular recordings on Columbia, Okeh, and other labels during 1920–22. Billy

Markwith and C. L. Brown were not the only entrepreneurs capable of deception.)

Early in the run, Theresa Valerio opened the second act with her own episode, but later her contribution disappeared, probably absorbed into the Dancing Fiends scene. A January appraisal of her act called her "about the prettiest young woman the Cincinnati stage has seen in a year, and she can sing as well as dance, although with her looks it is not very necessary to do either."[59] Among her numbers was an Italian dialect song called "Tony Caponi," harking back to her *Jack o' Lantern* specialty and selected for praise in several commentaries. But reviewers more often mentioned her beauty, voice, and dancing than her material. (Incidentally, Theresa's younger sister Adeline, known as Nina, was in the show's chorus, traveling under Theresa's wing just as Theresa had apprenticed in the Ringling circus under her older sister Rosa's protection.)

That Quartet, four heavyset men including the bass Aubrey Pringle, who had been the middle man in the first part, divided the newspaper critics into one camp that enjoyed their exuberant mix of ensemble and solo renditions of old favorites and another that was moved to describe them as "leather-lunged . . . probably the loudest quartet in existence"[60] or "the most clangorous male quartet in the world,"[61] a group that "simply yelped, where singing was indicated on the theater bill."[62] Nevertheless, as the critics felt bound to report, audience response was very positive, and "the louder they sang, the louder the applause."[63]

Julian Eltinge's episode, "Fads and Fancies of the Fair Sex," was the most consistent at eliciting critics' praise. No matter how many times critics and audiences had seen them, Eltinge's astonishingly rapid changes of wigs (often attached to hats), dresses, and footwear, just offstage or behind a drop, always seemed to approach the magical. He sang and danced his way through as many as six portrayals that at least overlapped, and perhaps duplicated, the characters he had created for his spring 1923 vaudeville tour. First onstage was "a sort of merry widow"[64] in a gown of "black and silver, a sumptuous creation of trailing draperies and glittering panels,"[65] crowned by "a big black hat with great plumes,"[66] from the midst of which Eltinge sang of "how he [would] break the hearts of the men who break the bank at Monte Carlo."[67] After an interval of mere seconds, the widow was replaced by Anna from Montana, "the Western show girl who smote Broadway amidship"[68] and "married a millionaire,"[69] whose wealth made it possible for her to dress in "an affair of white and delicate pastel shades that sparkle[d] with beads" as she sang her story "with the assistance of a feathery fan."[70] Another lightning transformation produced "a blonde and very buxom Cleopatra"[71] with "more beads and a new supply of huge fans"[72] to cash in on the fad for things Egyptian that swept the country in the aftermath of King Tut's disinterment. At some, but perhaps not all, venues, wearing "a lovely yellow velvet Spanish costume," he also did "a new song about an Irish lass who loved a Spaniard" and "a ditty about Crinoline days all done up as a colonial belle."[73] Eltinge closed the set as "a very young flapper, aged about eight,"[74] "in a pinafore, with a huge ribbon attached to his curls."[75] The costumes were "magnificent,"[76] "stunning,"[77] "perfectly heart-breaking,"[78] "the last word in sumptuousness."[79] The songs were "invariably clever, exceptionally 'catchy' and perfectly rendered,"[80] although one reviewer thought Eltinge had "lost considerable of his former freshness of voice."[81] Critics lauded the beauty of his shoulders, arms,[82] and back,[83] but few failed to notice—or to mention—that he was no longer "the dainty star of former years"[84] but getting to be a "big girl,"[85] "stouter than ever, and [that] a double chin add[ed] to the maturity of his charms."[86] Nevertheless, critics split on the question whether "the illusion of femininity is less perfect than in his young and slender days,"[87] one going so far as to claim that "no one would for one moment guess that he was not of the feminine sex."[88] And moral approval was not withheld, as it was noted that Eltinge could "mimic feminine mannerisms and graces without becoming effeminate,"[89] delineating his subjects in a way that was "always amusing and never overdone."[90]

After Eltinge's encores, the Six Brown Brothers took the stage, apparently doing the same "In the Land of King Tut" routine they had premiered in Chicago earlier in the year and incorporating the abandoned-bride number. With the Pyramids and the Sphinx in the background, the five Brothers in polka-dot clown suits performed a "musical invocation" to coax Tom, in blackface and a Tutankhamen headdress, from the tomb entrance in the foreground.[91] From that point on, according to a St. Louis journalist, the act was "note for note the same as it ha[d] been for years in other revues."[92] Instead of provoking commentary about its familiarity, however, the turn led some critics to elaborate praise:

> The Six Brown brothers make their saxophones do everything. Besides doing the conventional moaning and sobbing and wailing that most saxophones do, the Brown Brothers instruments have such an extensive though wordless vocabulary that in the novelty numbers they converse with all the ease they could if they actually did possess command of verbs, pronouns and the whatnot that goes to make up conversation. Their saxophone conversation act has robbed melodrama of its catch phrases, comedy of its stale jokes but preserved the spirit of both. There's a lilt and a dash and marvelous rhythm in their playing of popular numbers.[93]
>
> The performance of the Brown brothers suggests that if primitive man had had the saxophone, speech might never have been developed, for it would not have been needed. These horns do everything and with a quaint sufficiency.[94]
>
> The six Brown brothers . . . make one forget the bitter hatred which has been gathering for weeks in regard to the neighbor's boy who is resolved to study the saxophone. Their saxophones talk and laugh. They engage in repartee and weep when the repartee hurts.

Then, suddenly, they resolve to quit all nonsense and do some real music. And, as one listens, one grows tender hearted regarding the neighbor's boy, who is in the early stages of the saxophone, for the Brown sextette produces music as mellow and golden as sounds can be, that enchant the ear.[95]

The hilarity of the Brothers was succeeded by an attraction that realized a dream of Tom's going back at least six years.[96] Cast members who had appeared earlier as singers, dancers, or members of Eddie Pomeroy's Black and White Jazz Band now assembled onstage as Tom Brown's Saxophone Boys and Girls, a forty-piece (though gimlet-eyed newshawks sometimes counted as few as twenty-seven)[97] all-saxophone band that played a few popular tunes and then backed Tom as he played two numbers on his Adolphe Sax soprano. In San Francisco, the Duncan Sisters, guesting as newspaper critics, declared it a "sensation. And it made a gorgeous spectacle, with the saxophones illuminated by large numbers of tiny electric lamps when the stage was darkened."[98]

The finale of the show, originally a separate episode but later just the climax of the Saxophone Boys and Girls turn, brought the whole company back on the boards, supplementing the music with energetic dancing by the principals[99] and featuring Eltinge "in a towering headdress ornamented with pearls and roses, and the most dazzling costume of the evening."[100] With no book, no continuing characters, and no theme, the *Revue* struck many journalists as nothing more than a couple of star turns with inconsistently entertaining (and occasionally "amateurish")[101] padding. The inevitable comparison with Fred Stone's last three shows, which had played some of the same cities, left the *Revue* in very deep shade.

In a January letter, Eltinge told the *New York Morning Telegraph* that the *Revue* expected to open in a New York theatre in mid-February after a scheduled stand in Chicago.[102] Neither engagement ever came about. After short runs in Santa Barbara, San Diego, and Los Angeles, the troupe headed north to Stockton, California; Portland, Oregon; and Seattle before returning to the Golden State for a brief but lucrative run at San Francisco's Curran Theatre[103] and an even briefer one at the Victory in San Jose. Around Thanksgiving, they were in Beaumont, Texas, perhaps having entertained in a few cities en route.[104] Stands in Houston, Waco, Oklahoma City, and Tulsa were one- and two-nighters, but just before Christmas, the company settled in for a week's run at the Tulane Theatre in New Orleans, where the show played to big houses.

By the time of the Tulane engagement, Dockstader had left the troupe for health reasons. (He died of "a bone tumor" the following October 24.)[105] A New Orleans critic severely panned his replacement, Joe Rolly, "who has a liberal supply of jokes which were antique in the days of the brown derby, and equally depressing attempts at being frisky and jolly."[106] Three weeks later, Rolly fell ill just before a performance and was able to return to the cast only sporadically. Frank Morrell, a member of That Quartet, tried to fill in on an emergency basis and did an acceptable job until he essayed a monologue that fell flat and even "came as a dowse of cold water on some of the succeeding acts until a balance was recovered."[107]

A new series of one- and two-nighters followed a generally northbound trail through Memphis, Nashville, Chattanooga, Lexington (Kentucky), Cincinnati, St. Louis, Detroit, and Buffalo.[108] After Cincinnati, where Frank Morrell had subbed for Joe Rolly, Blackface Eddie Ross stepped in as the latter's replacement for the remainder of the tour, although their tenures overlapped during the St. Louis run. Ross was a relatively well known figure from the minstrel stage, a comedian and banjo virtuoso with several phonograph records on his resumé. A St. Louis journalist complained about his "ancient monologue,"[109] but others were much more receptive. To one, Ross was "more at sea, and therefore, more screamingly funny than ever, his reminiscences being set forth with a gravity which convulses his audience."[110] "With the most serious mien possible, Ross takes the audience into his confidence and talks of his family. Not a line of his patter has been heard in the city [London, Ontario] before and it really is something new in this line."[111] Another critic averred that Ross could "evoke more laughs per line of darky dialogue than it has ever been London [Ontario] theatergoers' privilege to hear."[112] Altogether, "Ross, with his great line of comedy, his banjo and his whistling talent, took up about three-quarters of an hour himself, and the audience laughed until they cried, dried their eyes, and then did it over again."[113]

About the time that Eltinge had predicted for the *Revue*'s New York opening, the show was occupied at the Princess Theatre in Toronto (where Allan Brown had once led the orchestra) and the Grand Opera Houses in the frozen Ontario cities of Hamilton and London. The company returned to the United States in late February, this time not to larger cities such as St. Louis and Detroit, but to Des Moines, Iowa; Madison, Wisconsin; Rock Island, Illinois; and Omaha, Nebraska. During this leg of the tour, it was announced from Los Angeles that *Black and White* had landed a return engagement at Philharmonic Auditorium, to begin in May.[114] Instead, the troupe finally disintegrated after a St. Joseph, Missouri, one-nighter late in March, scattering from coast to coast. The Browns landed in Chicago for a rest, Eltinge in Newark (where he opened in vaudeville at Proctor's), and Jacques Pierre and Eddie Pomeroy in Los Angeles.[115]

Tom Brown Jr. reports that his father told him that in the worst period of the tour, the show was losing about a thousand dollars a week. The senior Tom also recounted an anecdote that, while doubtless apocryphal, says something about his attitude. Just before opening in one of the smaller venues, Tom, peeking through the curtain to see an auditorium empty except for one man seated in orchestra center, decided a pre-show curtain speech was in order. Striding onto the apron in his end-man outfit, he assured the expectant audience that despite the small house the company would stage the entire spectacle with the same energy and enthusiasm as if the theatre were full to the roof. The seated man replied, "That's really nice of you, but I wonder if you could hurry it up a little. I'm the janitor, and I have to clean up after you're done."

Meanwhile in Manhattan, Fred Stone, along with Allene Crater and their daughter Dorothy, was filling the Globe Theatre nightly with the latest Dillingham show, *Stepping Stones*, which had opened November 6, the same day *Black and White* opened in San Jose, California. Teenaged Dorothy was a sensation, earning two standing ovations at the opening as she sang and danced the role of Rougette, a fatherless Red Riding Hood adopted at the end by Fred's character, Peter Plug. Although the general tone of the show recalled the fairy-tale ambience of *The Wizard of Oz*, *The Lady of the Slipper*, *Chin Chin*, and *Jack o' Lantern*, Dillingham eschewed the usual Fred Stone acrobatics, except for a horizontal-bar number, in favor of dancing. *Variety's* review remarked on the absence from the cast of any high-salaried attractions besides the three Stones.[116]

Black and White Revue of 1924 had some of the ingredients of a potential hit. Tom Brown and Julian Eltinge were both riding high, Tom through his long connection with Stone and Dillingham, Eltinge as a star of stage and screen, although the failure of *The Elusive Lady* had been a slight setback. Lew Dockstader, though recognized as a link with the nineteenth century, was still active in vaudeville and regarded as "the same old Lew" by its audience, an old-timer but not a has-been. In Theresa Valerio, the show had a rising star, although her featured appearances in *Tip Top* had been brief and overshadowed, like everything else in the play, by Fred Stone. The *Revue* had gorgeous costumes, elaborate sets, plenty of dancing and song, a good-looking chorus, a jazz band, and the World's Largest Saxophone Band. But after a promising launch in California, business sagged as the mid-continent winter wore on, and the long struggle ended with a one-nighter in St. Joseph. Many factors probably entered into the losing equation. Dockstader's departure was a serious blow, and some time was lost in finding an adequate replacement. Without a book or even a unifying theme, the format was too close to vaudeville to justify the higher prices, and one-night stands (on the minstrel or circus model), no matter how successful, don't bring audiences in by word of mouth, since people in Houston don't read the Waco papers. Then there was the air of staleness that hung over the production. Although the headliners were greeted with affection, their routines turned out to be only slight variations on material already familiar to many in the audience and almost all the reviewers. Some of the other material may have been fresher, especially Theresa's singing and dancing, but it was offset by the "rusty minstrel wheezes," the "jokes which were antique in the days of the brown derby," and the lack of new songs in the repertoire of That Quartet. Adding to the general tinge of outdatedness were Eltinge's heft and vocal problems, which only reminded audiences of his old allure. None of the reviews pointed it out, but another factor may have been that Eltinge could be seen for pennies on the nation's screens (albeit silent and in black and white), not only displaying his femininity, but confirming his masculinity by attacking any man who got too familiar. Cases like this, of flesh-and-blood artists losing out to their own simulacra in light and shadow, would soon grow ubiquitous with the advent of the early sound-movie processes such as Vitaphone and Photophone. Tom Brown Jr. also reports a theory that, during the six weeks or so the tour spent in Texas, Oklahoma, Louisiana, Tennessee, and Kentucky, part of the trouble may have lain in the title's suggestion of an interracial company.[117]

A pair of reunions on the road had recalled the past for Tom. In late November in Houston, he spent some time with H. G. Thayer, said to have been his first music instructor and the man who taught him how to play the clarinet.[118] In St. Louis in mid-January, Western Variety Managers' Association (WVMA) booker Joseph Erber brought together Tom and Billy Markwith, who was still doing his Tom Brown imitation as a member of one of three saxophone acts managed by C. L. Brown under the name "Original Brown Saxophone Six."[119] The WVMA had been booking the acts into midwestern movie houses with the help of "advance agent" Adelin (elsewhere called Adelaide) Lyle, who

> worked along lines which are deserving of study by psycho-analysts [sic]: She invariably emphasized that the acts she sold must not be billed as "The Six Brown Brothers," and that the acts she offered were "The Original Brown Saxophone Six," but she harped so much on this that she confused every manager and press agent and every phonograph shop manager until almost without exception the advertising would read "Six Brown Brothers."[120]

The Brown-Markwith meeting ended in a truce with the conditions that the WVMA would no longer book C. L. Brown's sextets and that Markwith would in future call his own group the Saxo-Sextette.[121] Apparently some kind of amity was expressed, since Variety reported that "Tom Brown felt that Clayton Leroy Brown, who cannot be located at present, had done him greater injury than Billy Markwith,"[122] and for that reason agreed to the encounter. As it turned out, Markwith was even included in Tom's next venture, a thirty-piece saxophone band for the vaudeville-and-movies market.

14

Between Showings

1924–27

B*lack and White Revue of 1924* stood at the beginning of a period of exper-imentation for Tom Brown. Except for two and a half months in the Australian summer of 1924–25 and a few weeks the following September, the Six Brown Brothers existed only as an adjunct to larger groups for the next four years, as Tom fronted, one after another, a large all-saxophone band, a minstrel show, and a dance-band stage attraction. As moving pic-tures grew to dominate show business, acts like Tom's new enterprises became interchangeable ingredients in the vaudeville sandwiched between films. Although Tom's acts could count on steady employment, their income declined along with their prestige.

Tom didn't stop long, if at all, to mourn the passing of *Black and White*, which was to be his last connection with a full-length stage production. On April 1, 1924, he signed a contract that would take the Six Brown Brothers to Australia the following December, with some idea (unrealized, as it turned out) of continuing on around the globe.[1] Meanwhile, his chief musical ven-ture was to be a version of a turn held over from *Black and White*, the Saxo-phone Boys and Girls, now billed as the Six Brown Brothers and Their Thirty-Piece Saxophone Band. A publicity photo in a Buescher ad in *Variety* shows all five living Browns, along with a tenor sax player who may be Harry Young, standing in front of twenty-two other saxophonists—Tom costumed as always, the other Brothers in a variation on their usual Pierrot outfits, and the supporting musicians in fox-hunting getups, like the Guy Brothers' Min-strels in their 1897–98 first part.[2] The photo shows the band to consist of seven women and twenty-one men, holding four sopranos, nine altos, nine tenors,[3] two baritones, and four basses (see figure 15). The personnel may have overlapped with that of the Saxophone Boys and Girls, but *Variety* implied that the group had been newly assembled, with musicians "recruited . . . from all parts of the country," and that it even included "Billy Markwith and his saxo players, formerly in vaudeville and with shows."[4] *Jacobs' Orches-tra Monthly* added that eleven of the players (six women and five men) had been recruited from the saxophone department at Tom Brown's Band and Orchestra School, a new adjunct to what had been Tom Brown's Saxophone Shop, now renamed the Tom Brown Music Company.[5] The new aggregation opened at Balaban and Katz's Chicago Theatre, just around the corner from the Tom Brown Music Company, on May 19, ultimately completing the same three-week tour of the Chicago, Tivoli, and Riviera Theatres that the Brothers had the previous year, in the same three-week time slot.[6] Just as in 1923, the Brown act was the only live attraction at the movie chain. *Variety's* business report on Windy City cinemas after the Browns' opening week opined that a return to normal business at the Chicago, despite five "miserable" rainy days out of the seven, was owed in considerable part to the Brothers' new production.[7]

After the June 8 closing at the Riviera, the group headed for New York, likely playing a number of engagements en route, including one at the Circle Theatre in Indianapolis. It was probably just before this trip that the Brothers' act was recorded on film in a one-reeler called *The Fine Art of Making Musical Instruments*, produced by the Atlas Educational Film Company of Chicago. The feature's main emphasis was upon the Buescher Band Instrument Company's manufacturing facilities in Elkhart, Indiana, and was slated to be "exhibited in all schools and Y.M.C.A. houses throughout the country, as well as in all of the better-class motion picture theatres."[8] When the Brown organization stopped in Elkhart to do two performances at the Bucklen Theatre on June 13, Buescher management hosted a luncheon for them at the Hotel Elkhart, in recognition of Tom's valuable endorsement of Buescher saxophones and his warm friendship with Gus Buescher.[9]

Advance buzz in *Variety* said that the new Brown venture would include thirty-two players, noting, "It is expected the band will parade daily on Broadway," where they were to play at the Mark Strand Theatre, just a block away from Dillingham's Globe.[10] The Buescher ad already mentioned inflated the figure even further, billing the group (under the photo with twenty-eight faces) as "Tom Brown and the Famous Six Brown Brothers with Their Stupendous Added Attraction—A 30 Piece Buescher True-Tone Saxophone Band." They opened at the Strand on June 29 for a two-week stand (whether with or without parades is not known), alternating with a Blanche Sweet film titled *Those Who Dance*. Although the live portion of the show also included an overture by the Mark Strand Symphony Orchestra, a tenor-soprano vocal duet, and a ballet danced by a company of twenty, the bill amounted to less than even the abbreviated vaudeville bills characteristic of the "State-Lake policy," so that *Variety* reviewed the Brown outfit's twenty-minute turn in its new "Presentations" department.

> Making use of the theatre's enlarged stage, heralded as being the biggest in any picture house in the world, this well known sextet lead off by their proverbial march around the area provided. Coming on in half stage, the six men render a quartet of numbers, closely adher-

ing to their former routine, and two of which are augmented by the
house orchestra, before the remaining 24 members are introduced.

Going to full stage, the entire ensemble plays three selections,
inclusive of one instance of vocalizing by a saxophonist and a comedy depiction of a hunt scene that was good for ripples but little else.
. . . One number had the mouths of the instruments rimmed by
miniature lighted bulbs that proved effective, but would be even
more so were all the small electrics working. . . .

As given here, the act shapes itself as an entertaining insertion
for a film theatre program that can class with the best. More does it
class as a solidly based addition to a program that is bound to please
a majority of the patronage.

The review is clearly favorable overall, in spite of the suggestion that the
comedy presented is partly familiar and partly unfunny. But the reviewer
("Skig") broaches a comparison that wouldn't have been important a few
years before:

As a stage attraction the saxaphone [sic] band is of undoubted value,
as proved by better than three-quarters of a house being present
downstairs on a sultry Sunday mid-afternoon [June 30], but it would
seem limited to such, with little chance of purveying the music for
the wax floor enthusiasts other than as a novelty.[11]

It was only during a short period leading up to 1924 that dance bands
started to be considered a part of show business and dancers (Skig's "wax floor
enthusiasts") a distinct audience that show journalism needed to take into
account. A turning point was Florenz Ziegfeld's decision to book Art Hickman's Orchestra for the finale of his *Follies of 1920*. Ziegfeld had hired Hickman, a San Francisco bandleader, the preceding year to play for dancing in
the nightclub atop the New Amsterdam Theatre, home of the *Follies* series,
but the inclusion of his orchestra in the downstairs revue itself was a crowd-
pleasing novelty that inspired emulators. Paul Whiteman, another San Francisco musician, and his orchestra appeared in *George White's Scandals of 1922*
and the 1923 *Follies*, and Charles Dornberger's Orchestra replaced them in
the 1923 *Scandals*.[12] Tom's advance publicity for the Strand engagement let
it be known that "several show producers are angling for the saxo band, with
Earl Carroll negotiating . . . for the musicians as one of the features with his
new 'Vanities.'"[13] Besides making rare appearances in prestigious Broadway
shows, dance bands also began to tour in vaudeville, as smaller, hot-jazz
bands had been doing since about 1917. *Variety* had just begun publishing
"Band and Orchestra Routes" as a department on a par with its long-estab-
lished listing of vaudeville artists' routes, along with reviews of dance-band
performances and recordings. From the commercial point of view, it mat-
tered a lot whether a musical organization like the big saxophone band could
win the affections of the ballroom-dancing public. And Skig thought not.

Nevertheless, the Brothers and their saxophone band had embarked on a successful tour, with some high points for their employers. After closing at the Strand on July 12, the group followed Fred Waring's Pennsylvanians into the Stanley Theatre in Philadelphia, where a break in the summer heat favored the bill, improving the Stanley's very good summer business even beyond the level it had reached with the help of Waring's popular group. *Variety* credited the "crackerjack surrounding program, headed by the Six Brown Brothers and their band" with pulling in the crowds.[14] Management held the act over for a second week, anticipating correctly that audiences and critics would not much like the feature that replaced Buster Keaton's magnificent *Sherlock Jr.*—a Claire Windsor melodrama called *For Sale*. "From the enthusiasm shown by audiences," reported *Variety*, it appeared that "many returned expressly to hear the saxophonists."[15] In August, the Brothers' act did for the Buffalo Hippodrome what it had done for the Stanley, drawing in some of the biggest audiences of the summer and playing matinees to sold-out houses with standees.[16] Venturing west, the act landed in Kansas City, Missouri, where a moribund Newman Theatre was revived in late September when the Browns "brought the smiles back to the Newman management and started the turnstiles clicking toward the normal mark."[17] *Variety's* reporter added that "it is reported the Browns received $3,500 for the week, but the takings jumped from around $10,000 for the preceding week to close to $16,000 last week, making it look like a good buy." In Australia the following winter (or summer, if the reader is in the Southern Hemisphere), Tom told an interviewer that the saxophone band had "created a furore all over America" and that he intended to reorganize it when he returned home.[18] But in fact the experiment was abandoned forever.

The Kansas City engagement at the end of September was apparently the last for the Six Brown Brothers and Their Thirty-Piece Saxophone Band, and the sextet seems to have stayed off the stage altogether during October. By the end of that month, Tom was back in Chicago, generating the paperwork necessary for the planned trip to Australia.[19] Neither the larger group nor the Brothers played the four-week return engagement at Balaban and Katz's Chicago houses that had been forecast in their advance publicity.[20] Instead, the October and November attractions at the Chicago, Riviera, and Tivoli Theatres were evidently in-house productions, sometimes with the generic title "B & K Stage Show." Like the Brothers' presentation, the more provocatively named "New Startling, Mysterious Radio Week," featuring the Mound City Blue Blowers (a novelty jazz group with a handful of successful Brunswick recordings, then appearing on WMAQ), and the "Giant Musical Production" "In a Song Shop" brightened each of the three theatres for a week while the remaining two relied on movies only.[21] Perhaps it was during this hiatus that Tom traveled to Omaha to visit H. A. Waggener and guest star in the Ak-Sar-Ben show for the year, *Bullfornia*.[22]

In mid-November, a slightly different version of the Brothers, without Alec and with two unknown non-Browns, gathered in San Francisco for a three-week cruise to Sydney, Australia, via Honolulu and Samoa, on the Oceanic Steamship Company's SS *Sierra*. Taking advantage of an opportunity presented to few, Theresa went along on the trip as a tourist rather than a performer and brought Tom Jr. with her. As the Browns awaited the *Sierra's* departure, they could have enjoyed former partner Blackface Eddie Ross's act on the movies-plus-continuous-vaudeville slate at the Golden Gate Theatre or caught Paul Ash's presentation at the Granada during the week of November 10–16, "Dancing Mad," with its fourteen dancing demons.[23]

The *Sierra* sailed from chilly San Francisco on the afternoon of November 18 and arrived in balmy Honolulu five days later. The Oceanic Steamship Company advertised "unsurpassed cuisine. Pleasure and entertainment the day long. Deck sports, golf, tennis, swimming tank, dancing, etc.,"[24] and indeed the trip was a pleasant one for the troupe. Tom, Theresa, and Tommy, from the evidence of a few snapshots, seem to have passed the time mostly with other show people, rather than with Bill, Vern, Fred, and the two unidentified replacements in the Brothers. Among their set were George Gee, a musical-comedy actor on his way to Australia to star in productions of *Good Morning, Dearie*, and *Kid Boots*, and Philip and Stella Wirth, two members of an eminent Australian circus-performer family. A snapshot and an old program among Theresa's memorabilia show that, besides the amusements provided by Oceanic management, there were bobbing for apples on the deck, shipboard visits from handome young Hawaiians, and a Grand Concert put on by the passengers on November 29. Among the twelve Grand Concert acts were a saxophone solo by Tommy, "A Mystery Show" by Theresa, a number by the Six Brown Brothers, a comic monologue by George Gee, and "Mr George Gee's 'Bum' Quartette," for which Tom provided one of the voices.

The Browns reached Sydney harbor on December 10. After a short rest, they took a train to Brisbane, where the Brothers entertained for a week at the Wintergarden Theatre, played to capacity houses and "created a furore."[25] On Christmas Day, they moved on to Melbourne's Tivoli Theatre, under management that almost exclusively hired non-Australian talent.[26] They remained for four and a half weeks, playing two shows a day to enthusiastic capacity houses. From Melbourne they moved to the Sydney Tivoli for five weeks, where they headlined "the strongest bill seen for many moons. . . . The acts getting the biggest applause were all Americans. The Six Brown Brothers stopped the show cold at their opening and have continued holding up each performance."[27] The two-a-day schedule and long runs must have been something of a relief after the summer's grind of four or five daily movie-house appearances and weekly moves from town to town.

A salary of 350 pounds per week and plenty of leisure time helped turn the Australian tour into something like a long vacation. Tom, Theresa, and Tom Jr. spent a lot of their spare time together at various tracks, betting on horses. A mock press release written for Tom by Harry Muller, apparently one of the Tivoli management, suggests that Tom's vacation activities also included deep-sea fishing, heavy drinking, and perhaps some skirt chasing. On a fishing cruise, when he got sick from the mix of wind, waves, and whiskey, "Tom Brown was shown a headland which was pointed out to him as the famous Gap from which many suicides had taken their last leap, but Mr Brown's feelings at the time compelled him to remark that he did not think it necessary to leave the boat, as he felt he was committing suicide by remaining." On the subject of alcohol, Muller puts the following words in Tom's mouth: "Australians don't drink. They pickle themselves in it. Even theatrical managers imbibe, and occasionally got the habit of asking me to do the same during business hours in the theatre—a most unique experience from an artist's point of view." On the subject of women (perhaps): "However, on the eve of my departure I arranged a date to see a very beautiful bird, but unfortunately could not make the connection, on account of other pressing engagements. Still, I understand these birds are plentiful in Australia, and I hope to catch another one on my return."[28]

Except for their brief tour of Keith houses in the summer of 1921, the Brothers hadn't had a real vaudeville run in a little over a decade, since they had first linked their fortunes to Dillingham and Fred Stone. It must have been exhilarating to reenter the old arena in the slightly old-fashioned Australian setting, where vaudeville hadn't taken a back seat to film to the extent it had in the United States. Cheering crowds would still turn up for a program of saxophone music and comedy, "colored talkers and steppers," two comedy teams, a magician, various singers, dancers, and instrumentalists, and a bicycle act for the last slot. In Australia, vaudeville had apparently moved very little beyond where it had been in England when the Brothers were part of the All American bill at the Finsbury Park Empire; but now the Brothers were at the top of the bill, thanks to the reputation they had built away from the vaudeville stage. Their experience on returning to North America was to be far different.

Between March 12 and April 2, the Browns crossed the Pacific on a British vessel, the SS *Aorangi*, arriving in Victoria, British Columbia, a year and a day after signing the contract. A notation in Tom's passport suggests that the group was offered twelve weeks' booking in New Zealand, but for unknown reasons Tom declined. Perhaps the problem was that twelve weeks would have carried the Browns beyond the expiration date on the papers granting them permission to reenter the United States. They got back to Chicago around April 20,[29] where Tom began work on his next project, one that, for the first time since the group was founded, didn't include the Six Brown Brothers.

Although the Brothers almost always drew favorable reviews, the few deprecatory remarks directed at them concerned the familiarity of their material. The song list always stayed up to date, but the stage business remained pretty much the same, even with Tom wearing a Tutankhamen headdress. One lesson experience in show business teaches is that novelty is generally a plus. Unfortunately, another lesson is that too extreme a departure from what audiences expect can alienate an established act's fan base altogether. After the Australian triumph as a two-a-day headliner, Tom probably didn't want to go back to playing five turns a day between films with a scattering of other acts. He tried instead to return to the presentation field, surprisingly separating himself from the Six Brown Brothers and making another attempt to mount a minstrel show, despite the failure of the minstrel-flavored Black and White Revue.

The new venture was a self-contained show billed at its May 25 introduction as "Minstrel Week With the One and Only Tom Brown of the Famous Six Brown Brothers And His 40 Famous Minstrels, A Regular Riot of Fun and Melody," presented at the Capitol Theatre on Chicago's South Side (Seventy-ninth and Halsted Streets).[30] Tom wrote to Waggener that among the musical arrangements used in the show were some Waggener had sent from Omaha. The show "went over so big that they booked us for the Stratford" for the following week.[31] The Tribune ad for the Stratford (closer in, at Sixty-third and Halsted) averred that "because of the tremendous crowds that stormed the Capitol last week, we are transferring the entire Minstrel Show with Tom Brown and His Famous Forty Minstrels to the Stratford[.] If you missed it at the Capitol see it any day this week at the Stratford."[32] Variety reviewed it at the Capitol on May 29, showing some enthusiasm for Tom, but not much for the rest. "Brown is still the master of the sax and coupled with the comedy that he dispenses came near tying up the proceedings. . . . Tom Brown's name is a big factor in putting this show over." It began with a full-cast parade across the stage, followed by a first part in which Tom, costumed and made up as usual, took the part of interlocutor. Tom's routine with the four end men was "ancient in spots but apparently new to this gathering." The opening comedy led to a succession of individual turns by dancers, singers, a vocal trio, a Chinese string band, a saxophone sextet (not the original Brothers, but led by Tom), and a ten-piece jazz and dance band. "The feature of the combination is a solo played by the trombonist utilizing his foot in operating the slide. This brought a spontaneous round of applause." The finale, again involving all forty participants, featured radium-treated uniforms that glowed in the dark. The anonymous reviewer, in closing, offered advice and held out hope for success. "The turn as it now stands needs more work up to whip it into shape. The comedy should be bolstered and with a little rearranging in the numbers will encounter no difficulty in continuing as a picture house attraction."[33]

The review says nothing about the commercial wisdom of framing and billing the presentation as a minstrel show, although one might think the minstrel format and brand, themselves as ancient as the end men's jokes, would be a liability. But minstrelsy was not as dead as it seemed, even though the few large touring companies left were on the far margins of show business. Variety reported later in the year that minstrelsy, in abbreviated form, is enjoying a revived vogue in the independently booked small-time vaude houses. Bookers are scrambling for any available offering of this type since several, recently routed over the independent time, chalked up new high grosses. . . . Prefacing the minstrels is a street parade. This generally is enlarged by the induction of local youngsters who don cork and line up in the march in exchange for passes to the show. Most of the outfits carry a jazz band which comes in handy in the parade and also for lobby dancing preceding and following the performances.[34]

Perhaps Tom's innovation was partly responsible for this limited comeback of the old form. There are no reports to indicate that he was joining a trend already launched.[35]

Except for a handful of dates, the Brothers were on hiatus for the next fourteen months, at first replaced to some extent by the saxophone six traveling with the Forty Famous Minstrels. Alec may have been with the Vincent Lopez Orchestra during this period and spending more time with Edith and the children in New Jersey, but it is unknown what Vern, Fred, and William were doing. Family members recall that William was married to a woman named Nettie in the mid-1920s. Perhaps he and Fred just enjoyed domestic life on their Australia savings. (Two possible members of the saxophone six and the subsequently revived Six Brown Brothers may have been a former Ringling bandsman named Lester Rush, who said he was a part of the group in the period 1925–27, and Jack Powell, later a solo blackface comedian in Murray Anderson's *Almanac*.)[36]

Whether the comedy was bolstered and the numbers rearranged is unknown, but the Forty Famous Minstrels folded in a few months, despite stands at major theatres such as the Missouri in St. Louis and Indianapolis's Circle.[37] Dillingham's 1919 warning had been right, it seems, but Tom was not ready to give up minstrelsy altogether. By September, the Six Brown Brothers were resurrected, filling small bills at picture houses on the East Coast[38] as Tom prepped the "jazz band" feature of the Forty Famous Minstrels, now called Tom Brown and His Merry Minstrel Orchestra, for an autonomous tour on the Keith (now called the Keith-Albee) circuit. Perhaps the Australian triumph had whetted Tom's appetite for big-time vaudeville (or what was left of it in the States by 1925). But instead of bringing back the tried, true, and somewhat too familiar Brothers, he fielded his version of one of the most marketable items on the current stage, the hot dance band.

In *Variety*'s 1924 year's-end review of the condition of show business, there appeared a piece called "Bands!" that addressed itself mostly to the success and bright prospects of dance bands in both vaudeville and movie-theatre settings. "Practically three out of every five vaudeville bills include band attractions. For mass popularity, from stage presentation, the band is a sure-fire commodity." The author noted that band shows that filled the entire space between movies were a great bargain for cinema managers, as the presentations could be paid $2,250 to $2,500 per week while boosting revenues by much more than that. The situation in vaudeville was different, because "the bookers, for one reason or another, assume that the bands are 'doubling' with a local dance job, and should therefore be content with a cut salary on the theory that both engagements in total should satisfy the organization's income." Bands who put on some sort of act, however, were said to be in better shape in vaudeville than ones who merely played dance music.[39] The Merry Minstrels belonged to the former category.

They opened on October 12 at the cavernous Hippodrome, once controlled by Dillingham but now another jewel in Keith-Albee's ever-growing Manhattan crown. Their compact version of a minstrel show, parade and all, blended with the latest dance tunes, elicited a strong endorsement from *Variety*: "The Tom Brown's minstrel orchestra is more than a stage band. Its consummate showmanship in blending comedy with unusual syncopation places a stamp of distinction on the organization. This . . . is a pliable unit, as readily pleasing for vaudeville as for production, picture houses, cafes or what not."[40]

Publicity photos, probably taken in the fall of 1925, show a generally young-looking band of two trumpets, trombone, four saxophones (counting Tom's), piano, banjo, sousaphone, and drums, a standard line-up for the mid-1920s. The photos don't, however, show the hedge of alternate instruments (baritone saxophones, oboes, slide whistles, English horns, and others) in front of the saxophonists that the Art Hickman and Paul Whiteman Orchestras had made popular. Tom has his alto and soprano saxes, and the two other alto players have sopranos as well as clarinets, but the tenor player has only a soprano as a double.[41] In one photo, the musicians are all in blackface, Tom dressed as always and the others in tailcoats with oversize lapels and buttons, light-colored trousers with broad stripes, dark satin capes with a lighter-colored lining and exaggerated stand-up collars, and top hats. As a final interlocutor touch, they all, except for Tom, carry canes. In four other shots, three with instruments, the band aside from Tom appears without makeup, wearing dark satin tuxedo jackets with white oversize cuffs and lapels, both decorated with a musical staff bearing a treble-clef sign and a few notes (see figure 16). Even Tom's lower sleeves carry this motif. The jackets are worn over dark satin vests and trousers with broad dark and light stripes. Wing collars, bow ties, and slicked-back hair create a perfect John Held look for the ensemble, especially standing on their giant dice chairs, instruments pointed ceilingward in simulation of an outburst of wild jazz. The backdrops may be photo-studio props, or they may be ones used in the act—one of tumbling dice roughly the size of the bandsmen's chairs, one of a hotel garden with Tom conducting the band drawn up in parade formation, and one of a sleepy Dixie river scene with the tumbling-dice drop furled to the sides.[42]

The week after the Hippodrome performance, the band was transferred to Keith's Riverside, on New York's Upper West Side, where they were placed last in an overlong show but were engaging enough to keep the audience in the theatre until the end. "Tom Brown and his orchestra . . . held them like the Army line," said an opening-night reviewer, alluding to the formidable West Point football team.[43]

One ingredient was still missing from the recipe for success as a dance band: a recording contract. Its potential importance went far beyond the prospects of extra income from sales of discs, for records were a way of creating demand for the band's performances in advance of their arrival at the local Keith-Albee house. Reciprocally, at least one recording company (Brunswick) reportedly supplemented the vaudeville salaries of bands under contract in order to create demand for the discs.[44] Tom managed to get a commitment from the Okeh company to wax some numbers in New York in November of 1925, possibly on the strength of the press's warm reception of his new group. Besides the two titles issued, "Forever and Ever with You" and "It's the Blues," Tom made a test recording of "At Dawn" to find out whether his Sax soprano would record well, and he was pleased with the result.[45] The issued disc seems not to have sold well, since the next Okeh date—which was also the last—resulted in only one issued side, "Good Night, I'll See You in the Morning."[46]

The arrangements on the three discs are lively and up-to-date, but neither as streamlined as Paul Whiteman's nor as hot as the previous year's West Coast crop from bands such as Art Hickman's and Henry Halstead's, let alone those played by coeval African American groups such as Fletcher Henderson's.[47] Tom's alto, with its wide vibrato and piercing tone, seems to be featured on the first chorus and second verse of "Forever and Ever with You" and on the bridge of the first chorus of "Goodnight," and he may be one of the clarinets playing a duet on "It's the Blues," but there are no saxophone or clarinet solos that sound like improvisations. The trombonist, very competent on all three pieces, is at his best on "It's the Blues," playing in a plausible black style. The engaging orchestration of the latter piece opens with an ensemble of four saxes and tuba that recalls Six Brown Brothers charts from the 1910s, with old-fashioned dotted rhythms and an ostinato bass that give way to a more swung rhythm in the balance of the performance, perhaps intentionally creating a then-and-now contrast to point up the difference between the Brothers and the Merry Minstrels. The texture of what follows keeps shifting, from full ensemble to solo trombone over rhythm to a brass trio to a duet for clarinets, one bending notes in the high register and the other slap-tonguing down in the chalumeau. Similarly varied, the other two arrangements have their attractive moments, including, on "Goodnight," eight bars of solo ukulele and almost a full chorus in which the saxophone section imitates a banjo. The Minstrels, however, don't have the cohesive sound of the period's top orchestras, and mistakes are plainly audible from time to time. If the discs represent them at their best, the group was not destined for dance-band stardom independently of its stage routines.

After touring Keith-Albee theatres for a couple of months, the Merry Minstrels switched to the Orpheum circuit, which, according to Tom, had promised them headliner status. For unknown reasons, the promise was not kept. When he reached Omaha, Tom wrote to Doc Waggener, who had just moved to Los Angeles,

> I doubt whether I shall be in Los Angeles with this show as I am changing my route this Saturday and may go back east. They started us out on the Orpheum circuit to be headlined and after we were out a week or two, switched us over to this road-show, which buries us to a certain extent on account of the headliners[48] already being in the show when we joined it; so unless they send us out by ourselves we will close Saturday night, here in Omaha.

Tom wrote also that the finale of the act was a performance of "Remember" in which he not only played the Sax soprano, but also sang. "Up to date there have been no bricks or tin cans from over the foot-lights."[49]

The broken promise was not the only indignity the Orpheum circuit visited on the Merry Minstrels. Every act in the unit show was required not only to do its regular turn, but also to stick around for a full-cast thirty-minute afterpiece at no extra pay, saving the circuit the cost of the additional two acts it would have taken to fill the bill. With vaudeville rapidly losing out to the movies as a favorite diversion for the American public, such penny-pinching had sadly become typical of even the major circuits. Tom decided not to put up with it and switched his outfit to the Pantages circuit; it had a pictures-and-vaudeville policy throughout its empire, which lay mostly on the Pacific coast. Perhaps to annoy Orpheum management, the Merry Minstrels' first stand was right in Omaha, at the World Theatre.[50] In another letter to Waggener, Tom indicated that there had been a substantial change in the personnel of the Minstrels: "I have all of my new men and we are rehearsing every day."[51]

By July of 1926, Tom and his band, now billed as the Lucky 'Leven Orchestra, had returned to Chicago in a pictures-and-vaudeville format, but not at a big Loop venue such as the State-Lake, the Chicago, or the lavish Oriental that Balaban and Katz had recently built as a showcase for Paul Ash. They were advertised to open at Lubliner and Trinz's Harding Theatre, far out at Milwaukee and Sawyer, while downtown houses featured dance bands such as Art Kahn's Novelty Syncopators, Ralph Williams and His Jazz Jesters, and the orchestras of Bennie Krueger and Sammy Kahn.[52] Perhaps because he was faced with such formidable competition on his home territory, Tom gave up on the Merry Minstrels as a self-sufficient unit, and subsequent advertisements announced "Tom Brown and the Lucky 'Leven Minstrel Orchestra with the Six Brown Brothers."[53] Though it is not known exactly what the personnel of the group was at this point, the Brothers were back, and back more or less for good. Evidence suggests that there were only fourteen members in the troupe at this point, so that two of the Brothers (besides Tom) must have been performing in both the sextet and the dance band.[54]

Over the next two months, Tom negotiated with the Tivoli management's American agents for a return to Australia with the Brothers and the

Minstrel Orchestra. At first Tom asked for 300 pounds weekly (probably just for the sextet), but the agent considered that excessive. Subsequent discussions included the whole fourteen-man combination, then returned to the idea of the Brothers alone, but the agent opined that the act would cost too much even at 150 pounds a week. Ultimately, the talks came to nothing.[55]

In August, Tom inverted the billing to read "The Original Six Brown Brothers and Their Augmented Orchestra" and left Chicago for a tour of Pantages houses on the West Coast. He was also leaving Theresa for the last time. Tensions in the Brown marriage had been increasing during the previous two years, Theresa reportedly charged, over Tom's heavy drinking. In October 1926, she filed a divorce suit, and six months later the writ was granted.[56] Factors besides Tom's "anti-Volstead"[57] penchant may have contributed to the breakup. After sixteen years, Theresa was no longer at her husband's side in show business, and so was probably resentful that he had a career while she didn't and possibly suspicious of his fidelity on the road. Tom Jr. also reports that Theresa was at some point (at least after the separation) courted by Will Morgan, one of the alto saxophonists in the Merry Minstrels, but decided against a relationship because of the difference between their ages; perhaps there was, already in 1926, some hint of Will's adoration in the air lending weight to the alternative of divorce. Tom was devastated by the collapse, but kept on working, newly obligated after the decree to pay Theresa a reported $400 a month in alimony.[58]

Newspaper descriptions of the Augmented Orchestra's performances are hard to find. The fading importance of vaudeville was mirrored in the dwindling amount of space given to reviews in the dailies, who now lovingly and at length detailed the plots of the movies shown in the same theatres. A brief review of their turn at the San Francisco Pantages in mid-August, however, indicates a partial return to the Thirty-Piece Saxophone Orchestra: "The sextet evokes sweet harmony on the brass, and they intersperse their numbers with band set-pieces in which fourteen saxophones, ranging from the ponderous B-flat to piccolo-sized trebles, join in."[59] The unidiomatic reference to saxophones as "brass" and the evocation, both unidiomatic and hyperbolic, of "piccolo-sized trebles" suggest that these are not the words of a press release, but an attempt to record what the reviewer actually saw. Another reviewer of the same performance failed to note the feature, however, but perhaps he didn't stay for the stage show.[60] For the second week of the San Francisco stand, Tom took a page from the Orpheum circuit's book and organized the stage performers into an afterpiece, somehow amassing a cast of forty to present a forty-five-minute capsule version of a minstrel show. Known members of the show were Burnum, a singer "who does female impersonations, dresses magnificently and puts his act over well"; the Four Pals, comedians and singers; Lillian Gonne and Roy La Pearl, "who offer a jumble of impromptu comedy"[61] that included bringing an Italian singer and a pianist up from the audience; and Billy Carmen, a xylophonist and monologist with "a spirited turn."[62] Details of the minstrel show, including the identities of the remaining sixteen performers, are not known, but it does not appear that Tom tried this experiment again on the Pantages tour.

The Brothers and Their Augmented Orchestra worked up and down the Pacific coast from Vancouver to San Diego until late November, when they started eastward through Salt Lake City, Denver, and Omaha.[63] In January and February, the orchestra marked time in the Midwest, awaiting a tour of the eastern Stanley circuit that was to begin in mid-March. Bookings were steady through all of 1927. A surviving itinerary for the year shows twenty-eight stands lasting a full week and nineteen more ranging from one to six days (totaling sixty-three days), so that the Augmented Orchestra was onstage 259 of the year's 365 days, working as many days as a person with a Monday-to-Friday job and two weeks' vacation. Pay started out at a respectable level, usually $2,000 for a week at big midwestern theatres such as the Missouri in St. Louis and the Capitol in Des Moines, and remained at that level through a series of Stanley circuit dates in April, May, and June that included a week each at the Brooklyn[64] and Manhattan Strand Theatres, where the Thirty-Piece Saxophone Band had triumphed three years before. But after a three-day run at the Earle in Atlantic City, New Jersey, something happened to break Tom's connection with Stanley, and the aggregation returned to the Pantages circuit for the balance of the year at reduced weekly pay—usually pegged at $1,500, but ranging from a stingy $1,200 at the Los Angeles Forum in September to $1,800 at the Omaha World in October. The decline in income must have been distressing.

On May 5, just before opening at the New York Strand, the Brown organization earned a whopping $3,000 for a single day's work, filming a short movie (or "record," as they were called at the time) for the Vitaphone Corporation, makers of the first commercially successful sound films. The process, which required a delicate synchronization of the projector running the film and the disc bearing the sound, yielded results of uneven quality. But it was so far superior to earlier attempts at a viable talking-picture technology that by February 1927 Vitaphone boasted in a two-page *Variety* ad of contracts with seventy-four theatres, including familiar Brothers venues such as Grauman's Egyptian in Hollywood, the Mark Strands in Brooklyn and Manhattan, the Chicago Capitol, and the Indianapolis Circle.[65] Hundreds more movie houses acquired the necessary apparatus before the original Vitaphone setup was superseded by the more reliable sound-on-film processes still used today. The Vitaphone Corporation itself soon became a division of Warner Brothers and lent its name to hundreds of films that didn't employ discs for sound.

A contract to make a Vitaphone short was not in itself a sign of fame. The quickly expanding market for product called for the filming of any professional-quality act passing through New York and willing to spend a few hours in the studio. The moving picture as a medium for the Brothers' act must have seemed an attractive alternative to the shrinking and progressively dishonored world of vaudeville. The until then ascendant entertainment technologies of radio and silent cinema were unsuited to an act that appealed to audiences as much for its visual as for its aural dimension (although the Brothers had worked in both those media).[66] But just behind the attractive surface lurked the same problem Tom had been dealing with since the end of his association with Fred Stone: the Six Brown Brothers had been doing substantially the same routine, though with a continually updated music playlist, since 1911; how could audiences be expected to keep coming back for what might appear to them to be the same thing over and over? Tom had dealt with the problem by doing his minstrel routine in *Black and White* and by mounting the Thirty-Piece Saxophone Band, the Forty Famous Minstrels, and the Merry Minstrel Orchestra—in short, by setting the Brown Brothers act aside in various ways. Vitaphone made the familiarity problem even worse by freezing the act in the form it had assumed on May 5, 1927. What would be the point, for a film producer, of doing a second or third Vitaphone of the Brothers, even if the tunes were different? In addition, Vitaphone created the new problem of competition against oneself. Not every potential customer who wanted to see the Six Brown Brothers would choose the real thing over the fascinating novelty of a giant booming simulacrum. When the Brothers played in one house and their images in another, the Vitaphone version would inevitably siphon off a portion of the receptive public. Tom Brown Jr. recalls that, during his stint with the Brothers in 1929–30, houses where they appeared would sometimes advertise "The Original Six Brown Brothers—Live, Not on the Vitaphone." There is a real question whether it was worth it to accept roughly ten times the normal performance fee (since royalties were not part of the deal) to make a short movie that would play many more than ten times, and occasionally take away a part of the act's public.

Sadly, the film made that day, *Six Original Brown Brothers, Saxaphonic [sic] Jazz Masters and Orchestra* is not known to exist, but at least one copy of the soundtrack disc survives, now in a private collection. The musicians were probably mostly the same as those in a photo taken during their March 13–16 engagement at the State Theatre in Lima, Ohio. Tom and Vern are the only Browns among the Brothers, who, aside from Tom, are dressed in diamond-checked clown suits with ruff collars and conical hats with a single pompon near the top. The four young-looking unknowns don't resemble any of the musicians in the Merry Minstrels photos, nor do the eight other players, generally older and somewhat careworn in the damp and cold Ohio alleyway. Although their faces are not made up, they also wear clownlike garb: a baggy one-piece satin garment in a plain pale color, its wide, limp collar draped over the shoulders, and pomponless conical hats in the same color. Many of the uniforms need ironing, and the tall sousaphone player's, descending only to midcalf instead of shoetops like the others', seems to have been recently inherited from a much shorter man. But the nine-minute soundtrack's music measures up to a much higher standard than that reached by the performances cut in 1925–26 by the much more snazzily dressed Merry Minstrel Orchestra. The dance band opens with one chorus of "Yankee Rose," a fast march, then yields to two short numbers by the sextet, Mabel Wayne's recent waltz hit "In a Little Spanish Town" and the Brothers' staple "The Bullfrog and the Coon." The arrangements bear no traces of the style of the sextet's Victor and Emerson recordings. Their "Spanish Town" sounds as streamlined as that of any 1927 hotel orchestra, and "Bullfrog" has been sweetened and ornamented to eliminate its former jerkiness. The electrical recording process makes it possible for the sextet to use a much wider dynamic range for expressive purposes and to play at a generally softer level without loss of detail. Unfortunately, these two pieces are the only sextet numbers in the film. After a quick reprise of "Yankee Rose," the band plays a lengthy fox trot based on themes from Leoncavallo's I Pagliacci, with a decorative overlay by the sextet, then turns to a version of "'Deed I Do" with an attractively cheerful vocal chorus by an unidentified member of the band.

Next comes Tom's abandoned-bride routine, the only surviving aural document of his amazing vocalization of the saxophone. The conversation's script hasn't changed much since Tom's sketch in his letter to Doc Waggener (see chapter 12), although the voice other than the bride's is now that of the whole band. And instead of replying to the band's "Oh, what a pal was Mary" with "Nobody knows and nobody seems to care," she bravely offers, "All by myself in the morning," following it with an anguished "All by myself in the night." Once her moaning and sobbing are done, a tenor sax plays "How Dry I Am." This then becomes the tune for Tom's Sousa parody, which closes with a ripping sound from the whole band. Comedy yields to sentiment as Tom picks up his soprano for "Rosy Cheeks" with the combined sextet and band. This version is shorter (consisting only of the chorus) and faster than the one described in chapter 12, but Tom emphasizes virtuoso display over emotion by adorning the melody with many more runs and fills than in the earlier reading. No sooner does he release the climactic high D-flat than the band begins its quick-stepping closer, "There's Something Nice about Everyone but There's Everything Nice about You," with the soprano leading and an a capella band vocal on the title phrase.

Variety's Mori reviewed the film in October 1928, after it had been in release for nearly a year, calling it "highly entertaining," noting its "speed" and "tuneful" playlist, and recommending it to exhibitors.[67] In the eyes of a show business professional like Mori, the film's only apparent value was its potential for filling movie houses. What good luck for us that the disc was not lost forever, as so many Vitaphones have been, and that it outlived its commercial value to become a historical treasure.[68]

15

Nothing Left to Do in Show Biz

1928–88

By the beginning of 1928, the Augmented Orchestra had disbanded for good. Tom seems to have given up performance altogether in the early part of the year for a period of rumination and retrenchment. No doubt the divorce and the declining revenues of the large traveling group weighed heavily in the deliberations leading up to the lengthy hiatus. On the other hand, one signal event of 1927 may have given him some encouragement: the resounding success of the first feature-length Vitaphone production, *The Jazz Singer*, starring fellow Dockstader alumnus Al Jolson. Not only did the first talkie (though it contained hardly any dialogue) open the prospect of a crossover from the moribund and marginalized variety stage to the ease and wealth of the movie business, but its star worked in burnt cork and sang the kind of material that could have graced a minstrel olio. Why couldn't the Brothers, or Tom by himself, find a place at the Hollywood table?

Tom turned up in Indianapolis at the end of January, where he dropped in at the Indiana Theatre.

> Those who attended the theater Saturday afternoon found an unscheduled attraction in a brief appearance of Tom Brown, noted band leader and director of the Brown Brothers Saxophone Sextet, who happened to be visiting Ace Berry, manager of the Indiana. Mr. Brown, unfamiliar out of blackface, made a short, amusing talk, and finally consented to borrow a saxophone from the Davis outfit [Charlie Davis and the Indiana Stage Band] and play a number with the band accompanying him. The unexpected novelty found enthusiastic favor.[1]

A few weeks later he was in Philadelphia visiting fellow saxophone pioneer and Victor artist, H. Benne Henton, who wrote to Doc Waggener that "our mutual friend Tom Brown was in town last week and as usual made our place his head quarters. We think a great deal of Tom around here and are always glad to have him stop in."[2]

There is no evidence in *Variety* listings that either of these visits was connected with a Brown performance in the vicinity. Indeed, there is no evidence that the Browns performed at all in 1928 until July, when they returned to the stage as a sextet without augmentation, probably including Tom, Fred, Alec, and Vern, and possibly William as well. They began touring on the Keith-Albee circuit, which had recently grown even larger by swallowing the huge Orpheum circuit. Although a very few Keith venues still played straight vaudeville, the Six Brown Brothers worked instead within the vaudeville-and-pictures format they had grown used to on the Balaban and Katz and Pantages time. Even *Variety* had acknowledged the steep decline of two-a-day by merging its listings of straight vaudeville performances with those of turns whose role was to entertain between showings of the week's movie. Still doing a version of the act developed in the 1910s, the Brothers appeared in cinemas from Louisville to Toronto, loved by their audiences and largely ignored by the newspapers. Even in Tom's birthplace, Ottawa, the reviewer for the *Citizen* managed only to repeat the usual stories about the Brothers' long association with Fred Stone and Tom's legendary status as the originator of the saxophone craze, for which, "on hearing and seeing [his] work and that of his associates, he can easily be forgiven. In their hands the instrument is one of melody and fun, and the latter aplenty."[3]

The vaudeville that the Brothers returned to in 1928 was in bad shape. A *Variety* piece in the year's first issue, looking back at the previous year, reported that big-time vaudeville "is generally accepted throughout the country as shot." There were plenty of vaudeville turns, the writer explained, perhaps more than ever before, but the old business apparatus of vaudeville, the system of circuits and bookings that kept it separate from other segments of show business, had practically disappeared. Vaudeville turns, he complained, had fallen far below the old average in quality. "Any steps now constitute a dancer; any mugger is accepted as a comic, and any person with nerve is still called a nut. If all were ground up together and the real performer extracted from the mass, the mass would develop a real performer in every 20." Acts that would formerly have been in vaudeville venues were now to be found in "legit" productions as well, both "drama" and comedy, "and more so than all the others combined, . . . in the picture houses." Even the elite Keith and Orpheum circuits had slowly gone over to a continuous vaudeville-and-pictures format in the great majority of their theatres, but they had been hampered in the transition by the number and size of their houses (generally smaller than the newer movie palaces) and their lack of a steady source of films, since most production companies, especially the ones employing recognized stars, had contracted their output elsewhere.

For vaudeville performers, the bright side of big time's plight was that picture houses exploited these advantages by offering higher salaries to acts and lower ticket prices to the public. "Where the vaudeville bookers sought to save $50 on a $300 turn or place the limit of $3,500 on any act, the picture houses raised the salary of the $300 turn to $400 and paid $6,000 for the act the vaudeville houses wouldn't give over $3,500." An evening of big-time vaudeville would set a customer back from $1.25 to $3.30, while a shorter bill, coupled with a visit to the Hollywood dream world, could be had for 50 to 99 cents. "There was no comparison in entertainment or price." Through the mid-1920s, as two-a-day houses converted almost universally to continuous vaudeville, big time lost the one major advantage, from a narrowly utilitarian point of view, that it once had, namely that it required only fourteen performances weekly, rather than the thirty or so exacted by the film houses. For the spreading format of continuous vaudeville called for about twenty-three performances over the week, leaving "little choice" for the artist who gave the matter careful consideration.[4]

A couple of surviving documents testify that the revived Brothers did fairly well in the new situation. An itinerary for June–December of 1929 shows them working 186 of the 213 days, about twenty percent more than the 151 days the Augmented Orchestra worked during the corresponding months of 1927. The 1929 itinerary unfortunately does not include salary figures, but a contract for a three-week engagement earlier in the year (March 30–April 20) promised them $1,500 a week to appear twice a day at the Chicago Stadium's Mid-Winter Circus, the same stipend the Augmented Orchestra, more than twice as large, had gotten on most of the Pantages circuit (for three or so shows a day) in the second half of 1927.[5] The sixty-act circus was an adjunct to a Wild West show called Miller Brothers 101 Ranch. The Six Brown Brothers were the only act billed by name in print advertising except for Zack Miller and His Famous Cowboys and Indians.[6]

The Brothers were playing the Lyric Theatre in Indianapolis on Black Thursday, October 24, 1929, when the economic depression that had been slouching across Europe and the farms of the United States since the Great War finally reached Wall Street, and the grossly inflated, credit-driven stock market went into a swoon that only another world war would awaken it from. The immediate effect on the act was negligible, since Tom's principal investments were the Tom Brown Music Company and an occasional wager on a horse race. But in a fairly short time, the rare vaudeville-only venues started closing, picture houses began to switch from stage-and-movie policies to pictures only (with the help of Vitaphone shorts of the turns they might otherwise have hired to perform live), and, worst of all, theatres began to close altogether as the shrinking money supply diverted the mass public's disposable income from entertainment to food and shelter.

Tom Jr. had joined the Brothers (replacing William) for the summer of 1929, between terms at Lake Forest Academy, and then for a longer stretch after he graduated in June 1930. He recalls that, at the onset of the depression, the Brothers gave up traveling by train, saving a few dollars by touring in two cars. Itineraries with short hops, carefully planned by theatre circuits to move artists from city to city in plenty of time to assure their availability, were replaced by schedules cobbled together by desperate agents from the few venues still hiring. During one especially bad period, Tom Jr. remembers, all the theatres the Brothers were booked at between Houston, Texas, and Montreal, Quebec, closed before the scheduled performance dates, resulting in a trip of about 2000 miles between gigs. But though the demand for vaudeville acts fell dramatically, the supply remained about the same, and fierce competition inevitably resulted in a buyer's market. By the end of 1930, the Brothers were back at the Indianapolis Lyric playing four shows a day at $900 for the week of December 27–January 2.[7]

The Brothers' membership shifted rapidly during what were to prove its death throes. The contract for the Lyric at the end of 1930 lists Tom, Fred, Alec, and Vern, along with Tom Jr. and Jack Carpenter (a Merry Minstrel Orchestra alumnus), both playing tenor sax. It was probably in 1932 that Alec, who had been handling hotel reservations, travel plans, and even some bookings, left the act permanently to return to his wife and family (now three daughters and a son) in Irvington, New Jersey. He was replaced by Chris Knutsen. Fred was the next to depart, replaced by Jesse Ewing. Gigs became ever scarcer. Tom Jr. recalled an agent telephoning with an offer of "the third in Kenosha and the tenth in Milwaukee and the seventeenth in Sheboygan." Tom Sr.: "Are these week stands?" The agent: "Hell, no. Sundays." Added Tom Jr., "And we played a few of them, too."[8] Gradually, work dried up altogether.

As the depression deepened, the Tom Brown Music Company became steadily more important for Tom, and not only as a source of income. Born in 1921 as Tom Brown's Saxophone Shop under the management of William H. Lyons, it became an Illinois corporation in December 1922, with Tom as president and Lyons as treasurer. Besides the lucrative retail trade in instruments and accessories, the corporation had a wholesale operation for the entire Chicago area in popular lines such as Buescher band instruments, Selmer woodwinds, Haynes flutes, Paramount banjos, Gibson guitars, and Leedy drums.[9] Tom, absent on the road most of the time, was involved hardly at all in the running of the firm. In early 1922, even before the incorporation, the company started offering music lessons to a half-dozen purchasers of instruments. Under the guidance of Lyons, his brother[10] Howard, and the sales manager, Howard Wallace, the teaching operation grew rapidly into the Tom Brown Band and Orchestra School, with about 500 pupils enrolled in the winter of 1923–24. Five teaching rooms and a rehearsal hall accommodating seventy-five musicians for various ensemble classes housed a thriving and expanding business, mostly centered on saxophones, but including instruction in other instruments and even in vaudeville technique.[11] By 1926, the quarters in the State-Lake Building had become so cramped that the store moved across the street, to 32–34 West Lake. At 9000 square feet, the new facility tripled the available space. Teaching studios were increased from five to nine, and a dance orchestra had been added to the list of ensembles in which group instruction was offered. About the same time, a branch store was opened farther south in the downtown area, at 222–224 West Madison, near Union Station,[12] and another, with its own Band and Orchestra School, in Valparaiso, Indiana.[13] (Among the throng of aspiring musicians at the Lake Street school was a twenty-year-old Cab Calloway, who took saxophone lessons there during the time that he was master of ceremonies at the Sunset Cafe on the South Side, probably in 1927.)[14] In 1928 or 1929, conflict among the management resulted in a further move.[15] The Lake Street store became the Lyons Music Company, run by William and Howard Lyons, and the Tom Brown Music Company, along with the Band and Orchestra School, under Howard Wallace's management, was established in somewhat smaller quarters at 315 South Wabash, in a district with a concentration of music stores.[16] When the depression engulfed Chicago, the music company and school both began to scale back their operations as potential customers started buying soup instead of saxophones. While the Lake Street store had offered one free lesson to any purchaser of an instrument, the despairing Wabash Avenue store almost reversed the proposition, offering an instrument rent-free for five weeks to anyone who would sign up for five $2 "test lessons," designed to interest buyers in further instruction and the acquisition of their own instruments by revealing their latent musical talent.[17]

As vaudeville got tougher and stingier, Tom began to spend more time at the store, interesting himself in ongoing management and occasionally acting as a salesman. When Tom Jr. came back to Chicago after his last year at suburban Lake Forest Academy (1929–30), father and son could no longer afford to live at the opulent Ambassador Hotel, so in 1931 they refurbished two of the little-used teaching and practice rooms on the third floor of the store into bedrooms, added a bathtub to the restroom, and took up residence in the Band and Orchestra School. Tom Jr., accustomed to the prices at the Ambassador's dining room, was astonished to find that 35 cents would buy ham, eggs, toast, and coffee at a Loop restaurant. Tom's enduring good cheer and belief that everything happens for the best kept the new living arrangement amicable for the next four years.

Besides working in the store as a clerk and saxophone instructor, Tom Jr. (also called Tommy) made his father proud by pursuing a career in music. By the end of 1932, he was leading and singing with a small band at the Allerton Hotel, broadcasting nightly over WCFL.[18] Tommy's continuing friendship with his uncle Vern, with whom he often played checkers in the latter's Near North Side apartment, resulted in another gig when Vern tipped him that a night spot called the Melody Club was about to open in the neighborhood. Tommy's cold call on the management netted him an agreement that he would open the club with a five-piece band to back the floor show, which included a line of eight chorus girls, a featured singer named Betty Burnett, and a comedian. The engagement was brief, however, since the band didn't get paid and, with some trepidation about what the somewhat shady owners might do, walked out one evening in late 1933. The budding saxophonist and singer's next engagement was closer to home, just down a flight of stairs at 315 South Wabash at the Century Dancing School. The floor between the music store and the Browns' apartment had been turned into a taxi-dancing establishment, "the kind where the girls wear out the front of their dresses," and Tommy was hired to lead a three-piece group for the grueling routine of very brief dance selections relieved by a five-minute break every hour. Seven nights a week, thirty to fifty good-looking, evening-gowned "instructresses" brightened the lives of assorted college boys, straying husbands, and other Chicagoans in search of human contact. Tommy's musician friends made the long grind fun by dropping by to sit in, but the extra income from the dime-a-dance lasted only about five months. After Tommy left for Manhattan in 1935, Tom frequently came down to the school, never dancing, but hanging out alone near the bandstand to listen to the music, watch the women, and talk to the young musicians who had taken the place of Tommy's group. Bob LaBelle, the new bandleader, said that Tom, who was still running the store, always left by 11:00.[19]

In a few interviews years later, Tom said that the Brothers broke up after performing at the Century of Progress Exposition in Chicago, held in 1933–34, but Tom Jr. thinks that the last engagement was at the Powers Theatre in Grand Rapids, Michigan, in February of 1933. In this case, the theatre stayed open long enough for at least one performance to take place, but not long enough for the check to clear.[20] A review pasted in Tom's scrapbook is worth quoting as a document of the end of the act:

> The vaudeville bill which opened at Powers yesterday is immeasurably better than the two preceding variety programs. It was favored by capacity audiences that generously applauded the acts.
>
> The six Brown brothers, headed by Tom Brown himself, who works in blackface, present saxophone entertainment which includes the playing of popular tunes such as "You're Telling Me" and "semi-classical" pieces like Victor Herbert's "Ah, Sweet Mystery of Life," and the popular "Trees," and Tom's crying and twittering novelty. This act is well known and reliable, having played here several times as Keith performers.[21]

According to Tom Jr., by 1929 Tom had become "the whole show"; the remaining Brothers only provided a background for his performance. To prepare Tommy for his debut with the Brothers, Tom carefully instructed him in how to apply the clown makeup, where to walk and stand, and how to walk while playing. Being somewhat unsure about his own musical prowess, Tom Jr. thought he should have a closer look at the arrrangements as well, even though he and Alec were the "Afterbeat Brothers," charged mostly with maintaining the ensemble's rhythmic pulse. "Poppa, what about the music?" he asked. Tom replied, "Oh well, just stay on D till it sounds bad, and then go to E-flat, and when it sounds bad, go back to D." Tom Jr. reminisced that "it worked out pretty good for a while, and then later on I did get the music."[22] A version of the bridal routine was still featured, but Tom Jr. doesn't remember any dancing or saxophone conversations or Sousa parody. The five clowns would enter the stage, tracing a figure 8 with their paths, and form up five abreast at center stage to play an introductory number. Then one of them (Tom Jr. during 1929–31) would retrieve a piano stool from the wings and place it in front of the clowns for Tom to sit on after his separate entrance. After some full-ensemble numbers and the bridal routine, Tom would play several selections, normally slower tunes such as "Ah! Sweet Mystery of Life," "At Dawning," or "Trees," on the Sax soprano to close the show with an upwelling of emotion. As the review quoted earlier reports, the sold-out house loved the well-known, reliable act, along perhaps with the singers, dancers, acrobats, and juggler that filled out the four-turn program, but they were loving it for the last time in person.

When the Brothers dissolved, Tom, with the music company to run, stayed on in Chicago, as did Vern. Fred and William may also have remained, although Tommy is not sure they did. Alec made a permanent move back to wife Edith's tightly controlled Irvington household. Born about 1894 into a family that ultimately included thirteen children, Edith had immigrated to the United States from Germany around 1910 and learned English in night school so well that she spoke with no trace of an accent. Even when Alec was making money on tour with the Brothers, not much of it found its way back to New Jersey, where Edith and the four children lived in a very modest house. Edith took in washing and ironing and sent the children out to do chores such as cleaning the neighbors' front stairs, hauling ashes from apartment buildings, and delivering groceries. Normal child's play was a luxury that receded even farther from reach after 1929. At the time of Alec's return, seven-year-old Allan was being sent across town every day on foot to a small workshop where he refinished furniture, and the family's meals were sometimes prepared from the contents of food baskets provided by charitable groups. Alec himself was out of work at first, but, after a period of odd jobs that included delivering newspapers and distributing handbills, he found a position in the shipping and receiving department of the Irvington Varnish and Insulating Company and stayed there until he retired in the 1950s. Strict, humorless Edith put an end to the heavy drinking habit her husband had perfected during thirty years in show business, probably prolonging his life by a couple of decades.[23]

Tommy, too, went east, drawn to New York in 1935 by his maternal uncle Louie Lotito's report of a possible music job in Manhattan. American Federation of Musicians rules, however, prevented members of other locals from taking a long-term engagement before the end of a waiting period, and the prospect vanished. Tommy filled time by working in the box office at the Center Theatre, one of several managed by Uncle Louie (the husband of Theresa's younger sister Adeline), finally getting a position selling instruments at the Selmer store in Manhattan until the German invasion of France cut off the flow of Selmer products.[24] Before getting his own apartment, Tommy lived for a while at the Lotitos' home in Mineola on Long Island, where his fellow lodgers included his mother, her sister Mary, and two of her out-of-work brothers, Don, who had been a circus wire-walker, and Clem, a saxophonist. Tommy and the Valerio brothers played golf and the horses together as they all waited for a break in the economic clouds.

Alone in the Wabash Avenue store, Tom sold little merchandise but kept his sense of humor. On slow days, he would sometimes hang out in the C. G. Conn Band Instrument store and school just around the corner on Van Buren. His pal Lynn Sams, the manager of the store at that time, always worried about what Tom might say to customers. When two nuns, from a parochial school where Conn sponsored Saturday band classes, were purchasing a cornet without using the installment plans that the depression had made ubiquitous, Tom introduced himself to them, explaining his forwardness by saying, "The reason I wanted to meet you is that you are the first people I ever saw pay cash for an instrument."[25]

In 1936 the Tom Brown Music Company went bankrupt. Early in 1937, Tom, now living at the Hotel Majestic on Quincy Street in the Loop, wrote to Doc Waggener in Los Angeles:

> It is high time that I was answering your Christmas card, which I appreciated very much way down deep in my heart. The principal reason for not answering sooner was because I have had untold trouble in the last few months. I have lost the store and turned it over to my creditors and settlement is now in progress thru the courts. The assets sold for a fair figure, however the creditors will not be paid in full and as for me I lose every thing. It has been a great heartache and I cannot tell you at this writing just what is going to happen to me.
>
> I organized a five piece band and I played in a hotel [the Woodruff] in Joliet, Illinois for about seventeen weeks. It was an orchestra consisting of string bass, trumpet, sax, clarinet and piano. The men were absolutely the best available, but we have disbanded as after leaving Joliet I was unable to get enough money to keep them going.
>
> The old soprano is even better than ever, and I have enjoyed playing several new numbers that I am sure you would like to hear. My great ambition, now that I am free, is to get out to Hollywood and make some tests with the hope that they could use me for different parts. If you happen to know anyone that you think might be interested in me, please let me know.[26]

After leaving the Majestic for a cheaper apartment on the Near North Side, Tom wrote again to Waggener, mentioning Hollywood again and reporting that their Omaha friend Paul Gallagher had sent him some food from the wholesale grocery firm he headed.

> Since I gave up the Store I have been sort of Free-lansing. I opened a fine night club for two nights and played in another Club for one night, then I broadcasted and expect to be put on the staff for the

NBC Minstrels which will be steady. . . . Vern Fred and Bill are on relief as there is absolutely nothing left to do in show Biz.[27]

The NBC Minstrels were a troupe broadcasting over the NBC network from Chicago radio station WENR for a half hour on Wednesday nights, presided over by the interlocutor Gene Arnold, who had written a couple of minstrel sketch books issued by the music publisher M. Witmark.[28] Most Wednesdays the program came on just before NBC's hit show "Amos 'n' Andy," probably riding on the tattered coattails of the latter's hugely popular caricatures of African Americans. Two surviving disc transcriptions at the Library of Congress show the broadcast as an adaptation of the traditional (and all-male) minstrel first part, with four dialect comedians playing against Arnold's middle man, skits involving just two of the end men (Vance McCune and Bill Thompson), songs without dialect by Thompson, a male chorus, a tenor, and a baritone, a sung-and-spoken number by McCune in Bert Williams's style, a dubious "tap-dancing chorus" number by the comedian Ken Christie, a banjo solo, and a medley of choral and solo songs for a grand finale. The comedy relies heavily on mispronunciation, puns, malapropisms, and a lineup of characters laden with the stereotypical baggage of stupidity, laziness, misinformation, bad marriages, and even cannibalism. On the other hand, neither the transcriptions nor a couple of surviving scripts from 1938 invoke razor fights or theft of watermelons and chickens. Prominent throughout as it accompanies the singers and "dancers" and presents feature numbers, Al Short's "minstrel band" plays (somewhat raggedly) in the style of 1937, even when doing material (such as "Some of These Days") from an earlier period, except for the program's circus-march theme music. A studio audience adds laughter, applause, gasps of amazement, and shouts of encouragement to the somewhat underrehearsed proceedings.[29]

Tom brought Waggener up to date in a May 3 letter, saying,

> I hope you get me on my next Broadcast which will be soon because I am going to be put on the staff tomorrow which means that I will be on hand to jump into any program whenever called and if any feature picture can use me my contract will be sold to the highest bidder and best of all it will take me to Hollywood where I can see you often. The little Sax is still wonderful and it is quite possible that I will broadcast with the sextette so if you have any arrangements send them on and I will have them copied and return the originals to you.[30]

Not much is known about Tom's relationship with the program—for example, what his on-air or staff role was, whether the Six Brown Brothers or perhaps a different sextet appeared on the show, or how long Tom kept the job. But the Hollywood dream seems almost to have materialized. On February 23, 1938, Tom wired Waggener, "INVITED TO HOLLYWOOD BY WARNER BROS PLEASE SEND ME TRANSPORTATION WESTERN

UNION PAID ON ARRIVAL." Waggener answered the same day but was notified two days later that his reply had been delivered to the Palmer House instead of Tom's apartment and never called for.[31] Evidently Waggener didn't try again to contact Tom about the money, since a later message repeated the appeal in stronger terms:

> Doctor I have A letter from Warner Brothers inviting me to come to Hollywood for a Test. But I am in urgent need of funds to get there. Just closed the Court proceedings regarding the Store and all my ready cash was lost in the shuffle, so here I am for the first time in my life help-less. With this letter and help from Fred Stone, Wallace Berry [Beery] and many others I know out there I am sure I will get a contract and will be able to pay you back with interest very soon. I would go on the Bus only I have to have my trunk so I will have to take the train. Fred Waring will be here at the Drake Friday the 26th. so I will get a letter from him as he just completed a picture for the Warners and has great influence. . . . P.S. Doctor I would'nt [sic] want to leave for about a month.[32]

The second call for help seems not to have wrested a loan from Waggener either. At any rate, even if there was an unrecorded Hollywood visit, it didn't issue in a screen career. A few weeks after the telegram to Waggener, Tom was in New York, living at the Palace Hotel (Percy's address when he died twenty years earlier), and made an appearance on Phillips Lord's interview broadcast, "We, the People."[33] Tom Jr., now securely employed selling instruments at Selmer, invited his father to share quarters in his apartment just off Times Square when his roommate, Carl Swift, left. Reunited, father and son lived together frugally as Tom presumably explored job possibilities in Gotham. Tommy reports that his father was his old cheerful and jovial self during this period, expressing no regrets about the death of the act, the wreck of the store, or the series of frustrating attempts to find a new niche in entertainment. But the new arrangement lasted only a few months. By August, Tom had returned to his Chicago apartment, and by the end of the year, to Lindsay, Ontario.

Failing to find steady work in the United States, Tom apparently decided to make his own opportunities, prevailing upon the Lindsay Citizens' Band to produce "the first real old time minstrel show" in Lindsay since 1922, with proceeds to go to the band. Billed as the "Tom Brown Minstrels," the company of fifty was made up of a handful of former professionals and avid amateurs drawn from organizations such as the Citizens' Band and the Girl Guides. On the bill was Tom Brown, with "His Famous Saxophone Sextette," very likely not including any of his actual brothers. Advance publicity stressed the "old-time" aspirations of the spectacle. It was to open with a half-hour concert by the minstrel band in front of the Academy Theatre. "There will be humorous end men and their songs, pretty ballads by the soloists, old time buck and wing dancers, musical acts that will make your toes tingle, old-time minstrel skits that bubble with laughter," and all at the "same old prices, 50 cents a ticket, no reserved seats." The two performances, on December 5 and 6, 1938 (Monday and Tuesday), were well attended by an enthusiastic audience that "rocked with laughter as Tom elicited cries and moans from his horn."[34] Tom sent his father, Allan, the founder of the Citizens' Band almost a half century earlier, a postcard after opening night, calling the show "a huge success" and "the talk of the town today" and saying he would try to visit Allie in Toronto the following Saturday.[35]

At some point in 1939–40, Tom probably took up residence in Toronto. A newspaper interview published in January 1941, saying he is "now of Toronto," reported that he was planning to produce an amateur minstrel show in St. Catharines, Ontario (near Niagara Falls), to benefit the St. Catharines Boys' Band.[36] He seems to have joined a Toronto club called the Originals' Association and performed both for them and, along with fellow Originals, for other social organizations. Further credits include solo appearances, one as the headliner in a three-act vaudeville between pictures at the Capitol Theatre in Galt, Ontario, where he was billed as "formerly with Montgomery and Stone Broadway Successes and The Primrose and Dockstader Minstrels." For a time he was even the bandmaster of the Boys' Band of Kingsway, a district of Toronto.[37] Tom Jr. adds that, during this period, when music gigs didn't bring in enough income, his father would also wait on tables and tune pianos.

During Tom's Canadian exile, the Six Brown Brothers made it into a major Hollywood production, though in an attenuated form. Twentieth Century–Fox's 1940 release *Tin Pan Alley*, a colossally inaccurate evocation of New York's popular-song business in the 1910s, included a sequence, about twenty minutes into the film, in which "You Say the Sweetest Things (Baby)" becomes a hit through the efforts of song pluggers, portrayed by John Payne and Jack Oakie. After a couple of choruses sung by Payne and Oakie, along with Betty Grable and Alice Faye, the tempo picks up for a montage of the piece's rise to popularity, performed by artists intended to epitomize the era. Eight bars of an Eddie Cantor–like song-and-dance man backed by a line of seated minstrels whacking tambourines are followed by eight bars of a Nora Bayes impersonator seated on a crescent moon, and then comes a saxophone sextet. Just as the Cantor and Bayes figures were not quite Cantor or Bayes, the sextet is not quite the Brothers, since there is no blackface character and their heads are variously topped with derbies, Mohawk haircuts, and a mop wig. But they wear clown suits, swing their horns in unison as they caper about the stage, and play pretty much as the Brown Brothers would have.[38]

Owing to a legal complication, Tom's stay in Canada was prolonged, perhaps by several years. Although he had begun the process of applying for U.S. citizenship years before, he had never finished it and, as a result, was refused reentry when he tried to return to Chicago. Dates and other details of this episode are unknown to the author. Alec and his son Allan paid a visit to Tom in Toronto in July of 1941, summed up in a postcard from fifteen-year-old Allan to Edith and his sisters in Irvington: "We have just returned from a visit of one of Tom's Friends. All are sober (hic)."[39] In 1943, the obituary of Tom's mother, Maria, referred to him as a bandleader in Toronto, and he appeared in the "New Members" listing of the Toronto local of the American Federation of Musicians.[40] He was probably back in Chicago by April 1944, when he entered into a royalty contract with Will Rossiter that granted the firm all rights to "Bull Frog Blues," "That Moaning Saxophone Rag," and "Chicken Walk" in return for royalties from performances and from sales of piano sheets and orchestrations. (The agreement included a $25 advance, probably important seed money for Tom's reentry into the States.)[41] By the following April, he was living at the same address (229 East Superior Street) as in 1937.[42]

Although Tom, marooned in Toronto, had to scuffle during World War II, the conflict gave his three unemployed brothers steady work. Vern and Bill, now living with their sister Myrtle in Chicago, found jobs in defense plants, and Fred, who had moved in with Alec's family in Irvington for a short time, enlisted in the Army and was stationed at Fort Dix, New Jersey, where Sergeant Brown played tenor sax in a band at the post.[43] Alec's children heard frequent news of Fred during his stay at Fort Dix, including a hair-raising AWOL story. Fred was away from the base longer than allowed, for the purpose of going on a toot. Incarcerated on his return, he was put to cleaning "GI cans," large metal vessels in which food was prepared for the mess hall. A sharp protrusion on one of the cans sliced Fred's arm open from elbow to wrist, landing him in the infirmary and preventing him from leaving for Europe with his regiment. Twenty-nine miles out into the Atlantic, a German torpedo sent the unlucky ship to the bottom, and none aboard survived.

Back in Chicago, Tom was playing a continuing engagement with a band at the Red Lion Inn at 61 East Adams, just around the corner from the shuttered Tom Brown Music Company, when he was interviewed by reporter Ruth Logan for the Sunday *Tribune*. It isn't known whether Logan's headline, "Real Granddad of Saxophone Found in Loop," boosted business at the club. Tom gave her a version of the standard Brothers story, but she included almost no details about the Red Lion gig itself, except that Tom was still playing both of his saxophones. She did note, however, that William and Vern were still living in Chicago.[44]

After the war ended and the defense plants closed, William moved from Myrtle's crowded house to a cheap hotel on the rundown Near North Side and found work in a Randolph Street restaurant. But his time was short. On Christmas Day 1945, his constitution weakened by years of alcohol abuse, he died of arteriosclerotic heart disease after two days in Cook County Hospital.[45] He was the first of four Brown Brothers to be buried at Mt. Hope Cemetery, in Worth, Illinois, at Chicago's southwest corner.

In Canada, father Allan, now married a second time, to Jennie Clark, was nearing ninety. He had moved from Ottawa to Toronto in 1925, after retiring from the Department of the Interior, and apparently had led a quiet life with his new wife and her daughter. There had been a few occasions to see his famous sons when they were still on the road, and after that Tom and Alec had visited him a couple of times before Tom's sojourn in Ontario. Presumably he and Tom saw a lot of each other during World War II. It isn't known whether he continued to work as a musician in later years, though none of his obituaries addresses the matter. In October 1947, at the age of eighty-eight or eighty-nine, Allan succumbed to old age at the home of his stepdaughter, Mrs. F. D. Crowder.[46]

As Tom aged, he had progressively less energy for finding work as a musician. He channeled some of his drive to perform into a minstrel group called the Triangle Club, made up of amateurs and retired professionals. Still attired in his red jacket, white bowleg pants, and burnt cork, Tom contributed humorous monologues, singing, and feature numbers on the saxophone.[47] Without savings or Social Security, and with no help from the zero pay of the Triangle minstrels, Tom found life in Chicago increasingly difficult. He seems also to have had a mild stroke at about this time, which made walking slow and labored for a period. C. L. Brown, who was then running a music school in nearby South Bend, Indiana, heard of the stroke and went to visit his old idol, with whom he had maintained a close friendship in spite of their legal clashes two decades earlier over Brown's Saxophone Six. In an interview years later, C. L. spoke sadly of Tom's straitened circumstances at the time, but stressed that, in spite of them, he was still "a hundred percent Tom," generously attempting to tip the waitress after C. L. had won the argument over who was to pay for lunch. She knew Tom and returned the coin, saying, "Tom Brown, I wouldn't take that quarter if somebody'd give me ten dollars." It was the last meeting for Tom and C. L.[48]

Shortly after Allan's death, during a visit to Tom Jr., who had married and settled in St. Louis, Missouri, father and son hatched a plan to reopen the Tom Brown Music Company. For a brief time after the Selmer store closed owing to the war in Europe, Tommy and a friend, Glenn Goodman, had met some success with their own music store in Manhattan, but the advent of the military draft in 1940 led them to close it. Tommy moved back to Chicago, where he worked (side by side with Myrtle's son Allan Elliott and ex-Brother Jesse Ewing) at Lyons Music Company, located at the address of the second Tom Brown Music Company, 32–34 West Lake Street, and run by his father's former partners, William and Howard Lyons. Goodman, meanwhile, had moved to St. Louis, where he was chief ordnance inspector in an ammunition plant. His letters drew Tommy south to a position as inspector in the same factory, where his future wife, Syrama, assembled bullets. Married in 1945, the Browns stayed on in St. Louis after the war, and Tommy, adaptable as ever, became an accountant for a while and then took a sales job at the Ludwig Music Company.

Increasingly concerned about Tom's situation in Chicago, Tommy proposed to his father that they open a music store in St. Louis, thinking that his own experience in accounting and their pooled wisdom about the music business would make success likely. They exploited their old contacts in the instrument and recording businesses and lined up a contract with Martin Band Instruments (the brand Tommy and Glenn Goodman had carried in their New York store) and a large initial stock of Victor, Decca, and Columbia discs. Overhead was to be covered by projected sales of records, with profits from instrument sales providing the margin of comfort. When the new Tom Brown Music Company opened in a downtown office building on St. Patrick's Day 1948, Tom finally had the prospect of a more comfortable retirement, with occasional opportunities to return to Chicago for performances with the Triangle Club.

Tommy had sensed that the Victor representative wanted to tell him something important during their negotiations over the supply contract and initial purchase of 78 r.p.m. discs. A short while after the store opened, he discovered what had been held back when the new long-playing format for records was announced to the public. The market for the soon-to-be-obsolete shellac discs wilted, and the Browns' inventory languished on the shelves. After six financially disastrous months, the business collapsed, Tommy returned to accounting, and Tom moved back to Chicago.[49] Perhaps through the good offices of someone in the Triangle Club, Tom got a job as night clerk at the Lake Lane Hotel. It was on the city's far northern edge, miles from the Loop but tied to it by the Chicago Transit Authority tracks that ran southward from just behind the hotel to cast their shadows on the old Lake Street and Wabash Avenue stores. The neighborhood, quiet and well maintained, was much preferable to the squalid Near North Side, where William had lived just across Clark Street from Fred's hotel. Tom kept some sort of connection with the Triangle Club, but it is not known whether he continued to perform in their shows. He wrote to Doc Waggener in March 1949 that he had been playing very little.[50]

Toward the end of January 1949, Fred, suffering from tuberculosis, entered Cook County Hospital. After two weeks' stay, on February 9, he died. A service was held at the same funeral parlor where his mother's had taken place, and he was buried a few yards from Bill's grave in Mt. Hope Cemetery.[51] Very few days remained for Tom himself. By the summer of 1950, he had moved to a small apartment not far from the Lake Lane Hotel, when the "Town Crier" column in the *Chicago Daily News* devoted a paragraph to him:

> Remember the Six Brown Brothers . . . that terrific vaudeville act of a past generation . . . six brothers in clown suits playing assorted saxaphones [*sic*]? Several of the brothers are dead now. The act hasn't been on any stage for a long while. And for many moons, Tom Brown has been night clerk at Chicago's Lake Lane hotel. Age is creeping up on old Tom Brown, and Sunday [August 20, 1950] he's leaving for the Masonic Home in Elmira, N.Y. But Thursday night, guests at the hotel are staging a party for Tom, one of those nostalgic,

sentimental affairs. And as a farewell gesture Tom will play one more show . . . he'll get out his treasure, the first saxophone ever built (given to him years ago by a medico friend) . . . and for a little while he [will] try to bring back the old days . . . when the Six Brown Brothers made melody.[52]

The following Monday's edition followed up with a brief piece about Tom, along with photos of the Brothers around 1921 and of Tom in 1950, looking gaunt and feeble and wearing a bathrobe. The reporter showed Tom some Brothers photos from the *Daily News* library, eliciting a smile and some reminiscences. Tom spoke of his plan to move to the Masonic home in September.[53] The article included Tom's new address, resulting in visits from some of his old show-business friends who hadn't known what bad shape he was in. Tommy had been planning to visit his father and finally rushed to Chicago after Tom called to say he didn't think he would last much longer. By the time Tommy arrived, Tom had died of a stroke at the Illinois Masonic Hospital, on August 29. The attending physician judged the underlying cause to be diabetes.[54]

The funeral, two days later, was well attended. Among the mourners was Wade Booth, a former vaudevillian who had become a Chicago theatrical agent. He told the *Daily News*, "Since Tom always played in blackface, and had a six-man act, we are having six Chicago minstrels as pallbearers."[55] It is not known whether the pallbearers carried out their duties in burnt cork. Booth arranged for Masonic rites to be included in the ceremony, delivered a short eulogy, and sang a couple of hymns. Much to the family's relief, expenses were paid by Booth, the Triangle Minstrels, and the Lake Lane Hotel management. The afternoon ended at Mt. Hope Cemetery, where Tom was interred near William and Fred in a grave that remained unmarked for the next half century.

After the services, Tommy went to his father's little apartment and opened his trunk. There lay Tom's costume, his Couesnon alto, the Sax soprano, and stacks of clippings, photos, scrapbooks, and other memorabilia from a lifetime in show business. With regret, Tommy left most of it behind, but he returned to St. Louis with the soprano and the keepsakes that made the present book possible. According to a letter from Booth to Doc Waggener, Myrtle, then working as a housekeeper's assistant at the Ambassador Hotel, may have claimed the rest of Tom's effects.

Booth regarded the Brown family with suspicion and hostility, for reasons mostly lost, but including a feeling that they should have paid something toward the funeral expenses. He wrote to Waggener, "There are many distressing circumstances which I do not care to express in writing. Maybe you will be through here [Chicago] some day or we may be able to talk on the phone." Paul Gallagher, Tom and Doc's mutual friend from the Omaha days, seemed to share Booth's attitude, telling Waggener that "after the Funeral Tom Jr went to old Toms apt and took all he could find."[56]

Both Gallagher's and Booth's letters seem to have been responses to inquiries from Waggener about the fate of the Sax soprano. Booth forwarded the inquiry to Tommy in St. Louis. The soprano had been the first Sax instrument that Waggener bought, although he had collected several others in the intervening three decades. In March 1949, Tom had written him about it: "About this old Sax, is it the oldest or have you one still older. Please let me know. I'm going to give it to Tommy my Son when I get through with it."[57] But in a letter sent in the month after the funeral, Waggener told Tommy that Tom had made an agreement whereby Waggener was to inherit the horn. Tommy replied that the "letter came as quite a surprise to me, because Dad had told me many, many times that he wanted me to have his old soprano. He was always very proud of the old horn, and he used to say 'Tommy, when I'm gone, pick up the old Adolph Saxe [sic] Soprano and play it once in a while. It's got a great tone—and you'll love it like I do.'" Waggener persisted, however, writing and phoning Tommy, and perhaps even threatening legal action. In 1952, having met only refusal for a couple of years, the doctor, now retired from practice and paying for two full-time nurses to care for his invalid wife, Ethel, offered to swap an item from his extensive collection, a gold-plated Buescher alto valued (by Waggener) at $600, for the soprano. By that time, Tommy was prepared to sell the instrument. Though uninterested in the alto, he wrote Waggener, "I have a strong hunch that if I contact the proper sources the old Adolph Sax Soprano will bring far more than Six Hundred Dollars. Nevertheless, I realize how very good a friend you were to my Dad, and with that thought in mind I would be pleased to let you have it for five hundred dollars."[58]

Waggener replied that $500 was too much for an instrument that "can have only a sentimental value." Besides repeating the exchange offer, he gave Tommy the option of accepting $300 cash for the horn. But the letter included much more than just a cold-blooded business proposition. It spoke of Waggener's love and esteem for Tom, of the artistic and financial contribution of the soprano to Tom's success, of the recent decline in the doctor's income, of his age (seventy-three) and his wife's illness, and finally of his belief that playing the instrument would be "about the only real pleasure I can hope to get out of life at my time." One short paragraph made Waggener's appeal less convincing than it might have been: "I believe that all of Brown Brothers have all passed on. Tom Sr., Alec, Fred, and Verne. As you will note I knew all of them very well." Tom had written to Waggener about William's death, and Alec and Vern were still among the living.[59] The letter's long fortissimo of emotion, genuine or calculated or both, failed to clinch the deal, and the soprano remained in Tommy's possession until 1998, when it passed into a private collection. In 1970, Waggener changed his tune a bit by telling Cecil Leeson, "When Mr. Pedersen died, his family gave the [Sax soprano] saxophone to me. And I, like a fool, I gave it away to Tom Brown."[60]

Theresa was not at Tom's funeral. When the Lotito family moved from Mineola to a much larger house in Spring Lake, New Jersey, Theresa moved with them and continued with her peaceful life among friends and relatives. She and Tommy visited back and forth between St. Louis and New Jersey, and she kept in touch with Alec's family in Irvington. She stayed beautiful and slim as she aged, but she never returned to the stage. On May 23, 1964, her life ended quietly. Just over two months later, Vern, thin as a string, left his Near North Side hotel with an inflammation of the lungs and spent twelve days at Cook County Hospital before dying on August 16. Vern's remains, like those of William and Fred, were taken from Cook County Hospital to Mt. Hope Cemetery for burial, but his grave, unlike theirs, was dug in the section set aside for paupers. Although the federal government is obligated to pay for veterans' headstones, no one arranged to get a marker for Vern.[61]

Alec, now the last of the Six Brown Brothers, had retired from his job at the Irvington Varnish and Insulating Company about ten years before Vern's passing.[62] He had become a venerable family man, with four grown children and numerous grandchildren, three of whom, sons of Allan, also lived in the Irvington area. Maybe because there had been no time for him to play with his own kids as they were growing up, Alec loved playing baseball with his grandsons. From time to time, the local newspapers would interview him about the old days and print one version or another of the Brothers' legend, stressing the group's antiquity in comparison with such vaudevillians-become-radio-stars as George Burns and Gracie Allen, Jack Benny, and Fibber McGee and Molly, all of whom Alec had known when they were just beginning. He played very little, although at parties his children and grandchildren could coax him into a few tunes on alto or C-melody (never on baritone). "Ramona" and "La Paloma" were the pieces he most liked to perform.

Taciturn Alec didn't reminisce much with his family, partly out of modesty and partly out of an aversion to offending Edith with tales of drinking and womanizing during twenty-five years on the road. But he would respond to their casual questions that, yes, he had sold peanuts for the Ringling Brothers, clowned before capacity houses from London to Los Angeles, and entertained New York's richest at opulent Long Island estates. He distanced himself from the past in another way as well, by dropping the name Alec and adopting his given first name, Allan. The family, with the exception of Edith, loved his old-fashioned sense of humor. Whenever Edith served apple pie with American cheese, his favorite dessert, he would say solemnly, "Apple pie without the cheese is like a kiss without the squeeze." If Edith asked him to pass the beans, he would hand her the bowl with the remark, "Have a few thousand beans." His son Allan recalled one of the many jokes his father got a kick out of telling. Alec went to the doctor. Doctor: "Hi there, Mr. Brown, how ya doing?" Alec: "Not so good. I think it's curtains for me." Doctor: "Mr. Brown, I know what your problem is. You drink too much." Alec: "Doctor, with all respect, you're mistaken. I spill half of it."

Because they were musicians, two of the sons of Allan and his wife Hazel, Jimmy and Tom, felt a special connection with their grandfather. Tom (born in 1952, when Alec was seventy) sent the author a touching sketch of Alec's old age:

> I remember him as having a generally sunny disposition that was often a foil for his wife's rather severe demeanor. He was fond of baseball, beer, cards and cigars. I think none of these affinities were shared conspicuously by Edith.
>
> While I was growing up, the grandparents Brown lived in a modest but comfortable cedar-shingled house on Maple Avenue in Irvington, New Jersey. There was a glider on the front porch where AB used to sit and smoke his El Productos and White Owls. He generally had a wonderful ashtray at his side—it was free-standing cast iron and incorporated a Chinese-looking dragon at least a foot and a half high.
>
> He was most in his element when at table, at least during the time I knew him. He loved making toasts, drinking toasts, entertaining those around him and just generally being social. He was generally the darling of the waitresses working the restaurants we visited, especially on his many birthdays. He was reliably charming. These displays of grace and savoir faire were not always met with unalloyed appreciation on Edith's part. It sometimes seemed she was somewhat jealous of all the attention paid to Alec.
>
> I don't recall Grandpa ever complaining about his health, although surely one doesn't get as old as he did without some substantial aches, pains, and dysfunctions. When he moved across from our house in Maplewood, NJ, he enjoyed walking to the delicatessen two and a half blocks away. He would stop, sit, and rest at a retaining wall made of railroad ties in front of one of the houses on the shady street. Sometimes, when he was 90 years old or better, he would pay the deli owner a quarter for a newspaper and a loaf of bread and then tell him to keep the change. The owner was a mensch with a sense of humor and never let on that he was being underpaid. Nor would he take money from my folks to cover the difference. I guess he was another victim of the Brown charm.
>
> There was, alas, never all that much musical communication between him and me. By the time I was really interested in music, Grandpa's overt musical behavior was pretty much limited to watching Lawrence Welk. . . . I am, in a vague way, an adherent to the practice of ancestor worship and I think of him sometimes in connection to my participation in music. My father told me that he dreamed of Alec in this context. He dreamed that Grandpa slid a saxophone across the floor (stage?) to me. Pretty nice dream.[63]

Probably owing at least in part to his moderate alcohol intake, Alec was still in relatively good physical shape at age ninety. Although he had lost his teeth, he could still read without glasses and bend over to touch his toes. After Edith died in 1974, he slowly declined, entering a nursing home in Jersey City about six months before his death, three weeks short of ninety-six, on August 18, 1978. Little sister Myrtle Elliott, at the time of Alec's passing a widow in Chicago, survived to a slightly older age, succumbing just past ninety-six on June 12, 1988.[64]

16

Maria Brown's Quilt

As the reader will remember from chapter 1, saxophone players and even saxophone ensembles were present on the American scene before the birth of the nucleus of the Brown Brothers in the Ringling aftershow, whether that event dates to 1906 (as in Sverre Braathen's story of the quartet) or, less likely, 1904 (as perhaps in Tom Brown's 1921 story suggesting a trio). International concert soloists such as Henri Wuille in 1853 and Edouard Lefèbre from 1873 onward, along with entertainers such as the Holbrooks, the Macks, and Billy Young in the early 1890s, had introduced the solo saxophone to a public whose extent can never be known. By 1903 and perhaps before, the saxophone quartet as a freestanding ensemble was introduced to American audiences as the Majestic Musical Four graced vaudeville stages.[1] By 1905, Lefèbre's sax quartet and the Apollo Concert Company, with such a foursome among its configurations, were on the road from the cities to the boondocks. In the 1904–6 period, the instrument, most often in its alto variety, was beginning to become standard in such bands as those of military units, police forces, streetcar drivers' unions, fraternal organizations, and larger municipalities. Although the sax was still regarded as a novelty or a curiosity outside the band context, it may seem that there was nothing left for the Brown Brothers to do, that they were boarding a train that had already left the station. Their legend may seem to have little substance.

But that reaction would misread the legend. The existence of the cited musicians and groups shows only that the most extreme form of the legend is false: Tom Brown wasn't "the bird who gave the saxophone its start,"[2] nor was he "the first explorer to learn that you can take nothing but saxos and make music out of them instead of using one incidentally,"[3] and neither the Brothers nor Rudy Wiedoeft "gave the saxophone a foothold in popular music."[4] By 1904–6, the saxophone was well started, the saxophone ensemble had been discovered, and the instrument had found its feet. But other parts of the legend, both more central and, understood in a certain way, less extravagant, can be given a fairly healthy color: they made the saxophone popular; they started the saxophone craze.

In the 1920s, the claim that the Brothers made the saxophone popular would have been understood in the context of the mania of the times, the instrument's "astonishing explosion in popularity."[5] The sax was not just popular, but wildly popular. Every dance band or jazz group had to include at least one. Touted as easy to learn and a way to gain the admiration of others, the horn was sold to tens of thousands of eager novices. Its sound became the musical voice of the 1920s. In 1926, the *San Francisco Chronicle* placed the Brothers in that context with a meteorological metaphor: the Browns "first taught a waiting world that a saxophone could be made to sit up and speak and thereby wafted that instrument on a breeze of popularity which has turned into a cyclone."[6] That is, their way of playing started a huge increase in the popularity of a horn that was already around, and the increase ultimately resulted in the craze it had become by 1926. The period between the breeze and the cyclone not only accommodates but calls for the participation of numerous others. So the assertion that they made the saxophone popular can be understood, not as the incredible one that they and they alone were responsible for public enthusiasm as of 1926, but as equivalent to the claim that they started the craze, not necessarily by being "from way back yonder at the head of Saxophone creek,"[7] but somehow or other. How? What could make such an idea plausible enough that it could be broached in print over and over in an era when people still remembered things about the upper reaches of Saxophone Creek?

The idea that a saxophone craze had begun was around already in 1915–16, when Clay Smith and Guy E. Holmes began talking about it (see chapter 1, note 6), so the initiation is to be looked for before that point, before Rudy Wiedoeft's virtuosity had astounded the public, before the birth of the "modern dance orchestras" of Art Hickman and Paul Whiteman, before the sax had become a jazz voice. But that restriction still leaves plenty of contenders for the originator's crown: at least Édouard Lefèbre's quartet, touring from about 1905 to 1910; the Apollo Concert Company, edifying Lyceum and Chautauqua audiences starting about the same time; the Four Cates; the Musical Spillers; and the Brown Brothers (with or without Hopkins and Doc Kealey). These are the contenders not only because of their early start and national exposure, but also because they played as ensembles rather than just as soloists, so that they could demonstrate more of the instrument's possibilities to future players and fans alike. One aspect of the craze suggests eliminating Lefèbre, the Apollos, and the Cates from the list. The 1910s and 1920s were crazy about the saxophone as a vehicle for popular music rather than for transcriptions of von Suppé overtures or the quartet from *Rigoletto*. Although many listeners inspired to buy and learn the instrument, or only to seek opportunities to hear it, may have had tastes that ran to the symphonic and operatic, the overwhelming majority of enthusiasts wanted to produce or consume ragtime, musical-comedy songs, one-steps, two-steps, and fox-trots. The saxophone was popular not just in the sense that large numbers of people took it up or liked listening to it, but also in the sense that it lent itself to the music of the people, the lowbrow and middle-brow consumers whose preferences weighed heavily in the market.

With that restriction, only two of the contenders, the Browns and the Spillers, remain in the contest. Both presented the latest in popular music, both began about the same time (1906), both reached a sextet form at about the same time (1910 for the Spillers, 1911 for the Browns), and they broke through to big-time vaudeville almost neck and neck (winter 1910–11). Choosing the Browns over the Spillers could be seen as just another manifestation of American racism, but one substantial difference between the groups (a difference perhaps itself stemming from racial discrimination) makes the choice attractive: the Five Brown Brothers were available on records, and the Spillers weren't.

Sales figures for the 1911 Columbia disc and U-S Everlasting cylinders have not survived, but the disc, at least, must have sold well. A likely explanation of Columbia's rewaxing of the two numbers in March 1912 (though under false colors) is that the stampers (the metal negatives or dies used to make the disc) had worn out from use. An additional sign of wide diffusion is that the disc was reissued on at least two other labels (United in the United States and Regal in England). Besides that, the Browns' first discs and cylinders were the only sax ensemble records available from 1911 until their next efforts were released in 1914, and no recording by another sax group (except the crypto-Browns of 1912) was on the market until 1917.

Records have the potential to increase an act's audience in important ways. In cities where the artists might appear, the recording can entice the public into the theatre for more of what they've heard on the gramophone at home or at a friend's. In places where the act is never booked, it can still please listeners in the comfort of their own parlors. Besides increasing projection, discs and cylinders also have the power to fuel enthusiasm by repeated listening. How many teenagers have worn out their favorite records by playing them over and over, with a growing attachment to each phrase, each note (before the less clearly mortal CD was marketed)? A fan who purchased the Browns' Columbia disc would have no trouble working up his or her appetite for playing a saxophone when exacting an encore was as easy as swinging the tone arm away from the center and carefully placing the needle again in the first groove. The Brothers' early bow as recording artists and six-year monopoly in the field, added to the features they shared with the Spillers—national presence, a popular repertoire, and a large dose of comedy—tip the historical balance in their favor. If anyone started the saxophone craze, most likely it was the Brown Brothers.

If anyone started the saxophone craze. A more judicious position is that nobody started it. The small army of saxophonists around 1905 grew by platoons, then by regiments, into the invincible force of the mid-1920s in the way of all fads, to follow this line of thought. One neophyte joined the fold because he heard Lefèbre, another because she heard the Apollos or the Spillers, another because of Tom Brown, or Arthur Rackett, or Billy and

Lilly Mack. Turning into performers themselves, the neophytes gathered yet more recruits, as in a pyramid scheme, while the seasoned musicians continued to light new fires, and the process repeated itself. Saxophonists proliferated, lines of inspiration crossed and blurred, and the tracing of causal chains back from, for instance, Duke Ellington's 1928–32 sax section (Johnny Hodges, Harry Carney, and Barney Bigard) to particular players a quarter of a century earlier becomes not just a practical impossibility, but a literally inconceivable task.

Still, even if a narrative along those lines is more defensible, surely the Brown Brothers must be conceded a leading role in it, at least through 1916. And even in the late 1910s and early 1920s, as the spotlight shifted to other figures on the ever more crowded stage, the Browns remained a significant influence. Only in 1925, when Tom dropped the group to experiment with other turns, do they seem to have been swamped by the wave they did so much to raise. Although their 1926–33 revival prospered at first, they were clearly no longer a major force in the continuing craze.

Besides the credit due the Browns for their place in the saxophone craze, perhaps they should be given some for the origination, and certainly for the foreshadowing, of the standard alto-alto-tenor (AAT) sax section of mid-1920s dance bands, just such a section as the melodic component of the Six Brown Brothers. If, as many believe, the standard sax section began with the two-voice combination of Art Hickman's Orchestra in 1919, it was a scant two years before three voices started to be heard on the 1921 recordings of the bands of Isham Jones (July), Paul Whiteman (August), Gene Rodemich (October), Ray Miller, the California Ramblers (both November), and (Jan) Garber-(Milton) Davis (December).[8] Many more followed in 1922. Most, though not all, of these groups used the AAT configuration for melodic exposition, with other reed voices (for example, soprano and bass clarinet, oboe, or soprano and baritone saxophone) thrown in from time to time for timbral variety. Once the AAT array became established, around 1923, it was ubiquitous in published orchestrations and only somewhat less ubiquitous in the dance bands themselves.[9] As early as 1914's "Virginia Lee" and "La Paloma," the Browns had shown how well suited this combination was to the kind of music that dominated the popular market, and on later sides such as "Walkin' the Dog" (1916), the "Pretty Baby" segment of "Chin Chin Medley" (1916), "The Darktown Strutters' Ball" (1917), and "For Me and My Gal" (1917), the AAT combination sounds just like a mid-to-late-1920s sax section except for the occasional jerkiness of the rhythm.

Paul Whiteman's orchestra, probably the strongest immediate influence on the instrumentation of the leading dance bands of the early 1920s, may well have picked up its AAT configuration from the Browns. Although Art Hickman's 1919 group is often cited as the first dance band with a saxophone section, its two saxophonists (Clyde Doerr doubling alto and baritone and Bert Ralton doubling tenor and soprano) seldom played as a section—one leading, the other harmonizing—on their numerous recordings. Dance bands of the 1920s followed Whiteman's path rather than Hickman's, thereby also putting aside possible three-horn teams such as soprano-alto-tenor, alto-tenor-baritone, and so on, that would have provided interesting opportunities for arrangers. Because dance-band musicians virtually always doubled (and many tripled and quadrupled), such alternatives were used from time to time, but AAT was the standard.

In a remark that has probably shaped many people's perception of the Brown Brothers, Brian Rust said that "it should be obvious that a fair number of them [the Brothers' recordings] were not designed for dancing,"[10] but, even counting the cylinders and discs of 1911, it isn't apt. Of the forty-three selections commercially issued (not counting the two sound-film discs), only thirteen were not designated as dance records (see appendix), and, from 1916 on, all but two of the thirty-two sides released ("Rigoletto Quartet" and "The Concourse March") were aimed at the dance market. Victor and Emerson sold the Browns as a dance band, and the public bought. In the aural context of 1920s dance bands, this fact may seem odd. But in 1914–20, the Brothers' discs were every bit as danceable as the competition, and their AAT lineup seems to have left its mark on the minds of early arrangers.

From about 1917 to 1923, Maria Brown, touring with her famous sons, worked on a signature quilt with the help of Alec's wife, Edith.[11] Sometimes in person, sometimes by letter, Maria would offer prominent figures in show business and public life swatches of silk or cotton and ask them to sign their names on the cloth. The two women then embroidered over the 145 or so signatures and stitched the pieces together into a quilt top measuring seventy-two by eighty inches—a grid of nine squares by ten, with an imposed diagonal grid of larger squares whose sides slice each smaller square neatly into halves. The mostly pastel colors are in no discernible order, except that two swatches of the same color never touch. A signature might occupy the triangular half of a square (though most of them are left blank), the diagonal bar that slices it, or an edge bar running along two squares. Although many of the respondents may have been personal friends of the Browns—as were Lew Dockstader, Ethel Levey, Raymond Wylie, and Fred and Allene Stone—others, such as Theodore Roosevelt, Herbert Hoover, Thomas Edison, Rabindranath Tagore, and Al Smith, must have helped Maria out because of her boys' prestige.

Roosevelt gets pride of place, just above the quilt's center, his two-square edge piece framed by a full diagonal square made of American-flag fabric. The Six Brown Brothers have their strip, of course, along with separate ones for Tom Brown and Theresa Valerio. Enrico Caruso signed, as did the soprano Amelita Galli-Curci. John Drew, Ethel and Lionel Barrymore, and De Wolf Hopper are among the prominent thespians represented. The newspaper magnate William Randolph Hearst's strip is discreetly separated from that of his lover, the film actress (and former bareback rider) Marion Davies. Other movie luminaries such as Mary Pickford, Charlie Chaplin, Jackie

Coogan, and Alice Brady make appearances, and entertainers from Joe Weber (of Weber and Fields) and Lillian Russell to Al Jolson and the Original Dixieland Jazz Band can be found. The professional environment of Maria's sons is evoked by the names of John Ringling, Dockstader, Wylie, Josie Heather, the Stones, Violet Zell, R. H. Burnside, Oscar Ragland, the Duncan Sisters, and Julian Eltinge. Billie Burke, David Belasco, Harry Lauder, Ina Claire, George M. Cohan, Norma Talmadge, Nora Bayes, Evelyn Nesbit, and Leo Carrillo are names that ring sometimes faint bells today, sewn among the many forgotten and illegible ones. Occasionally only part of a signature will remain visible, partly covered by a later addition; Bert Levy robs Bob N—— of his surname, and John Drew does the same for Florence Sh——. In one case (and who knows how many others) a strip (Jackie Coogan Jr.) once completely concealed an earlier one beneath it (Walter Brown), though the latter now peeks through the tatters.

Although the quilt has been lovingly preserved over the decades, here and there a swatch will be in shreds or flakes, consumed by internal forces such as microbes and chemical dyes. The strips for the Brothers and Theresa seem to have worn away in spots from repeated touching, but Tom's, like most of the others, has remained bright and intact. With Edith's help, Maria produced a remarkable artifact, somewhere in the borderland between mute craft object, such as Gustave Stickley sofas or the Navajo trade rugs produced for the Fred Harvey Company, and historical document. As a document, it doesn't say much. On the strictest reading, it may seem to be just a collection of names, with an occasional salutation such as "Good luck," "Best wishes," or "Sincerely yours" or a brief identifier such as "French Flying Corps" or "R. F. C." (Royal Flying Corps). Nothing is predicated of the bearers of the names; no assertions are made. The quilt's informational content is that of a laundry list or an inventory of the items in a detainee's pockets. But a more generous reading, one that makes an obvious guess at Maria's reasons for the labor, may discern a vague predicate attached to all the names, something hovering between real importance and mere fame, between being worthy of remembrance and being assured of it, something like candidacy for inclusion in future histories.

One history succeeds another as the future becomes the present and then the past. On the generous reading of the quilt, and at the current historical moment, Maria's implied judgments have been in many cases borne out. Teddy Roosevelt, Harry Houdini, Hoover, Chaplin, Edison, and Caruso are still vivid in American collective memory. Mary Pickford, Lillian Russell, Al Smith, and George M. Cohan live there too, if paler and farther in the background. Personalities such as Galli-Curci, the ODJB, Joe Weber, and Julian Eltinge also survive, though mostly in the recollection of specialist devotees of opera, early jazz, comedy teams, and female impersonation. But Maria seems, for the moment, to have been wrong about Valeska Surratt, Major H. Johnston, Jack Gardner, and a host of others, and even about most of the figures in the present volume. How many (besides you, who have read to the end) attach any reference to the names of Billy Mack, Violet Zell, or Theresa Valerio, or even Fred Stone, who had a later career in Hollywood, or Lew Dockstader, who made a president laugh at himself? How many who aren't saxophonists or record collectors remember the Six Brown Brothers? Yet all these men and women have claims, weaker or stronger, to be embroidered on the constantly renewed quilt of collective memory. Biographies of the forgotten are, among other things, arguments in support of this kind of claim, with the hope that the claimants will not only be restored to the quilt but also, if only for a time, be remembered for what they actually did and who they really were. The present book invites its readers to embroider a strip of fine durable cloth with the name of the Six Brown Brothers, once famous entertainers, said to be the originators of the saxophone craze.

Appendix: Discography

As far as I know, the only primary sources for discographical information on the Six (or Five) Brown Brothers are the Columbia Graphophone Company file cards that Brian Rust used for the *Columbia Master Book*, the Victor Talking Machine Company's recording books, currently housed at Bertelsmann Music Group, New York, and the Emerson catalog cited in chapter 10, note 45. There are no known archives for Emerson, according to Allan Sutton, who has studied the company's history. Only the Emerson catalog lists personnel for the sessions. For the Columbia and Victor discs, the best one can do is conjecture from what is known about the group's makeup from other sources, such as theatre programs, newspaper articles, and photographs. There may have been substitutes on some of the recording sessions (Billy Markwith is pictured in place of William Brown in some Victor publications), but I have found no evidence for the presence of Guy Shrigley, Harry Cook, Slap White, or Sunny Clapp, although Shrigley, Cook, and White all get composer credit on various titles. Nor have I found any evidence that the instrumentation ever included a C-melody sax or, before 1919, a soprano sax. No soprano sax is audible on any of the titles below, except for Tom Brown's solo side of "Rosy Cheeks" and the soundtrack disc for Vitaphone no. 549.

The first known personnel list for the Five Brown Brothers, published in *Variety*, December 11, 1909, includes Tom Brown and Fred Brown, alto sax; Billy Markwith, tenor sax; Alec Brown, baritone sax; Vern Brown, bass sax. The Brothers made their first records in 1911, including four cylinders for the United States Phonograph Company, described in chapter 6. The exact recording date for the cylinders, released in October 1911, is unknown. The personnel may have been as it is given above, but it may also have included one or both of the other two Brown brothers, Percy and William. Percy is pictured with the Six Brown Brothers in December 1911 playing baritone sax, and William at various times from 1912 onward played both baritone and tenor with the sextet. The 1911 personnel of the quintet may also have included Harry Fink (who was born Harry Finklestein and later went by the name Harry Brown), who sometimes played baritone, sometimes tenor.

Each entry below gives (1) the name of the group as it appears on released discs, (2) the location and recording date of the selections, (3) the matrix and take number (underlined take numbers indicating that the take was mastered, that is, used to create a metal negative that in turn could be used to manufacture records), (4) the overall title of the side, followed by the type (fox-trot, waltz, etc.) when that is not part of the title, followed by names of selections included in a medley, followed by the names of the composer(s) and arranger, when known, and (5) information about the fate of the take(s) (rejected, mastered though never issued, or released on the disc specified). All the information under (4) is given at the first occurrence of a title, but only a short title is given for repetitions, except when two different record companies are involved. When there is a conflict between information given on a record label and that given by the corresponding documentation, preference is given to the record-label version. Composer's names are given as they are presented on labels and in documentation. They have not been corrected, although I have allowed myself an occasional "*sic*." Where no composer is identified in the sources, "n.c." appears where the name(s) would otherwise appear.

Brown Brothers' Saxophone Quintette

New York, June 26, 1911

19433-1	That Beautiful Rag (n.c.)	rejected
19434-1	American Patrol (Meacham)	Columbia A-1041
19435-1	Tramp, Tramp, Tramp— Theme and Variations (n.c.)	rejected
19436-1	The Bullfrog and the Coon— Medley ("Chicken [Reel]," "Cubanola Glide," When the Moon Plays Peek-a-Boo," "The Bullfrog and the Coon") (n.c.)	Columbia A-1041

These two released titles were remade on March 7, 1912, and issued on discs with the same release number as the June takes. The matrix numbers of the remakes were respectively 19790 and 19789. But the March 1912 group couldn't have been the real Brown Brothers, since the latter were not in New York at that time and had by then become the *Six* Brown Brothers. There is some reason to believe that the March 1912 group included Billy Markwith.

Six Brown Brothers

New York, November 10, 1914

From contemporary photos, the most likely personnel for this group includes Tom Brown and Fred Brown, alto sax; William Brown, tenor sax; Harry Fink and Alec Brown, baritone sax; Vern Brown, bass sax. However, Billy Markwith appears in some photos during this period instead of William Brown.

15360-1-2	Chicken Reel Comedy Medley ("Chicken Reel," "He's a Devil in His Home Town,"	rejected

                   "While the Angelus Is Ringing,"
                   "Bull Frog and the Coon") (n.c.)

15361-1-2	La Paloma (Yradier)	rejected
15362-1-2	That Moaning Saxophone Rag (Harry Cook—Tom Brown)	rejected
15363-1-2	Dill Pickles Rag (Johnson)	rejected

New York, November 20, 1914

15360-3	Chicken Reel Comedy Medley	rejected
15361-3	La Paloma	Victor 17822, 72326
15362-3	That Moaning Saxophone Rag	Victor 17677
15363-3	Dill Pickles Rag	mastered, not issued
15414-1	Independentia—Medley March ("Independentia," "Under [the] Double Eagle," "When You Wore a Tulip") (n.c.)	rejected

New York, December 8, 1914

15414-2-3	Independentia—Medley March	rejected

New York, February 15, 1915

15360-4-5	Chicken Reel Comedy Medley ("Poet and Peasant," "Chicken Reel," "Virginia Lee," "Bull Frog [sic: Bullfrog] and the Coon") (n.c.)	Victor 17799
15361-4	La Paloma	rejected
15363-4	Dill Pickles Rag	rejected
15414-4-5	Independentia—Medley March	rejected

New York, June 11, 1915

15414-6-7-8-9-10	Independentia—Medley March ("Independentia," "Under the Double Eagle," "Billboard March") (n.c.)	Victor 17822

New York, June 25, 1915

16141-1-2-3	American Patrol (n.c.)	mastered, not issued
16142-1-2-3	Down Home Rag (Wilber C. S. Sweatman)	rejected

New York, July 8, 1915

16142-4-5-6	Down Home Rag	Victor 17834
16178-1-2-3	A La Carte (Abe Holtzman)	rejected

New York, August 13, 1915

| 16178-4-5-6 | A La Carte | rejected |
| 16355-1 | The Hustler March (Harry L. Alford) | rejected |

Camden, N.J., June 19, 1916

The instrumentation has probably changed by this date, but not the personnel:
    Tom Brown and Fred Brown, alto sax; Harry Fink and William Brown, tenor sax; Alec Brown, baritone sax; Vern Brown, bass sax. Some of the arrangements for this series of dates are by F. Henri Klickmann, according to the Victor recording books.

17894-1-2	Pussyfoot March (In Fox Trot Time) ("Slap" White, arr. FHK)	Victor 18097
17895-1-2	Chin Chin—Medley Fox Trot ("Pretty Baby," "Chin-Chin Open Your Heart and Let Me In") (Van Alstyne [sic]—Seymour Brown)	rejected
17896-1-2	Rigoletto Quartet (Verdi, arr. G. E. Holmes)	rejected

Camden, N.J., June 20, 1916

17895-3-4-5	Chin Chin—Medley Fox Trot	Victor 18149
17897-1-2	Bull Frog Blues (In Fox Trot Time) (Tom Browne [sic]—Guy Shrigley, arr. FHK)	Victor 18097
17898-1-2	Walkin' the Dog—Fox Trot (Brooks—Shrigley, arr. FHK)	rejected
17899-1-2-3	Chicken Walk—Eccentric Fox Trot (Tom Brown, arr. FHK)	Victor 18189

Camden, N.J., June 21, 1916

17895-6-7	Chin Chin—Medley Fox Trot	rejected
17898-3-4	Walkin' the Dog	rejected
17899-4-5	Chicken Walk	rejected
18006-1-2	Passion Dance (La Danza Appassionata) (Parisian Fox-Tango) (Clarence M. Jones, arr. FHK)	rejected
18007-1	Saxophone Sobs—Fox Trot (E. Erdmann, arr. FHK)	rejected

Camden, N.J., June 22, 1916

17896-3-4-5	Rigoletto Quartet	Victor 18217
17898-5-6	Walkin' the Dog	Victor 18140
18006-3-4	Passion Dance	rejected
18007-2	Saxophone Sobs	Victor 18140

| 18014-1-2 | Tambourines and Oranges— | rejected |
| | Fox Trot (F. Henri Klickmann) | |

Camden, N.J., June 23, 1916

17895-8-9	Chin Chin—Medley	rejected
17896-6-7-8	Rigoletto Quartet	rejected
18006-5-6	Passion Dance	Victor 18217
18007-3	Saxophone Sobs	rejected
18014-3	Tambourines and Oranges	mastered, not issued

New York,[1] May 7, 1917

Personnel and instrumentation are probably the same as those on the 1915 sessions, except that a cornet or trumpet is audible on "For Me and My Gal."

19696-1-2	Tom Brown's Saxophone (Waltz)	mastered, not issued
	(Tom Brown, arr. FHK)	
19697-1-2	Daughters of American Revolution	mastered, not issued
	(National March) (n.c.)	
19698-1-2-3	Saxophone Sam—Fox Trot	Victor 18309
	(Paul Biese—F. Henri Klickmann)	
19840-1-2-3	My Fox Trot Girl (Paul Biese—	Victor 18310
	F. Henri Klickmann)	

New York, May 8, 1917

19699-1-2	Comedy Tom (In One-Step Tempo)	Victor 18385
	(Gus King)	
19843-1-2-3	The Aunt Jemimas [sic] Slide	mastered, not issued
	(Fox Trot) (Karl Johnson)	
19844-1-2	Ghost of the Saxophone—Fox Trot	rejected
	(F. Henri Klickmann)	
19845-1-2	A Wonderful Thing (Valse Hesitation)	mastered, not issued
	(n.c.)	
19846-1-2	Saxophonology (One Step)	rejected
	(Ernie Erdman, arr. FHK)	

New York, May 9, 1917

19844-3-4	Ghost of the Saxophone	Victor 18309
19846-3	Saxophonology	mastered, not issued
19847-1-2-3	The Darktown Strutters' Ball—	Victor 18376
	Fox Trot (Shelton Brooks)	
19848-1-2	For Me and My Gal—Medley Fox Trot	mastered, not issued
	("From Here to Shanghai," "For Me	
	and My Gal") (George W. Meyer—	
	Irving Berlin)	

19849-1-2-3-4-5   Smiles and Chuckles (Jazz Rag)   Victor 18385
                   (In One-Step Tempo)
                   (F. Henri Klickmann)

New York, May 10, 1917

19848-3-4-5-6   For Me and My Gal   Victor 18310

New York, June 4, 1918

At this point, Vern Brown may already have been in the military, though Fred was not inducted until September 1918. A possible substitute for Vern is Matthew Amaturo. Otherwise, the personnel is probably the same as for the 1917 sessions.

21945-1-2	Minstrel Days March (G. E. Holmes)	rejected
21946-1-2	Oh! Babe!—Fox Trot (F. Henri Klickmann, arr. FHK)	rejected
21947-1-2	When Aunt Dinah's Daughter Hannah Bangs on That Piano—One Step (James (Slap) White, arr. FHK)	Victor 18476
21948-1-2	A Georgia Moan—Fox Trot (Frank Fuhrer)	mastered, not issued
21949-1-2	Come Along Ma Honey (Down Upon the Swanee)—Fox Trot (Harold Weeks, arr. FHK)	mastered, not issued

New York, June 5, 1918

21945-3	Minstrel Days March	mastered, not issued
21950-1-2	Chasing the Chickens— Fox Trot (Walker—Olman)	rejected
21951-1-2-3	Drafting Blues—Fox Trot (Maceo Pinkard)	rejected
21952-1-2	Cute and Pretty—Fox Trot (Melville Morris)	rejected
21953-1-2	Sand Dunes—One Step (Will Rossiter [sic])	rejected
21954-1-2-3	At the Funny Page Ball— Fox Trot (Robert Sparcey)	rejected
21955-1-2	The Courtier March (G. E. Holmes)	rejected

New York, June 6, 1918

21952-3-4	Cute and Pretty	mastered, not issued
21953-3	Sand Dunes	rejected
21955-3-4	The Courtier March	mastered, not issued
21956-1-2	Cry Baby—A Jass Fox Trot (Tom Brown—Ernie Erdman)	mastered, not issued

21957-1-2	Play It Again—One Step	mastered, not issued
	(Ernie Erdman—Tom Brown)	
21958-1-2	Moovie [sic] Blues—Fox Trot	mastered, not issued
	(Harry Brown)	
21959-1-2	Hello Central, Give Me No Man's Land	rejected
	(Jean Schwartz)	
21960-1	Saxophone Caprice	mastered, not issued
	(F. Henri Klickmann)	

New York, June 7, 1918

21946-3-4	Oh! Babe!	mastered, not issued
21950-3	Chasing the Chickens	Victor 18476
21951-4-5	Drafting Blues	mastered, not issued
21953-4-5	Sand Dunes	mastered, not issued
21954-4	At the Funny Page Ball	mastered, not issued
21959-3-4	Hello Central, Give Me No Man's Land	mastered, not issued
21960-2-3-4	Saxophone Caprice	rejected

Camden, N.J., May 12, 1919

At this point, both Fred and Vern Brown may still have been in the military, although the war had ended the previous November. So there could be subs on second alto and bass sax, possibly including Billy Markwith and Matthew Amaturo, or the personnel could be the same as in 1914–1917: Tom Brown and Fred Brown, alto sax; Harry Fink and William Brown, tenor sax; Alec Brown, baritone sax; and Vern Brown, bass sax.

21956-3-4	Cry Baby	mastered, not issued
22826-1-2-3	Peter Gink—One Step (George L. Cobb)	rejected
22827-1-2	Missouri Blues—Fox Trot (Harry Brown)	mastered, not issued
22828-1-2	Oriental Fox Trot (Vincent Rose)	mastered, not issued
22842-1-2	Off Again On Again Gone	mastered, not issued
	Again Finnegan (F. Henri Klickmann)	

Camden, N. J., May 13, 1919

22826-4	Peter Gink	Victor 18562
22843-1-2-3	Pershing Patrol (Herbert Phillips)	rejected
22844-1-2	Sweet Jazz o' Mine—Rag One Step	mastered, not issued
	(Jack Frost, arr. FHK)	
22850-1-2	Rajah One Step (N. M. [sic])	rejected
22851-1-2-3	Egyptland—Fox Trot	Victor 18562
	(James W. Casey, arr. FHK)	

New York, 1919, probably after May 1

Personnel and instrumentation, according to the Emerson catalog, are the same as in 1916–17. The cornet or trumpet soloist on "I'll Say She Does" may be Harry Fink. A cornet or trumpet is also audible on "Rainbow of My Dreams." The takes marked as issued are those on discs known to the author. There may be others.

4437-1-2-3	I'll Say She Does (Medley) ("Smiles," "I'm Forever Blowing Bubbles") (Fox Trot) (De Sylva—Kahn—Jolson —Lee S. Roberts—Kenbrovin—Kellett)	Emerson 1056
4438-1-2	Carolina Sunshine (Waltz) (Hirsch—Schmidt)	Emerson 1055
4439-1-2-3	The Concourse March (G. E. Holmes)	Emerson 10106
4440-1-2-3	Peter Gink (One Step) (George L. Cobb)	Emerson 1055
4441-1-2	Missouri Blues (Fox Trot) (Harry Brown)	Emerson 1056

New York, 1919–20

4688-1-2-3-4	Twelfth Street Rag (Fox Trot) (C. E. Wheeler [sic])	Emerson 10205

New York, spring 1920?

41105-1-2-3	Fatima (One Step) (Curtis—Van Alstyne)	Emerson 10205
41106-1-2	Jazz Band Blues (Fox Trot) (James White)	Emerson 10195
41107-1	Lazy Jazz Waltz (Sweet Hawaiian Moonlight) (F. Henry [sic] Klickmann)	Emerson 10186
41108-1-2	Rainbow of My Dreams (Medley) ("Norse Maid") (Fox Trot) (Freed—Wallace)	Emerson 10195
41109-1-2-3	Alexandria (One Step) (Anselm Goetzl)	Emerson 10186

New York or Camden, N.J., November 22, 1920

24702-1-2-3	Tip Top—Medley Fox Trot ("Wonderful Girl, Wonderful Boy," "The Girl I Never Met") (Ivan Caryll)	Victor 18714
24703-1-2	If a Wish Could Make It So— Medley Fox Trot ("TickleMe") (Herbert Stothart)	Victor 18714
24704-1-2-3	Shivaree—One Step (Geo. L. Cobb)	mastered, not issued*

New York, c. 1920

Disc for a sound movie short produced by the Talking Picture Company of New York; title of film and musical selections are unknown; see "Pat" Ballard, "Making the First Talking Picture of a Jazz Orchestra," *Metronome*, November 1929, 40.

Tom Brown Accompanied by Brown Brothers

Location and date unknown [probably 1921-25]

Rosy Cheeks (Squires)   not commercially issued*

Six Original Brown Brothers

New York, May 5, 1927

This Vitaphone soundtrack disc, entitled *Saxaphonic* [sic] *Jazz Masters and Orchestra* in Vitaphone's distributor's catalog but copyrighted as *The Original Six Brown Brothers, Saxophone Orchestra Headed by Tom Brown, Offering* . . . (completed by the playlist), is slightly longer than nine minutes. Only two pieces are played by the Six Brown Brothers; others are by Their Augmented Orchestra (with or without the addition of the sextet), a "modern dance orchestra" including Tom Brown on soprano and alto saxophones and possibly other members of the Six Brown Brothers, which at the time probably included Tom on soprano and alto, Vern Brown on bass sax, and four unidentified musicians, possibly including Lester Rush, on alto, two tenors, and a baritone. No composers are given in the Vitaphone catalog, which is the only written source I know of for information about the short. I have added their names where known, but have omitted "n.c."

Yankee Rose (Abe Frankl): band   Vitaphone 549
In a Little Spanish Town(Mabel Wayne): sextet
The Bullfrog and the Coon (Joseph S. Nathan): band
Yankee Rose: band
Pagliacci (Dance Orchestration)(Leoncavallo): band
'Deed I Do (Walter Hirsch—Fred Rose): band
Abandoned-bride routine: Tom Brown and band
How Dry I Am: band
Rosy Cheeks (Harry D. Squires): Tom Brown and band
There's Something Nice About Everyone
    (Arthur Terker—Alfred Bryan—Pete Wendling): band

*"Shivaree" and "Rosy Cheeks" are the selections on the two sides of a privately made disc designated Six Brown Bros Saxophone Records 1000, recorded by Electric Recording Laboratories, New York, at an unknown date. The former seems likely to be a dub of the November 1920 Victor "Shivaree." The latter sounds as if it were recorded acoustically, which makes a date of 1925 or earlier likely, and the song bears a 1921 copyright. Since the date of the Brothers' short film for the Talking Picture Company of New York (see chapter 12) is unknown, but probably lies in the period 1920–23, and since "Pat" Ballard, on whose testimony knowledge of the film relies, characterized the music in it as "subdued and organ-like," perhaps "Rosy Cheeks" is a dub of the soundtrack disc. The artist credit on the "Shivaree" side reads "Played by

Six Brown Brothers"; the corresponding line on the reverse is "Solo Played by Tom Brown Accompanied by Brown Brothers." The disc is inscribed "Gift from Dorothy Stone" and may have entered the collection of the National Music Museum, Vermillion, South Dakota, via the private collection of Tom Brown's friend H. A. Waggener.

Notes

Abbreviations Used in Notes

BMG   Victor Talking Machine Company documents, Bertelsmann Music Group, New York

BRTC   Billy Rose Theatre Collection, New York Public Library for the Performing Arts

CBD   Charles Bancroft Dillingham Papers, Manuscripts and Archives Division, New York Public Library

CWM   Robert L. Parkinson Library and Research Center, Circus World Museum, Baraboo, Wisconsin

KAA   Keith/Albee Collection, University Libraries, University of Iowa, Iowa City, Iowa

MMC   Private collection of Mark Miller, Toronto, Ontario

NMM   Cecil B. Leeson Collection, National Music Museum, Vermillion, South Dakota

TBS   Tom Brown scrapbooks, author's collection

Chapter 1

1. "The Power of the Drama," *Life*, October 21, 1920, 724.
2. Gilbert Seldes, *The Seven Lively Arts* (1924; reprint, Mineola, N.Y.: Dover, 2001), 348, 251, 256. A version of the judgment about vaudeville, already including the Six Brown Brothers as an example, had appeared earlier in Seldes, "The Damned Effrontery of the Two-a-Day," *Vanity Fair*, October 1922, 51.
3. "Minstrels Delight Crowded Audience," *Ottawa Citizen*, March 29, 1913, n.p., author's collection.
4. The claim is found in numerous advertisements for the Buescher Band Instrument Company, whose saxophones the group endorsed, for example *Jacobs' Orchestra Monthly*, October 1921, 83; *Metronome*, June 1921, 27. Tom Brown did not play a Buescher instrument: his alto was a Couesnon with a Buescher logo, and his soprano was made by Sax.
5. Alexander Woollcott, "The Play," *New York Times*, October 6, 1920, 13.

6. Percy A. Scholes, *The Oxford Companion to Music*, 10th ed., ed. John Owen Ward (Oxford: Oxford University Press, 1970), 914. The passage is held over from the 1938 edition. Scholes goes on to lament, "To the judicious this was a grief, as the members of the family were often made to perform feats for which providence had not intended them, and the tone quality that resulted was often trying to sensitive ears" (914). The earliest printed references to the saxophone craze known to the author are in a series of articles in the *Dominant* for 1915–16 by Guy E. Holmes and Clay Smith, speaking of Americans "crazy over saxophones" ("Saxophone Article," November 1915, 72) or "saxophone mad" ("Saxophone Article," January 1916, 74), and finally, in "Saxophone Celebrities," May 1916, 71, using an equivalent of "saxophone craze" itself: "The craze for saxophones for all purposes continues, and about twenty per cent of all new wind instruments purchased in the past three months were saxophones." The bandmaster J. H. McClure uses the phrase "saxophone craze" in "The Saxophone in the Orchestra," *Metronome Orchestra Monthly*, May 1916, 20. Unfortunately, Holmes and Smith didn't say when they consider the craze to have begun. Tom Brown staked his claim to the office of creator a few months later: "To make a long story short they [C. G. Conn saxophones] satisfy the Six Brown Brothers and the musical world knows we started the Saxophone craze." The sentence is represented as taken from a telegram sent from Milwaukee, Wisconsin, on February 22, 1917 (advertisement, *Musical Truth*, September 1917, 28).
7. Paul Lindemeyer, *Celebrating the Saxophone* (New York: Hearst Books, 1996), 33.
8. Mark Hulsebos, *Cecil Leeson: The Pioneering of the Concert Saxophone in America from 1921 to 1941* (Ann Arbor, Mich.: University Microfilms, 1989), 15–16. Hulsebos is repeating the opinion of his mentor, the pioneer concert saxophonist Cecil Leeson (1902–1989), given in a transcript of a 1986 interview in Hulsebos, 186. More recently and more judiciously, Richard Ingham, in *The Cambridge Companion to the Saxophone*, ed. Richard Ingham (Cambridge: Cambridge University Press, 1998), 71–72, says, "The popularity of the instrument itself in the early twentieth century can be traced to saxophone ensembles touring the vaudeville circuit. One of the most celebrated groups was that led by Tom Brown."
9. Sime Silverman, "Tip-Top," *Variety*, October 8, 1920, 17.
10. Edward Haffel, "B. F. Keith's Palace New York," *Billboard*, July 2, 1921, 9.
11. Advertisement, *San Francisco Call and Post*, June 18, 1923, 12.
12. H. W. Schwarz, *The Story of Musical Instruments: From Shepherd's Pipe to Symphony* (Elkhart, Ind.: Pan-American Band Instruments, 1938), 139–40.
13. Arthur Lange, *Arranging for the Modern Dance Orchestra* (New York: A. Lange, 1926), ix, 40.
14. These are of course the author's favorites. Readers may compile their own lists.
15. See Fred Hemke, *The Early History of the Saxophone* (Ann Arbor, Mich.: University Microfilms, 1975).
16. Lindemeyer, *Celebrating the Saxophone*, 30. Harry R. Gee, *Saxophone Soloists and Their Music, 1844–1985* (Bloomington: Indiana University Press, 1985), 13–14, gives the soloist's name as Henri Wuille and the date as December 19, 1853.

17. Margaret Hindle Hazen and Robert M. Hazen, *The Music Men: An Illustrated History of Brass Bands in America, 1800–1920* (Washington, D.C.: Smithsonian Institution Press, 1987), 42.
18. Hazen and Hazen, *The Music Men,* 98–99, 106–7, 194.
19. Hazen and Hazen, *The Music Men,* 98–99.
20. Lindemeyer, *Celebrating the Saxophone,* 30. The information regarding Lefèbre's stint with Sousa comes from Margaret Downie Banks's research on the instrument manufacturer C. G. Conn (personal communication).
21. Michael Eric Hester, *A Study of the Saxophone Soloists Performing with the John Philip Sousa Band: 1893–1930* (Ann Arbor, Mich.: University Microfilms, 1995), 35, 89.
22. Hazen and Hazen, *The Music Men,* 98–99.
23. See Arthur A. Clappé, *The Wind-Band and Its Instruments* (New York: Henry Holt, 1911), 36–37, 39, and 72.
24. The first roster of the Ringling Brothers Circus band to include a saxophone, for example, is the 1905 list (compiled many years after the fact by Sverre O. Braathen, an apparently tireless researcher whose papers are housed at the Robert L. Parkinson Library and Research Center of the Circus World Museum, Baraboo, Wisconsin). Only one member of the group, F. Barney, is named as a saxophonist. Exceptions show up in advertisements in the show-business weekly *New York Clipper.* Among the hundreds of help-wanted notices and boasts about such traveling shows each year in the period 1890–95, only two mention saxophones in 1890 (February 22, 1890, 834; November 29, 1890, 603), two in 1891 (September 12, 1891, 461; August 15, 1891, 395), none in 1892, four in 1893 (February 4, 1893, 782; February 18, 1893, 810; June 3, 1893, 211; September 23, 1893, 475), five in 1894 (January 20, 1894, 746; June 9, 1894, 221; August 4, 1894, 351; August 11, 1894, 364, repeated on August 25, 1894, 398; December 1, 1894, 628), and one in 1895 (April 20, 1895, 108). Carl Clair, bandmaster of the Barnum and Bailey circus from 1892 to 1906, seems to have used one or more saxophones in his band during that whole period, and before that when he led the King and Franklin Circus band in the 1890 season (advertisements, *New York Clipper,* February 22, 1890, 834; January 9, 1892, 738; June 3, 1893, 211; January 20, 1894, 746).
25. G. E. Holmes and Clay Smith, "The Saxophone Is Coming Fast," *Dominant,* July 1915, 66. "Gorten's Golden Band Minstrels" probably refers to the company managed by Joseph Gorton in the late nineteenth and early twentieth centuries, starting some time after 1867 and still performing in 1910. See Edward Le Roy Rice, *Monarchs of Minstrelsy* (New York: Kenny, 1911), 108. W. C. Handy, primarily a cornetist, recalled buying a tenor sax around 1897, when he was with Mahara's Minstrels, only to have it "appropriated" by W. N. P. Spiller, later the founder of the Musical Spillers, a rival of the Brown Brothers, for which see chapter 6 (W. C. Handy, *The Father of the Blues: An Autobiography* [New York: Macmillan, 1941], 63–64).
26. To give a couple of typical examples, rosters published in advertisements in the *New York Clipper* show fourteen musicians in the orchestra traveling with W. S. Cleveland's All-United Monster Minstrels, only three of whom don't list doubles (October 22, 1892, 535), and ten in the Famous Bartholemew's

Equine Paradox Band and Orchestra, seven of whom double (January 21, 1893, 716).

27. In advertising a tenor and a baritone sax for sale in the *New York Clipper* for June 28, 1890, 254, Sam O'Bannon tells his potential customers: "Fine turn for variety artists."

28. The examples in this paragraph represent the total number of advertisements for variety turns including saxophones in the *New York Clipper* during the period 1890–95, based on the author's survey. Note that there are no such ads in 1890. Not included are a handful of ads in which a variety turn or traveling show seeks to hire a saxophonist, since it may have failed to find one.

29. Advertisements, *New York Clipper*, February 7, 1891, 767; February 28, 1891, 812.

30. Advertisement, *New York Clipper*, October 22, 1892, 532.

31. Advertisement, *New York Clipper*, February 18, 1893, 810.

32. Advertisements, *New York Clipper*, August 19, 1893, 388; October 28, 1893, 551.

33. Advertisement, *New York Clipper*, October 14, 1893, 524.

34. Advertisement, *New York Clipper*, September 22, 1894, 463. See also advertisement, *New York Clipper*, April 13, 1895, 94.

35. Advertisements, *New York Clipper*, October 20, 1894, 533; October 27, 1894, 550.

36. Advertisement, *New York Clipper*, October 12, 1895, 514.

37. "Frank Mudge" [obituary], *Variety*, March 25, 1942, 54. Obituaries are notoriously inaccurate about dates, but perhaps this one is correct about Mudge's having been first. However, Billy Young's American Musical Tramp act seems to have played vaudeville theatres.

38. "B. C. and Louise Linden Bent," *New York Clipper*, May 22, 1897, 191. The Bents "have won the heartiest recognition for their artistic skill."

39. "Banjo Pickings," *Gatcomb's Musical Gazette*, April–May 1898, 6. Since *Gatcomb's* was a journal for players of mandolins, guitars, and banjos, Farrell probably specialized on one of those instruments and used the saxophone as a supplementary gimmick. Farrell played a song titled "You Have a Girl of Your Own."

40. Advertisement, *New York Clipper*, July 7, 1900, 413.

41. Photograph caption, *New York Clipper*, August 3, 1901, 482. Hagenbeck's was one of the best-known circuses of the era. It seems likely that this Rackett is the same as the Arthur Rackett who played with John Philip Sousa's band, mentioned in Hemke, *The Early History of the Saxophone*, 422.

42. Advertisement, *New York Clipper*, May 16, 1903, 296. W. C. Handy, then bandmaster with Frank Mahara's Minstrels, an African American company under white management, hired a saxophone quartet from Chicago during the 1902–3 season long enough for it to play in a single morning parade, but it is not known whether the group continued to play professionally (Handy, *Father of the Blues*, 63). I am grateful to Larry Gushee for the citation.

43. "Gray and Graham," *New York Clipper*, May 13, 1905, 311; "The Famous Four Emperors of Music," May 20, 1905, 181; "Lew Wells" (photo caption), February 25, 1905, xiii. From later descriptions, Graham's saxophone seems to have been a contrabass.

44. Thomas W. Smialek Jr., *Clay Smith and G. E. Holmes: Their Role in the Development of Saxophone Performance and Pedagogy in the United States, 1905–1930* (Ann Arbor, Mich.: University Microfilms, 1991), 21. In Clay Smith and G. E. Holmes, "The Saxophone and Its Advantages," *Dominant*, April 1915, 8, the authors claim to have had a saxophone quartet as early as 1900, but Smialek's evidence indicates that this is an error.

45. "Map as of 1915," in Irene Briggs Da Boll and Raymond F. Da Boll, *Recollections of the Lyceum and Chautauqua Circuits* (Freeport, Me.: Bond Wheelwright, 1969), 52.

46. Smith and Holmes, "The Saxophone Is Coming Fast," 67. Hemke, *The Early History of the Saxophone*, 417, says that Lefèbre had formed his saxophone quartet by 1905 and toured almost until the end of his life, in 1911. Lefèbre's obituary in *Metronome*, April 1911, 16, indicates that the quartet's first tour began in 1905, though the context creates a faint ambiguity.

47. The data on early saxophone recordings come from Jim Walsh, "Favorite Pioneer Recording Artists," *Hobbies*, November 1973, 37–38, 122–23, with the exception of the Berliner "Annie Laurie," noted in Paul Charosh, comp., *Berliner Gramophone Records: American Issues, 1892–1900* (Westport, Conn.: Greenwood Press, 1995), 46. Charosh also notes that some of the Moeremans sides were recorded in 1897 (93).

48. The date of Conn's first saxophone comes from C. G. Conn Company, *C. G. Conn's New Invention Saxophones* (Elkhart, Ind.: C. G. Conn, 1915). The date for Buescher's departure comes from an open letter of resignation from the Conn Company written and published by Buescher, dated September 26, 1893. For knowledge of both items, I am indebted to Margaret Downie Banks's unpublished research on Conn (personal communication). The report that Buescher built Conn's first saxophone comes from Lynn Sams, interview by Cecil Leeson, tape recording, July 26, 1970, NMM. Sams was a later president of the Buescher Band Instrument Company.

49. Smith and Holmes, "The Saxophone and its Advantages," 8. See also "Clay Smith and Guy E. Holmes," *True-Tone* 17:2, n.d. [1922?], 10.

50. Smith and Holmes, "The Saxophone Is Coming Fast," 66.

51. "Saxophones Here to Stay," *True-Tone* 9:3, n.d. [1914?], 10.

52. Lindemeyer, *Celebrating the Saxophone*, 45.

53. Smith and Holmes, "The Saxophone Is Coming Fast," 66.

54. Smith and Holmes, "The Saxophone Is Coming Fast," 67.

55. "Send For Our Free Booklet," by ———— Kenny and [Harry?] Reser. The piece seems not to have been copyrighted, but it was recorded by Six Jumping Jacks (a group led by the banjoist Harry Reser) in 1930 and released on Brunswick 4759.

56. Isador Berger, "The Saxophone: Siren of Satan," *San Francisco Chronicle*, January 14, 1917, magazine section, 1.

Chapter 2

1. Margaret Hindle Hazen and Robert M. Hazen, *The Music Men: An Illustrated History of Brass Bands in America, 1800–1920* (Washington, D.C.: Smithsonian Institution Press, 1987), xviii, 27.

2. Information on birth and death dates comes from "Band Leader Cornetist Dies in 89th Year," *Toronto Telegram*, October 18, 1947, n.p.; William Brown's tombstone in the Mt. Hope Cemetery, Worth, Illinois; the death certificates of William, Tom, and Percy Brown; "Percy Brown" [obituary], *New York Times*, December 22, 1918, 17; the Canadian census of 1881; Tom and Alec's birth registrations; and various newspaper stories that cite the Browns' ages. Percy's death certificate gives his date of birth as October 31, 1882, but that conflicts with Alec's birth registration, a more nearly contemporaneous and so prima facie more reliable document, which gives the date in the text. In an early photo of the Brown children, Percy clearly appears a year or so younger than Alec (see figure 2).

3. "Six Browns Now Five," *Philadelphia Public Ledger*, April 27, 1919, sec. 1, pt. 2, 9.

4. "Musical Musings," *Billboard*, January 5, 1924, 48–49.

5. "Band Leader Cornetist Dies in 89th Year."

6. Birth dates for Fred and Myrtle come from Ontario birth registrations. Vern's place of birth is taken from his death certificate and his date of birth from the United States government's Social Security database.

7. Tom Brown, *Borrow an Instrument from Me for Five Weeks without Rental Charge* (Chicago: Tom Brown Band School, n.d. [c. 1930]), [4]. In Tom Brown, "Stage Tales On and Off" (*San Francisco Call and Post*, June 20, 1923, 15), Tom says that his first job as a boy was playing clarinet in a traveling minstrel show. The photo also appears in A. C. E. Schonemann, "The Tom Brown Band and Orchestra School," *Jacobs' Orchestra Monthly*, n.d. [c. 1924], n.p., labeled "The original Six Brown Brothers. As they appeared in 1897." The date can't be accurate, however, since the children appear too young. Tom Brown Jr. identified the children as in the present text. A copy of the photo in the author's collection, made in the 1920s or 1930s, bears the date 1894 (see figure 2).

8. An undated obituary of Allan, probably from a Lindsay newspaper, says, without giving dates, that he also directed a band in Trenton, Ontario, east of Cobourg along the shore of Lake Ontario.

9. Watson Kirkconnell and Frankie L. MacArthur, *County of Victoria Centennial History*, 2d ed. (Lindsay, Ont.: Victoria City Council, 1967), 103.

10. Kirkconnell and MacArthur, *County of Victoria*, 100, 109.

11. Kirkconnell and MacArthur, *County of Victoria*, 111.

12. Kirkconnell and MacArthur, *County of Victoria*, 115.

13. Kirkconnell and MacArthur, *County of Victoria*, 131.

14. "Witmark Minstrel Overture" (New York: Witmark, 1915), for instance, follows this pattern, although the curtain rises only after a few bars have been sung behind it.

15. Edward Le Roy Rice, *Monarchs of Minstrelsy* (New York: Kenny, 1911), 11. One of the four was Dan Emmet, the author of "Dixie" (1859), which became the Confederate States of America's war anthem.

16. The phrase, but not the claim about minstrel shows, comes from Harry Birdoff, *The World's Greatest Hit: Uncle Tom's Cabin* (New York: S. F. Vanni, 1947), 130. He means it seriously; I do not.

17. Frank Dumont, a producer and prolific author of minstrel shows, advises amateurs in his book, *The Witmark Amateur Minstrel Guide and Burnt Cork Encyclopedia* (New York: M. Witmark, 1899), as follows: "Do not use dialect, nor allow

it to be used, as it spoils the stories and is often unintelligible to the audience. It is for this reason that the gags, etc. [in the *Guide*], have not been written in dialect form. A mannerism of speech can be assumed without using the thick dialect of the Southern darkey, which is seldom heard among the latter-day children of Ham" (8). He qualifies this advice later on: "Speak naturally, without dialect, as it is not used by the end men. Keep the dialect for your imitations of colored preachers or old darkies" (18). "Many entertainers in the [eighteen-]eighties, and long after, appeared in blackface with no attempt at dialect or impersonation. Some of these were Lew Dockstader, Leopold and Bunnell, Frazer and Allen, Carroll and Nealey, Keating and Sands, Smith and Byrne, and Bryant and Saville. They did monologues or other specialties, jig, clog, and so on, and used blackface make-up. But they were not Negro impersonators; they were blackface entertainers" (Douglas Gilbert, *American Vaudeville: Its Life and Times* [1940; reprint, New York: Dover, 1963], 80–81).

18. James H. Dormon, "Shaping the Popular Image of Post-Reconstruction American Blacks: The 'Coon Song' Phenomenon of the Gilded Age," *American Quarterly* 40 (1988): 450–71. The passage quoted is on p. 455. Dormon's failure to define "coon song" makes his conclusions apply only with some doubt to the whole genre, but I think he nevertheless identifies and gives a sound historical interpretation of one very prevalent kind of coon song.

19. Dormon, "Shaping the Popular Image," 466.

20. Henry J. Wehman, *Wehman's Minstrel Sketches, Conundrums and Jokes* (New York: Henry J. Wehman, 1890), 107.

21. Dave Reed Jr. and Chas. B. Ward, "I'll Make Dat Black Gal Mine (Coon Song)" (New York: New York Music, 1896), in *Primrose and West's Musical Album* (New York: New York Music, n.d. [contents copyrighted 1897 and earlier]), [3]. The Pickaninny Cake-Walkers may have been African American child entertainers; Marshall Stearns and Jean Stearns, in *Jazz Dance: The Story of American Vernacular Dance* (New York: Da Capo Press, 1994), 80–82, give examples of white vaudeville acts in the early part of the twentieth century that carried with them "a group of Negro kids that really could sing and dance" to provide "a sock finish." Following p. 240 of the same book, an undated Primrose and West's poster is pictured, advertising "70 performers—40 white and 30 black—70." The company existed under that name from 1889 until 1898.

22. Dailey Paskman and Sigmund Spaeth, *"Gentlemen, Be Seated!": A Parade of the Old-time Minstrels* (Garden City, N.Y.: Doubleday, Doran, 1928), 28, 80, 176.

23. Dumont, *Witmark Minstrel Guide*, 1.

24. Marian Hannah Winter, "Juba and American Minstrelsy," in *Inside the Minstrel Mask: Readings in Nineteenth-Century Blackface Minstrelsy*, ed. Annemarie Bean, James V. Hatch, and Brooks McNamara (Hanover, N.H.: Wesleyan University Press, 1996), 223–41. The citation is from p. 239.

25. Wehman, *Wehman's Minstrel Sketches*, 75, specifies the following for the two-person sketch "Stocks Up, Stocks Down": "ORLANDO—*Exaggerated evening dress, but shabby and the seams whitened with French chalk; the coat buttoned up to the neck from the waist with scanty ruffles in bosom; coat-collar turned up on one side; one sleeve out at elbow.*"

26. Wehman, *Wehman's Minstrel Sketches*, 23. Jake is also furnished with a broken umbrella.

27. Wehman, *Wehman's Minstrel Sketches*, 75.
28. This version of the story comes from Rice, *Monarchs of Minstrelsy*, 7–10, which purports to reprint an article in *Atlantic Monthly* by Robert P. Nevin. Nevin's version mentions the song, but not the dance. Other versions of the legend, for example Robert Toll's account in *Blacking Up: The Minstrel Show in Nineteenth Century America* (New York: Oxford University Press, 1974), 28, have Rice costuming himself in the clothing of the same person from whom he copied the song and dance, in effect appropriating Jim Crow's very identity. Toll places the incident in 1828.
29. Toll, *Blacking Up*, 45.
30. Rice, *Monarchs of Minstrelsy*, 162.
31. Fred Stone, *Rolling Stone* (New York: McGraw-Hill, 1945), 94.
32. The most famous seems to have been Mme. Rentz's Female Minstrels, mentioned, e.g., in Paskman and Spaeth, *Gentlemen, Be Seated!*, 172–73.
33. Rice, *Monarchs of Minstrelsy*, 20.
34. Rice, *Monarchs of Minstrelsy*, 142–44.
35. Paskman and Spaeth, *Gentlemen, Be Seated!*, 80.

Chapter 3

1. Tom Brown, "Stage Tales On and Off," *San Francisco Call and Post*, June 20, 1923, 15. Although these recollections appeared under Tom's byline, they have the flavor of newspaperman's prose and make errors that would be surprising for Tom to make, for example calling Bowmanville and Janetville, Ontario, "Bowmansville" and "Jennetville." They can fairly be regarded as as-told-to sources.
2. Tom Brown, "Stage Tales On and Off," *San Francisco Call and Post*, June 23, 1923, 9.
3. Brown, "Stage Tales," June 23, 1923, 9.
4. See "Guy Brothers' Minstrels Notes," *New York Clipper*, January 11, 1896, 710; December 26, 1896, 682; February 27, 1897, 828. George Guy Sr., the father of the Guy Brothers, was said to have been one of the founders of the Elks ("Mr. and Mrs. Guy of Minstrel Fame were Married 50 Years Ago June 21," *Springfield [Mass.] Union*, June 11, 1932, n.p. [Springfield Scrapbook 14:26, Springfield {Mass.} Museums]).
5. Brown, "Stage Tales," June 23, 1923, 9.
6. Tom Brown, "Stage Tales On and Off," *San Francisco Call and Post*, June 21, 1923, 18.
7. "On the Road" [list of the week's minstrel engagements], *New York Clipper*, shows Guy Brothers' Minstrels playing Lindsay on October 15, 1896 (October 17, 1896, 518), and October 14, 1897 (October 16, 1897, 540). These published itineraries appear only sporadically, however, never covering an organization's entire tour. Judging from the published itineraries from 1896 through 1900, the Guys seem to have made annual tours of southern Canada during September, October, and November. It is likely that the Guys played Lindsay annually during these tours, between dates that appeared in the *Clipper*. However, one document casts some doubt on whether Tom worked for Ringling Brothers' Circus in the summer of 1899: an "Application to Reenter the

United States" he filed with the U.S. Department of Labor on October 28, 1924, gives his original date of entry into the United States as November 15, 1899, after the circus season had ended.

8. The description is a composite of accounts in "Guy Brothers' [or "Bros.'"] Minstrels Notes," *New York Clipper*, August 1, 1896, 342; September 5, 1896, 425; September 19, 1896, 452. Some or all of the banner-carrying boys probably did not travel with the troupe but more likely were hired locally, like Tom.

9. "Guy Brothers' Minstrels Notes," *New York Clipper*, September 17, 1898, 477; November 12, 1898, 625.

10. There is no Main Street in Lindsay.

11. Brown, "Stage Tales," June 20, 1923, 15.

12. "Guy Brothers' Minstrels Notes," *New York Clipper*, September 18, 1897, 474. No Guy Brothers' item in the *Clipper* mentions a concluding burlesque, so it is likely they didn't do one. Nor is one mentioned in a Guy Brothers' Minstrels program in BRTC. The program is probably from the period 1900–1905, since the cast includes Arthur Guy, who left in 1905 to form his own company, Arthur L. Guy's Novelty Minstrels; see "Notes from Guy Brothers' Minstrels," *New York Clipper*, September 17, 1904, 675; "Arthur L. Guy's Minstrels," *New York Clipper*, June 10, 1905, 404.

13. "Guy Bros.' Minstrels Notes," *New York Clipper*, December 11, 1897, 674.

14. "Guy Bros.' Minstrels Notes," *New York Clipper*, May 2, 1896, 134.

15. During at least part of a season early in the century, however, George and William were not in the show, as indicated by the Guy Brothers' poster mentioned in note 12 of this chapter.

16. "Guy Brothers' Minstrels Notes," *New York Clipper*, September 17, 1898, 477. The illustrated-song alternative (with Arthur Guy as the singer) is explicit in a poster (undated, probably from 1900–1905) and a poster (undated, probably 1900–1905, mentioned in note 12 of this chapter) for Guy Brothers' Minstrels in BRTC.

17. Charles Philip Fox, *A Ticket to the Circus: A Pictorial History of the Incredible Ringlings* (New York: Bramhall House, 1959), 111

18. "Guy Brothers' Minstrels Notes," *New York Clipper*, November 12, 1898, 625; "Guy Bros.' Minstrels Notes," *New York Clipper*, October 21, 1899, 692.

19. "Guy Bros.' Minstrels Notes," *New York Clipper*, October 21, 1899, and the first of two Guy Brothers' Minstrels posters mentioned in note 16 of this chapter.

20. "On the Road," *New York Clipper*, May 6, 1896, 164.

21. Harry Birdoff, *The World's Greatest Hit: Uncle Tom's Cabin* (New York: S. F. Vanni, 1947), 257.

22. Birdoff, *World's Greatest Hit*, 76.

23. Birdoff, *World's Greatest Hit*, 5.

24. Advertisement, *New York Clipper*, July 25, 1896, 338.

25. Birdoff, *World's Greatest Hit*, 324–25.

26. Birdoff, *World's Greatest Hit*, 320, 318.

27. *Washington (D.C.) Colored American*, November 11, 1896, n.p., quoted in Henry T. Sampson, *Blacks in Blackface: A Source Book on Early Black Musical Shows* (Lanham, Md.: Scarecrow Press, 1980), 5.

28. At the Hamilton, Ontario, Grand Opera House, April 11, 1896. The program is in the collection of the Toronto, Ontario, Public Library.

29. "Darkest America," *New York Clipper*, January 18, 1896, 729.

30. Sampson, *Blacks in Blackface*, contains biographies of Chenault (352–54) and Rucker (423–24) and two mentions of Fidler (2, 62). Both Chenault (as Liza Hotfoot) and Fidler (as Mamma Toodle) played drag roles in the playlets.

31. "Darkest America."

32. "Six Browns Now Five," *Philadelphia Public Ledger*, April 27, 1919, sec. 2, pt. 2, 9. It is probably no coincidence that Canadian compulsory education in those days ended at age fourteen (Watson Kirkconnell and Frankie L. MacArthur, *County of Victoria Centennial History*, 2d ed. [Lindsay, Ontario: Victoria City Council, 1967], 212). I amend the quotation to "[some of] his brothers" because in 1895–96, when Tom was fourteen, Vern would have been only about six years old and Fred only about five.

33. It would have been natural for Tom to specify that the troupe was Guy Brothers', given that the story about the fire had been in the *Call and Post* just three days before this one, but he doesn't. In favor of the company having been Guy Brothers' is the near agreement between Tom's declaration (cited in note 7 of this chapter) that he first entered the United States on November 15, 1899, and the Guys' itinerary ("On the Road," *New York Clipper*, November 25, 1899, 811), according to which they returned (to Medina, New York) from their 1899 Ontario tour on November 23, 1899.

34. Brown, "Stage Tales," June 23, 1923, 9.

35. The date is uncertain. "Six Browns Now Five," 9, says, "Twenty years ago Tom left home with a traveling orchestra and in Springfield, Mass., played with the Guy brothers' minstrels."

36. "Notes from the Al. G. Field Big White Minstrels," *New York Clipper*, April 18, 1896, 102; "Notes from W. A. Mahara's Minstrels," *New York Clipper*, September 5, 1896, 422; and "Barlow Bros.' Minstrels Notes," *New York Clipper*, July 25, 1896, 326. The conjecture is based on two clues: in press releases in the *Clipper*, Guy Brothers' never boasts, as other shows often did, about having railroad cars, and the show traveled in very short hops.

37. Dexter W. Fellows and Andrew A. Freeman, *This Way to the Big Show: The Life of Dexter Fellows* (New York: Viking, 1936), 347. The incident took place on July 16, 1896, in Massillon, Ohio.

38. Al. G. Field [Albert Griffith Hatfield], *Watch Yourself Go By* (Columbus, Ohio: Printed by Spohr and Glenn, 1912), 510–11. Employment ads in the *New York Clipper* in the 1890s routinely advise "boozers" and "lushers," along with "mashers," "chippy chasers," and "kickers," to "save your stamps."

Chapter 4

1. "Six Musical Browns at B. F. Keith's Real Brothers," *Cincinnati Commercial*, March 6, 1912, n.p.; "Sensational Saxaphone [*sic*] Sextet," *Louisville Times*, March 12, 1912, n.p.; Brown Brothers file, BRTC. The two items' near-identity in content suggests that they both came from the same press release.

2. "Browns Are 'Sax' Veterans," unidentified newspaper, n.d. [c. 1926], n.p., TBS. According to Edward Le Roy Rice, *Monarchs of Minstrelsy* (New York: Kenny, 1911), 340, 356, Cohan and Harris's Minstrels began in July 1908 and ended c. March 1910, when it became the property of George "Honey Boy" Evans, a principal with the troupe.

3. Ringling Brothers' Circus performers' ledgers record the weekly pay of all performers in the organization, thus providing the best possible evidence for someone's presence in the show, but members of a performing group (such as the Brown Brothers or a sideshow band) are not separately listed per se, so that absence from the ledger is not conclusive evidence of absence from the show. Ledgers for 1906 and 1907 are preserved in the Robert L. Parkinson Library at the Circus World Museum in Baraboo, Wisconsin, but ledgers for 1904–5 and 1908–9 are not known to exist. The clear evidence in the case of the 1909 season is a photograph labeled "Al Sweet's Concert Band—Ringling Bros.' Shows—Season 1909," at the Parkinson Library, which shows Vern holding a clarinet, Tom holding a tenor sax, and Alec holding a bass sax (see figure 4).

4. Wilton Eckley, *The American Circus* (Boston: Twayne, 1984), 185.

5. George C. Warren, "Mother Gone, Her Boys Are Running Wild," *San Francisco Chronicle*, June 16, 1923, 8.

6. Eckley, *American Circus*, 185.

7. "Guy Bros.' Minstrels Notes," *New York Clipper*, September 5, 1896, 425; "Guy Brothers' Minstrels Notes," *New York Clipper*, May 15, 1897, 170. For twelve weeks beginning June 10, 1901, Guy Brothers' also played a summer outdoor season in parks ("Guy Brothers' Minstrels Notes," *New York Clipper*, May 4, 1901, 209). This may have been their first.

8. "Tom and Percy Brown," *New York Clipper*, August 29, 1903, 624; "Guy Brothers' Minstrels Notes," *New York Clipper*, September 5, 1903, 647.

9. Roger Lewis (words) and Harry Cook and Tom Brown (music), "That Moaning Saxophone Rag" (Chicago: Will Rossiter, 1913).

10. The fully developed legend is related in, for example, "Six Browns Now Five," *Philadelphia Public Ledger*, April 27, 1919, sec. 1, pt. 2, 9; "How Many Browns?," *New York Times*, October 24, 1920, sec. 6, 1. In the *Ledger*, the Brothers gather in Guy Brothers', while in the *Times*, they gather in the Ringling show.

11. Rice, *Monarchs of Minstrelsy*, 36.

12. William's and George Jr.'s dates are from Rice, *Monarchs of Minstrelsy*, 242, 263, except for George Jr.'s date of death, which comes from "George R. Guy, Old Trouper, Dies in Home," *Springfield (Mass.) Union*, June 12, 1942, n.p. (Springfield Scrapbook 4:180, Springfield [Mass.] Museums). Arthur's dates are from Rice, *Monarchs of Minstrelsy*, 346; "Arthur Guy" [obituary], *Variety*, October 13, 1937, 62. Rice gives 1903 as the date Arthur Guy's Novelty Minstrels began, but the *Clipper* lists Arthur as one of the end men in Guy Brother's Minstrels for the season of 1904–5 ("Notes from Guy Brothers' Minstrels," *New York Clipper*, September 17, 1904, 675) and first mentions Arthur L. Guy's Minstrels as a twelve-man troupe playing the summer season of 1905 ("Arthur L. Guy's Minstrels," *New York Clipper*, June 10, 1905, 404).

13. "Percy Brown" [obituary], *Lindsay (Ontario) Post*, January 3, 1919, 10, says, "Percy signed up with Guy Bros.' Minstrels when leaving Lindsay"; and a piece called "The Browns' Rise" in a program for the Sydney, Australia, Tivoli Theatre in early 1925 quotes Tom, for the moment laying the legend aside, as follows: "Then, when I left school, I took it [music as a profession] up, and played here and there. One of my brothers joined me, and after all kinds of small engagements we went with a circus."

14. "Mr. and Mrs. Guy of Minstrel Fame were Married 50 Years Ago June 21," *Springfield (Mass.) Union*, June 11, 1932, n.p. (Springfield Scrapbook 14:26,

Springfield [Mass.] Museums). The clipping also confirms Tom Brown's presence in the orchestra.

15. Eckley, *American Circus*, 36: "No better picture of circus hierarchy could be had than in the cookhouse. Ticket sellers, candy butchers, and front-door men were high in the caste system because they often were promoted to management positions. The performers, too, had their positions of status—equestrians, aerialists, animal trainers, acrobats, clowns, and sideshow freaks—in that order. The band was more or less an entity in itself. Democracy ruled only in the food served; all got the same and as much of it as they wanted."

16. Charles Philip Fox, *A Ticket to the Circus: A Pictorial History of the Incredible Ringlings* (New York: Bramhall House, 1959), 129. Fox indicates that the "Suggestions and Rules" are from "50 years ago," but doesn't give an exact date.

17. Fox, *A Ticket to the Circus*, 103. Sources don't report whether male performers were similarly treated.

18. Dexter W. Fellows and Andrew A. Freeman, *This Way to the Big Show: The Life of Dexter Fellows* (New York: Viking, 1936), 168. Fellows was a publicist who worked for the Ringlings after many years with the rival Barnum and Bailey Greatest Show on Earth. The nickname suggests (facetiously?) that Ringling management required its performers to substitute "ting-a-ling" for "piss."

19. Alfred Ringling, *Life Story of the Ringling Brothers* (Chicago: R. R. Donnelley & Sons, 1900), 236–37; these claims, drawn from a book intended to create excitement about the show, are probably not entirely reliable. In a 1919 article in the *American*, John Ringling defended the essential honesty of circus advertising thus: "there is no effort to deceive the public—but to express the hugeness of everything in figures that carry the idea. If we have fifty elephants, and say a hundred, it pleases rather than offends" (quoted in Fox, *A Ticket to the Circus*, 45–46).

20. Isaac F. Marcosson, *Autobiography of a Clown* (New York: Moffat, Yard, 1910), 59–60.

21. Dixie Willson, *Where the World Folds Up at Night* (New York: D. Appleton, 1932), 62. Willson is describing the Ringling show in the 1921 season.

22. Willson, *Where the World Folds Up*, 158.

23. "Notes from Ringling Brothers' World's Greatest Shows," *New York Clipper*, July 16, 1904, 473; July 30, 1904, 519.

24. Courtney Ryley Cooper, *Under the Big Top* (Boston: Little, Brown, 1923), 182–91.

25. Fox, *A Ticket to the Circus*, 79–80.

26. Carl Landrum, "George Gauweiler, Band Master," *Bandwagon*, January–February 1981, 17. Gauweiler (more usually called Ganweiler) led the Ringling big-top band 1897–1905. In "Tom Brown Back in Town—This Time at Woodruff," unidentified newspaper [Joliet, Ill.], n.d. [c. 1938], n.p., TBS, the writer says that Tom "suffers a strange nostalgia for the mount he once rode as the featured soloist in a mounted band, and for the elephants whose act he shared."

27. Robert Edmund Sherwood, *Here We Are Again: Recollections of an Old Circus Clown* (Indianapolis: Bobbs-Merrill, 1926), 139–40.

28. W. N. Merrick, "The Evolution of the Circus Band," *Billboard*, April 15, 1911, 12.

29. Fox, *A Ticket to the Circus*, 110.

30. "Notes from the Walter L. Main Show," *New York Clipper*, April 11, 1903, 169.
31. "Our Chicago Letter," *New York Clipper*, April 18, 1903, 185. The same spectacle was mounted in both 1903 and 1904.
32. Ringling Brothers' Circus. *Offical Program, Ringling Bros.' World's Greatest Shows* (n.p.: 1904), [3], CWM.
33. Fox, *A Ticket to the Circus*, 139.
34. Thomas J. Hatton, *Karl L. King: An American Bandmaster* (Evanston, Ill.: The Instrumentalist, 1975), 37.
35. Fox, *A Ticket to the Circus*, 111. H. H. Whittier, "Circus Bands and Leaders of the Past," *Billboard*, December 7, 1929, 101, describes the bandsman's life as follows: "The old circus trouper will always remember the daily routine—up one hill, down another, just one continual round of jollification. Parade, 10 A.M.; (sometimes) a hastily eaten dinner; concert before the 'big show'; then the performance, 2 to 2½ hours long; then the after-show or concert; another meal, up town for a short concert; parade back to the 'lot' and then the same routine as in the afternoon. It was a real day's work and the poor 'windjammer' . . . certainly earned his money."
36. Margaret Hindle Hazen and Robert M. Hazen, *The Music Men: An Illustrated History of Brass Bands in America, 1800–1920* (Washington, D.C.: Smithsonian Institution Press, 1987), 30.
37. Fox, *A Ticket to the Circus*, 45, quoting John Ringling in 1919. The Walter L. Main Shows contract for the 1903 season read: "When you sign this Contract you do [so] with the understanding that you engage to make yourself generally useful. . . . Anyone refusing to do anything the Manager requests that is reasonable will forfeit all money due and be discharged."
38. Willson, *Where the World Folds Up*, 106, 122.
39. "How Many Browns?"; "Tom Brown at Lions," unidentified newspaper [St. Catharines, Ont.?], n.d. [January 29, 1941?], n.p., TBS.
40. Paul Luckey to Lester E. Rush, July 31, 1964, CWM, says that Les Roser, a Ringling office wagon employee from 1906 to 1913, "knew another [Brown] brother or two [besides those who played in the big show band] that played in side show band." Luckey was the superintendent of displays at the Circus World Museum at the time. Lester E. Rush was a member of the Six Brown Brothers in 1925–27.
41. A route book is a souvenir commemorative volume brought out at the end of the season and contains much valuable information about personnel, equipment, programs, and interesting incidents. Normally, it lists all the organization's performers, and sometimes it lists workingmen as well.
42. The roster is one of hundreds of circus band rosters compiled by the historian Sverre O. Braathen and now part of the Sverre O. Braathen papers, CWM. In many cases, the source of the roster can be identified as a route book, a performers' ledger, an article in a contemporaneous periodical such as *Billboard*, the *New York Clipper*, or *Variety*, or a letter in Braathen's correspondence, also included in the Braathen papers. I have not been able to identify the source of the 1905 Ringling Brothers' roster. The fact that the roster includes only twenty-four musicians suggests that it is incomplete, since the Ringling band normally carried a number closer to forty.
43. These are both partial rosters, one with only five names, one with thirteen, compiled by Braathen from unknown sources.

44. "The Story of the Saxophone," *Billboard*, September 17, 1921, 74. Tom's would not have been the first saxophone in the Ringling show. Although Braathen's rosters for Ringling show bands include no saxophones before 1905 (when F. Barney played one), the 1903 sideshow, "Ringling Brothers' Annex and Ethnological Congress," included Charlotte Rutherford, saxophone soloist, along with a double-bodied boy, a three-legged boy, a midget, a ventriloquist, and a snake charmer, according to *The Circus Annual[,] Season 1903: A Route Book of Ringling Brothers' World's Greatest Shows* (Baraboo, Wis.: Ringling Brothers' Circus, 1903), 51, CWM. Rutherford herself later became a snake charmer.

45. Warren, "Mother Gone, Her Boys Are Running Wild."

46. If Percy had had a saxophone at the time, he would almost certainly have displayed it in a photo intended to show prospective employers and customers what the duo had to offer.

47. A tentative date of 1904–5 can be assigned, since Tom claimed to have bought his first saxophone no earlier than 1904 and vaudeville itineraries show the Brown Brothers becoming the Brown Brothers and Hopkins in January–February 1906 ("Vaudeville Route List," *New York Clipper*, February 3, 1906, 1275; and "Routes Ahead," *Billboard*, February 17, 1906, 35). Since neither Guy Brothers' Minstrels nor the Main show included Chicago on its itineraries, there is no reason to suppose that Percy and Tom would have visited the city before joining the Ringlings.

48. The caption under a photo of Theresa in *Town and Country*, April 10, 1918, n.p., Teresa [*sic*] Valerio file, BRTC, says, "She is a member of an old theatrical family and her brothers and sisters have been touring the country for several years as The Valerio Family, in a musical, balancing and acrobatic act." Tom Brown Jr., interviewed by the author, added that Theresa's three oldest siblings had been born in Liverpool, England, and that her younger sister, Adeline, and her brother, Don, were born respectively in Brookfield, Illinois, and Sherman, Texas.

49. Harry D. Kline, "The Press Agent's Story," unidentified newspaper [Philadelphia?], November 20, 1917, n.p., Teresa [*sic*] Valerio file, BRTC, says that the Valerio family arrived in the United States "thirty years ago." Theresa's baptismal certificate, drawing upon parish records, places her birth on March 30, 1888, but on other documents, she consistently gives her birthday as April 6, with varying years.

50. Both Rosa and Theresa (as a ballet girl) are in the 1906 performers' ledger for the Ringling circus. Rosa began the season as a ballet girl at $8 per week, but was raised to $10 on May 29, when she became a snake handler, according to the ledger. Absence of documentation for the Ringling show in 1904 and 1905 leaves open the possibility that Rosa, Theresa, or both traveled with the troupe during those seasons. Two pieces of evidence indicate 1903: two sources give Theresa's age at the time of the meeting as fifteen (Tom Brown, "Stage Tales On and Off," *San Francisco Call and Post*, June 21, 1923, 18; Leah Durand, "Charming Sisters Bright Bit in 'Black and White Review' at the Berchel," unidentified Des Moines, Ia., newspaper, n.d. [probably February or March 1924], n.p., in TBS), and Tom claimed in the first of the two sources that nine years passed between the meeting and their January 30, 1912, wedding. Complicating matters further, he said in the same source that they met when he was

"going on for 18," that is, shortly before March 1899 (when Theresa was ten years old).

51. According to Tom, this incident took place while he was "a clarinet player in the 10 cent show," that is, the sideshow (Brown, "Stage Tales," June 21, 1923, 18).

52. Durand, "Charming Sisters."

53. Brown, "Stage Tales," June 21, 1923, 18.

54. "How Many Browns?," 1.

55. Rice, *Monarchs of Minstrelsy*, 6, 19.

56. Fellows and Freeman, *This Way to the Big Show*, 213.

57. Majorie [sic] Moss, "Tom Brown and his Temperamental Shoes," source unknown, but probably a page from a publication of the Buescher Band Instrument Company, c. 1926, NMM. The article bears page number 16. Tom Brown Jr. says that he saw these same shoes in Tom's trunk at the time of Tom's death.

58. Marcosson, *Autobiography of a Clown*, 61–62.

59. Marcosson, *Autobiography of a Clown*, 23.

60. "Circus Gossip," *Billboard*, May 12, 1906, 33.

61. Fellows and Freeman, *This Way to the Big Show*, 308–9. Some details in my description come from a thoughtful section on Johnson in Robert Bogdan, *Freak Show: Presenting Human Oddities for Amusement and Profit* (Chicago: University of Chicago Press, 1988), 134–42. The popular comic-strip character Zippy the Pinhead is very loosely based on Johnson.

62. So characterized in Alice Ringling Coerper, "The Ringlings of Baraboo," in Fox, *A Ticket to the Circus*, 18. Coerper was the daughter of Ringling brother Gus.

63. Ringling, *Life Story of the Ringling Brothers*, 242, title page.

64. Ringling, *Life Story of the Ringling Brothers*, 150–51. Two other brothers, Gus and Henry, had become involved in the family business by the time the book was written, but neither is mentioned in the story, which concentrates on the early years.

65. Ringling, *Life Story of the Ringling Brothers*, 10.

66. Ringling, *Life Story of the Ringling Brothers*, 204.

67. Ringling, *Life Story of the Ringling Brothers*, 91–99.

68. Ringling, *Life Story of the Ringling Brothers*, 83, 110, 122–23, 195.

Chapter 5

1. Douglas Gilbert, *American Vaudeville: Its Life and Times* (1940; reprint, New York: Dover, 1963), 113.

2. I draw these terms from Elias E. Sugarman, "Is the Vaudeville Situation Hopeless?," *Billboard*, December 7, 1929, 80, 103.

3. Sime Silverman, "Four Rubes," *Variety*, October 31, 1914, 20.

4. "Like many other improvident circus men of my day, I was forced during the winter or off season, to 'join out' as the saying goes with a 'hall show.' The theater with circus men is known as a 'hall show' to distinguish it from the 'tent show.'" Robert Edmund Sherwood, *Here We Are Again: Recollections of an Old Circus Clown* (Indianapolis: Bobbs-Merrill, 1926), 237.

5. Isaac F. Marcosson, *Autobiography of a Clown* (New York: Moffat, Yard, 1910), 41.
6. The locations and dates are given in "Vaudeville Route List," *New York Clipper*, January–April 1905. The Ringling Brothers started their season at the Chicago Coliseum on April 8, 1905 ("Circus Routes," *New York Clipper*, April 15, 1905, 205).
7. The inscription on the back, "Merry Xmas and Happy New Year / To Father from your Sons / Tom & Percy," suggests that Maria was separated from Allan, whom she divorced at some point, and, less strongly, that she was already traveling with the act, as she had done "since they first went on the stage," according to "Six Browns Now Five," *Philadelphia Public Ledger*, April 27, 1919, sec. 1, pt. 2, 9. It is hard to resist the speculation that she designed and sewed her boys' outfits.
8. Advertisement, *Chicago Tribune*, January 28, 1906, pt. 10, x.
9. "Show to Help Zoo," *Milwaukee Journal*, February 12, 1906, 2. The Brown Brothers and Hopkins were one of two acts featured in the olio of an otherwise amateur minstrel show put on by the Garfield Lodge of the Knights of Pythias in order to raise money to purchase a baby elephant for Milwaukee's Washington Park zoo.
10. "Correspondence[:] Chicago, Ill.," *Variety*, February 3, 1906, 12.
11. Sverre O. Braathen, "Circus Windjammers," *Bandwagon*, May–June 1971, 18. Although Braathen doesn't say so, the cited portion of the article sounds as if it were based on an interview with Sweet. Sweet may have thought (wrongly) that the debut of Brown Brothers and Hopkins in the Ringling after-show was its first appearance anywhere. Braathen makes a number of apparent factual errors in the article, for example, placing the Brothers' vaudeville debut in December 1907.
12. Ringling Brothers' Circus, *Official Program, Ringling Bros' [sic] World's Greatest Shows* (n.p. [Baraboo, Wis.?: Ringling Brothers' Circus, 1905]), [9], CWM.
13. "Majestic Packed Daily," *Madison, Wisconsin State Journal*, January 2, 1907, 4.
14. Advertisement, *Davenport (Iowa) Democrat and Leader*, December 23, 1906, 7. The same (Family) theatre's advertisement the next day indicates that the Brown Brothers and Doc Kealey, along with most of the rest of the bill, did not appear for the engagement.
15. "The Bell," *Oakland (California) Tribune*, March 31, 1908, 3. According to unpublished research by Prof. Lawrence Gushee of the University of Illinois, a vogue for saxophones in cabaret bands seems to have begun in the San Francisco Bay region around 1910 and to have spread to Los Angeles and Chicago by 1914. Such a current would have been an important contribution to the rising flood of the saxophone's popularity. We might speculate that the Brown Brothers and Kealey's long stay in the Bay Area two years earlier had something to do with it: either Bay Area audiences were receptive to them because they were already eager to hear saxophones, or Bay Area musicians cultivated the saxophone in emulation of the Brown Brothers.
16. C. L. Brown, interview by Cecil Leeson, tape recording, August 18, 1970, NMM.
17. Tivoli Theatre, "The Browns' Rise," in an untitled program (Sydney, Australia: [Tivoli Theatre, early 1925]), n.p., MMC.

18. "Minstrels Delight Crowded Audience," *Ottawa Citizen*, March 29, 1913, n.p., author's collection.
19. "The Browns' Rise," n.p.
20. Advertisement, *Variety*, February 27, 1909, 35.
21. "Hoboken, N.J.," *Variety*, March 6, 1909, 29.
22. "The Browns' Rise," n.p.
23. One detail of the *Variety* ad cited in note 20 suggests that Tom was already using dialect humor, however: its headline reads, "A-ha! A-ha! 'Ketched right up to you!!!'"
24. The Brothers' first listing in "Variety Artists' Routes" with *Broadway Gaiety Girls* is October 18, 1909, indicating that they didn't finish the whole circus season with the Ringlings ("Variety Artists' Routes," *Variety*, October 18, 1909, 18).
25. Robert C. Allen, *Horrible Prettiness: Burlesque and American Culture* (Chapel Hill: University of North Carolina Press, 1991), 165.
26. "Eastern Wheel Manager Analyzes Burlesque," *Variety*, May 7, 1910, 8.
27. While the Brown Brothers were traveling with *Broadway Gaiety Girls*, for example, the future *Ziegfeld Follies* stars Fannie Brice and Leon Errol were traveling with other burlesque companies.
28. Rush [pseud.], "Broadway Gaiety Girls," *Variety*, January 15, 1910, 18.
29. Barbara Stratyner, *Ned Wayburn and the Dance Routine: From Vaudeville to the Ziegfeld Follies* (n.p.: Society of Dance History Scholars, 1996), 20.
30. "It didn't take us long [after we met] to decide that we were going to work double for the rest of our lives" (Tom Brown, "Stage Tales On and Off," *San Francisco Call and Post*, June 21, 1923, 18). "Work double" could be a show-business metaphor for staying together, but it could also mean "work double," that is, "appear in the same show." Documents show that Tom and Theresa did in fact work double most of the time from 1914 until 1924.
31. Leah Durand, "Charming Sisters Bright Bit in 'Black and White Review' at the Berchel," unidentified Des Moines, Ia., newspaper, n.d. [probably February or March 1924], n.p., TBS.
32. First described in a 1919 review of *Jack o' Lantern* at the American Theatre in St. Louis, unidentified St. Louis newspaper, n.d. [1919], n.p., TBS. It is interesting to speculate that this routine ultimately derived from the sideshow band directing of Zip, the What-Is-It, on the Ringling show.
33. Rush [pseud.], "New Acts," *Variety*, January 15, 1910, 14.
34. Photograph, *Variety*, December 11, 1909, 50. A similar photograph in the *New York Clipper*, February 18, 1911, n.p., Brown Brothers file, BRTC, gives the first specific information on their repertoire: "They are featuring Jerome H. Remick's latest rag, 'Cotton Time.'" "Cotton Time," by Charles N. Daniels (also known as Neil Moret), was copyrighted in 1910.
35. The affidavit is described in "Permanent Injunction Issued against Brown and Markwith," *Variety*, December 9, 1921, 5, 19.
36. "Six Browns Now Five," 9; "How Many Browns?," *New York Times*, October 24, 1920, sec. 6, 1. These sources spell the surname "Finkelstein," as does Harry's death certificate in giving Harry's father's name, but Harry's nephew, Jack Eagleson, says the family spelled it "Finklestein" (personal communication).

37. Harry Fink's birthplace and the dates of his birth and death are taken from his death certificate. In the early 1920s, when he had left the Brothers for the Vincent Lopez Orchestra, Fink continued to work under the name Harry Brown.
38. Marcosson, *Autobiography of a Clown*, 8–9.
39. A photo in the author's collection shows several of the brothers in an informal pose with a number of other vaudeville artists in Flint, Michigan, on June 13, 1910.
40. "The Five Brown Brothers," *Variety*, June 11, 1910, 7.
41. "Sternad's the Hustling Kid," *Variety*, March 6, 1909, 8.
42. "Now at the Orpheum," unidentified newspaper, n.d. [1910–11?], n.p., TBS. Since the act reviewed is a quintet, rather than a sextet, and the theatre is an Orpheum, the season must be that of 1910–11, before the Brothers came east.
43. Advertisement, *Variety*, December 31, 1910, 28.
44. Dash [pseud.], "Alhambra," *Variety*, February 18, 1911, 18.
45. Dash [pseud.], "Brighton," *Variety*, May 20, 1911, 23, reviewing their performance at the Brighton Theatre, Brooklyn.
46. Jess [pseud.], "Hammerstein's Roof," *Variety*, July 8, 1911, 22.
47. All the citations and details in these two paragraphs come from Sime Silverman, "The Folies Bergere," *Variety*, May 6, 1911, 23, 25, except for the characterization of the posing models, which is from a later review by Silverman: "They [the audience] like her [Simone De Beryl] for the little clothes she wears. [Jean] Marcel's posers in the niches have even less, but they are farther away" (Sime Silverman, "The Folies Bergere," *Variety*, August 5, 1911, 22).

Chapter 6

1. For example: advertisement, *Variety*, December 31, 1910, 34, which also gives these three names.
2. Advertisement, *Variety*, December 11, 1909, 30. The range is unlikely because saxophones in those days normally had ranges beginning one or two chromatic steps below their fundamental note (the one after which they were named), so a likely lowest note for an E-flat instrument would be a D or D-flat. However, the ad may have meant to specify a range from written low B-flat to written high G altissimo, that is, from low D-flat to high B-flat altissimo, still a bit unlikely, but not impossible.
3. Advertisement, *Variety*, September 17, 1910, 30.
4. Advertisement, *Variety*, October 22, 1910, 34.
5. Six: reviewer for the *Winnipeg Press* (quoted in advertisement, *Variety*, April 16, 1910, 32); seven: reviewer for the *Nashville (Tennessee) American* (quoted in advertisement, *Variety*, October 15, 1910, 34); eight: reviewer for the *Waco (Texas) Times-Herald* (quoted in advertisement, *Variety*, January 10, 1910, 34). A review from the *New Castle (Indiana) Daily Courier* describes it as "large enough to form the rainspout on the Singer Building in New York" (quoted in advertisement, *Variety*, November 5, 1910, 34).
6. These selections are mentioned in advertisements, *Variety*, October 1, 1910, 34; April 16, 1910, 32; September 24, 1910, 30; September 10, 1910, 34; October 30, 1909, 34. Many of the theatres in question may have been Chautauqua

venues rather than small-time vaudeville houses. Advertising material in the collection of the library of the University of Iowa shows that, at least part of the time, the Cates traveled as a Chautauqua attraction. Their model seems to have been the Apollo Concert Company of Clay Smith and Guy Holmes, noted in chapter 1.

7. Quoted in advertisement, *Variety*, April 16, 1910, 32.

8. Quoted in advertisement, *Variety*, September 24, 1910, 30.

9. Quoted in advertisement, *Variety*, October 8, 1910, 30.

10. Advertisement, *Variety*, July 9, 1910, 26. This Cates ad quotes a review in the *Denver Times* for June 26, 1910.

11. Advertisement, *Variety*, April 3, 1909, 32.

12. Advertisement, *Variety*, September 4, 1909, 36.

13. Advertisement, *Variety*, October 9, 1909, 35.

14. Advertisement, *Variety*, May 7, 1910, 34. B. J.'s original response to Batchellor is in "Artist's Forum," *Variety*, May 21, 1910, 11. In "Harry Batchellor," *Variety*, November 19, 1910, 7, Batchellor is identified as "a musician from the Coast."

15. "Forum," *Variety*, November 26, 1910, 15.

16. Advertisement, *Variety*, October 22, 1910, 34.

17. "Terms of Musical Challenge," *Variety*, December 24, 1910, 8.

18. Advertisement, *Variety*, January 7, 1911, 34.

19. Advertisement, *Variety*, December 31, 1910, 28.

20. Advertisement, *Variety*, January 14, 1911, 34. "Championship Rag" seems never to have been registered for copyright or published.

21. Advertisement, *Variety*, January 21, 1911, 34.

22. Advertisement, *Variety*, May 13, 1911, 34.

23. "The Four Musical Cates," *Variety*, July 8, 1911, 7; "The Four Musical Cates," *Variety*, July 15, 1911, 18; W. Buchanan Taylor, "London Notes: The Musical Cates," *Variety*, September 23, 1911, 13.

24. Advertisement, *Variety*, December 10, 1912, 196. Brinton J. Cate died at age fifty on July 3, 1915, of Bright's disease, according to "Brinton J. Cate" [obituary], *Variety*, July 9, 1915, 7.

25. G. E. Holmes and Clay Smith, however, praised Tom's musicianship in 1916: "There is no question but what the grand old LeFevre [Edouard Lefèbre] was a great artist on the saxaphone [*sic*], and perhaps no one has ever surpassed him in tone production. However, when it comes to execution, Harry Lewis, Ben Vereecken, Homer Dickinson, Tom Brown, Benne Henton and a score of others have him tied to a post" (Holmes and Smith, "Saxophone Celebrities," *Dominant*, May 1916, 74).

26. Dash [pseud.], "Hammerstein's," *Variety*, August 5, 1911, 22. Young Alabama, in the opinion of *Variety's* Dash, was "the slickest of the shoulder-and-foot dancers. An easy grace and a dandy personality make him a certainty" (Dash [pseud.], "American Roof," September 16, 1911, 20). The Grizzly Bear was a popular dance of the era, often criticized as coarse and sexual.

27. Caroline Caffin, *Vaudeville* (New York: Mitchell Kennerley, 1914), 18–19.

28. Information on the Spillers, unless otherwise footnoted, comes from Rainer Lotz, "Musical Spillers," in Lotz, *Black People: Entertainers of African Descent in Europe and Germany* (Bonn, Germany: Birgit Lotz Verlag, 1997), 125–49. The quote is from p. 130.

29. Advertisement, *Variety*, December 10, 1910, 158.

30. Jazz cornetist Rex Stewart, who was with the Seven Spillers c. 1921–23, gives a hilarious account of learning how to dance and play at the same time in his autobiography, Rex Stewart, *Boy Meets Horn*, ed. Claire P. Gordon (Ann Arbor: University of Michigan Press, 1991), 38–43.
31. Sime Silverman, "Six Musical Spillers," *Variety*, July 29, 1911, 20.
32. United Booking Office, "United Booking Office Managers' Reports," bk. 15, 36, KAA. The quote is from the manager's report at Keith's Theatre, Cincinnati, for April 6, 1913.
33. Roland Gelatt, *The Fabulous Phonograph 1877–1977*, 2d ed. (New York: Collier Books, 1977), 156.
34. Gelatt, *The Fabulous Phonograph*, 167.
35. Information about Columbia saxophone recordings and the quote from the Columbia supplement both come from Jim Walsh, "Favorite Pioneer Recording Artists: Rudy Wiedoeft and Other Saxophone Players," *Hobbies*, November 1973, 37–38, 122–23.
36. Gelatt, *The Fabulous Phonograph*, 204. The quoted passage is attributed to J. P. Maxfield.
37. Gelatt, *The Fabulous Phonograph*, 166. Gelatt here contrasts the lateral-cut method for producing discs employed by Columbia and Victor with the vertical-cut method used by Edison for discs and by all manufacturers for cylinders.
38. Titles and recording date are from Brian Rust, comp., *The Columbia Master Book Discography*, volume 2, *Principal U.S. Matrix Series, 1910–1924* (Westport, Conn.: Greenwood Press, 1999), 18. George F. Root published his very popular "Tramp, Tramp, Tramp, or The Prisoner's Hope" in 1864.
39. Jim Walsh, "Favorite Pioneer Recording Artists," 122.
40. See, for example, "Ragtime vs. Classical," *Variety*, December 23, 1911, 40, 110; and an extensive study of the question in Edward A. Berlin, *Ragtime: A Musical and Cultural History* (Berkeley: University of California Press, 1980), 1–20.
41. Quoted in Jim Walsh, "Favorite Pioneer Recording Artists," 122. The Saxo Sextet may have included Billy Markwith, one of the Five Brown Brothers in 1909. They may also overlap with an unknown group, possibly including Markwith, who recorded as the Brown Brothers Saxophone Quintet for Columbia on March 7, 1912, remaking the two titles already released. These new efforts were then brought out on a disc with the same release number as the one by the real Five Brown Brothers (A-1041). (See Rust, *Columbia Master Book*, 36.) The March 1912 Brown Brothers could hardly be the real ones, since by that time the original act had become the *Six* Brown Brothers and was on tour in the Midwest. If the March 1912 group is indeed Markwith's, that fact would partly explain why Brown's Saxophone Six, a group he was later featured with, advertised itself as "Columbia Phonograph Artists."
42. Jim Walsh, "Favorite Pioneer Recording Artists," 122. I am indebted to Tim Gracyk for correcting Walsh's versions of the cylinder titles and for information about the U.S. Phonograph Company. Bill Klinger's articles, "U-S Everlasting Record" and "U-S Phonograph Co.," in *Encyclopedia of Recorded Sound in the United States*, ed. Guy A. Marco (New York: Garland, 1993), 730–31, provide a detailed account of the company's 1908–14 career. He remarks that "some collectors consider the U-S cylinders to have remained unsurpassed throughout the acoustic recording era" (731).
43. Gelatt, *The Fabulous Phonograph*, 168.

44. "Dogfight," too convenient a term to forgo in describing many of the Six Brown Brothers' recordings, is used by band musicians to denote an antiphonal section, usually eight bars long, between two statements of a strain, in which the initial harmony threatens a key change, though none comes.
45. "The Brown Brothers," *Variety*, July 29, 1911, 7.
46. Photograph caption, *Variety*, December 23, 1911, 161.
47. Robert J. Landry, "Pat Casey: Man Behind the Scenes," *Variety*, n.d., n.p., Pat Casey file, BRTC.
48. Wynn [pseud. (John J. O'Connor)], "Majestic," *Variety*, August 5, 1911, 23.
49. Tivoli Theatre, "The Browns' Rise," in an untitled program (Sydney, Australia: [Tivoli Theatre, early 1925]), n.p., MMC.
50. See the United Booking Office, "United Booking Office Managers' Reports," bk. 13, 114, 184, 210, KAA.
51. The marriage certificate gives Chicago as the residence of both Tom and Theresa.
52. "The Browns Prevail upon Majestic Bill," unidentified newspaper, n.d. [February 1912], n.p., TBS. The review is identifiable as referring to the February 1912 engagement because it mentions Eva Tanguay, and, in the elided sentence, Caesar Rivoli and Edgar Atchison-Ely, all of whom were on the Majestic's program that week.
53. Anthony Slide, "Eva Tanguay," in Slide, *The Vaudevillians: A Dictionary of Vaudeville Performers* (Westport, Conn.: Arlington House, 1981), 146–48; Slide, *Selected Vaudeville Criticism* (Metuchen, N.J.: Scarecrow Press, 1988), 180–81.
54. Jolo [pseud.], "Colonial," *Variety*, June 1, 1912, 23.

Chapter 7

1. Biographical details are drawn from "A Famous Team," *Gatcomb's Musical Gazette*, April–May 1898, 2; Edward Le Roy Rice, *Monarchs of Minstrelsy* (New York: Kenny, 1911), 236, 273.
2. Rennold Wolf, "Primrose & Dockstader Reunited to Appear at Frolic Tonight," *New York Morning Telegraph*, June 27, 1912, n.p., Lew Dockstader scrapbook, BRTC.
3. Rice, *Monarchs of Minstrelsy*, 236.
4. Though succeeded as Charles's stage sibling by William Lee (alias W. L. Dockstader), according to Rice, *Monarchs of Minstrelsy*, 303, Lew kept the name under which he had won his first measure of fame.
5. Rice, *Monarchs of Minstrelsy*, 275. Most of the information in this paragraph comes from Rice's biography of Dockstader on 274–76, with some bits from "Lew Dockstader," *New York Clipper*, January 11, 1896, 710.
6. Dailey Paskman and Sigmund Spaeth, *"Gentlemen, Be Seated!": A Parade of the Old-Time Minstrels* (Garden City, N.Y.: Doubleday, Doran, 1928), 231.
7. "Lew Dockstader" [obituary], *Variety*, October 29, 1924, 43.
8. "Six Musical Browns at B. F. Keith's Real Brothers," *Cincinnati Commercial*, March 6, 1912, n.p.; "Sensational Saxaphone [*sic*] Sextet," *Louisville Times*, March 12, 1912, n.p.; Brown Brothers file, BRTC.
9. "Tom Brown," C. G. Conn's *Musical Truth*, June 1913, n.p., NMM.

10. F. H. Young, "Providence Opera House," *Providence Journal*, March 14, 1913, n.p., Lew Dockstader scrapbook, BRTC. Information about the general plan of the performance is drawn from program, Harmanus Bleecker Hall, Albany, N.Y., September 26, 1912, Lew Dockstader scrapbook, BRTC. Details are added from Young, "Providence Opera House"; Amy Leslie, "Funny Minstrel Show," *Chicago News*, November 5, 1912, n.p.; "George P. and Lew D. Have a Good Show," *Brooklyn Daily Eagle*, March 4, 1913, n.p. (the latter two in the Lew Dockstader scrapbook, BRTC); "Minstrels Delight Crowded Audience," *Ottawa Citizen*, March 29, 1913, n.p., author's collection.

11. "George P. and Lew D. Have a Good Show."

12. Program, Harmanus Bleecker Hall.

13. "George P. and Lew D. Have a Good Show."

14. Review [title and byline missing from clipping], *Terre Haute Tribune*, March 10, 1914, n.p., Primrose and Dockstader file, BRTC.

15. "Belasco—Primrose and Dockstader," *Washington Post*, October 7, 1913, n.p., Primrose and Dockstader file, BRTC.

16. "Tom Brown's Minstrel Days," unidentified newspaper [Philadelphia?], n.d. [1919?], n.p., TBS.

17. Program, Harmanus Bleecker Hall; later reviews don't mention his singing, perhaps because it was not worthy of mention, perhaps because he no longer sang.

18. Wylie was later billed as "The Male Tetrazzini."

19. Leslie, "Funny Minstrel Show."

20. Young, "Providence Opera House."

21. Ibid. Program, Harmanus Bleecker Hall, lists them as "the Four Humorists," but every other source consulted used "Harmonists."

22. "Lew Dockstader, who could give a practically perfect impersonation of Theodore Roosevelt, was the fine flower of minstrel stump speakers. The travesty motif was strong in minstrelsy, and the mock political speech during the olio was always a hit. Dockstader got the thing down so fine that when he had his own show he used to send Vince Bryant, his gag man, ahead to study local politics and prepare fresh inserts for his speech" (Edward B. Marks [as told to Abbott J. Liebling], *They All Sang: From Tony Pastor to Rudy Vallee* [New York: Viking, 1934], 68).

23. "Most of the minstrel men worked in dialect as well as blackface, but Dockstader talked white out of the black, as did Primrose" (Marks, *They All Sang*, 68). Both men seem to have sung in dialect, however.

24. Leslie, "Funny Minstrel Show."

25. "A Famous Imitation," *Ohio State Journal*, February 17, 1915, n.p., Lew Dockstader scrapbook, BRTC.

26. "My Policies," *Stage Pictorial*, September 1914, n.p., Lew Dockstader scrapbook, BRTC.

27. Colgate Baker, "Lew Dockstader Organizes the Herogettes," *New York Review*, July 2, 1910, n.p., Lew Dockstader scrapbook, BRTC. Carrie Chapman Catt was a prominent fighter for women's rights, especially the right to vote.

28. "George P. and Lew D. Have a Good Show."

29. Young, "Providence Opera House."

30. Leslie, "Funny Minstrel Show."

31. "George P. and Lew D. Have a Good Show."
32. "Minstrels Delight Crowded Audience."
33. In September 1912, the Brothers' act had been placed between Dockstader's and Primrose's, probably to allow for scene shifting between "The Bull Moose Dream" and the dancing trio, and the olio had closed with the Famous Sensational De Onzo Brothers, a barrel-jumping duo. By November, the De Onzos were gone, Dockstader's turn had become a monologue so there was less scenery to shift, and the Browns had moved to the end of the olio. Robert Speare, "Minstrels Make Things Merry," *New York Morning Telegraph*, April 7, 1914, 5, indicates that all six Browns wore burnt cork for the performance he reviewed, although the photograph printed on the cover of the piano sheet of Tom Brown, Harry Cook, and Roger Lewis, "That Moaning Saxophone Rag," (Chicago: Will Rossiter, 1913), published during their Primrose and Dockstader tenure, shows only Tom in blackface, as do advertising photographs posted in front of the Belasco Theatre for a Primrose and Dockstader performance, visible in a photograph of the Brothers in the author's collection.
34. Strauss is probably mentioned because he had included a quartet of saxophones in the orchestra for his *Domestic Symphony* (1903).
35. "Minstrels Delight Crowded Audience."
36. Young, "Providence Opera House."
37. "Minstrels Delight Crowded Audience."
38. Tom Jr. scratched the offending name off his diploma from Thorpe Academy, the exclusive Lake Forest, Illinois, elementary school he attended. Later he discovered that his birth certificate instead bore the middle name Alexander, the given name of Theresa's father and the middle name of his uncle Alec.
39. The photo, from TBS, is of a minstrel parade band at rest in front of a Westchester Theatre bearing posters for a performance of George Primrose's Minstrels on Wednesday, August 6, a day-date combination that places it in 1913. The circumstances surrounding this performance by Primrose without Dockstader, in the middle of their new period of partnership, are unknown.
40. Advertisement, *Variety*, May 11, 1912, 28.
41. Recall that the Brothers didn't sing in their act and so would have had no use for a song per se. A feature found in many songs adapted from instrumental rags is that the rhythm has been changed to fit the lyric. The slight rhythmic differences between the song and instrumental versions of "That Moaning Saxophone Rag" seem likely to have had the same origin.
42. "Back to Dixie with Burnt Cork Friends," *Brooklyn Daily Eagle*, January 20, 1914, picture and sporting section, 8.
43. The description of the party comes from "Mr. Eddy Entertains," *Ottawa Citizen*, March 29, 1913, n.p., MMC.
44. "Music and Drama," *Ottawa Citizen*, March 22, 1913, n.p., TBS.
45. Information drawn from Ottawa and Toronto city directories (thanks to Mark Miller), "Band Leader Cornetist Dies in 89th Year," *Toronto Telegram*, October 19, 1947, n.p., MMC; "Allan Brown, 89[;] Former Ottawa Bandsman Dies," *Ottawa Journal*, October 20, 1947, 8; Martin J. Lane (curator, Regimental Museum of the Governor General's Foot Guards, Ottawa) to Bruce Vermazen, December 10, 1993; "Maria Brown" [obituary], unidentified newspaper, n.d. [1943], n.p., in the collection of Tom Brown Jr.

46. Rennold Wolf, "Harry Fox and Jennie Dolly Quit Garden after Row," *New York Morning Telegraph*, June 10, 1913, 4.

47. Wynn [pseud.], "Brown Brothers," *Variety*, June 6, 1913, 21. There had been another two-person Brown Brothers prior to Tom and Percy's act, a pair of "Lancashire clog dancers" mentioned from time to time in the *New York Clipper*, e.g., December 14, 1895, 646. There was also an act called Brown and Brown, the Real Indian College Boys (sometimes listed as Brown Brothers), in 1905, rendering *Billboard* itineraries confusing.

48. "Minstrels on Broadway Again, after All These Years," *New York Tribune*, March 18, 1913, n.p., Lew Dockstader scrapbook, BRTC.

49. Arthur, "Correspondence: Long Branch, N.J.," *Variety*, August 15, 1913, 30. The turn had by early 1914 inspired what seems to be the first of a legion of imitators: the Five Melody Boys, reviewed by *Variety*, February 20, 1914, 19, at New York's Fifth Avenue Theatre: "Four straight instrumentalists and one blackfaced comedian. They play brass, then a little crossfire talk, the sextet from 'Lucia' in ragtime (one playing the piano), saxophone solo in which all later join, a little more comedy and pop melodies. They qualify as instrumentalists, but there isn't sufficient comedy."

50. "Minstrels Stop Show," *Variety*, April 24, 1914, 5.

51. Robert Toll, *Blacking Up: The Minstrel Show in Nineteenth Century America* (New York: Oxford University Press, 1974), 154.

52. Al. G. Field (Albert Griffith Hatfield), *Watch Yourself Go By* (Columbus, Ohio: Printed by Spohr and Glenn, 1912), 474–76.

53. At the Eleventh Street Opera House in Philadelphia, lasting until May 1909, according to "Home of Minstrelsy Forced to Close," *Fort Worth Record*, May 16, 1909, n.p., Lew Dockstader scrapbook, BRTC, and perhaps longer.

54. Frank Dumont, *The Witmark Amateur Minstrel Guide and Burnt Cork Encyclopedia* (New York: M. Witmark, 1899), 32–33, 38–39.

55. Charles N. Young, "Lew Dockstader Says That Minstrel Field Is Forever Barred to Women," *Boston Traveler*, January 16, 1909, n.p., Lew Dockstader scrapbook, BRTC.

56. Quoted in Toll, *Blacking Up*, 154–55.

57. Majestic Theatre [city unknown], program for George Primrose Minstrels, August 28, 1905, n.p., George Primrose file, BRTC. Toll, *Blacking Up*, 155, points out similar yesterday/today contrasts in first parts, going back to 1857, and says, "After 1880, such 'histories of minstrelsy' or 'Ethiopian Renaissances' became common minstrel features."

58. "George Primrose Retires," *Variety*, May 29, 1914, 7.

59. Brander Matthews, "The Rise and Fall of Negro-Minstrelsy," *Scribner's*, May 1915, 754–59.

Chapter 8

1. "Sailings," *Variety*, June 26, 1914, 4.

2. Barbara Stratyner, *Ned Wayburn and the Dance Routine: From Vaudeville to the Ziegfeld Follies* (n.p.: Society of Dance History Scholars, 1996), 10–11.

3. "Wayburn Puts It Over," *Variety*, January 2, 1914, 4.

4. Information about Melville Gideon comes from "Melville Gideon" [obituary], *Variety*, November 14, 1933, 55.

5. In Joe Smith (as told to Aaron Fishman), "Two Americans Abroad," *Variety*, January 5, 1955, 247ff.

6. George Gottlieb, "Psychology of the American Vaudeville Show from the Manager's Point of View," in *American Vaudeville as Seen by its Contemporaries*, ed. Charles W. Stein (New York: Alfred A. Knopf, 1984), 179–81. Reprinted from *Current Opinion*, April 1916, 257–58. Gottlieb discusses a hypothetical nine-act bill rather than an eight-act bill such as the present one.

7. This is the author's conjecture, based on study of a large photo of what is apparently the whole All American Vaudeville troupe, which includes only three of the blood Bards. Another piece of evidence is that slightly earlier photos of the Bards show three men with clear facial resemblances to each other and a fourth who looks as if he came from another family.

8. Sime Silverman, "American," *Variety*, January 14, 1911, 20.

9. "Princess," *St. Louis Globe*, February 20, 1911, n.p., Four Bards file, BRTC.

10. Silverman, "American."

11. "Some Feat," *Variety*, December 4, 1909, 10.

12. Silverman, "American." I am deeply indebted to two gymnastics coaches at Western Illinois University, Judy Gedney and Don Carney, for translating *Variety*'s shop-talk descriptions of the tricks into something comprehensible to an outsider. Gedney suggests another possibility for the last trick described, in which the pitcher-catchers face each other and the fliers are thrown backward through the air to alight in hand-to-hand stands in which they face in the opposite direction from their respective catchers.

13. Clipping [title missing], *New York Telegraph*, August 8, 1914, n.p., Dooley and Sales scrapbook, BRTC.

14. "'Frolics at Seashore' Feature at the Penn," *Philadelphia North American*, December 1, 1914, n.p., Dooley and Sales scrapbook, BRTC.

15. "A Nonsense Comedian," *Pittsburgh Leader*, August 30, 1913, n.p., Dooley and Sales scrapbook, BRTC.

16. "Amusements," *Louisville Herald*, June 21, 1909, n.p., Dooley and Sales scrapbook, BRTC.

17. Thomas J. Grey, "Tommy's Tattles," *Variety*, August 31, 1917, 9.

18. Advertisement, *Variety*, October 26, 1917, 47, quoting a review from an unidentified New Orleans newspaper. Other information in this paragraph comes from the same ad and from "Josie Heather" [obituary], *Variety*, April 22, 1942, 54; and a review of the Finsbury Park Empire show [clipping, title missing] from the *New York Morning Telegraph*, August 8, 1914, n.p., Dooley and Sales scrapbook, BRTC.

19. Alfred Bryan (words) and Fred Fischer (music), "Who Paid the Rent for Mrs. Rip Van Winkle?" (New York: Leo Feist, 1914).

20. Smith and Fishman, "Two Americans Abroad."

21. "Free Chewing-Gum for Theatre-Goers," *Times* (London), July 14, 1914, 5.

22. Clipping from an unidentified Cincinnati newspaper, November 18, 1913, Charles and Fannie Van file, BRTC.

23. Untitled clipping, *Toledo Blade*, October 28, 1913, n.p., Charles and Fannie Van file, BRTC.

24. "Charles and Fannie Van," *Dayton News*, February 14, 1912, n.p., Charles and Fannie Van file, BRTC.
25. "Receives a Roughing in 'Case of Emergency,'" *Louisville Times*, February 29, 1912, n.p., Charles and Fannie Van file, BRTC.
26. "Three Good Headliners," *Milwaukee Wisconsin* [sic], January 23, 1912, n.p., Charles and Fannie Van file, BRTC.
27. "Receives a Roughing."
28. [Untitled clipping (different from the one cited in note 24, this chapter)], *Dayton News*, February 14, 1912, n.p., Charles and Fannie Van file, BRTC.
29. Ibid.
30. Anthony Slide, *The Encyclopedia of Vaudeville* (Westport, Conn.: Greenwood Press, 1994), 472. The characters' names and some details of the routine are drawn from a 1924 recording of a condensed version of the act: Avon Comedy Four, "The New School Teacher" (Camden, N.J.: Victor Talking Machine Company, 1924). The original release number of this disc was Victor 35750.
31. Smith and Fishman, "Two Americans Abroad."
32. Clipping [title missing], *New York Morning Telegraph*, August 8, 1914, n.p., Dooley and Sales scrapbook, BRTC.
33. Caroline Caffin, *Vaudeville* (New York: Mitchell Kennerley, 1914), 110.
34. Gottlieb, "Psychology of the American Vaudeville Show," 181.
35. Clipping [title missing], *New York Morning Telegraph*, August 8, 1914, n.p., Dooley and Sales scrapbook, BRTC.
36. Wynn [pseud.], "Ethel Mae Barker," *Variety*, December 5, 1914, 18.
37. "American Bill Success," *Variety*, July 17, 1914, 4.
38. Clipping [title missing], *New York Morning Telegraph*, August 8, 1914, n.p., Dooley and Sales scrapbook, BRTC.
39. Richard and Paulette Ziegfeld, *The Ziegfeld Touch: The Life and Times of Florenz Ziegfeld, Jr.* (New York: Harry N. Abrams, 1993), 51–52.
40. Dillingham's travels are sketchily chronicled in a series of items in *Variety*: "Dillingham's Jugglers," May 1, 1914, 4; "Dillingham Has Relapse," May 22, 1914, 4; "Dillingham Improved," May 29, 1914, 4; "Dillingham, Improved, in Paris," June 12, 1914, 4; "Sailings," July 24, 1914, 4.
41. Armond Fields and L. Marc Fields, *From the Bowery to Broadway: Lew Fields and the Roots of American Popular Theatre* (New York: Oxford University Press, 1993), 296.
42. "Tom Brown at Lions," unidentified newspaper [St. Catharines, Ont.?], n.d. [January 29, 1941?], n.p., in TBS.
43. C. B. Dillingham [unsigned] to Pat Casey, February 10, 1914; Pat Casey to C. B. Dillingham, February 11, 1914, February 21, 1914; Pat Casey to Bruce Edwards, April 11, 1914; Bruce Edwards [unsigned] to Pat Casey, April 11, 1914; Pat Casey to Bruce Edwards, April 13, 1914, Box 10, CBD.
44. "How Many Browns?," *New York Times*, October 24, 1920, sec. 6, 1.
45. See "News in Brief . . . Music-Hall Artists and the War," *Times* (London), August 10, 1914, 9; Martin Harvey to the editor, *Times* (London), August 12, 1914; 6, "Items of War News," *Times* (London), August 31, 1914, 2.
46. "American Players Abroad Held There by the Battle," *Variety*, August 7, 1914, 3.
47. "Americans Won't Cut," *Variety*, August 28, 1914, 4.
48. Bruce Edwards to Tom Brown, September 7, 1914, Box 13, CBD.

Chapter 9

1. "Orpheum Circuit Not Paying Transportation Next Season," *Variety*, July 10, 1914, 5.
2. "More 'Cut Weeks' Than Ever Next Season, East and West," *Variety*, June 5, 1914, 5.
3. "'Chin Chin' a Real Hit," *Variety*, October 3, 1914, 10.
4. "How Many Browns?," *New York Times*, October 24, 1920, sec. 6, 1. In 1920, *Variety* suggested the verb "to Dillingham" for this kind of brightening, since "whenever there is a 'sag' in one of [Dillingham's] productions, he brings in a vaudeville act, and he does it so deftly that his name is associated with the practice" ("Vaude Artists," *Variety*, June 12, 1920, 25).
5. This costuming decision was fateful for saxophone ensembles, as scores, perhaps hundreds, of them donned clown garb in the subsequent nine decades. Even Rudy Wiedoeft, a giant of the instrument after his 1917 debut in New York, dressed as a clown (though without makeup) in a 1931 Warner Brothers Vitaphone short called *Darn Tootin'*, accompanied by a quartet of similarly togged saxophonists whose upper bodies emerged from the tone holes of a giant sax.
6. "Montgomery and Stone," *New York Clipper*, November 26, 1898, 657.
7. The competition included such celebrated shows as Victor Herbert's lavish operetta *Babes in Toyland*, Bert Williams and George Walker's *In Dahomey* (with an African American cast), and *Whoop-Dee-Do* (a Joe Weber and Lew Fields vehicle with Lillian Russell).
8. Biographical details come from "Montgomery and Stone"; Edward Le Roy Rice, *Monarchs of Minstrelsy* (New York: Kenny, 1911), 342; "David Montgomery" [obituary], *Variety*, April 27, 1917, 14; Charles Darnton, "Montgomery and Stone Together for 22 Years; No One for Dave's Place," *New York Evening World*, April 28, 1917, 9; Roger D. Kinkle, *The Complete Encyclopedia of Popular Music and Jazz, 1900–1950* (New Rochelle, N.Y.: Arlington House, 1974), 3:1463; Anthony Slide, *The Vaudevillians: A Dictionary of Vaudeville Performers* (Westport, Conn.: Arlington House, 1981), 143–44.
9. Caroline Caffin and Charles H. Caffin, *Dancing and Dancers of Today: The Modern Revival of Dancing as an Art* (New York: Dodd, Mead, 1912), 267–68.
10. Rice, *Monarchs of Minstrelsy*, 342. This was Stone's professional debut. According to Armond Fields, *Fred Stone: Circus Performer and Musical Comedy Star* (Jefferson, N.C.: McFarland, 2002), 22, he had appeared as the Big Bad Wolf in an earlier amateur performance of *Red Riding Hood*.
11. "Rapid Fun Makes 'Chin Chin' a Go," *New York Times*, October 21, 1914, 11.
12. Katherine Richardson, "Laughfest with 'Chin, Chin' Opens at the Jefferson," unidentified newspaper [St. Louis], n.d. [1916–17], n.p., TBS; "'Chin Chin' Joyous Succession of Fun," unidentified newspaper [St. Louis], n.d. [1916–17], n.p., TBS.
13. "'Chin-Chin,'" unidentified newspaper [Buffalo, N.Y.], n.d. [1916–17], n.p., TBS.
14. Stella Flores, "The Six Brown Brothers and Other Fascinations of 'Chin Chin,'" at the Globe," *New York Evening Journal*, February 12, 1915, n.p., TBS.
15. Archie Gunn, "'Clown Band' in 'Chin Chin' Adds Fame to Name of Brown, Archie Gunn Discovers," *New York American*, December 15, 1914, n.p., Six Brown Brothers file, BRTC.

16. Richard Spamer, "Chin Chin, Slow to Start, Speeds Up as Stars Appear," unidentified newspaper [St. Louis], n.d. [1916–17], n.p., TBS.

17. "'Chin Chin' Joyous Succession of Fun."

18. Fred Stone, *Rolling Stone* (New York: McGraw-Hill, 1945), 190–91. The song was written by John Golden and Mike Roarke but passed off as the work of a (fictitious) British soldier, Terence Lowrey, in an elaborate hoax on Dillingham engineered by Golden.

19. "'Chin Chin' Joyous Succession of Fun." "Montgomery and Stone Film," *Variety*, September 11, 1914, 10, says the 600-foot film was shot by Kinemacolor.

20. Kinkle, *The Complete Encyclopedia*, 1:67–69.

21. "Shows at the Box Office in New York and Chicago," *Variety*, December 5, 1914, 11.

22. "Vaudevillians in Revues; Several Now Preparing," *Variety*, December 5, 1914, 7.

23. "Broadway's Rush of Revues Calling on Vaudeville," *Variety*, December 19, 1914, 11.

24. "The Six Brown Brothers' Clown Band in 'Chin Chin,' at the Globe Theatre," *New York Evening Journal*, December 11, 1914, n.p., TBS.

25. "In 'Chin Chin' at the Globe Theatre" [photographs], unidentified New York newspaper, n.d., n.p., TBS. The photos are identified as products of White Studios, a famous theatrical photographic concern that also made a series of photos of the Six Brown Brothers in costume (see, for example, figures 7 and 8).

26. The copyright date on the sheet music is 1917, but Will Rossiter also published an orchestration of the piece with a 1916 copyright. The sheet music's copyright line sandwiches the last "I" in "MCMXVII" between the other "I" and the word "by," as if it had been added as an afterthought. The date on the cover of the sheet music, however, is a straightforward MCMXVII, and the piece was actually registered with the U.S. Copyright Office in March 1917.

27. "Big Minstrel Show," *Variety*, October 31, 1914, 8.

28. "Life Members," *Variety*, July 2, 1915, 12.

29. C. G. Child to Tom Brown [contract], October 31, 1914, BMG.

30. Victor Talking Machine Company, Recording Book: Jan. 2, 1913 to Dec. 31, 1914; Recording Book, 1915–1916 [unpublished documents], 942, 952, 965 in the former and 1021 in the latter, BMG. The information in these primary documents differs somewhat from that given in the standard reference work, Brian Rust, *American Dance Band Discography 1917–1942* (New Rochelle, N.Y.: Arlington House, 1975), 2:1708–10. Rust, for example, says that the sessions took place in Camden, New Jersey.

31. James Lincoln Collier, *Benny Goodman and the Swing Era* (New York: Oxford University Press, 1993), 33–34; Richard M. Sudhalter, *Lost Chords: White Musicians and Their Contribution to Jazz* (New York: Oxford University Press, 1999), 88.

32. Sales figures for the disc are unknown, but they may have been low, since the "La Paloma" side was reissued in 1919 on Victor's ethnic-music series under the Lithuanian title "Balandis," played by what translates as the Samogitian Sextet (Card for Victor 72326, Victor Talking Machine Company numerical card file, BMG). The Samogitians are a linguistic group dwelling mostly in the lowlands of Lithuania. Thanks to Professor Alan Timberlake for the translation.

33. Card for Victor 17677, Victor Talking Machine Company numerical card file, BMG. The contract is in the author's collection. According to Tim Brooks, "Columbia Records, 1901–1934: A History," in Brooks, *The Columbia Master Book Discography* (Westport, Conn.: Greenwood Press, 1999), 1:17, a hit Columbia record c. 1915 "might ship 20,000 copies." Victor sales were probably not much different.

34. C. G. Child to Tom Brown [contract], June 23, 1915, BMG.

35. Recording Book 1915–1916, 1125.

36. "'Chin-Chin' Comes Back," *New York Times*, August 17, 1915, 9.

37. C. B. Dillingham [unsigned] to Tom Brown, May 13, 1916; Tom Brown to C. B. Dillingham, May 15, 1916; C. B. Dillingham [unsigned] to Tom Brown, May 18, 1916, Box 20, CBD.

38. "Contract, June 30, 1916," under "6 Brown Bros" in the first gathering of "Charles B. Dillingham: Index to Correspondence," Box 32, CBD, n.p..

39. Advertisement, *Variety*, October 22, 1915, 35.

40. Advertisement, *Variety*, December 24, 1915, 50. These groups stood at the beginning of a trend that enhanced Tom Brown's prestige and income. By the end of 1917, besides the Musical Harvards, there were Tom Brown's Blackface Revue (like the Harvards, traveling on the Interstate circuit), Tom Brown's Clown Band (replicating the Brothers' routines with a road company of *Chin Chin*), Tom Brown's Princeton Five (working the Midwest on the small-time Western Vaudeville Managers' Association circuit), and Tom Brown's Seven Musical Highlanders on United time (advertisement, *Variety*, November 2, 1917, n.p. [back cover]).

41. C. G. Child to Tom Brown [contract], March 15, 1916, BMG.

42. According to Victor's numerical card file, BMG, "Tambourines and Oranges" was to have been one side of Victor 18096, a release number that went unused, backed by "Cielo Andaluz," a title never attempted by the Brothers.

43. Victor Talking Machine Company, *Victor Records for September 1916* (n.p. [Camden, N.J.?]: [Victor Talking Machine Company?, 1916]), 14. The tenor player resembles photos of Markwith, but not enough to make a definitive identification. The author lacks a reliably identified photo of Shrigley. The Victor Supplement may have printed an outdated photo of the group, since there is some reason to think that, by the time of the 1916 recordings, the instrumentation had shifted from two baritones to two tenors. See this chapter, note 47.

44. Probably on the joint basis of the popular idea that the Six Brown Brothers weren't all really brothers and the fact that James "Slap" White was the composer of "Pussyfoot March," "When Aunt Dinah's Daughter Hannah Bangs on That Piano," and "Jazz Band Blues," all recorded by the group, Rust, *American Dance Band Discography*, 2:1708, says that White plays C-melody saxophone on the June 1916 sessions. White's presence is very unlikely, however, since he was an African American from Canada, and, while vaudeville turns occasionally were racially integrated in the 1910s, print sources would probably have remarked on the fact.

45. U.S. Copyright Office, *Catalog of Copyright Entries, Part 3, Musical Compositions*, 1916, no. 7, 9103. Three of the other pieces weren't registered until even later, "Bull Frog Blues" and "Walkin' the Dog" in September 1916, and "Chicken Walk" in March 1917!

46. Victor Talking Machine Company, *Victor Records for September 1916*, 14. According to John Chilton, *Sidney Bechet: The Wizard of Jazz* (New York: Oxford University Press, 1987), 32, hearing the Brothers' record of "Bull Frog Blues" led the famed New Orleans clarinetist and soprano saxophonist Sidney Bechet to buy his first saxophone. Chilton doesn't assign a date to the event but places it close to the record's first appearance.

47. There is conflicting evidence about the instrumentation of the Six Brown Brothers in 1916. NMM has a set of manuscript parts for "La Danza Appassionata," obtained from the estate of Tom Brown's longtime friend H. A. Waggener, to whom Tom used to send copies of the music used by the Brothers. All the parts except the first alto sax have "(Brown Bros.)" written after the title, indicating that the music was either used by the Brothers or copied from music they used. But the instrumentation—two altos, two tenors, baritone, and bass—differs from the instrumentation in Victor Talking Machine Company, *Victor Records for September 1916*, 14 [photograph], and *Victor Records for September 1917*, n.p. [photograph], private collection, in which there are two baritones and one tenor. (One of the baritones is Harry Fink; the tenor player appears to be Billy Markwith, and neither William nor Percy Brown is in the photo.) However, between those two printings, a different photo appeared in another Victor supplement (n.d., but datable between the other two because of the records announced), 12, with the Brothers in their *Chin Chin* costumes, posed around a Victrola, over the caption "Six Brown Bros. on tour." In this photo, there are two tenors. (The faces in the small, blurry half-tone image are unidentifiable.) Since the tour lasted from December 1915 until April 1917, they could have made the change before the June 1916 Victor sessions, in which case the "La Danza Appassionata" parts could be originals or copies of originals rather than later revisions for a new instrumentation.

48. Uriel Davis to Charles B. Dillingham, August 29, 1916; Bruce Edwards [unsigned] to Uriel Davis, August 30, 1916; Uriel Davis to Bruce Edwards, September 1, 1916. Box 30, CBD.

49. The publisher E. B. Marks supports the view that saxophone parts began to appear in theatre orchestrations around 1916 (Edward B. Marks [as told to Abbott J. Liebling], *They All Sang: From Tony Pastor to Rudy Vallee* [New York: Viking, 1934], 174). In its March 1916 number, the widely circulated *Metronome Orchestra Monthly* began to include two saxophone parts in the two orchestrations that came with each issue. In April 1916, the New York publisher Leo Feist announced that all its future theatre orchestrations would include parts for alto and tenor saxes (advertisement, *Metronome Orchestra Monthly*, April 1916, 22). The author knows of a handful of earlier theatre orchestrations, all of marches, that include alto and tenor sax parts.

50. Information from Myrtle (Brown) Hendrickson's baptismal certificate.

51. "The Chicago Record," *Variety*, June 16, 1916, 7. Fields, *Fred Stone*, 179, reports that the tour included twenty-five cities.

52. "Tom Brown's Saxophone Band," *Variety*, March 30, 1917, 20, mentions record sales as a factor in the show's prosperity.

53. Tom Brown Jr., interviewed by the author. The date was November 25, 1916, and Tom Jr. was paid $20 for his appearance.

54. Harry D. Kline, "The Press Agent's Story," unidentified newspaper [New York], November 20, 1917, n.p., Teresa [sic] Valerio file, BRTC. The quote is from "Teresa [sic] Valerio," *New York Times*, October 1917 [?], n.p., TBS.

55. "Chicago," *Variety*, March 23, 1917, 36. Fields, *Fred Stone*, 170, 180, reports that Montgomery had begun experiencing persistent abdominal pain as early as 1914.

56. "Montgomery's Fight for Life," *Variety*, April 20, 1917, 4.

57. "David Montgomery" [obituary].

58. "Montgomery is Dead; Stone at Pal's Bedside," *Chicago Tribune*, April 21, 1917, 13.

59. Stone, *Rolling Stone*, 194.

60. "Dave Montgomery Laid to Rest in Woodlawn," *New York Tribune*, April 24, 1917, n.p.; "Actors Mourn at Bier of David Montgomery," *New York Evening Telegram*, April 23, 1917, n.p.; both clippings in Anna Laughlin scrapbook, BRTC.

Chapter 10

1. C. G. Child to Tom Brown [contract], May 1, 1917, BMG.

2. That is, these are the months in which the discs were announced to the trade in *Talking Machine World*, a monthly magazine aimed at manufacturers and dealers in the phonograph and record business. Victor 18097, coupling "Bull Frog Blues" and "Pussyfoot March," was the first of the batch to be announced, in "Record Bulletins for September 1916," *Talking Machine World*, August 1916, 100. Victor 18217, with "Rigoletto Quartet" and "Passion Dance," was the last, in "Record Bulletins for March 1917," *Talking Machine World*, February 1917, 117.

3. Victor Talking Machine Company, Recording Book: 1917–1918 [unpublished document], 1996–97, 2000–2001, 2003, BMG. Advertisement (for Will Rossiter), *Jacobs' Orchestra Monthly*, September 1918, 54, says that both "Comedy Tom" and "Tom Brown's Saxophone" were later used in *Jack o' Lantern*.

4. Victor 18255, coupling the ODJB's "Dixieland Jass Band" with "Livery Stable Blues," was announced in the "Record Bulletins for May 1917," *Talking Machine World*, April 1917, 124, with a note saying of it and another disc, "The Following Two Records Were Listed as a Dance Special in March and Are Repeated Here for Convenience of Dealers." The listing mentioned is not, however, in *Talking Machine World*. It may instead be in a special Victor Talking Machine Company supplement circulated in April 1917.

5. Tim Gracyk brought to the author's attention a puzzling reference to *Chin Chin* on the record sleeve for Edison Diamond Disc No. 50423, announced in "Record Bulletins for July 1917," *Talking Machine World*, June 1917, 129, but bearing a number that is compatible with its having been released months earlier. The copy concerning one side, "That Funny Jas Band From Dixieland," sung by Arthur Collins and Byron G. Harlan, reads, "What do *you* know about a 'Jas Band?' They had a little one in the operetta 'Chin Chin;' did you see it? Also there is one playing at one of New York's big restaurants." Gracyk suggests

that perhaps the Brothers did a jazz number during the show's road tour. Out-of-town jazz bands (including the nucleus of the ODJB) had appeared in Chicago cabarets before the ODJB's advent at Reisenweber's (see Richard M. Sudhalter, *Lost Chords: White Musicians and Their Contribution to Jazz* [New York: Oxford University Press, 1999], 5–12), so an interpolation would have had local appeal for Windy City audiences in 1916. According to reviews, a Hawaiian band was interpolated into the show for its St. Louis run a year later. But there is no documentary evidence to indicate that *Chin Chin's* Jas Band was the Six Brown Brothers, except a hint in Tivoli Theatre, "The Browns' Rise," in an untitled program (Sydney, Australia: [Tivoli Theatre, early 1925]), n.p., MMC, where Tom says, "We were the first to give them jazz music, but for a long time they didn't want it." In context, however, this remark seems to be about the pre-1909 period!

6. "Record Bulletins for August 1917," *Talking Machine World*, July 1917, 140. A cornet or trumpet is faintly audible in some ensemble passages of "For Me and My Gal"!

7. The announcements were made both in the Columbia Graphophone [formerly "Phonograph"] Company catalog for May 1917 and in "Record Bulletins for May 1917," *Talking Machine World*, April 1917, 124.

8. Four titles had been attempted in November 1916, but none of the twelve takes was successful. Two more unreleased titles were attempted in May 1917. The group is not known to have recorded after that date (Brian Rust, *The Columbia Master Book Discography*, vol. 2, *Principal U. S. Matrix Series*, *1910–1924* [Westport, Conn.: Greenwood Press, 1999], 197, 202–4, 214). The disc pairing "American Patrol" and "Bull Frog Blues" must have sold well, since the company had it remade by the Columbia Saxophone Sextette, masquerading as the Saxo Sextette, in July 1919 (Rust, *Columbia Master Book*, 282–83). Although the 1917 discs were Columbia's first saxophone releases since 1911, they were not its first saxophone recordings since that date. Fred Brown recorded several solos in August and September of 1916 that were released after the Saxo Sextette sides. Fred's records are described later in the present chapter.

9. Brian Rust, *Jazz Records, 1897–1942* (New Rochelle, N.Y.: Arlington House, 1978), 2:1516. Although Rust says there are two altos and one tenor on the recording, a photograph of the group in the Pathé catalog cited clearly shows the instrumentation given in the present text. The recording is too muddy to resolve the question which makeup is correct. The Sweatman group is notable also as probably the first African American jazz ensemble to record, setting aside semantic problems about the word "jazz." The record was announced in "Record Bulletins for May 1917," *Talking Machine World*, April 1917, 124. Another Sweatman Pathé item with a lower release number (20145) wasn't announced in the magazine until June.

10. The recording dates come from Rust, *Columbia Master Book Discography*, 2:188. According to Rust's introduction, 1, the information given in the volume was transcribed directly from file cards made by Columbia at the time of the recording. It is intriguing that, although the discs released bore two separate artist's names, both the August 29 and the September 1 cards are headed "Fred H. Brown (as Fred Allen)" (although the first interpolates the phrase "of the Six Brown Brothers" after "Brown").

11. C. G. Child to Tom Brown [contract], May 1, 1917; Tom Brown et al. to Victor Talking Machine Company, May 10, 1917, both items in BMG.

12. I am grateful to Doug Caldwell, who is writing a biography of Wiedoeft, for the information in this paragraph.

13. The arrangements were registered for copyright in February 1917. The arranger was composer Mayhew Lester Lake (1879–1955), editor-in-chief of the band and orchestra department at Carl Fischer from 1913 until 1948. He used the pseudonym Lester Brockton.

14. The claim that they played for dancing appears in an untitled item, *Ragtime Review*, August 1917, 19, which also names two other orchestras playing at the Bismarck Gardens. Tom Brown's son, Tom Jr., doubts that the group played for dancing. The starting date (July 16) comes from Tom Brown to Bruce Edwards [telegram], June 26, 1917, Box 20, CBD. The "dowager" characterization comes from "Marigold Room Is Dowager of City's Cabarets," *Chicago Tribune*, June 11, 1922, n.p. "The Marigold Gardens," *Variety*, March 28, 1919, 20, called the Bismarck (by then renamed Marigold) Gardens "undoubtedly the largest and most pretentious cabaret in Chicago." It seated 2600, according to the *Tribune* article, and stood at the corner of Grace and Halsted Streets.

15. "Marigold Room Is Dowager" and "Marigold Gardens Sold for $125,000," *Chicago Tribune*, October 10, 1950, n.p., clippings courtesy of Chuck Sengstock.

16. Mary C. Henderson, *The New Amsterdam: The Biography of a Broadway Theatre* (New York: Hyperion, 1997), 165–68.

17. "Contract, May 12, 1917" under "Valerio, Theresa" in fifth gathering of "Charles B. Dillingham: Index to Correspondence," Box 32, CBD, n.p.

18. Richard L. Stokes, "Fred Stone Glistens in 'Jack o' Lantern,'" unidentified newspaper [St. Louis], n.d. [December 1919], n.p., TBS. The detail about Stone's somersault comes from Sime Silverman, "Jack o' Lantern," *Variety*, October 19, 1917, 15, a review of opening night. The author's description of the show is pieced together from the reviews cited as sources for the direct quotations, in full consciousness that, like any theatrical piece, *Jack o' Lantern* must have changed in many respects during its two and a half years of life.

19. Ashton Stevens, "Fred Stone Brings Us a Fairyland," unidentified newspaper [Boston or Chicago], n.d., n.p., TBS.

20. Stokes, "Fred Stone Glistens."

21. "The New Play," unidentified newspaper [New York], n.d. [fall 1917], n.p., TBS. The use of film is suggested in "Theaters: English—'Jack o' Lantern,'" unidentified newspaper [Indianapolis], n.d. [1919–20], n.p., TBS: "He . . . goes away, showing the children the time of their young lives by means of plenty of candy, picture shows and other luxuries that are dear to the heart of a kiddie."

22. A New York reviewer sniffed, "The presence of several dwarfs as a feature of the otherwise pleasing Candyland scene . . . did not appeal to The Playgoer. They have a disagreeable matured precocity that is abnormal and in striking contrast to the joyous naturalness of the rest of this entertaining show" ("The Theatre," unidentified newspaper [New York], n.d. [October 1917], n.p., TBS).

23. Stokes, "Fred Stone Glistens."

24. Ibid.

25. "English's—'Jack o' Lantern,'" unidentified newspaper [Indianapolis], n.d. [early 1920?], n.p., TBS. By early 1920, the word "jazz" was being applied to many more kinds of popular music than just the kind played by the Original Dixieland Jazz Band and its imitators.

26. H. E. Cherrington, [title missing], unidentified newspaper [Columbus, Ohio], n.d. [December 1919], n.p., TBS.

27. H. H. Ryan, "News of the Playhouses," unidentified newspaper [Milwaukee], n.d. [December 1919], n.p., TBS.

28. "English's—'Jack o' Lantern.'"

29. [No author, no title] [review of *Jack o' Lantern* at the Grand Theatre, Kansas City, Missouri], unidentified newspaper [Kansas City, Mo.], n.d. [mid-January 1920], n.p., TBS.

30. H. E. Cherrington, [title missing].

31. H. W. G., "Fred Stone in Jack o' Lantern," unidentified newspaper [Milwaukee], n.d. [1919–20], n.p., TBS.

32. H. E. Cherrington, [title missing].

33. "English's—'Jack o' Lantern.'" The skater described is Katie Smith.

34. Ibid.

35. "Shubert Majestic," unidentified newspaper [Providence, R.I.], n.d. [May 1920], n.p., TBS.

36. Silverman, "Jack o' Lantern."

37. L. G. S., "New Detroit—Fred Stone in 'Jack o' Lantern,'" unidentified newspaper [Detroit], n.d. [September 1919], n.p., TBS.

38. L. G. S., "New Detroit."

39. E. A. J., "The Stage: 'Jack o' Lantern'" [review of performance at Macauley's Theatre], unidentified newspaper, n.d., n.p., TBS.

40. "Theresa Valerio Makes Musical Hit," unidentified newspaper [Philadelphia], n.d., n.p., TBS.

41. "Contract, dated Apr. 23, 1918" under "Valerio, Theresa" in fifth gathering of "Charles B. Dillingham: Index to Correspondence," Box 32, CBD, n.p.

42. "In the Service," *Variety*, June 8, 1917, 8. He was accompanied by Steve Spears, the manager of the Palace Hotel (near the Globe Theatre), where the Browns may have been living; at the time of writing (2003) it is the Best Western Ambassador. It was Percy's residence at the time of his death, and Tom lived there in 1914 and 1938.

43. "Draft Acceptances," *Variety*, August 17, 1917, 7; "The Six Brown Brothers," *Variety*, August 17, 1917, 9.

44. "Drafted," *Variety*, March 15, 1918, 8, says, "Verne Brown (Six Brown Bros.) is in Class A and subject to call in the last quota." There is no information on when he entered the service, but a postwar list "of the men attached to the staff of the Hippodrome . . . who went to the front" includes Vern ("What the Hip Did," *Variety*, December 27, 1918, 156). His connection with the Hippodrome is not known; perhaps he, like Percy, was in Tom Brown's Clown Band in *Everything*, which opened August 22, 1918. It is unlikely that he was in the Hippodrome show of the 1917–18 season.

45. Emerson Phonograph Company, *New Gold Seal Emerson Records November 1919* [catalog] (n.p. [New York]: Emerson Phonograph Company, 1919), 3. The catalog entry for the Brothers' records uses one of the 1914 White Studio photos of the group, showing two baritones, in contradiction of the verbal

description of the group as using two tenors. It is the same photo as the inset of the Brothers in figure 8.

46. *Band Masters with Circus and Seasons, 1841 through 1958* [pamphlet] (Sheridan, Wyo.: Circus History, n.d.), [13]. This source lists two 1915 bandmasters for Hagenbeck-Wallace, suggesting a change during the season.

47. "How Many Browns?," *New York Times*, October 24, 1920, sec. 6, 1.

48. Harry R. Gee, *Saxophone Soloists and Their Music, 1844–1985* (Bloomington: Indiana University Press, 1986), 70. Gee says that Amaturo was a member of the group specifically during the run of *Jack o' Lantern*, making the claim more credible than similar but less specific ones, in other sources and on behalf of other artists, that they were once in the Six Brown Brothers.

Chapter 11

1. "'Jack o' Lantern's' Record," *Variety*, May 24, 1918, 12. After completing *Under the Top*, he also starred in *Johnny, Get Your Gun* (Fred Stone, *Rolling Stone* [New York: McGraw-Hill, 1945], 213–15) and *The Goat* (Armond Fields, *Fred Stone: Circus Performer and Musical Comedy Star* [Jefferson, N.C.: McFarland, 2002], 193).

2. "The Six Brown Brothers," *Variety*, June 7, 1918, 9. Ziegfeld's request is in Florenz Ziegfeld to C. B. Dillingham, May 8, 1918, Box 30, CBD. The contract called for two to six weeks at $600 per week ("Contract, June 3, 1918 between C. B. D. and Florenz Ziegfeld, Jr." under "6 Brown Bros" in first gathering of "Charles B. Dillingham: Index to Correspondence," Box 32, CBD).

3. C. G. Child to Tom Brown [contract], May 4, 1918, BMG.

4. Victor Talking Machine Company, Recording Book, 1917–1918 [unpublished document], 2434–36, 2439, BMG, for these dates names F. Henri Klickmann as the arranger of this selection and three others, but doesn't specify an arranger for "Chasing the Chickens."

5. "Bert Williams," *Variety*, July 12, 1918, 11; advertisement, *Variety*, July 19, 1918, 18. General information about the *Frolic* and *Follies* comes from Mary C. Henderson, *The New Amsterdam: The Biography of a New York Theatre* (New York: Hyperion, 1997), 168, 177–78.

6. "Cabarets," *Variety*, May 3, 1918, 17. The review doesn't mention Fannie Brice, who must have joined the cast later in the run.

7. John J. O'Connor, "Who's Who—and Why—in Vaudeville," *Variety*, July 4, 1919, 9.

8. "Cabarets."

9. Bert Williams and George Walker, "The Stage Negro," *Variety*, December 14, 1907, 30.

10. "Chicago Correspondence," *Variety*, September 6, 1918, 22.

11. "In the Service," *Variety*, September 13, 1918, 8.

12. "English Actors of Draft Age Have 60 More Days to Enlist," *Variety*, August 2, 1918, 4.

13. "Shows and Bills Canceled as Cities Fight Epidemic," *Variety*, October 4, 1918, 7, 24.

14. *Jack o' Lantern*'s progress and the spread of Spanish influenza can be followed in *Variety*: "Shows in Chicago," September 20, 1918, 13; "Shows in Chicago,"

October 11, 1918, 14; "The Show Business," October 18, 1918, 11; "Shows in Chicago," October 18, 1918, 13; "Epidemic Fast Breaking Up," November 1, 1918, 3, 18; "Shows in Chicago," November 8, 1918, 12; "Shows in Chicago," November 15, 1918, 14; "Shows out of Town," November 22, 1918, 14; "Shows at the Box Office," December 13, 1918, 20.

15. "Epidemic Casualties," *Variety*, October 11, 1918, 5. The "best male voice" opinion is in Ibee [pseud.], "Everything," *Variety*, August 30, 1918, 16.

16. Information drawn from Percy's death certificate; "Percy Brown" [obituary], *New York Times*, December 22, 1918, 17; "Percy Brown" [obituary], *Lindsay (Ontario) Post*, January 3, 1919, 10. The death certificate gives what is probably the wrong date for Percy's birth (October 31, 1882), since it conflicts with Alec's birth date as given on his birth registration (September 9, 1882), a prima facie much more reliable document. (Alec's birth was registered in February 1883.) It may also be unreliable as to his place of birth, given as Potsdam, New York. A possible motivation for providing misinformation, if it is that, comes from the decree making British subjects over thirty-one, such as Percy, liable to the American draft after September 28, 1918.

17. Items in *Variety*: "The Fred Stone," November 29, 1918, 11; Len Libbey, "Boston," January 10, 1919, 35; "Boston's Unexplained Drop," February 21, 1919, 13; Len Libbey, "Boston," February 28, 1919, 44; Len Libbey, "Boston," April 11, 1919, 42; Len Libbey, "Boston," April 18, 1919, 40; "Shows in Philly," May 16, 1919, 15.

18. Omaha newspapers reported, erroneously, that Tom and Waggener had been friends in college.

19. The date is an estimate based on interpolating the instrument's serial number (27409) into the series of numbers of other surviving Sax instruments. According to Malou Haine and Ignace De Keyser, *Catalogue des instruments Sax au Musée Instrumental de Bruxelles* (Brussels: Musée Instrumental, 1980), 242, surviving instruments with serial numbers 27403 and 27741 were built in 1863.

20. Clay Smith, "Saxophone Article," *Dominant*, July 1919, 75–78. The title of the show and the information that the cast and audience were limited to men come from Arvid E. Nelson Jr., *The Ak-Sar-Ben Story: A Seventy-Year History of the Knights of Ak-Sar-Ben* (Lincoln, Neb.: Johnsen, 1967), 90, 107.

21. The privately issued recording may be a dub of a lost soundtrack disc made c. 1920–21. See appendix.

22. "Resenting Grieg in Ragtime," *Literary Digest*, December 11, 1920, 37.

23. The original parts for this arrangement are in NMM. They include notations, not in the same hand as the rest of the arrangement, calling for tempo changes and ritardandos, although the record retains the same tempo throughout. Tom's part is for alto saxophone, not soprano. These parts probably came from H. A. Waggener.

24. Sime Silverman, "The Ziegfeld Frolics," *Variety*, December 13, 1918, 15.

25. "The Six Brown Brothers," *Variety*, May 23, 1919, 17. A flyer for both the *Frolic* and the *Nine o' Clock Revue* inserted in the printed program for the *Follies* for the week beginning July 28, 1919, lists a collective line-up of Lillian Lorraine, the Brothers, Oscar Shaw, W. C. Fields, Savoy and Brennan, Evan B. Fontaine, Green and Blyler, and Hal Hixon, along with the "50 most striking American beauties ever assembled on any stage" (private collection).

26. Henderson, *The New Amsterdam*, 169. Henderson gives an opening date of June 16, but "'Follies' Opened to $3,250," *Variety*, June 13, 1919, 13, reports that the *Follies* opened on June 11.
27. "Brown Brothers Score Hit in 'Ziegfeld Frolic,'" unidentified New York newspaper, n.d. [c. June 10, 1919], n.p., TBS.
28. Silverman, "The Ziegfeld Frolics."
29. "Shows in New York and Comment," *Variety*, June 27, 1919, 15.
30. "Shows in New York and Comment," *Variety*, July 11, 1919, 15; "Outcome of Actor's Strike Still in Doubt This Week," *Variety*, August 15, 1919, 3.
31. "Shows in New York and Comment," *Variety*, August 22, 1919, 14.
32. Although I have not seen the "Advance Record Bulletins for November 1919" in *Talking Machine World*, October 1919, the highest Emerson 1000-series release number announced in "Advance Record Bulletins for October 1919," *Talking Machine World*, September 1919, 196, is 1054, while the lowest in "Advance Record Bulletins for December 1919," *Talking Machine World*, November 1919, 195, is 1070, making it all but certain that the Brothers discs, 1055 and 1056, were announced in October.
33. C. G. Child to Tom Brown [contract], July 25, 1919, 2, BMG; Tom Brown to Victor Talking Machine Company, October 15, 1919, BMG.
34. Allan Sutton, "The Many Sides of Victor Emerson," *Victrola and 78 Journal* 12 (winter 1997–98): 46.
35. Information about the Emerson Phonograph Company comes from Allan Sutton, "The Emerson Phonograph Company," *Victrola and 78 Journal* 12 (winter 1997–98): 39–45. The citations are from 39. Sutton quotes from an Emerson ad in *Talking Machine World*, aimed at dealers rather than primary consumers.
36. "Some New Emerson Artists," *Talking Machine World*, September 1919, 181.
37. "Smiles" had been copyrighted in late 1917.
38. Tom Brown to Charles B. Dillingham, November 26, 1919; C. B. Dillingham [unsigned] to Tom Brown, November 28, 1919, Box 21, CBD. The problem with the Emerson discs may have been a noticeably inferior sound quality on the first releases, owing to a "universal cut" recording method that made the records playable on machines designed only for standard lateral-cut discs or only for vertical-cut ones such as Edison and Pathé issues. Although, according to Sutton, "Emerson Phonograph Company," 40, the firm abandoned the universal cut some time in 1919, an Emerson ad for their first Six Brown Brothers release, in the *Saturday Evening Post*, October 4, 1919, 104, includes the line "Play on all phonographs—no attachments."
39. Brian Rust, *American Dance Band Discography, 1917–1942* (New Rochelle, N.Y.: Arlington House, 1975), 1:339–41.
40. Michael Eric Hester, *A Study of the Saxophone Soloists Performing with the John Philip Sousa Band, 1893–1930* (Ann Arbor, Mich.: University Microfilms, 1995), 51, 55, 58.
41. "It's the biggest hit we have ever played since we have been in the show business" (advertisement, *Variety*, June 27, 1919, 34).
42. The complete itinerary is in *Charles Dillingham: Season 1918–19* [sic], a routing book in Box 32, CBD.
43. Lily Carthew, "Cleveland," *Variety*, September 26, 1919, 49.
44. Information on *Jack o' Lantern Upside Down* comes from a printed program, n.p. (St. Louis, Mo.), n.d. [December 31, 1919], in TBS.

45. C. B. Dillingham [unsigned] to Tom Brown, May 13, 1916, Box 20, CBD; Tom Brown to C. B. Dillingham, October 13, 1919; C. B. Dillingham [unsigned] to Tom Brown, October 14, 1919; Tom Brown to Chas. B. Dillingham, November 22, 1919; C. B. Dillingham to Tom Brown, November 24, 1919; Tom Brown to Charles B. Dillingham, November 26, 1919, Box 21, CBD.

46. "A Brown Brother to Marry," New York Morning Telegraph, March 10, 1920, n.p., Brown Brothers file, BRTC.

47. "Advance Record Bulletins for July, 1919 . . . Columbia Graphophone Company . . . May Mid-month List," Talking Machine World, June 1919, 155.

48. Sutton, "The Emerson Phonograph Company," 42.

49. Advertisement, Talking Machine World, July 1923, 72.

50. C. G. Child to Tom Brown [contract], July 25, 1919, BMG.

51. The disc, bearing in grease pencil the inscription "Gift of Dorothy Stone" (most likely Fred Stone's daughter), is of unknown date, although the credit line for the Electric Recording Laboratories, New York, suggests that it was manufactured no earlier than 1925, when electrical recording passed from the laboratory into the stream of commerce. "Shivaree" is backed by a very brief reading of "Rosy Cheeks," a Harry D. Squires composition copyrighted in 1921, which Tom featured in Tip Top during 1922. It seems likely that "Shivaree" is a dub from a Victor test pressing of the 1920 recording, although none of the numbers stamped, engraved, or printed on the disc corresponds to the Victor matrix numbers for the November 22 session.

52. "Peter Gink" does abandon the sixteen-bar custom in its second strain, which is only twelve bars long. Cobb may have been inspired to use the Schubert piece as the basis for a ragtime saxophone transformation by the fact that the nationally known saxophonist E. A. Lefèbre had transcribed it for accompanied alto saxophone in 1904 and (I conjecture) programmed it in his concerts. As of August 2002, the saxophone part of the transcription was still in print, in Paul DeVille, Universal Method for Saxophone (New York: Carl Fischer, 1908 [sic]), 304.

53. Card for Victor 18714, Victor numerical card file, BMG. The Columbia Saxophone Sextette continued to record, but only until March 1921, according to Rust, American Dance Band Discography, 1:341. For the 1921 crisis in the record business, see Tim Brooks, "Columbia Records, 1901–1934: A History," in Brooks, The Columbia Master Books Discography (Westport, Conn.: Greenwood Press, 1991), 1:17–18.

54. For an early discussion of the distinction between hot and sweet and its importance in the early 1920s, see Henry O. Osgood, So This Is Jazz (Boston: Little, Brown, 1926), 108 and passim.

55. Card for Victor 18694, Victor numerical card file, BMG.

Chapter 12

1. "Brown to Be Busy," Billboard, June 26, 1920, 19. Dillingham's contract with the Browns for Tip Top had, however, already been announced in advertisement, Variety, June 4, 1920, 22.

2. "Tom Brown's Saxophone Band," Variety, March 30, 1917, 20.

3. Advertisement, *Variety*, April 2, 1920, 69.
4. Details of the benefit come from a souvenir program in the author's collection.
5. "Pat" Ballard, "Making the First Talking Picture of a Jazz Orchestra," *Metronome*, November 1929, 40. Ballard seems to claim that his own jazz band made a film for the firm in 1920, but he also says that one of the selections was "Minnie the Mermaid." B. G. DeSylva's well-known song by that name was copyrighted in 1923, so it is at least possible that Ballard misstated the date. He says that the Six Brown Brothers and Harry Lauder had done earlier shorts for the company. If the Ballard movie dates from 1923 rather than 1920, the Brothers' disc of "Rosy Cheeks," discussed later in this chapter, becomes a candidate for the soundtrack. See appendix.
6. "Thousands See Ak-Sar-Ben Show," *Billboard*, June 19, 1920, 21.
7. "Brown to be Busy"; "Styles at Marigold," *Billboard*, August 7, 1920, 21.
8. "New York Hippodrome Opens Monday Evening, August 9th," *Billboard*, August 7, 1920, 6.
9. *Billboard*, August 28, 1920, 32. The item has a dateline of August 20.
10. Sime Silverman, "Tip-Top," *Variety*, October 8, 1920, 17.
11. Alexander Woollcott, "The Play," *New York Times*, October 6, 1920, 13.
12. Earle Dorsey, "Fred Stone in 'Tip Top' at the National," unidentified newspaper [Washington, D.C.], n.d. [April 1922], n.p., TBS.
13. Up to this point, my summary has been based on the script in BRTC, from which the quoted dialogue is drawn. From this point on, the description relies primarily on a souvenir program from the Colonial Theatre in Boston for performances on February 27 and 28, 1922, in the author's collection, but also on numerous newspaper reviews in TBS.
14. "Fred Stone at Globe in New Dancing Show," unidentified newspaper [New York], n.d. [October 1920], n.p., TBS.
15. Arthur Sheekman, "Metropolitan," unidentified newspaper [Minneapolis or Seattle?], n.d. [probably season of 1922–23], n.p., TBS.
16. "Nixon—Fred Stone, 'Tip Top,'" unidentified newspaper [Pittsburgh, Pa.], n.d. [probably season of 1922–23], n.p., TBS.
17. "The Power of the Drama," *Life*, October 21, 1920, 724.
18. "Nixon—Fred Stone, 'Tip Top.'"
19. Thomas Nunan, "Fred Stone Delights in Great Show," *San Francisco Examiner*, March 13, 1923, 11.
20. Fred Stone, *Rolling Stone* (New York: McGraw-Hill, 1945), 220.
21. "Fred Stone's Unexpected Effects Make Hit in 'Tip Top' at the Globe Theatre," *New York Evening Telegram*, October 6, 1920, 22.
22. Tom Brown to H. A. Waggener, March 10, 1921, NMM. The detail about unison movement of the instruments was contributed by Myrtle Hendrickson, Alec Brown's oldest daughter, who saw the show at the Globe.
23. Ibid.
24. Tom Brown to H. A. Waggener, March 10, 1921, NMM. My description of Tom's performance is based on the soundtrack of the Vitaphone film discussed in chapter 14.
25. Woollcott, "The Play."
26. Tom Brown to H. A. Waggener, October 9, 1920, NMM.
27. Advertisement, *Metronome*, n.d. [c. May 1921], 27, TBS.

28. Tom Brown to Charles B. Dillingham, November 26, 1919, Box 21, CBD.

29. Contract dated March 29, 1920, author's collection.

30. "Contract July 28–20" under "Valerio, Theresa" in fifth gathering of "Charles B. Dillingham: Index to Correspondence," Box 32, CBD, n.p.

31. For Thomas Healy's, see advertisement, *New York Times*, February 18, 1921, 16. The quoted material is from Tom Brown to [Bruce] Edwards, February 28, 1920 [*sic*: 1921], Box 21, CBD. The year on Tom's letter is evidently a mistake, since it is on Globe Theatre letterhead and the Six Brown Brothers were playing in Hagerstown, Maryland, on February 28, 1920.

32. "Harry Fink (Columbia, Victor)," *True-Tone* 12:2 (second quarter of 1922), 2.

33. So identified by an ailing Tom in "Old Days as Sax Star Still Live for Clerk, 68," *Chicago Daily News*, August 21, 1950, n.p., NMM. But there are several inaccuracies in the article, including Tom's statement that Young "took my brother Percy's place when Percy died during the flu epidemic back in the first World War." The photo printed with the *Chicago Daily News* article was published in a souvenir program for *Tip Top*, Colonial Theatre, Boston, February 27–28, 1922, [48], author's collection, and was shot in Chicago, giving it a likely date of August–December 1921, when the Brothers are known to have been in Chicago.

34. "Fred Stone Due Back at the Globe Monday," *Variety*, April 29, 1921, 17.

35. "Fred Stone Breaks Ankle," *Variety*, April 8, 1921, 13; "Stone Out Four Weeks," *Variety*, April 15, 1921, 12. Despite the title of the former article, the latter (as well as subsequent articles) states that the fractured bone was in Stone's toe. Armond Fields, in *Fred Stone: Circus Performer and Musical Comedy Star* (Jefferson, N.C.: McFarland, 2002), 209, opts for the ankle.

36. "Stone Out Four Weeks." A *New York Times* writer, said by Marshall and Jean Stearns (in *Jazz Dance* [New York: Da Capo Press, 1968], 205) to have been playwright George S. Kaufman, wrote a long piece praising Dixon's efforts and reporting that the audience called him out for a curtain speech the night of his first appearance in Stone's role ("Dixon as Successor to Stone," *New York Times*, April 17, 1921, sec. 6, 1). It was probably during the Globe's temporary closing that the Browns "doubled for three days at the Hippodrome, filling in for [comedian] Joe Jackson who was out owing to illness" ("Cabarets," *Variety*, April 22, 1921, 21).

37. "Expect Stone Back," *Variety*, April 22, 1921, 13; "Fred Stone Due Back."

38. "'Tip-Top' Closing Run at Globe This Week," *Variety*, May 6, 1921, 14.

39. "Cabarets," *Variety*, April 22, 1921, 13; "Closing 'Frolic,'" *Variety*, May 20, 1921, 1.

40. Mary C. Henderson, *The New Amsterdam: The Biography of a Broadway Theatre* (New York: Hyperion, 1997), 178.

41. "Vaudeville Notes," *Billboard*, June 25, 1921, 13.

42. "Browns over Keith Circuit," *Billboard*, June 18, 1921, 8; "Routes in Advance," *Billboard*, July 9, 1921, 58; July 16, 1921, 59; July 23, 1921, 57.

43. Edward Haffel, "B. F. Keith's Palace New York," *Billboard*, July 2, 1921, 9.

44. Jack Lait, "Jack Lait's Reviews," *Variety*, July 1, 1921, 15.

45. "'Tip-Top' Rehearsing," *Billboard*, July 23, 1921, 34.

46. "Admission Scales in Chi Stay at $3.85," *Variety*, August 19, 1921, 14.

47. "'Cat' Scene at Fields'," *Variety*, September 30, 1921, 9.

48. "Cabaret," *Variety*, September 23, 1921, 8.

49. Items in *Variety*: "Chicago Theatres Can't Sell Upstairs," September 30, 1921, 14; "One Chicago House Dark This Week," October 21, 1921, 14; "Chicago Disappoints Two Big Shows," November 11, 1921, 14.

50. "'Tip Top' Going Out," *Variety*, November 25, 1921, 9.

51. "Statelake Opens March 4," *Variety*, December 13, 1918, 6; Jack Lait, "Magnificent New State-Lake Starts Its Amusement Career," *Variety*, March 21, 1919, 6, 26; Jack Lait, "The New State-Lake Theatre and the People Who Built It," *Variety*, March 28, 1919, 6, 30; Floyd B. Scott, "Inside the State Lake," *Variety*, March 28, 1919, 30.

52. "Tom Brown Music Co. Organized," *Music Trade Review*, December 9, 1922, n.p.; "Tom Brown Increases Capital," *Music Trade Review*, January 24, 1925, n.p.; "Tom Brown Music Co.: A Record of Five Years of Progress," *Music Trade Review*, August 7, 1926, 3 (author's collection).

53. "Permanent Injunction Issued against Brown and Markwith," *Variety*, December 9, 1921, 5, 19.

54. From a copy of the injunction published by the Buescher Band Instrument Company on an undated flyer advertising the Brothers' endorsement of their products, NMM.

55. Items in *Variety*: "Cold Wave in Boston Hurt Attendance," February 3, 1922, 16; "Slump Hits Boston, Big Storm Blamed," February 24, 1922, 14; "Boston Houses Hold Up Despite Lent," March 10, 1922, 16.

56. "Business' Bad Break; All Philly's Shows Off," *Variety*, March 31, 1922, 16; "Philly Jammed with Heavy Dramatics," *Variety*, April 7, 1922, 16.

57. Fields, *Fred Stone*, 216, provides more details on the company's woes in the following season, that of 1922–23.

58. The remarks come respectively from Sheekman, "Metropolitan"; Val Sherman, "Metropolitan," unidentified newspaper [Minneapolis or Seattle?], n.d. [1922–23?], n.p., TBS; and "Metropolitan," unidentified newspaper [Minneapolis or Seattle?], n.d. [1922–23?], n.p., TBS.

59. "Now You Know Where the Saxophone Arrangements Used by the Six Brown Brothers Come From," *Sharps and Flats*, January 1922, 1. The other selections listed are "All By Myself" (an Irving Berlin piece that became a standard), "Nobody's Baby," "Wabash Blues," "My Sunny Tennessee," "Sweetheart," "June Moon," and "Mississippi Cradle."

60. The contract, dated October 18, 1921, is in the author's collection.

61. Details of the Balaban and Katz engagements are drawn from advertisements, *Chicago Tribune*, May 20, 1922, 12; May 30, 1922, 18; June 12, 1922, 24; June 20, 1922, 18; July 4, 1922, 18; July 11, 1922, 18. During the eight weeks, Balaban and Katz acquired a fifth theatre, the Roosevelt (across State Street from Marshall Field's), but the Brothers did not appear there. Later in the summer, Tom "gave a number of saxophone concerts" at a music dealers' convention on Chicago's Navy Pier ("Six Brown Bros. and Buescher," *Music Trade Review*, August 6, 1922, 6).

62. Ralph Holmes, "White Sisters and Brown Brothers Help Make Colorful Show," unidentified newspaper [Detroit], n.d. [probably spring 1923], n.p., TBS.

63. John Corbin, "The Play," *New York Times*, November 29, 1922, 20.

64. Waters, "The Bunch and Judy," *Variety*, November 10, 1922, 16–17.

65. "Lively Week-End in Philly Last Week," *Variety*, November 24, 1922, 13; "Dooley, 'Bunch and Judy,'" *Variety*, December 1, 1922, 11.

66. "Musical Musings," *Billboard*, December 23, 1922, 43. The anecdote about Voltaire and Barnet is in Charlie Barnet and Stanley Dance, *Those Swinging Years: The Autobiography of Charlie Barnet* (Baton Rouge: Louisiana State University Press, 1984), 4–5. Barnet was under the impression that Voltaire was a member of the Six Brown Brothers, so perhaps at one point he was. The saxophone lessons took place in 1923.

67. Sime Silverman, "Bunch and Judy," *Variety*, December 15, 1922, 18.

68. "Shows in N.Y. and Comment," *Variety*, January 19, 1923, 16.

Chapter 13

1. Armond Fields, *Fred Stone: Circus Performer and Musical Comedy Star* (Jefferson, N.C.: McFarland, 2002), 155. *The Old Town* played as far west as San Francisco and Los Angeles.

2. Val Sherman, "Metropolitan," unidentified newspaper [Minneapolis or Seattle?], n.d. [1922–23], n.p., TBS.

3. For example, "Stone's Company Has Family Tinge," unidentified San Francisco newspaper, n.d. [March 1923], n.p., TBS.

4. Advertisement, *Variety*, May 10, 1923, 37.

5. Dates and other details of the Chicago and San Francisco engagements come from print ads in the *Chicago Tribune* and *San Francisco Chronicle* for May–June 1923.

6. Caricature caption, *San Francisco Call and Post*, June 18, 1923, 12.

7. George C. Warren, "Mother Gone, Her Boys Are Running Wild," *San Francisco Chronicle*, June 16, 1923, 8.

8. "Grauman's Metropolitan," unidentified newspaper [Los Angeles], n.d., n.p., TBS.

9. Walter N. Brunt, "The Buford Trip," *The Buford Cruise to the Far North* [pamphlet], (n. p. [San Francisco?]: n.d. [1923?], [3–6]). The quote is from p. [2] of the pamphlet.

10. So says E. B. (Elwyn Brooks) White, in "The Years of Wonder," in White, *The Points of My Compass: Letters from the East, the West, the North, the South* (New York: Harper and Row, 1962), 205–40. "Alaska, The Country of a Thousand Wonders; Arctic Cruise 1923" (San Francisco: Alaskan-Siberian Navigation Company, 1923), a brochure advertising the trip, mentions a jazz band.

11. White, "The Years of Wonder," 213. The six weeks projected in "Alaska, Country of a Thousand Wonders" stretched to seven.

12. [Author and title missing], *Juneau (Alaska) Daily Empire*, n.d. [July 30, 1923], n.p., TBS.

13. White, "The Years of Wonder," 214.

14. White, "The Years of Wonder," 221.

15. See this chapter, note 12.

16. One of these snapshots inspired a California saxophone ensemble in recent years to name itself the Nuclear Whales. On the back of another, in Theresa's hand, is the inscription, "Some whale! guess that's where the saxophone got its wail. Ha!"

17. White, "The Years of Wonder," 231–32; the quote is from p. 232.

18. White, "The Years of Wonder," 232.
19. Brunt, "The Buford Trip," [4–5].
20. White, "The Years of Wonder," 233–34.
21. Snow was "a big-game hunter, who brought along his elephant gun, his movie camera, and his son Sydney," according to White, "The Years of Wonder," 213; Snow's lectures provided the only on-board entertainment aside from that furnished by the Brothers.
22. Brunt, "The Buford Trip," [5].
23. Brunt, *The Cruise of the Buford to the Far North*, [2].
24. "Nome Chamber of Commerce Entertains San Francisco Chamber of Commerce Delegation at the Log Cabin," *Nome (Alaska) Nugget*, August 18, 1923, n.p., TBS.
25. Brunt, "The Buford Trip," [6].
26. White, "The Years of Wonder," 238–39.
27. Brunt, "The Buford Trip," [6].
28. "Brown Brothers Purchase Expensive Gift," *Nome (Alaska) Nugget*, n.d., n.p., TBS.
29. Tom Brown to Chas. B. Dillingham, November 22, 1919, Box 21, CBD.
30. C. B. Dillingham [unsigned] to Tom Brown, May 13, 1916; October 14, 1919; respectively in Box 20 and Box 21, CBD.
31. Advertisements, *Los Angeles Times*, July 1, 1923, pt. 3, 31, 34.
32. "Julian Eltinge's Plans," *New York Telegraph*, July 10, 1922, n.p., Julian Eltinge scrapbook, BRTC.
33. "Geo. Primrose Dead," *Variety*, July 25, 1919, 5.
34. "Dockstader Home Burns," *Variety*, January 9, 1920, 6; "Save Wife's Body in Dockstader Home Fire," *Los Angeles Times*, January 9, 1920, 5.
35. This is the date on his birth certificate. "Julian Eltinge" [obituary], *New York Times*, March 8, 1941, 19, gives a date of May 14, 1883, and another early source, Edward Le Roy Rice, *Monarchs of Minstrelsy* (New York: Kenny, 1911), 363, gives 1884. I am grateful to Susan Walter for showing me a copy of the birth certificate.
36. He had appeared on the New York stage as John Smith in 1904 in the play *Mr. Wix of Wickham*, characterized by a review headline as "A Poor Show, Poorly Acted, with No Redeeming Features" (*New York Times*, September 20, 1904, 9). There is no indication in the review that Eltinge appeared in female drag. The Eltinge Theatre opened in 1912. Renamed the Empire and partially restored, it still stood near Times Square as of 2003, although it had been moved to a new location.
37. Anthony Slide, in Slide, *The Vaudevillians: A Dictionary of Vaudeville Performers* (Westport, Conn.: Arlington House, 1981), 46, says the film began as "a 1920 film titled *An Adventuress*, which was reedited and reissued in 1922." In Slide, *The Encyclopedia of Vaudeville* (Westport, Conn.: Greenwood Press, 1994), 159, he gives the title instead as *The Adventurers*.
38. Details of Eltinge's career come principally from "Julian Eltinge" [obituary]; Rice, *Monarchs of Minstrelsy*, 363; Slide, *The Vaudevillians*, 46–47; Slide, *The Encyclopedia of Vaudeville*, 158–61.
39. The three quotes are respectively from Jolo [pseud.], "The Fascinating Widow," *Variety*, September 16, 1911, 20; "Eltinge Succeeds in 'Crinoline

Girl,'" *New York Times*, March 17, 1914, 11; Johnny O'Connor, [untitled], *Dramatic Mirror*, August 16, 1921, 663; the last reprinted in Anthony Slide, *Selected Vaudeville Criticism* (Metuchen, N.J.: Scarecrow Press, 1988), 77.

40. "Julian Eltinge in Klein's Last Play," *New York Times*, August 28, 1915, 7. In *The Isle of Love*, Eltinge's character, Cliff Townsend, disguised as Julie, warns Prince Halbere, "Remember—I am a lady!," and, when the Prince persists in his wooing, beats him, strangles him, and leaves him for dead.

41. Slide, *The Vaudevillians*, 47.

42. Slide, *Encyclopedia of Vaudeville*, 160. It should be noted that the author of the present book is interested in Eltinge's sexual orientation because he is himself homosexual.

43. The three quotes are respectively from Slide, *The Vaudevillians*, 46; and Slide, *Selected Vaudeville Criticism*, 75, 76.

44. Rush [pseud.], "A Dressing Room Marvel," *Variety*, December 11, 1909, 153.

45. "Eltinge's Plans," *Variety*, March 15, 1918, 5; "Julian Eltinge," *New York Star*, April 21, 1923, n.p.; the latter item is in the Julian Eltinge scrapbook, BRTC.

46. "An Effective Local Tie-Up," *Music Trade Review*, October 27, 1923, 51, reports that during the Los Angeles engagement the company staged "a regular old-time minstrel parade from Philharmonic Auditorium to the main store of the Southern California Music Co., on Broadway," featuring the show's large all-saxophone band.

47. "Julian Eltinge Here at Tulane," unidentified newspaper [New Orleans], n.d. [December 1923], n.p., TBS.

48. Grace Kingsley, "Bright Offering," unidentified newspaper [Los Angeles], n.d. [September 1923], n.p., TBS.

49. "Eltinge, Brown Revue at Tulane," unidentified newspaper [New Orleans], n.d. [December 1923], n.p., TBS.

50. Henry Segal, "Brown Brothers Score," unidentified newspaper [Cincinnati], n.d. [January 1923], n.p., TBS.

51. "Eltinge, Brown Revue at Tulane."

52. Richard L. Stokes, "Eltinge's New Show Is an Odd Patchwork," unidentified newspaper [St. Louis], January 14, 1924, n.p., TBS.

53. Vivian Duncan and Rosetta Duncan, "Big Company in the 'Black and White Revue,'" unidentified newspaper [San Francisco], n.d. [November 1923], n.p., TBS.

54. Leone Cass Baer, "Revue at Heilig Staged with Snap," unidentified newspaper [Portland, Ore.], n.d. [October 1923], n.p., TBS.

55. "Black and White Revue of 1924 Is Solid Hit," unidentified newspaper [San Diego], n.d. [September 1923], n.p., TBS.

56. Kingsley, "Bright Offering."

57. Baer, "Revue at Heilig."

58. E. C. Waterworth, "Eltinge Charms; Spark Plug Hit," unidentified newspaper [New Orleans], n.d. [December 1923], n.p., TBS.

59. "Eltinge and Browns Score in Revue," *Cincinnati Times*, January 7, 1924, n.p., TBS.

60. "Eltinge, Brown Revue at Tulane."

61. Stokes, "Eltinge's New Show."

62. "Eltinge and Browns Score in Revue."

63. "Eltinge, Brown Revue at Tulane."

64. Stokes, "Eltinge's New Show."
65. "Orpheum Features Julian Eltinge With His Gowns," *San Francisco Chronicle*, March 12, 1923, 9.
66. Stokes, "Eltinge's New Show."
67. "Orpheum Features Julian Eltinge With His Gowns."
68. "At the Majestic," unidentified newspaper [Buffalo, N.Y.?], n.d. [January–February 1924?], n.p., TBS.
69. Waterworth, "Eltinge Charms."
70. "Orpheum Features Julian Eltinge with His Gowns."
71. Stokes, "Eltinge's New Show."
72. "Orpheum Features Julian Eltinge with His Gowns."
73. Baer, "Revue at Heilig."
74. "At the Majestic."
75. Stokes, "Eltinge's New Show."
76. "'Black and White' Brilliant Revue," unidentified newspaper [Hamilton, Ont.], n.d. [February 1924], n.p., TBS.
77. "Grand," unidentified newspaper [Hamilton, Ont.], n.d. [February 1924], n.p., TBS.
78. Dorothy Ashby, "Entertainments: Black and White Revue," unidentified newspaper [Des Moines, Ia.], n.d. [February–March 1924], n.p., TBS.
79. Stokes, "Eltinge's New Show."
80. "'Black and White' Brilliant Revue."
81. "Eltinge, Brown Revue at Tulane."
82. "Black and White Revue of 1924 Is Solid Hit."
83. Ashby, "Entertainments: Black and White."
84. "Grand."
85. W. D. L., "Brown-Eltinge Revue Big Hit," *St. Joseph (Missouri) Gazette*, March 22, 1924, n.p., TBS.
86. Stokes, "Eltinge's New Show."
87. Ashby, "Entertainments: Black and White."
88. "Black and White Revue of 1924 Is Show Supreme," unidentified newspaper [London, Ont.], n.d. [February 1924?], n.p., TBS.
89. Stokes, "Eltinge's New Show."
90. "'Black and White' Brilliant Revue."
91. Waterworth, "Eltinge Charms."
92. Stokes, "Eltinge's New Show."
93. "Glorified Vaudeville with at least three Top-Notchers and Julian Added—Berchel," unidentified newspaper [Des Moines, Ia.], n.d. [February–March 1924], n.p., TBS.
94. "Eltinge and Browns Score in Revue."
95. "At the Majestic."
96. See chapter 12.
97. "'Black-White Revue,' Eltinge and Browns, Are at the American," unidentified newspaper [St. Louis?], n.d. [January 1924], n.p., TBS.
98. Duncan and Duncan, "Big Company." The oversize saxophone ensemble was not a new idea, even in 1917. In 1914, *True-Tone* reported that Ed Wetmore, of Los Angeles, had already succeeded in recruiting 50 of the 100 saxophonists he was aiming to use in an all-sax group for the Panama Pacific International Exposition in San Francisco the following year (Guy E. Holmes and Clay

Smith, "Saxophones Here to Stay," *True-Tone* 9:3 [third quarter of 1914], 10).
A few months later, the same magazine ran a short piece on the thirty-piece
Seattle Saxophone Band, under the direction of A. A. Bronson ("Seattle Sax-
ophone Band," *True-Tone* 10:1 [first quarter of 1915], 2). These two groups
seem to have been composed of amateurs, but, on the professional side, Burt
Earle beat Tom to the punch when his Twenty Saxophone Girls "appeared at
the Pageant of Progress Exposition" in Los Angeles in 1922 (advertisement,
Variety, December 29, 1922, 24K).

99. Don Short, "Eltinge's Show Makes Big Hit in San Diego," unidentified newspaper [San Diego], n.d. [September 1923], n.p., TBS.

100. Stokes, "Eltinge's New Show."

101. "Eltinge, Brown Revue at Tulane."

102. "Eltinge on the Way," *New York Morning Telegraph*, January 8, 1924, n.p.,
Julian Eltinge scrapbook, BRTC.

103. "Frisco Gets Sample of Drawing Power," *Variety*, November 8, 1923, 16,
reports that the play earned a "very nifty" $13,000, only slightly worse than the
Duncan Sisters' smash hit *Topsy and Eva* ($15,000), then in its sixteenth week.

104. For example, Tucson, Arizona, where a young Pee Wee Russell subbed in the
group for one evening at about that time, according to Robert Hilbert, *Pee Wee
Russell: The Life of a Jazzman* (New York: Oxford University Press, 1993), 23.
But Hilbert's chronology is too unclear to place the event squarely in 1923.

105. "Lew Dockstader" [obituary], *Variety*, October 29, 1924, 43.

106. "Eltinge, Brown Revue at Tulane."

107. Harold Wilson Coates, [title of review missing], unidentified newspaper
[Cincinnati], n.d. [January 1924], n.p., TBS.

108. A *Black and White* program for the week beginning January 28, 1924, at the
Majestic Theatre in Buffalo, BRTC, gives the personnel of the Six Brown
Brothers as Tom, Alec, Fred, Vern, Harry, and Earl Brown. It is not known
whether this Harry is the Harry of the *Buford* voyage, and Earl's real surname is
not recorded.

109. "'Black-White Revue,' Eltinge and Browns, Are at the American."

110. "'Black and White' Brilliant Revue."

111. "Black and White Revue of 1924 Is Show Supreme."

112. "Wonderful Show at the Grand," *London (Ontario) Free Press*, n.d. [February
1924?], n.p., TBS.

113. W. D. L., "Brown-Eltinge Revue Big Hit."

114. "Brown-Eltinge Return Date," *Variety*, March 12, 1924, 12.

115. "Brown's Road Show Closes," *Variety*, April 2, 1924, 15.

116. Fred [pseud.], "Stepping Stones," *Variety*, November 8, 1923, 19–20.

117. Two years later, for example, *Variety* printed a short notice of *White and Black
Revue*, a show on the Columbia burlesque wheel with a mixed Caucasian and
African American cast, as "like most of the mixed shows with the white people
doing the first act and the colored the second" ("Mixed Color Choristers in
Burlesque Show," *Variety*, April 28, 1926, 61).

118. "Musical Musings," *Billboard*, January 5, 1924, 48–49.

119. "Tom Brown's Title Will Be Left Alone," *Variety*, January 31, 1924, 6.

120. "Chicago Correspondence," *Variety*, February 7, 1924, 31.

121. Another reason to suppose that the Saxo Sextette that recorded for Columbia
in 1916–17 was a Markwith enterprise.

122. "Tom Brown's Title." Sidney Burton, "Buffalo," *Variety*, February 28, 1924, 33, announces that the Brown Saxophone Six is about to open at the Lafayette Square Theatre in Buffalo, New York. C. L. Brown was not so easily discouraged. The Original Brown's Saxophone Six was still on the road in 1925, according to a handwritten date on a photo of C. L. Brown in the collection of his grandson, Larry Larkins. The photo also shows a sandwich board advertising the group.

Chapter 14

1. Contract between Musgrove's Theatres Proprietary Ltd. and Original Tom Brown Sextette, April 1, 1924, author's collection. The possibility of an around-the-world trip, to take up to six months, is stated in the Applications to Reenter the United States (U.S. Department of Labor Immigration Service Form 681), dated October 28, 1924, of Tom, Theresa, and Tom Jr., also in the author's collection.
2. Advertisement, *Variety*, June 25, 1924, 37.
3. Some of the apparent altos and tenors may be C-melody saxes, which had become very popular by 1924, but including them would have unnecessarily complicated life for those playing them.
4. "Brown's 30 Saxos on B'way for 2 Weeks," *Variety*, July 2, 1924, 9. In a photo of the group in the author's collection, there is a musician at the extreme right of the second row who looks a bit like Markwith, holding an alto sax (see figure 15).
5. A. C. E. Schonemann, "The Tom Brown Band and Orchestra School," *Jacobs' Orchestra Monthly*, n.d. [November? 1924], n.p., TBS.
6. Advertisements, *Chicago Tribune*, May 16, 1924, 22; May 26, 1924, 24; June 2, 1924, 24.
7. "'Loop' Houses Pick Up Again; Last Week in Chi. Not So Bad," *Variety*, May 28, 1924, 21.
8. "Manufacture of Saxophones Shown in Moving Picture," *Talking Machine World*, June 1924, 170; "Saxophone Making Shown in an Industrial Film," *Music Trade Review*, May 24, 1924, 103. The short also showed Clyde Doerr's Orchestra at the Congress Hotel in Chicago. The quotation is from the *Music Trade Review* report.
9. "Entertainers Guests of F. A. Buescher at Luncheon," *Elkhart (Indiana) Truth*, June 13, 1924, 2. See also "Six Brown Brothers Play," *Music Trade Review*, June 7, 1924, 101.
10. "Sax Band at Strand," *Variety*, June 11, 1924, 26.
11. Skig [pseud.], "Brown Brothers' Band," *Variety*, July 2, 1924, 28.
12. Roger Kinkle, *The Complete Encyclopedia of Popular Music and Jazz, 1900–1950* (New Rochelle, N.Y.: Arlington House, 1974) 1:128, 1:136, 1:138; Bruce Vermazen, "Hickman, Art, and His Orchestra (13 June 1886–16 January 1930)," in *The Encyclopedia of Popular American Recording Pioneers 1895–1925*, ed. Tim Gracyk (Granite Bay, Calif.: Victrola and 78 Journal Press, 1999), 166–71.
13. "Brown's 30 Saxos." This same piece says that the group had tentative contracts for stands in Baltimore, Washington, Rochester, Cleveland, and St.

Louis. Itineraries during this period have proved difficult to reconstruct, since *Variety* had not yet begun listing acts playing in "picture houses."

14. "Stanley Ran Up $26,000 With Added Browns," *Variety*, July 23, 1924, 22.

15. *Variety*, July 30, 1924, 21. The following week's report on Philadelphia cinemas opined that "absence of Brown Brothers hurt" the Stanley's gross ("$13,000 Last, Jazz Week, at Fox's, Philly, in Terrific Heat," *Variety*, August 6, 1924, 20).

16. "$20,000 at Buffalo Hip with Brown's Band," *Variety*, August 20, 1924, 18.

17. "Brown Bros. Pushed Newman Up to $16,000," *Variety*, October 1, 1924, 20.

18. The interview is reported in "Saxophone Playing as an Art," source unknown [Tivoli Theatre program?, Melbourne, Australia], n.d. [December 1924–January 1925], n.p., MMC.

19. His Application to Reenter the United States is dated October 28, 1924, and his new British passport is dated October 29, 1924; both were issued in Chicago (author's collection).

20. "Brown's 30 Saxos."

21. Advertisements, *Chicago Tribune*, October 1, 1924, 26; October 12, 1924, pt. 10, 4; October 19, 1924, pt. 8, 4; November 3, 1924, 24; November 9, 1924, pt. 9, 4; November 16, 1924, pt. 10, 4.

22. "All Trolleys to Ak-Sar-Ben Den," unidentified newspaper [Omaha, Neb.?], n.d. [1924?], n.p., TBS.

23. Advertisements, *San Francisco Examiner*, November 8, 1924, 10; November 9, 1924, editorial section, 2.

24. Advertisement, *San Francisco Examiner*, November 15, 1924, 6.

25. "Australia," *Variety*, February 4, 1925, 7. The dispatch is dated January 8, 1925.

26. "Australia," *Variety*, January 21, 1925, 3. The opening date is taken from an advertising card in the author's collection. Another source suggests that they opened on December 26.

27. "Australia," *Variety*, March 18, 1925, 3. The dispatch is dated February 20, 1925.

28. Harry Muller, "Form of Interview for Universal Issue to the Press on Mr Tom Brown's Return from Australia to the U.S.A.," n.d. [1925], 4, 6, 5 (TS, author's collection).

29. Tom Brown to H. A. Waggener, April 21, 1925, NMM.

30. Advertisement, *Chicago Daily Tribune*, May 25, 1925, 18.

31. Tom Brown to H. A. Waggener, June 5, 1925, NMM.

32. Advertisement, *Chicago Daily Tribune*, June 1, 1925, 24.

33. "Tom Brown's Minstrels," *Variety*, June 3, 1925, 30.

34. "Minstrelsy's Come-Back," *Variety*, November 4, 1925, 7.

35. The preceding October, however, the Lubliner and Trinz chain of Chicago film houses had mounted a Minstrel Week at two of its theatres, the Pantheon and Senate. It is not reported whether the show, of nine acts, none well known, was successful (advertisements, *Chicago Tribune*, October 19, 1924, pt. 8, 4; October 26, 1924, pt. 8, 4). Perhaps Tom, who was probably in Chicago at the time, was inspired by the Lubliner and Trinz presentation.

36. Lester Rush to Sverre O. Braathen, July 20, 1964, CWM; Abbe Niles, "Enter the Musical Shows," *Theatre Guild Magazine*, November 1929, 18–21, 64–65.

37. "Picture House Bills," *Variety*, August 5, 1925, 15; August 19, 1925, 17.

38. "Picture House Bills," *Variety*, September 9, 1925, 35; "Features and Stage Acts in Picture Theatres," *Variety*, September 23, 1925, 40.
39. Abel [pseud.], "Bands!," *Variety*, December 31, 1924, 26B.
40. Abel [pseud.], "Palace," *Variety*, October 14, 1925, 15.
41. On their recording of "Forever and Ever with You," however, there is a featured spot for an instrument that sounds like a baritone saxophone.
42. The musicians are identified by nickname on the blackface shot, so, with some help from Tom Brown Jr., fairly certain identifications of who played what are possible. The trumpet players are Ted Morse, head of the trumpet department at Tom Brown Music Co., and "Smithy." Will Morgan plays alto and soprano saxophones and clarinet. I. J. (Jack) Carpenter plays tenor and soprano saxophones. The other saxophonist (alto, soprano, clarinet) is "named" in the photo with a question mark. The trombonist is "Ponzi," which was the nickname of Thurlow Cranz (or Crans), who played with the Charles Dornberger Orchestra, and so may be Cranz; both men wore mustaches, a fairly unusual adornment in the mid-1920s. The rhythm section is composed of "Bartz," piano; "Dee Dee," banjo; "Tuschof," sousaphone; and "Dick," drums. "Tuschof" might be Elmer Tuschoff, a Chicago musician of that era.
43. Con [pseud.], "Keith's Riverside," *Variety*, October 21, 1925, 13.
44. Abel [pseud.], "Bands!"
45. Tom Brown to H. A. Waggener, January 18, 1926, NMM.
46. Brian Rust, *American Dance Band Discography 1917–1942* (New Rochelle, N.Y.: Arlington House, 1975), 1:212. The piece was recorded in New York on April 30, 1926, so was probably performed by a somewhat different band than the November selections.
47. Don Redman was Henderson's chief arranger at the time. In 1925–26, Henderson had the additional advantage of featuring solo voices of tremendous heat and astonishing originality, such as Louis Armstrong, Joe Smith, Charlie Green, Buster Bailey, and Coleman Hawkins.
48. The headliners were Ted and Betty Healy, whose act incubated the Three Stooges.
49. Tom Brown to H. A. Waggener, January 18, 1926, NMM.
50. "Brown Quits Orpheum Time; 'Afterpiece' Work without Pay," *Variety*, January 27, 1926, 9.
51. Tom Brown to H. A. Waggener, February 2, 1926, NMM.
52. Advertisements, *Chicago Daily Tribune*, July 25, 1926, pt. 7, 4. Art Kahn had been recording for Columbia, Ralph Williams for Victor, and Bennie Krueger for Brunswick. The Sammy Kahn group seems not to have recorded.
53. Advertisement, *Chicago Daily Tribune*, July 27, 1926, 30.
54. The two bits of evidence are that the August–September 1926 negotiations with the Tivoli in Australia (see next paragraph) included a proposal to pay "fourteen fares—his original Saxophone Six and his Jazz Band" (text of cable reported by Australian researcher Mike Sutcliffe, personal communication) and that a March 1927 photo of the troupe (author's collection) shows only fourteen musicians, divided into six Brothers and eight others, leaving the Lucky 'Leven three short. The instruments held in the photo make it very likely that the three assigned double duty are Tom and two saxophone players.

55. Details of the negotiation come from Australian researcher Mike Sutcliffe, reported in a letter to the Canadian popular-music historian Mark Miller dated July 15, 1994.
56. "Wife Charges Tom Brown with Drinking," *Variety*, October 20, 1926, 72; "Money and Alimony Wrenched from Tom Brown by Mrs. Tom," *Variety*, March 30, 1927, 29.
57. "Money and Alimony."
58. The alimony amount was reported in "Money and Alimony" and in "Divorces Saxophone Expert; $400 a Month for Alimony," *Chicago Tribune*, March 25, 1927, 19. The former source also states that Theresa "fixed her husband's income at $3,000 a month and his personal fortune at $100,000." Tom's state of mind was reported by Tom Jr. and in Harry L. Alford to H. A. Waggener, January 31, 1927, NMM: "Tom was in last Saturday—he certainly does not look very well—he looks very worried indeed and I am very sorry to hear about the divorce proceedings."
59. "Saxophonists Topping New Pantages Bill," *San Francisco Chronicle*, August 16, 1926, 8.
60. "Brown Tops Pantages Bill," *San Francisco Bulletin*, August 16, 1926, 9.
61. The quoted phrases are from "Pantages Shows 'Three Bad Men,'" *San Francisco Examiner*, October 25, 1926, 17. Other details come from "Tom Brown on Pantages Stage," *San Francisco Bulletin*, October 23, 1926, 8; "Western Picture on 'Pan' Screen," *San Francisco Bulletin*, October 25, 1926, 6; "Pantages Fills House With 'Three Bad Men,'" *San Francisco Chronicle*, October 25, 1926, 9.
62. "Tom Brown on Pantages Stage."
63. "Alphabetical Routes," *Variety*, September–December 1927.
64. Tom and the Augmented Orchestra played the Brooklyn Strand March 26–April 1. During that time—on March 29, two days after Tom turned forty-six—the Browns' marriage was officially dissolved.
65. Advertisement, *Variety*, February 9, 1927, 29.
66. The Six Brown Brothers' few known radio appearances, sporadic and incidental to their touring, are not noted in the text.
67. Mori [pseud.], "Six Brown Bros., (14), Vitaphone no. 549," *Variety*, October 17, 1928, 16. I owe a huge debt of gratitude to Gary Scott for making the soundtrack available to me. Newspaper reviews of the act suggest that it was the same as what is found in the Vitaphone film, although it is likely that the stage presentation was longer than nine minutes. See, for example, A. F. Gillaspey, "'Passion' Returns to Screen," *San Francisco Bulletin*, August 15, 1927, 5.
68. The other side is "Shivaree," described at the end of chapter 11.

Chapter 15

1. "'The Valley of the Giants'—Indiana," unidentified newspaper [Indianapolis], n.d. [January 27, 1928], n.p., TBS.
2. H. Benne Henton to H. A. Waggener, February 21, 1928, NMM.
3. R. M. M., "At B. F. Keith's," *Ottawa Citizen*, October 8, 1928, 16. See also "Tom Brown with the Original Six Brown Brothers," *Ottawa Citizen*, October 4, 1928, 21. A surviving snapshot, dated 1928, of Alec in costume (author's

collection) indicates that he was in the revived act. It is likely that Fred, William, and Vern were also on board.

4. "Year in Vaudeville," *Variety*, January 4, 1928, 17.
5. Both the itinerary (untitled TS, 2) and the contract between the Chicago Stadium Corporation of Chicago and Tom Brown, Manager of the Brown Brothers Saxaphone [*sic*] Sextette, January 23, 1929, are in the author's collection. The contract was actually drawn for March 24–April 14, but the new Chicago Stadium, the run's venue, was delayed in opening until March 28, when it housed a prize fight (Don Maxwell, "New $7,000,000 Stadium Opens; Draws 15,000," *Chicago Tribune*, March 29, 1929, 1).
6. Advertisement, *Chicago Tribune*, March 30, 1929, 9.
7. Contract between Radio-Keith-Orpheum Western Vaudeville Exchange and Tom Brown, December 23, 1930, author's collection. The last line on the reverse of the contract, with a little cuffed hand pointing to it, says "DON'T TRAVEL BY MOTOR—LATE ARRIVAL WILL RESULT IN A SALARY DEDUCTION."
8. Tom Brown Jr., interviewed by the author, December 8, 1996; August 26, 1999. The personnel after Tom Jr.'s departure is not known.
9. "Tom Brown Music Co.[:] A Record of Five Years of Progress," *Music Trade Review*, August 7, 1926, 3; "Tom Brown Music Co. Organized," *Music Trade Review*, December 9, 1922, 115.
10. Tom Brown Jr., who later worked for the Lyonses, remembers them as the Lyons brothers, although "Tom Brown Music Co.: A Record" says they were cousins.
11. A. C. E. Schonemann, "The Tom Brown Band and Orchestra School," *Jacobs' Orchestra Monthly*, n.d. [November? 1924], n.p., TBS.
12. "Tom Brown Music Co. Moves to New and Larger Quarters," *Talking Machine World*, April 1926, 106.
13. "Unique Announcement Sent by Tom Brown Co.," *Music Trade Review*, June 5, 1926, 326.
14. Cab Calloway and Bryant Rollins, *Of Minnie the Moocher and Me* (New York: Thomas Y. Crowell, 1976), 61. The book's chronology is somewhat unclear. Calloway reported that his instructor was "one of the famous Brown Brothers," but Tom Brown Jr. assured the author that none of the brothers ever taught there. Calloway continued: "They had a studio in downtown Chicago where they gave lessons during the day; in the evening they played in Chicago nightclubs. There were five of them in a saxophone quintet, and they made some very unusual melodic music—a totally original kind of jazz and blues."
15. The date comes from Tom Brown Jr. (personal communication).
16. Information about the move comes from Tom Brown Jr. (personal communication), September 23, 2000.
17. Tom Brown, *Borrow an Instrument from me for 5 weeks without-rental-charge* (Tom Brown Band School: Chicago, n.d. [early 1930s?]), [5–6], author's collection.
18. Tom Brown to H. A. Waggener, December 29, 1932, NMM. In the same letter, Tom writes that he plans to play the Sax soprano during an engagement from December 31, 1932 through January 2, 1933. The other information in this paragraph comes from the author's interviews with Tom Brown Jr.
19. The phrase about the "girls" wearing out the front of their dresses comes from Tom Brown Jr. (personal communication). Bob LaBelle, on whose correspon-

dence some of the present description of the School is based, says that, during his tenure at the Century (December 1935–July 1936), management discouraged the kind of frottage implied in Tommy's description, though it would happen from time to time in the hall's darker corners.

20. The check, in the author's collection, is drawn on the Wolverine Theatres Corporation's account at the Old Kent Bank in Grand Rapids, in the amount of $139.43. It's possible that this represents one day's pay at a weekly rate of $1000 (i.e., $142.86) minus an agent's commission or some other small fee. The Powers, incidentally, was the theatre at which *Tip Top* had opened its 1921–22 road season.

21. "Saxophone Sextet Tops Powers' Bill, Which is Best Yet," unidentified newspaper [Grand Rapids, Mich.?], n.d. [February 13, 1933?], n.p., TBS.

22. Tom Brown Jr., interviewed by the author, December 8, 1996. Musicians will note that the prescription works pretty well for selections in B-flat and E-flat if the chords are mostly tonics and dominants. But no doubt Tom was making a point about how easy it was to supply afterbeats, not offering a literally reliable guide to the novice.

23. Myrtle (Brown) Hendrickson and Allan Brown, interviewed by the author, September 24, 1999. Mrs. Hendrickson and Mr. Brown are two of Alec's children.

24. Tom Brown Jr. (personal communication). The Center Theatre post gave Tommy a brief moment of celebrity when the newspapers reported his box-office encounter with the father of Moss Hart, the producer of *The Great Waltz*, then playing at the theatre. A man walked up to the box office and said, in a heavy accent, "I'm Moss Hart's father." Tommy asked him to repeat it, and he did. Puzzled, Tommy walked over to his supervisor and said, "Man here says he's Mozart's father."

25. Lynn Sams, interviewed by Cecil Leeson, tape recording, July 26, 1970, NMM.

26. Tom Brown to H. A. Waggener, February 4, 1937, NMM.

27. Tom Brown to H. A. Waggener, n.d. [1937], NMM. Other passages in the letter clearly place it between letters dated February 4, 1937, and May 3, 1937.

28. Gene Arnold, *Complete Modern Minstrels*, bks. 1–2 (New York: M. Witmark and Sons, 1933). Arnold had also been the master of ceremonies on the earlier NBC show, "The Sinclair Minstrels."

29. The two Library of Congress transcriptions of broadcasts of "NBC Minstrels," July 28, 1937, and August 4, 1937 (shelf nos. RWA 2127 A1–2 and A3–4), are close in time to Tom's involvement with the show, but there is no indication on the recordings that he was connected with the broadcasts. However, announcer Norman Barry does not give the sort of credits at the end of the half hour that later became normal on network shows. The 1938 scripts for "NBC Minstrels of 1938," dated July 6, 1938, and July 20, 1938, are in the collection of the Library of American Broadcasting. They give writer credit to Albert Barker. Tom Brown was no longer connected with the program in July 1938.

30. Tom Brown to H. A. Waggener, May 3, 1937, NMM. A search of the ongoing *Chicago Tribune* feature "Today's Radio Broadcasts" through April–December 1937 turned up no mentions of any participation by Tom, although it does name Gene Arnold, Eddie Dean, Vance McCune, Clark Dennis, Harold Peary (who later portrayed The Great Gildersleeve for many years), Mark Love, Edward Davies, and the orchestras of Al Short and Harry Kogen ("Today's

Radio Broadcasts," *Chicago Tribune*, June 2, 1937, 21; August 4, 1937, 19; September 22, 1937, 16).

31. Tom Brown to H. A. Waggener, telegram, February 23, 1938; Western Union Telegraph Company to H. A. Waggener, telegram, February 25, 1938, NMM. Waggener subsequently wrote Tom's Superior Street address on the latter telegram, as if preparing to telephone Western Union to redirect the original reply.

32. Tom Brown to H. A. Waggener, n.d. [February–August 1938?], NMM. A date between February 23, 1938 and August 26, 1938 seems likely. The former date is that of the telegram, which, because of the contents of the two messages, seems to be earlier. The latter date is the only Friday the 26th in 1938. There is a weak case for Friday the 26th being in November 1937, but, according to "Variety Bills," *Variety*, February 17, 1937, 60, and February 24, 1937, 52, either Vincent Lopez or Paul Whiteman was playing at the Drake on that date. Fred Waring, along with his orchestra, had been a featured player in the Warner Brothers picture *Varsity Show*, released September 4, 1937, according to Barrie Roberts, "Priscilla Lane, All American," on the Classic Images website, http://www.classicimages.com/1999/february99/lane.html, consulted September 8, 2002.

33. Edmund F. Kahn, of Phillips H. Lord, Inc., to Tom Brown, April 2, 1938, author's collection. Tom's fee was $150.

34. "Minstrels Will Be at Academy," *Lindsay (Ontario) Post*, November 30, 1938, 4; advertisement, *Lindsay (Ontario) Post*, December 5, 1938, 3; "Young Musicians" and "Minstrel Show Fine Success," both *Lindsay (Ontario) Post*, December 7, 1938, 1. Besides Tom, participants noted in the *Post* were the comedians "Hi" Meehan, Bruce Maidens, and Guy Mills, and the musicians Murray Wright and Donald and Cecil Hughes.

35. Tom Brown to Allan Brown, postcard, December 6, 1938, author's collection.

36. "Tom Brown at Lions," unidentified newspaper [St. Catharines, Ont.?], n.d. [January 29, 1941?], n.p., TBS.

37. "Kingsway Boys' Band W. Tech. String Band Have Fine Concert"; "Originals' Smoker Attracts Visitors"; "'Originals' Captivate Legion Crowd"; advertisement (Capitol Theatre, Galt, Ont.); all from unidentified newspapers [Toronto, Ont.? and Galt, Ont.?], n.d., n.p., TBS. References to the London Blitz, movie titles such as *The Roaring Twenties*, and song titles such as "Scatterbrain" and "White Cliffs of Dover" make it likely that the clippings date from the early 1940s.

38. "You Say the Sweetest Things (Baby)" was written for the film by Mack Gordon and Harry Warren. Another difference between the film sextet and the Brothers lies in instrumentation. The Twentieth Century–Fox clowns play a curved soprano, two altos, tenor, baritone, and bass.

39. Allan Brown (Alec's son) to Edith Brown and family, postcard, July 2, 1941, author's collection.

40. "Local Reports," *International Musician*, April 1943, 19.

41. Royalty Contract between Will Rossiter and Tom Brown, April 24, 1944, author's collection. The copy I have is a carbon, signed by Rossiter but not by Tom Brown. Entering into the contract would not, of course, have required Tom's physical presence in Chicago, but another indication that he returned in 1944 is that the Toronto local of the A.F.M. issued a transfer to Tom some

time before July 1944, according to "Local Reports," *International Musician*, September 1944, 18. The magazine's "Local Reports" are wildly sporadic during 1944 and 1945, so there is no indication when Tom rejoined the Chicago local.

42. Ruth Logan, "Real Granddad of Saxophone Found in Loop," *Chicago Tribune*, April 29, 1945, pt. 3, 2. Tom may have returned to the U. S. for a short while after the Lindsay Citizens' Band minstrel show; Alec's children Allan and Myrtle remember Tom starring in an amateur minstrel show at the Elks Club in Irvington, New Jersey, in about 1940. Allan performed Rudy Wiedoeft's virtuoso piece "Saxophobia," but Alec didn't appear. "Mother wouldn't have allowed it," said Myrtle (Allan Brown and Myrtle [Brown] Hendrickson, interviewed by the author).

43. Logan, "Real Granddad of Saxophone." Although the article, based on an interview with Tom, says that Fred was a bandmaster, Alec's children Myrtle and Allan (personal communication) are sure he was not. A photo from the period, in the author's collection, shows Fred in uniform, carrying a tenor sax.

44. Logan, "Real Granddad of Saxophone."

45. Information on William's address, illness, and death come from his death certificate. His occupation is recorded both on the death certificate and in "William Brown" [obituary], *Chicago Tribune*, December 27, 1945, 10.

46. Information drawn from "Band Leader Cornetist Dies in 89th Year," *Toronto Telegram*, October 18, 1947, n.p.; "Allan W. Brown" [obituary], *Ottawa Journal*, October 20, 1947, n.p.; author's collection.

47. Tom Brown Jr. (personal communication) and "Hit Show of the Year Presented by Triangle Minstrels" [program] (Chicago: Triangle Minstrels, December 5, 1947), author's collection. Tom Jr. reported that he painted an oil portrait of his father in costume that hung in the Triangle clubhouse (probably the Triangle Tavern, 3633 Fullerton Avenue, Chicago, "The Home of the Famous Triangle Minstrels," as the program calls it; "Hit Show of the Year," [4]).

48. C. L. Brown, interviewed by Cecil Leeson, tape recording, August 18, 1970, NMM. Brown does not give a date for his last lunch with Tom, but various features of the surrounding story suggest strongly that it took place when Tom was still living in downtown Chicago, so very likely before 1948.

49. Most of the information in this paragraph and the three before it comes from interviews with Tom Brown Jr. The detail about plans to return to Chicago to participate in Triangle Club performances comes from H. A. Waggener to Tom Brown, September 9, 1948, author's collection.

50. Tom Brown to H. A. Waggener, March 3, 1949, NMM.

51. Information from Fred's death certificate.

52. Tony Weitzel, "Town Crier," *Chicago Daily News*, August 17, 1950, 40.

53. "Old Days as Sax Star Still Live for Clerk, 68," *Chicago Daily News*, August 21, 1950, 9.

54. The cause of death comes from Tom's death certificate. The detail about the phone call comes from Tom Brown, Jr. (personal communication).

55. "Tom Brown, Vaudeville Sax Star, Bows Out," *Chicago Daily News*, August 30, 1950, 13.

56. Details of the funeral and its immediate aftermath come from Tom Brown Jr., interviewed by the author, and two letters in NMM: Wade Booth to H. A.

Waggener, September 5, 1950, and Paul Gallagher to H. A. Waggener, n.d., but written shortly after Tom's funeral, which Gallagher had attended.

57. Tom Brown to H. A. Waggener, March 3, 1949, NMM.

58. Tom Brown Jr. to H. A. Waggener, September 29, 1950; October 22, 1950; September 21, 1952; NMM. In fairness, it must be said that Waggener's side of this correspondence is not known to exist, so that his position can only be inferred from Tommy's responses.

59. H. A. Waggener to Tom Brown Jr. (file copy in Waggener's hand), September 23, 1952, NMM.

60. H. A. Waggener, interviewed by Cecil Leeson, tape recording, August 5, 1970, NMM.

61. Information on Theresa's last days comes from Tom Brown Jr. (personal communication). Information on Vern's illness, death, and interment comes from his death certificate. The signature on the contracts for both William's and Fred's headstones is that of Myrtle Elliott.

62. Harry Fink, long a member of the early Brothers, had died in Woodbridge, New Jersey, on November 2, 1951, according to his death certificate. He had been living in Newark.

63. Thomas E. Brown to the author, March 15, 1999, author's collection.

64. Almost all the information about Alec was furnished by interviews with three of his children, Allan E. Brown, Myrtle Hendrickson, and Helene Bleibdrey. The newspaper interviews referred to are clippings, in the author's collection, from unidentified sources, undated and without page numbers.

Chapter 16

1. Although John Philip Sousa featured a freestanding saxophone ensemble in his concerts from 1919 to 1928, he seems not to have done so before that period. See Michael Eric Hester, *A Study of Saxophone Soloists Performing with the John Philip Sousa Band: 1893–1930* (Ann Arbor, Mich.: University Microfilms, 1995), 51, 55, 58, 79–80.

2. Caricature caption, *San Francisco Call and Post*, June 18, 1923, 12.

3. Sime Silverman, "Tip-Top," *Variety*, October 8, 1920, 17.

4. Paul Lindemeyer, *Celebrating the Saxophone* (New York: Hearst Books, 1996), 33.

5. Ibid.

6. "Saxophonists Topping New Pantages Bill," *San Francisco Chronicle*, August 16, 1926, 8.

7. "Back to Dixie with Burnt Cork Friends," *Brooklyn Daily Eagle*, January 20, 1914, picture and sporting section, 8.

8. Brian Rust, *American Dance Band Discography, 1917–1942* (New Rochelle, N.Y.: Arlington House, 1975), 1:885, 2:1919, 2:1524, 2:1246, 1:227, 1:546. W. C. Handy claimed credit for introducing the saxophone into dance orchestras, when, in 1909, he fielded a dance combination in Memphis with violin, clarinet, cornet, trombone, tenor sax, guitar, and bass. So successful was it that he soon formed two more with the same lineup. Handy's original saxophonist was James T. Osborne, and the new hires were William King Phillips and William

Singleton (W. C. Handy, *Father of the Blues: An Autobiography* [New York: Macmillan, 1941], 95, 100). I am grateful to Larry Gushee for directing me to this text.

9. Other configurations, with a few exceptions, seem to have been treated as extensions of AAT. The bass sax often found in the 1920s was normally employed as a variant on the tuba or string bass and so should be counted as a part of the rhythm section rather than the sax section.

10. Rust, *American Dance Band Discography*, 2:1708.

11. The quilt is currently in a private collection. The story of its making comes from the author's interviews with Tom Brown Jr., Helene Bleibdrey, and Myrtle Hendrickson, three of Maria Brown's grandchildren.

Discography

1. Brian Rust (personal communication) told the author that he is certain that all the Six Brown Brothers Victors from 1917 onward were recorded in Camden, N.J., but, except for 1919, the recording books seem to indicate New York or, in the case of the 1920 session, are ambiguous as to location.

General Index

Index of Musical Compositions